Comparing Political Regimes

COMPARING POLITICAL REGIMES

A THEMATIC INTRODUCTION TO COMPARATIVE POLITICS THIRD EDITION

ALAN SIAROFF

UNIVERSITY OF TORONTO PRESS

LIBRARY AND ARCHIVES CANADA CATALOGUING IN PUBLICATION

Siaroff, Alan, 1962–, author
Comparing political regimes: a thematic introduction to comparative politics / Alan Siaroff.—Third edition.
Includes bibliographical references and index.

Issued in print and electronic formats. ISBN 978-1-4426-0767-5 (bound).—ISBN 978-1-4426-0700-2 (pbk.).—ISBN 978-1-4426-0701-9 (pdf).—ISBN 978-1-4426-0702-6 (epub)

1. Comparative government—Textbooks. I. Title.

JF51.S53 2013   320.3   C2013-903286-X   C2013-903287-8

We welcome comments and suggestions regarding any aspect of our publications—please feel free to contact us at news@utphighereducation.com or visit our Internet site at www.utppublishing.com.

North America
5201 Dufferin Street
North York, Ontario, Canada, M3H 5T8

2250 Military Road
Tonawanda, New York, USA, 14150

ORDERS PHONE: 1–800–565–9523
ORDERS FAX: 1–800–221–9985
ORDERS E-MAIL: utpbooks@utpress.utoronto.ca

UK, Ireland, and continental Europe
NBN International
Estover Road, Plymouth, PL6 7PY, UK
ORDERS PHONE: 44 (0) 1752 202301
ORDERS FAX: 44 (0) 1752 202333
ORDERS E-MAIL: enquiries@nbninternational.com

The University of Toronto Press acknowledges the financial support for its publishing activities of the Government of Canada through the Canada Book Fund.

Printed in Canada

Throughout my education and then my academic career, my parents were always full of support and pride, and so this edition is dedicated, in loving memory, to my mother and my father.

Contents

Figures

Tables

Acknowledgements

It remains a pleasure to work with the University of Toronto Press. I wish to thank personally Michael Harrison, freelancer Ashley Rayner, and Beate Schwirtlich for their efficiency and professionalism. Particular gratitude goes to freelance copyeditor Karen Taylor for her tireless and careful editing and comments.

This book builds on a long career of research and teaching in comparative politics. It was first written—and has been twice revised—with students fully in mind in the hopes that it will answer most or at least many of their questions about comparative politics and perhaps inspire further questions.

Alan Siaroff
The University of Lethbridge

CHAPTER ONE

Introducing Comparative Politics

IN THIS CHAPTER YOU WILL LEARN

▶ why we study comparative politics;

▶ what a political regime is;

▶ what a sovereign state is;

▶ how, where, and why the number of sovereign states has increased over time and may continue to increase in the future; and

▶ how to define the head of government versus the head of state.

Comparing Political Regimes

This textbook compares and contrasts the political regimes of the countries of the world. It is thus relevant for any core course in comparative politics. That said, the field of comparative politics does have varied foci. Sometimes the term "comparative politics" merely refers to the study of any country outside of one's own, such as, for instance, focusing on the government and politics of China, Germany, or Russia. However, if only one such country is studied, then any actual cross-country comparisons are usually only implicit. Comparative politics has also involved the study of specific regions or subregions, such as "Politics in Western Europe." Such regional foci may simply be called "area studies," especially if broader theoretical perspectives are lacking. Comparative politics can and should be more than just a description of the government and politics of a country, a few countries, or a region—and in this textbook it is indeed more. First, this text analyses every country now in the world; it is intentionally thorough in this regard. Second, it follows a rigorous comparative methodology in outlining the different political regimes that have existed, in placing every country into this typology, and in comparing and contrasting the roles of key political actors (such as national "leaders"), political institutions (such as legislatures and, where these exist, regional governments), political processes (such as elections and democratic transitions), and patterns of political competition (such as the type of party system where there is democratic competition).

Studying comparative politics, and in this case studying all the countries of the world, has at least two main benefits for a student. First, it provides the broad context needed for analysing the political phenomena of whatever country interests you or is a matter of "current events." Take, for example, the possibilities of Egypt or Libya becoming—or some other country remaining—democratic. This issue begs certain questions: What do we mean by democracy? How do non-democracies (what we shall call "autocracies") become democracies? What makes for a stable democracy? These are only some of the questions answered in this book. Second, studying comparative politics counteracts ethnocentrism, that is, the limited perspective of knowing only one's own country. To this end, your sense of what is unique or supposedly great (or flawed) about your country politically may well change as you read about other countries.

As for the concept of a "political regime," by this we mean a method or system of government as opposed to the specific individuals in power. This definition is a simplified version of the following more elaborate explanation of a **political regime** as

> the formal and informal structure of state and governmental roles and processes. The regime includes the method of selection of the government and of representative assemblies (election, coup, decision within the military, [royal prerogative,] etc.), formal and informal mechanisms of representation, and patterns of repression. The regime is typically distinguished from the particular incumbents who occupy state and governmental roles, the political coalition that supports these incumbents, and the public policies they adopt (except of course policies that define or transpose the regime itself).[1]

Sovereign States

Our focus on "countries" means that we are limiting our detailed analysis to sovereign states, excluding, for example, subnational governments such as Canadian provinces. The concept of a **state,** as you may remember from your introductory politics textbook, involves the combination of a fixed territory, population, and sovereign control (based in a capital), so that the sovereign power effectively rules over the population within this territory. (This notion of "a state" overlaps somewhat with that of "the state," that is, the organizationally differentiated political, bureaucratic, legal, and usually military system of a country, which, as will be shown, can vary in its strength and effectiveness. In the first sense, generally either a state exists or it does not; in the second sense, states can vary along a continuum of capacity.) With fixed territories there are consequent borders between one state and the next, for example, the border between Canada and the United States. Population refers to the people who are being governed by the state or, perhaps, those who are citizens of a state with resulting political rights. Sovereignty is the most complex of these three aspects. Generally, it refers to being the highest authority in an area and thus being, as Max Weber stressed, an organization with the monopoly on the legitimate use of force within a territory.[2]

Sovereignty itself is a term with somewhat varying meanings. Krasner notes four of these.[3]

▸ *Domestic sovereignty* refers to sovereignty *within* a state, wherein the structures of authority or "the state" effectively control the behaviour of the population, at least in the sense of establishing law and order. The lack of such domestic sovereignty in the context of religious wars was what motivated the writings and philosophies of Bodin and Hobbes.

▸ *Interdependence sovereignty* refers to the right of states to control their borders and to police and, if they wish, limit the movement of people, goods, capital, information, and other resources. Here is where the issue of globalization is relevant, because aspects of globalization—international air travel, the Internet, capital flows, and so on—clearly seem to impede the ability of states to exercise interdependence sovereignty while international agreements may even limit their rights in this area. However, one has to remember here that borders were less relevant in nineteenth-century Europe than in the twentieth and that borders barely existed in pre-colonial Africa but are certainly salient factors there today.[4]

▸ *Westphalian* or *Vattelian sovereignty* refers to the absence of any external sources of authority over a sovereign state, in which case it would not be sovereign. The term "Westphalian" comes from the Treaty of Westphalia of 1648 that ended the Thirty Years War and from which came, we assume, the notion that states refrain from interfering in the internal affairs of other states. In fact, as Krasner points out, the Treaty of Westphalia was hardly this far-reaching; the broad principle of international non-intervention actually comes a century later in the works of two international legal theorists, Emer de Vattel and Christian Wolff.[5]

▸ Finally, *international legal sovereignty* involves the notion that any and all states are free and able to enter into international agreements with other states on military, trade, or other matters. Moreover, such agreements are considered binding on the signatories as long as they were not coerced into signing (as per a contract involving individuals).

Although the first two aspects of sovereignty tend to go hand in hand, generally, it is possible to have some but not all of these. In particular, a **de facto state**, such as Somaliland in East Africa, the Turkish Republic of Northern Cyprus, Trans-Dniester, Abkhazia, and South Ossetia in post-communist Europe, or even Taiwan, has effective internal and border controls and domestic legitimacy but lacks international recognition.[6] If such recognition eventually occurs, then the state will no longer be de facto. Conversely, without international recognition, a de facto state can be conquered by (or forced back into) the state with formal sovereignty over its territory and thus disappear as a de facto state. Such was the fate of the de facto state of Tamil Eelam, which for decades controlled much of the ethnic-Tamil territory of north and east Sri Lanka until it was defeated by the Sri Lankan military in 2007–2009.[7] Of course, international recognition of a breakaway territory is not determined solely by neutral "merit" based on the extent of domestic and interdependence sovereignty of the territory; rather, especially for major powers, it is based on the foreign policy interests of recognizing (or not) a specific new country.[8] In contrast, a **de jure state** is recognized as a state by the international community but is so weak or illegitimate that it cannot control its own people or its borders.[9]

Part of the rise of sovereignty in European history involved replacing the widespread (but diffuse) control of the Catholic Church. The other part involved the centralization of power. Under the system of feudalism that structured mediaeval Europe, power resided at the level of the local lord or noble, of whom there were thousands on the continent. Jurisdictions differed not only in terms of currency (if they used one at all) but also in terms of weights and measures. Trade across even a moderate area was thus very problematic. The sovereign state was, however, not the only system that arose out of the ashes of feudalism. In Italy, there were city-states, centred on a dominant city (e.g., Florence or Venice) but including smaller neighbouring cities as well. These city-states at least had fixed borders. There were also **confederations** (on this concept see Chapter 6), which sometimes lacked borders altogether. One example, the Hanseatic League, was an alliance of cities around the Baltic Sea. Not only were the members of this league not geographically contiguous, as the league was formed because of function rather than geography, but also they were never constrained by membership; cities simply "joined" and left as they wished.[10] Neither city-states nor confederations had effective, legitimate central control. Consequently, they were not as successful as sovereign states in raising revenue, which was needed to fight wars. Moreover, sovereign states were better in a wide range of areas, such as standardizing weights and measures, introducing a common currency, and establishing centralized justice (including clear property rights and contractual obligations), all of which facilitated trade, economic growth, and, ultimately, tax revenues. Finally, sovereign states could credibly enter into agreements with other sovereign states (but only with these) because states with international legal sovereignty were more likely to honour their commitments; consequently, the international utility of this political structure, the sovereign state, was reinforced.[11]

Although the need to fight wars was not new, with the evolution of warfare toward more professional and thus more expensive armies by the sixteenth century, the financing of war became a (if not *the*) central concern for European political entities. Here the sovereign state showed its superiority in terms of organization and resource extraction. Other political structures, or even sovereign states, that could not "compete" in this regard tended to be conquered by states that were better organized. Thus, war not only arose from greater state capacity but provided a strong incentive to increase this capacity. In Charles Tilly's classic summation, "war made the state, and the state made war."[12] So, by the end of the Napoleonic era, there were considerably fewer political entities in Europe, and these surviving states tended to be relatively effective. However, these European patterns should not be generalized globally. Centeno has shown that "[w]ar did not make states in Latin America" because the main Latin American wars of the nineteenth century "occurred under very different historical circumstances than during the European 'military revolution.'"[13] As for Africa and Asia, as we shall see, most of the countries therein achieved independence, and thus sovereignty, after World War II, and they have thus existed only in an era when the international order discouraged wars against one's neighbours. Consequently, many of the countries in these areas have survived despite having **weak states** (on this concept see Chapter 3).

Geographical and Historical Classifications of States

Today, there are almost 200 sovereign states. Specifically, after the additions of Timor-Leste (East Timor) and Switzerland in 2002, Montenegro in 2006, and South Sudan in 2011, the United Nations (UN) has 193 members. UN membership is a pretty clear measure of the international recognition of a state, although Kosovo and Taiwan merit inclusion in any list of independent states given that both are broadly acknowledged as such even though they do not have UN membership or, in the case of Taiwan, formal diplomatic recognition. At one level, a student could be interested in the specifics of any one of these. Consequently, Table 1.1 gives geographical and historical data for all 195 sovereign states. However, in terms of getting a sense of the countries of the world, we need more than just an alphabetical list. How are we to group all of these states? One way is by placing them into five broad geographic regions—Africa, the Americas, Asia, Europe, and Oceania—as is done in Table 1.1. These five regions now have respectively 54, 35, 43, 49, and 14 states (although these numbers would change slightly if North Africa or the three Transcaucasian states were reclassified).[14] Historically, perhaps the most important factor in contrasting countries is simply their duration, as long-established countries will have had time to consolidate and develop themselves in ways that newly independent states cannot obviously match.[15] Thus, the fact that they joined the UN in the same recent year disguises the reality that Switzerland is one of the world's oldest states whereas Timor-Leste is the fourth newest. (Denmark, France, and Portugal, in that order, are in fact the three oldest states in the world.)

The following historical patterns come from examining the years of independence or state formation of the states that exist today and from looking only at continuous independence through today. First, only 20 states date back to before 1800. These states are mostly European, although the United States also became independent in this era. The United States is thus the contemporary world's nineteenth oldest state. Then in the first half of the nineteenth century, or more precisely from 1804 to 1847,

TABLE 1.1 The Countries of the World: Geographical and Historical Data (as of 2012)

Country	Geographic Region	Geographic Subregion	Year of Modern Independence or State Formation	State Independence Achieved From[1]	Year of First Constitution	Year of Current Constitution or Last Major Revisions
Afghanistan	Asia	South Asia	1921	(formerly a British protectorate)	1923	2005
Albania	Europe	South-Eastern Europe	1912	Ottoman Empire	1914	1998
Algeria	Africa	North Africa	1962	France	1963	2008
Andorra	Europe	Western Europe	1993	(formerly a French-Spanish protectorate)	1993	1993
Angola	Africa	Southern Africa	1975	Portugal	1975	2010
Antigua and Barbuda	Americas	Caribbean	1981	United Kingdom	1981	1981
Argentina	Americas	South America	1816	Spain	1819	1994
Armenia	Europe	Transcaucasus	1991	Soviet Union	1863	2005
Australia	Oceania		1901	United Kingdom	1901	1901
Austria*	Europe	Central Europe	1526		1867	1945
Azerbaijan	Europe	Transcaucasus	1991	Soviet Union	1978	2009
Bahamas	Americas	Caribbean	1973	United Kingdom	1973	1973
Bahrain	Asia	Middle East	1971	(formerly a British protectorate)	1973	2002
Bangladesh	Asia	South Asia	1971	Pakistan	1972	1972
Barbados	Americas	Caribbean	1966	United Kingdom	1966	1966
Belarus	Europe	Eastern Europe	1991	Soviet Union	1919	2004
Belgium	Europe	Western Europe	1830	Netherlands	1831	1994
Belize	Americas	Central America	1981	United Kingdom	1854	1981
Benin	Africa	West Africa	1960	France	1959	1990
Bhutan	Asia	South Asia	1949	United Kingdom (formerly a British protectorate)	2008	2008

* The date of Austria's state formation refers to the consolidation of the Hapsburg Empire; the first Republic of Austria was established in 1919.

Country	Geographic Region	Geographic Subregion	Year of Modern Independence or State Formation	State Independence Achieved From[1]	Year of First Constitution	Year of Current Constitution or Last Major Revisions
Bolivia	Americas	South America (Andean)	1825	Spain	1825	2009
Bosnia-Herzegovina*	Europe	South-Eastern Europe	1992	Yugoslavia	1910	1995
Botswana	Africa	Southern Africa	1966	(formerly a British protectorate)	1960	1966
Brazil	Americas	South America	1822	Portugal	1824	1988
Brunei	Asia	South East Asia	1984	(formerly a British protectorate)	1959	1984
Bulgaria	Europe	South-Eastern Europe	1908	Ottoman Empire	1879	1991
Burkina Faso	Africa	West Africa	1960	France	1960	2000
Burma/Myanmar	Asia	South East Asia	1948	United Kingdom	1947	2011
Burundi	Africa	Central Africa	1962	Belgium	1961	2005
Cambodia	Asia	South East Asia	1953	France	1947	1993
Cameroon	Africa	Central Africa	1961	(divided between France and the United Kingdom)	1961	2008
Canada	Americas	North America	1867	United Kingdom	1791	1982
Cape Verde	Africa	West Africa	1975	Portugal	1975	1999
Central African Republic	Africa	Central Africa	1960	France	1962	2004
Chad	Africa	Central Africa	1960	France	1959	2005
Chile	Americas	South America	1818	Spain	1818	2004
China	Asia	East Asia	1368		1908	1982
Colombia	Americas	South America (Andean)	1819	Spain	1811	2005
Comoros	Africa	Southern Africa	1975	France	1961	2001
Congo, DR (Kinshasa)	Africa	Central Africa	1960	Belgium	1960	2006

* Bosnia-Herzegovina was under Ottoman rule for centuries, then occupied by the Austro-Hungarian Empire in 1878, then awarded to the Kingdom of Serbs, Croats, and Slovenes (later Yugoslavia) in 1918.

Country	Geographic Region	Geographic Subregion	Year of Modern Independence or State Formation	State Independence Achieved From[1]	Year of First Constitution	Year of Current Constitution or Last Major Revisions
Congo, R (Brazzaville)	Africa	Central Africa	1960	France	1960	2002
Costa Rica	Americas	Central America	1821/1838	Spain/United Provinces of Central America	1825	1949
Croatia*	Europe	South-Eastern Europe	1991	Yugoslavia	1947	2001
Cuba**	Americas	Caribbean	1899	Spain	1901	2002
Cyprus (Greek)***	Europe	South-Eastern Europe	1960	United Kingdom	1960	1960
Czech Republic	Europe	Central Europe	1918/1992	Austrian Empire/ Czechoslovakia	1920/1993	1993
Denmark	Europe	Northern Europe	899		1849	1953
Djibouti	Africa	East Africa	1977	France	1981	2010
Dominica	Americas	Caribbean	1978	United Kingdom	1978	1978
Dominican Republic	Americas	Caribbean	1821/1844	Spain/Haiti	1844	2010
Ecuador	Americas	South America (Andean)	1822/1830	Spain/Colombia	1830	2008
Egypt	Africa	North Africa	1922	United Kingdom	1923	2012
El Salvador	Americas	Central America	1821/1838	Spain/United Provinces of Central America	1841	1983
Equatorial Guinea	Africa	Central Africa	1968	Spain	1968	2011
Eritrea[†]	Africa	East Africa	1993	Ethiopia	1997	1997
Estonia[‡]	Europe	Northern Europe	1918/1991	Russia/Soviet Union	1918/1992	1992
Ethiopia	Africa	East Africa	1682		1931	1995
Fiji	Oceania	Melanesia	1970	United Kingdom	1966	1998

*   Croatia was under Hungarian rule prior to the creation of the Kingdom of Serbs, Croats, and Slovenes (later Yugoslavia) in 1918.

** Cuba was a de facto protectorate of the United States until 1933.

*** Since 1974, Cyprus has been divided de facto between the Greek Cypriot–controlled majority area (the government of which has legal sovereignty over the entire island) and the Turkish minority area that declared itself an independent republic in 1983 (recognized only by Turkey).

[†]   Eritrea was an Italian colony until World War II.

[‡]   Estonia was independent in the interwar period.

Country	Geographic Region	Geographic Subregion	Year of Modern Independence or State Formation	State Independence Achieved From[1]	Year of First Constitution	Year of Current Constitution or Last Major Revisions
Finland*	Europe	Northern Europe	1918	Russia	1906	2000
France	Europe	Western Europe	987		1791	2000
Gabon	Africa	Central Africa	1960	France	1961	1991
Gambia	Africa	West Africa	1965	United Kingdom	1970	1997
Georgia	Europe	Transcaucasus	1918/1991	Russia/Soviet Union	1921/1995	1995
Germany**	Europe	Western Europe	1871		1871	1949
Ghana	Africa	West Africa	1957	United Kingdom	1925	1993
Greece	Europe	South-Eastern Europe	1832	Ottoman Empire	1822	2001
Grenada	Americas	Caribbean	1974	United Kingdom	1973	1974
Guatemala	Americas	Central America	1821/1839	Spain/United Provinces of Central America	1851	1993
Guinea	Africa	West Africa	1958	France	1958	2010
Guinea-Bissau	Africa	West Africa	1973	Portugal	1973	1984
Guyana	Americas	South America	1966	United Kingdom	1792	1980
Haiti	Americas	Caribbean	1804	France	1789	1987
Honduras	Americas	Central America	1821/1838	Spain/United Provinces of Central America	1825	1982
Hungary***	Europe	Central Europe	1867	(as a union with Austria)	1848	2012
Iceland	Europe	Northern Europe	1918	Denmark	1874	1944
India	Asia	South Asia	1947	United Kingdom	1950	1950
Indonesia	Asia	South East Asia	1945	Netherlands	1945	2002
Iran	Asia	Middle East	1501		1906	1989

* Finland was Swedish until 1809, then Russian.

** Germany was divided into the Federal Republic of Germany (West Germany) and the German Democratic Republic (East Germany) in 1949, following World War II. The 1949 constitution of West Germany became the constitution of the united Germany in 1990.

*** The union (Dual Monarchy) with Austria ended in 1918, and a separate Hungarian state was established by 1920.

Country	Geographic Region	Geographic Subregion	Year of Modern Independence or State Formation	State Independence Achieved From[1]	Year of First Constitution	Year of Current Constitution or Last Major Revisions
Iraq	Asia	Middle East	1932	(formerly a British protectorate)	1925	2005
Ireland	Europe	Western Europe	1921	United Kingdom	1922	1937
Israel	Asia	Middle East	1948	(formerly part of a British protectorate)	Unwritten Constitution	
Italy	Europe	Western Europe	1861		1861	1948
Ivory Coast	Africa	West Africa	1960	France	1960	2000
Jamaica	Americas	Caribbean	1962	United Kingdom	1884	1962
Japan	Asia	East Asia	1609		1889	1947
Jordan	Asia	Middle East	1946	United Kingdom	1928	1952
Kazakhstan	Asia	Central Asia	1991	Soviet Union	1993	2007
Kenya	Africa	East Africa	1963	United Kingdom	1954	2010
Kiribati	Oceania	Micronesia	1979	United Kingdom	1979	1979
Korea, North*	Asia	East Asia	1945/1948	Japan/Soviet Union	1948	1972
Korea, South**	Asia	East Asia	1945/1948	Japan/USA	1948	1988
Kosovo	Europe	South-Eastern Europe	2008	Serbia	1974	2008
Kuwait	Asia	Middle East	1961	(formerly a British protectorate)	1938	1962
Kyrgyzstan	Asia	Central Asia	1991	Soviet Union	1993	2010
Laos	Asia	South East Asia	1953	(formerly a French protectorate)	1947	2003
Latvia***	Europe	Northern Europe	1918/1991	Russia/Soviet Union	1922/1991	1993
Lebanon	Asia	Middle East	1943	France	1926	1990
Lesotho	Africa	Southern Africa	1966	(formerly a British protectorate)	1966	1993

*　North Korea was under Soviet occupation from 1945 to 1948.
**　South Korea was under US military government from 1945 to 1948.
***　Latvia was independent in the interwar period.

Country	Geographic Region	Geographic Subregion	Year of Modern Independence or State Formation	State Independence Achieved From[1]	Year of First Constitution	Year of Current Constitution or Last Major Revisions
Liberia	Africa	West Africa	1847		1839	1986
Libya*	Africa	North Africa	1951	Italy	1951	2011
Liechtenstein	Europe	Western Europe	1719		1818	2003
Lithuania**	Europe	Northern Europe	1918/1991	Russia / Soviet Union	1922 / 1990	1992
Luxembourg	Europe	Western Europe	1867	Netherlands	1868	1919
Macedonia***	Europe	South-Eastern Europe	1991	Yugoslavia	1991	2009
Madagascar	Africa	Southern Africa	1960	France	1959	2010
Malawi	Africa	Southern Africa	1964	United Kingdom	1966	1995
Malaysia	Asia	South East Asia	1963	United Kingdom	1957	1957
Maldives	Asia	South Asia	1965	United Kingdom	1968	2008
Mali	Africa	West Africa	1960	France	1960	1992
Malta	Europe	Western Europe	1964	United Kingdom	1964	1974
Marshall Islands	Oceania	Micronesia	1986	(formerly a United States protectorate)	1979	1979
Mauritania	Africa	West Africa	1960	France	1959	2006
Mauritius	Africa	Southern Africa	1968	United Kingdom	1968	1992
Mexico	Americas	North America	1810	Spain	1824	1992
Micronesia	Oceania	Micronesia	1986	(formerly a United States protectorate)	1979	1979
Moldova†	Europe	Eastern Europe	1991	Soviet Union	1994	1994
Monaco	Europe	Western Europe	1861	France	1911	2002
Mongolia	Asia	East Asia	1921	China	1924	1992

* Libya was under Anglo-French administration as a UN protectorate after Italy's defeat in World War II.
** Lithuania was independent in the interwar period.
*** Macedonia was under Ottoman rule for centuries until it was conquered by Serbia in 1912-1913.
† Most of Moldova was part of Romania until World War II.

Country	Geographic Region	Geographic Subregion	Year of Modern Independence or State Formation	State Independence Achieved From[1]	Year of First Constitution	Year of Current Constitution or Last Major Revisions
Montenegro*	Europe	South-Eastern Europe	2006	Yugoslavia	1905	2007
Morocco	Africa	North Africa	1956	France	1962	2011
Mozambique	Africa	Southern Africa	1975	Portugal	1975	1990
Namibia	Africa	Southern Africa	1990	(formerly a South African protectorate)	1990	1990
Nauru	Oceania	Micronesia	1968	(formerly an Australian protectorate)	1968	1968
Nepal	Asia	South Asia	1769		1951	2007
Netherlands	Europe	Western Europe	1581		1814	1983
New Zealand	Oceania	Polynesia	1907	United Kingdom	Unwritten Constitution	?
Nicaragua	Americas	Central America	1821/1838	Spain / United Provinces of Central America	1826	2009
Niger	Africa	West Africa	1960	France	1960	1999
Nigeria	Africa	West Africa	1960	United Kingdom	1914	1999
Norway**	Europe	Northern Europe	1814	Denmark (as a union with Sweden)	1814	1814
Oman	Asia	Middle East	1971	(formerly a British protectorate)	1996	1996
Pakistan	Asia	South Asia	1947	United Kingdom	1956	2010
Palau	Oceania	Micronesia	1994	(formerly a United States protectorate)	1981	1981
Panama***	Americas	Central America	1821/1903	Spain / Colombia	1904	2004
Papua New Guinea	Oceania	Melanesia	1975	(formerly an Australian-administered UN protectorate)	1975	1975
Paraguay	Americas	South America	1811	Spain	1813	1992
Peru	Americas	South America (Andean)	1821	Spain	1823	1993

* Montenegro was independent from 1878 to 1918, when it joined the Kingdom of Serbs, Croats, and Slovenes (later Yugoslavia); from 2003 to 2006, Montenegro was in a confederation with Serbia.
** The royal union between Norway and Sweden ended in 1905.
*** Panama was a de facto protectorate of the United States until 1936.

Country	Geographic Region	Geographic Subregion	Year of Modern Independence or State Formation	State Independence Achieved From[1]	Year of First Constitution	Year of Current Constitution or Last Major Revisions
Philippines	Asia	South East Asia	1898/1946	Spain/United States	1899	1987
Poland	Europe	Central Europe	1919	(divided among Austria, Germany, and Russia)	1815	1997
Portugal	Europe	Western Europe	1143		1822	1989
Qatar	Asia	Middle East	1971	(formerly a British protectorate)	1970	2005
Romania	Europe	South-Eastern Europe	1878	Ottoman Empire	1866	2003
Russia	Europe	Eastern Europe	1480		1906	2008
Rwanda	Africa	Central Africa	1962	(formerly a Belgium-administered UN protectorate)	1962	2003
Saint Kitts and Nevis	Americas	Caribbean	1983	United Kingdom	1976	1983
Saint Lucia	Americas	Caribbean	1979	United Kingdom	1979	1979
Saint Vincent and the Grenadines	Americas	Caribbean	1979	United Kingdom	1979	1979
Samoa (Western)	Oceania	Polynesia	1962	(formerly a New Zealand protectorate)	1962	1962
San Marino	Europe	Western Europe	1631		1600	2002
São Tomé and Príncipe	Africa	Central Africa	1975	Portugal	1975	1990
Saudi Arabia*	Asia	Middle East			Unwritten Constitution	
Senegal	Africa	West Africa	1960	France	1958	2001
Serbia**	Europe	South-Eastern Europe	1878	Ottoman Empire	1835	2006
Seychelles***	Africa	Southern Africa	1976	United Kingdom	1976	1993
Sierra Leone	Africa	West Africa	1961	United Kingdom	1961	1991
Singapore†	Asia	South East Asia	1965	United Kingdom	1959	2010

*   Saudi Arabia has no written constitution per se, and the Koran is the formal source of authority; however, in 1992 three royal decrees outlined a "basic system of government" (that is, political institutions).

** Serbia was autonomous from 1815; the Kingdom of Serbs, Croats, and Slovenes formed in 1918 and was renamed Yugoslavia in 1929; Serbia and Montenegro formed a confederation from 2003 to 2006.

*** Originally a French colony, the Seychelles came under British control in 1814.

†   Singapore was part of the Malaysian Federation from 1963 to 1965.

Country	Geographic Region	Geographic Subregion	Year of Modern Independence or State Formation	State Independence Achieved From[1]	Year of First Constitution	Year of Current Constitution or Last Major Revisions
Slovakia	Europe	Central Europe	1918/1992	Hungarian Empire/Czechoslovakia	1939	1998
Slovenia*	Europe	Central Europe	1992	Yugoslavia	1991	2000
Solomon Islands	Oceania	Melanesia	1978	United Kingdom	1978	1978
Somalia	Africa	East Africa	1960	(divided between the United Kingdom and Italy)	1960	none in force
South Africa	Africa	Southern Africa	1910	United Kingdom	1909	1997
South Sudan	Africa	East Africa	2011	Sudan	2005	2011
Spain	Europe	Western Europe	1479		1812	1978
Sri Lanka	Asia	South Asia	1948	United Kingdom	1833	2010
Sudan	Africa	East Africa	1956	United Kingdom	1952	2005
Suriname	Americas	South America	1975	Netherlands	1975	1987
Swaziland	Africa	Southern Africa	1968	United Kingdom	1968	2006
Sweden	Europe	Northern Europe	1388		1809	2011
Switzerland**	Europe	Western Europe	1291		1848	2000
Syria***	Asia	Middle East	1944	France (previously Ottoman)	1930	2012
Taiwan†	Asia	East Asia	1947		1947	2005
Tajikistan	Asia	Central Asia	1991	Soviet Union	1994	1994
Tanzania	Africa	East Africa	1961	UK-administered UN trusteeship	1961	1992
Thailand	Asia	South East Asia	1782		1932	2007
Timor-Leste (East Timor)	Asia	South East Asia	1975/2002	Portugal/Indonesia	2002	2002
Togo	Africa	West Africa	1960	French-administered UN trusteeship	1963	1992

* Slovenia was under Austrian (Hapsburg) rule prior to the creation of the Kingdom of Serbs, Croats, and Slovenes (later Yugoslavia) in 1918.
** Swiss independence was not formally recognized until 1648.
*** Syria was in a political union with Egypt as the United Arab Republic from 1958 to 1961.
† The People's Republic of China claims Taiwan (officially The Republic of China) as a province.

Country	Geographic Region	Geographic Subregion	Year of Modern Independence or State Formation	State Independence Achieved From[1]	Year of First Constitution	Year of Current Constitution or Last Major Revisions
Tonga	Oceania	Polynesia	1970	(formerly a British protectorate)	1875	1988
Trinidad and Tobago	Americas	Caribbean	1962	United Kingdom	1949	1976
Tunisia	Africa	North Africa	1956	France	1861	2002
Turkey*	Europe	South-Eastern Europe	1473		1876	2010
Turkmenistan	Asia	Central Asia	1991	Soviet Union	1992	2008
Tuvalu	Oceania	Polynesia	1978	United Kingdom	1978	1986
Uganda	Africa	East Africa	1962	United Kingdom	1955	2005
Ukraine	Europe	Eastern Europe	1991	Soviet Union	1919	1996
United Arab Emirates	Asia	Middle East	1971	(formerly a British protectorate)	1971	1996
United Kingdom	Europe	Western Europe	1707		Unwritten Constitution	
United States	Americas	North America	1776	United Kingdom	1781	1789
Uruguay	Americas	South America	1811/1825	Spain / Brazil	1830	2004
Uzbekistan	Asia	Central Asia	1991	Soviet Union	1992	2002
Vanuatu	Oceania	Melanesia	1980	(formerly under Anglo-French joint rule)	1980	1980
Venezuela	Americas	South America (Andean)	1821/1830	Spain / Colombia	1811 / 1830	2009
Vietnam	Asia	South East Asia	1954	France	1946	1992
Yemen**	Asia	Middle East	1967	United Kingdom (South Yemen)	1964	2001
Zambia	Africa	Southern Africa	1964	United Kingdom	1964	1996
Zimbabwe***	Africa	Southern Africa	1980	United Kingdom	1923	1990

* The date of Turkey's independence refers to the creation of a centralized Ottoman Empire based in Istanbul (Constantinople); the modern Turkish Republic was founded in 1923.

† North Yemen became independent in 1918 after the collapse of Ottoman rule; North and South Yemen joined in 1990.

‡ A unilateral declaration of independence was made by the white minority of Zimbabwe (then Rhodesia) in 1965.

NOTE: Some countries were divided after independence and later reunified (Germany, Vietnam, Yemen). Information on the country from which independence was achieved is given only when relevant.

22 more states, overwhelmingly in Latin America, were formed or became independent.[16] However, in the *second* half of the nineteenth century, or more precisely from 1852 to 1878, only nine new and still ongoing states came into existence, and these few new states were overwhelmingly in Europe. Indeed, after the Treaty of Berlin in 1878, which recognized the independence of Romania, Serbia, and Montenegro, there was more than a 20-year break until the formation of Australia in 1901. That said, the latter half of the nineteenth century did see the creation of Canada, which is tied for 46th in terms of longevity. Then from 1901 (Australia) through 1944 (Syria), another 17 new states were added. These were scattered over various regions but, at the end of this period, many arose in the Middle East. The real explosion in the number of states came after World War II, starting with Indonesia in 1945.[17] Indeed, from 1945 (Indonesia) to 1990 (Namibia) no fewer than 100 of today's states were formed or became independent—over half of the total extant today. These states arose first throughout Africa and Asia and later (from 1962 onwards) also in the Caribbean and Oceania. This sudden increase in the number of states largely reflected the processes of decolonization in these regions.[18] Finally, the period from 1991 to the present has seen a relatively high number of new states, 27, overwhelmingly in Europe but also in Central Asia, due to the **dissolution** (complete break-up) of the Soviet Union,[19] Yugoslavia, and Czechoslovakia.

Future States and How These Might Arise

In the future, new states are likely to emerge in one of three ways (but two main ones). First, places that are still colonies or territories under the control of existing states could be granted their independence. For example, we might soon see an independent New Caledonia and, further in the future, an independent Greenland. Chapter 6 will note some of these relationships. Second, a part of a current country could secede and form a new country. Palestinian independence from Israel, Scottish independence from the United Kingdom, and Serbian (Srpska Republic) independence from Bosnia-Herzegovina could be achieved in this way. Also, although less possible now than decades ago, Quebec could gain independence from Canada. That said, if unilateral **secession** (that is, secession occurring against the will of the existing "host" state) is a reality on the ground but is not followed by diplomatic recognition, this process would produce more de facto states but not truly sovereign ones. The third and least likely way in which new states could occur would be through **dissolution**, that is, a current state dissolving completely into two or more separate parts. However, the only two states for which dissolution seems even remotely possible are Belgium and Yemen. Conversely, the number of sovereign states could decrease marginally if two currently sovereign states merged in some way, as might occur someday with the Koreas and as did occur in 1975 when North Vietnam conquered South Vietnam, in 1990 when North and South Yemen merged, and in 1990 when East Germany was dissolved and Germany was reunited.

Outline of This Book

This textbook takes the following approaches and sequence. Chapter 2 discusses what is meant by development across a wide range of aspects, including bureaucracies and civil-military relations, and how these aspects of development ideally should occur. Chapter 3 examines variations in state effectiveness and the related issues of political economy and economic development. In Chapter 4, we outline in detail what is meant by liberal democracy, which involves five components, and more generally categorize the regimes of the countries of the world today. All of these national regimes can be put into one of four categories: liberal democracies, electoral democracies, semi-liberal autocracies, and closed autocracies. These categories are defined and contrasted. In Chapter 5, explanations and statistical analyses are made of the factors conducive to *individual* countries being more or less democratic. We focus on democracies more closely in Chapter 6 through Chapter 8, grouping together the liberal and electoral democracies and going into more detail about their political institutions, party politics, and patterns of power—specifically, whether power is concentrated or diffused, centralized or decentralized. Chapter 9 examines the autocracies (non-democracies), which can be totalitarian, sultanistic, or authoritarian, although, in fact, these divide further into eight different subtypes of autocracies. Chapter 10 looks at transitions to democracy and includes both an examination of the notion of global democratic "waves" (and "reverse waves") and an assessment of the prospects for new democracies to become "consolidated." Conversely, we shall see why and how democracies "break down." Finally, in Chapter 11, we assess the potential for various countries, and thus the world as a whole, to become either more democratic or less democratic in the future—or indeed to oscillate back and forth in this regard.

Head of Government versus Head of State

One initial distinction to be clear on is that between the head of government, defined as the most powerful politician (the one who runs the country), and the head of state, defined as the symbolic national head (the one who awards honours and receives the credentials of foreign diplomats). These may be separate or fused positions. A separate head of state can take many forms. However, one key distinction is whether or not the head of state is a hereditary monarch and thus the country is a monarchy. If not—no matter the resulting nature of the position—then the country is a **republic**. Although the nature of the head of state in this regard can be quite important and even politically divisive, it does not determine the overall regime type. In other words, monarchies can be democratic (as in the Netherlands or the United Kingdom) or autocratic (as in Brunei or Saudi Arabia), and, likewise, republics can be democratic (as in France or the United States) or autocratic (as in China or Sudan).

A Note on Mathematical Formulae

Political science students are rarely fans of mathematics, and, in this book, mathematical calculations are kept to a minimum. However, you will need to note a few of these. The first such calculation is the *t-test,* which is used to assess differences amongst (the means of) two groups of data. A higher (absolute) number indicates a greater difference. That said, as is the nature of statistical calculations, what really matters is whether the t score is statistically significant, by which we mean whether its level of significance is .05 or *less.* Consequently, ever-lower values—down to .000—would indicate ever-higher significance. Second, there is the *Pearson chi-square test,* used when data are grouped into an "N by N" (at least, and usually, a "2 by 2") table. A higher number here indicates the tendency of one specific category of a given variable to be associated with one specific category of another variable. Again, what is key here is the significance level. Third, there is *multiple regression.* This calculation assesses the combined explanatory nature of several independent variables on one dependent variable (in what is called a "model"). A variable that may "explain" (relate to) some other variable on its own may in fact lose this causal relationship when other, stronger, variables are included. A multiple regression will thus establish what, collectively, are the most useful explanatory variables for the dependent variable in question. A multiple regression will still provide t scores and significance levels for each independent variable in the model, as well as for a constant. In addition, the overall relationship is given in the form of an adjusted r^2, which ranges from 0 (absolutely no relationship with the dependent variable) to 1 (a full explanation of absolutely all the variation in the dependent variable, which is, of course, "too much to expect"). An adjusted r^2 of 0.500 or higher is generally seen as indicating a strong explanatory relationship.

A separate relevant calculation is that of the "effective number" of something. If we count something by integers (1, 2, 3, 4, etc.), then we are counting each with the same value of 1. This is fine if we want to treat everything the same, but problematic if the "things" are of greatly different size. Thus, the effective number of something, indicated by N, is a calculation that weights each item by size (as a percentage of the overall total). Where everything is of the same size, then the effective number is the same as the actual integer number; otherwise, though, it is different.

A concrete example that uses the "effective number" calculation will help us understand the concept. Let us imagine we are talking about the effective number of political parties in a country and determining this by seat shares. In the case of party A and party B each getting exactly half of the seats, we would say the effective number of political parties is 2. But when party A has 90 per cent of the seats and party B has 10 per cent, the effective number of political parties measured by seat count is closer to 1 (1.22 to be exact).

Some examples of this calculation are as follows (to two decimal places):

WITH TWO THINGS:

A has 50%	A has 66.7%	A has 90%
B has 50%	B has 33.3%	B has 10%
N = 2.00	N = 1.80	N = 1.22

WITH THREE THINGS:

A has 33.3%	A has 44%	A has 70%	A has 90%
B has 33.3%	B has 44%	B has 20%	B has 5%
C has 33.3%	C has 12%	C has 10%	C has 5%
N = 3.00	N = 2.49	N = 1.85	N = 1.23

WITH FOUR THINGS:

A has 25%	A has 40%	A has 44%	A has 70%
B has 25%	B has 30%	B has 44%	B has 10%
C has 25%	C has 20%	C has 8%	C has 10%
D has 25%	D has 10%	D has 4%	D had 10%
N = 4.00	N = 3.33	N = 2.53	N = 1.92

Note that N can never be less than 1.00, which occurs when there is only one thing: that is, A has 100%.

Notes

1 Ruth Collier and David Collier, *Shaping the Political Arena: Critical Junctures, the Labor Movement, and Regime Dynamics in Latin America* (Princeton, NJ: Princeton University Press, 1991), 789.

2 Max Weber, *Max Weber: The Theory of Social and Economic Organization*, ed. Talcott Parsons, trans. A.M. Henderson and Talcott Parsons (New York, NY: The Free Press, 1964), 156.

3 Stephen D. Krasner, "Abiding Sovereignty," *International Political Science Review* 22, no. 3 (July 2001): 229–51, especially 231–33.

4 On Africa, see Jeffrey Herbst, *States and Power in Africa: Comparative Lessons in Authority and Control* (Princeton, NJ: Princeton University Press, 2000), 252.

5 Krasner, "Abiding Sovereignty," 232.

6 Because de facto states are still officially part of (various) internationally recognized sovereign states, they amount to "states within states," in the phrasing of Kingston, Spears, et al. See Paul Kingston and Ian S. Spears, eds., *States-Within-States: Incipient Political Entities in the Post–Cold War Era* (New York, NY: Palgrave Macmillan, 2004).

7 The various aspects of this de facto state were created at different times. On the building of the Tamil Eelam de facto state, see Kristian Stokke, "Building the Tamil Eelam State: Emerging State Institutions and Forms of Governance in LTTE-Controlled Areas in Sri Lanka," *Third World Quarterly* 27, no. 6 (September 2006): 1021–40.

8 Bridget Coggins, "Friends in High Places: International Politics and the Emergence of States from Secessionism," *International Organization* 65, no. 3 (Summer 2011): 433–67.

9 Robert H. Jackson calls these entities "quasi-states." See his *Quasi-States: Sovereignty, International Relations and the Third World* (Cambridge, UK: Cambridge University Press, 1990).

10 League membership was flexible in this way until 1667.

11 This paragraph is drawn from Hendrik Spruyt, *The Sovereign State and Its Competitors: An Analysis of Systems Change* (Princeton, NJ: Princeton University Press, 1994).

12 Charles Tilly, "Reflections on the History of European State-Making," in *The Formation of Nation-States in Western Europe*, ed. Charles Tilly, 3–83 (Princeton, NJ: Princeton University Press, 1975), 42.

13 Miguel Angel Centeno, "Blood and Debt: War and Taxation in Nineteenth-Century Latin America," *American Journal of Sociology* 102, no. 6 (May 1997): 1565–1605; see abstract on page 1565 for quotation.

14 North African states are often grouped with the Middle Eastern states of Asia for historical
    (Ottoman control) and religious reasons. The three Transcaucasian states (Armenia, Azerbaijan,
    and Georgia) are on the border between Europe and Asia, as is Turkey.

15 This distinction obviously leaves aside all of those historical states that no longer exist today, at least
    not independently.

16 Although the term "Latin America" is commonly used in analysis, one should note that this descrip-
    tor does not refer to a geographically based subregion of the Americas but rather to a cultural
    grouping together of countries whose inhabitants speak primarily a Romance language—Spanish,
    Portuguese, or French (in that order of frequency)—and are predominantly Catholic. Consequently,
    "Latin America" normally refers to (only) 20 of the 35 states of the Americas, as follows: Argentina,
    Bolivia, Brazil, Chile, Colombia, Costa Rica, Cuba, the Dominican Republic, Ecuador, El Salvador,
    Guatemala, Haiti, Honduras, Mexico, Nicaragua, Panama, Paraguay, Peru, Uruguay, and Venezuela.

17 Technically speaking, World War II was not quite over in Asia when Indonesia proclaimed its inde-
    pendence in August 1945.

18 As Holsti emphasizes, decolonization produced "the greatest explosion of state creation in world his-
    tory." K. J. Holsti, *Taming the Sovereigns: Institutional Change in International Politics* (Cambridge
    UK: Cambridge University Press, 2004), 273.

19 On the Soviet Union, see Edward W. Walker, *Dissolution: Sovereignty and the Breakup of the Soviet
    Union* (Lanham, MD: Rowman & Littlefield, 2003).

CHAPTER TWO

Development and Political Development

IN THIS CHAPTER YOU WILL LEARN

- how development (or modernization) has cultural, economic, and political aspects;
- how the level of national political culture relates to a regime's legitimacy and thus to the likelihood of military intervention to displace that regime;
- how civil-military relations vary on a continuum, and how this continuum relates to (liberal) democracy;
- what is meant by political development and the central role of institutionalization in this;
- what factors facilitate national identity;
- how and why scholars feel political development should be sequenced; and
- which countries have exemplified this ideal sequence of political development.

Traditional versus Modern Societies

The classic way of distinguishing between traditional and modern societies is Max Weber's theory of authority. Weber documents a shift from *traditional authority*, which is based on the personal authority of the chief (or hereditary monarch) that is passed down to those whose authority is an extension of that of the chief or monarch, to *(rational) legal authority*, which is based on legal rules and wherein the authority to determine these rules is set by the occupants of hierarchical political and bureaucratic offices (not personally by the specific individuals who happen to occupy them). Weber also notes a third type of authority, *charismatic authority,* based on the unique or indeed superhuman personal qualities of an individual who is seen to have divine inspiration. Charismatic authority can occasionally be the basis for political organization, but this type of government rarely outlasts the individual with charisma.[1] Moreover, as Weber notes, over time, there is a "routinization of charisma" inasmuch as "in its pure form charismatic authority may be said to exist only in the process of originating. It cannot remain stable, but becomes either traditionalized or rationalized, or a combination of both."[2] Thus, ultimately, we are left with traditional versus legal-rational authority.

More broadly, in traditional society or what Weber calls "status societies," one's birth determines one's social position, not just for monarchs but for everyone. In such societies, kinship is paramount. People are also more oriented to the past and tend to be fatalistic, if not superstitious. In contrast, in modern society or what Weber calls "class societies," one's social position is determined, and thus can be raised (or lowered), by hard work and achievement (or the lack of these). In theory, all are equal before the law. Individualism is important; family ties are less central. People tend to be forward oriented and rational, generally rejecting tradition as a valid reason in itself. Individuals and society as a whole believe in progress (both personally and collectively), leading to emphases on entrepreneurialism and science. Interpersonal behaviour is likewise generally based on the impersonal rationality of contracts and assessments of others' qualifications rather than on family or personal ties.[3]

In summary, then, modern political societies will differ from traditional ones in terms of what is considered a legitimate decision—these decisions will be based on legal-rational procedures and not on traditional authority. This distinction between traditional and modern political societies can be seen as a difference in **political culture**, that is, in the attitudes, values, and beliefs that individuals have with respect to their political regime or system and to the ways it allocates power and resolves political conflicts.

Political Culture and Military Intervention

Alagappa suggests that countries with high levels of political culture are less prone to military intervention.[4] As noted, countries vary in terms of their political cultures; specifically, they differ as to what is considered legitimate decision-making behaviour. Would any political culture ever consider a military coup to be legitimate, then? It would not if that culture were based on either traditional or legal-rational authority. But, perhaps a leader with charismatic authority could mount a legitimate coup. Usually, though, military coups are staged by rather "faceless" generals. The issue becomes the inverse, that is, whether a military coup would be seen as particularly *illegitimate.* To evaluate this illegitimacy, Finer argues that one can assess and rank national political cultures according to the following three criteria:

▸ Does there exist a wide public approval of the procedures for transferring [political] power, and a corresponding belief that no exercise of power in breach of these procedures is legitimate?

▸ Does there exist a wide public recognition as to who or what constitutes the sovereign authority, and a corresponding belief that no other persons or centre of power is legitimate or duty-worthy?

▸ Is the public proportionality large and well-mobilized into private associations? Do we find cohesive churches, industrial associations and firms, labour unions, and political parties [that are capable of acting independently of the state]?[5]

The higher a nation ranks on the first two criteria, the more likely it is that a military coup (or any other seizure of power) would be seen as illegitimate. The higher a nation ranks on the third criterion—essentially what can be called the level of civil society—the more a society can mobilize itself in defence of the legitimate holders of power. Consequently, the strength of social mobilization (civil support) for civilian structures, leaders, and policies acts as a deterrent to military action by increasing the costs of intervention and reducing the military's bargaining power. Short of a fully revolutionary situation, military interventions would be limited somewhat by the prospect of large-scale civil-military conflict. Thus, the massive mobilization of opposition would undermine or ideally prevent military intervention.[6]

Finer goes further and outlines four categories of national political culture: mature, developed, low, and minimal.[7] (Note that "developed" is not the highest term here.) In countries with a *mature political culture,* such as Canada, the United States, or those of north-western Europe, a military coup is simply unthinkable, even by the military itself. If one were actually tried, it would have no legitimacy. Countries with a *developed political culture* also have an established civil society, but there is some question or dispute as to how power should be transferred and who or what should be the legitimate sovereign authority. In these countries, such as Weimar Germany or the French Fourth Republic, a military coup is, in fact, thinkable but would be broadly resisted by well-mobilized associations (although presumably not so broadly as in countries with a mature political culture). Thus, with a developed political culture a military coup certainly may be tried or threatened, but it would be most unlikely to succeed (fully). For example, the Kapp *putsch* of March 1920 in Germany failed—although it did cause the government to flee Berlin—and was ultimately abandoned in the face of widespread strikes in support of the Weimar Republic. In Spain in February 1981, only a few years after democratization and in the midst of political instability, rebel civil guards seized the *Cortes* (parliament), holding the deputies at gunpoint for 36 hours. The rebels hoped others on the far right would rally to their cause of reversing democracy. Instead, there was widespread public revulsion and an effective condemnation of the uprising by King Juan Carlos. The uprising was quickly thwarted. In August 1991 in the Soviet Union, selected hard-line communists and generals staged a coup to overthrow Mikhail Gorbachev. Gorbachev was placed under house arrest for a couple of days, but there were public demonstrations against the coup (led by Russian president Boris Yeltsin, who escaped capture), and most of the military did not support it. The "August *putsch*," as it was known, fizzled out after three days. Of course, it probably did not help the coup leaders that they were drunk when they addressed the country on television!

In countries with a *low political culture,* such as many Latin American countries during the twentieth century and Pakistan still today, no governing system is seen as unquestionably legitimate; that is, there is an ongoing dispute regarding political institutions and procedures. The level of civic mobilization is moderate to low. In these countries, coups have not only been frequent but usually successful—provided that there are issues, even short-term ones, which produce dissatisfaction with the civilian government (as discussed above). In countries with a *minimal political culture,* for example many Latin American countries during the nineteenth century or places in Central Africa today, political structures lack institutionalization, and society is so localized and unorganized that legitimacy is not really a relevant concept. Coups occur without any broad justification or resistance. Finally, Finer notes that kinship societies with *traditional monarchies* constitute a largely historical fifth class, one in which the monarchical structure has legitimacy but there is no civic organization. Presumably, any military forces would act in the name of the ruling dynasty.

Finer's categories are generally comprehensive, but, to them, we could add cases of, let us say, a *polarized* (intermediate) *political culture*, one that has high political mobilization (as in the first two of Finer's categories) but that combines this with a *major* dispute about the legitimacy of the regime (or alternative regimes). Such political polarization may well lead to a successful military coup (in the sense of the military seizing power), but, to maintain power, the military in such mobilized societies will have to repress—to a greater or lesser extent violently—a well-organized and hitherto influential labour movement, a political left, or likely both. This was the pattern in the "bureaucratic authoritarian" regimes of the 1960s to the 1980s that occurred mainly in Latin America. Specifically, Munck lists six such regimes that fit this pattern: Argentina from 1966 to 1973 and again from 1976 to 1983, Brazil from 1964 to 1985, Chile from 1973 to 1990, Greece from 1967 to 1974, and Uruguay from 1973 to 1985.[8] Indeed, it was no coincidence that, of these regimes, the two that were less modern in a socio-economic sense—Brazil and Greece—were clearly less repressive than the others, where sustained repression, including political "disappearances," were needed to break the left.

In summary, then, the military has difficulty exerting influence when there is high political culture; the government is seen as having a legitimate and moral right to govern; there are high levels of public involvement in and attachment to civil institutions; and a state has widespread public approval, legitimacy, and a procedure for transferring power.[9] Kohn offers a warning here, however:

> even in democracies with rich traditions of unbroken civilian dominance, war and security can (and have) become so important in national life and so central to the definition of the state that the military, particularly during or after [said] crisis or war, can use its expertise or public standing to limit civilian influence into military affairs.[10]

The Basic Problem of Civil-Military Relations

As noted, the military is an actor that can potentially invalidate responsible government. However, most countries determine that they require some sort of military force for national protection. The resulting trade-off has been made clear by Muthiah Alagappa, who comments that "the central paradox of the modern state is how to create a military strong enough to protect the nation-state from external and internal threats but at the same time prevent it from dominating the state or becoming an instrument for internal repression."[11] Richard H. Kohn seconds this view, noting that "the purpose of the military is to defend society, not define it."[12]

In a modern democracy, the military must be not only institutionally separate from other parts of government but also subordinate to the state, and civil authorities must have legitimate control over the means of forcible coercion. In other words, there must be civilian control over the military. By civilians, we mean all organizations and individuals that are not attached to the military, including the majority of the state administrative structure and civil society. Civilian control is thus generally defined as governments and their agencies having the authority to determine the organization, resources, and purpose of the armed forces without threat of military interference.[13] Civilian control and military influence are consequently two sides of the same issue and are often measured by plotting their relationship with each other along the spectrum of a continuum, as we shall do in the next section of this chapter.

Felipe Agüero, however, downplays the term "civilian control," suggesting that it indicates some potential for "antagonistic relations" between the two actors.[14] The armed forces, presumably, have behaved in some fashion that requires not only checks and balances to be imposed by the civilian regime but also constant civilian intervention in military affairs to ensure harmonious relations between the two actors. Instead of the term civilian control, Agüero recommends that social scientists use the term "civilian supremacy" in their analyses; in fact, we shall use both (with supremacy the stronger category) in our continuum below. Specifically, Agüero defines **civilian supremacy** as the "ability of a civilian, democratically elected, government to conduct general policy without interference from the military, to define the goals and general organization of national defense, to formulate and conduct defense policy, and to monitor the implementation of military policy."[15]

Ideally, the civilian supremacy model requires non-military decision makers to determine such things as the military's function or purpose, its extent and composition, its allocation of resources, and its involvement in domestic politics and foreign affairs (including war and defence). Although the military may retain jurisdiction in determining its own professional functions, it must necessarily be under the policy control of civilian authorities and remain subordinate to the rule of law. The military must be subordinate not only to executive politicians such as the president or prime minister but also to the entire structure of government.[16]

Lyle N. McAlister points out that all armed forces (even those traditionally controlled by civilians) are political to some degree. Consequently, he defines military intervention as "the armed forces or parts thereof deliberately participating in governmental processes for purposes transcending legitimate service interests."[17] Military intervention ranges from brief and limited military incursions into civilian affairs to complete military control of the state. States themselves vary from democracies with long histories of civilian supremacy to others where the military has customarily dominated society and those that have yet to develop any institutional apparatus for restraining the armed forces from political activities.

Finally, at what point is civilian supremacy over the military achieved? Agüero suggests that there are four conditions that must be satisfied before the armed forces can be deemed subordinated.[18] First, there must be some regularity in the sense of repeated practice over time of civilian supremacy. Second, the roles and privileges of the military must be codified in the nation's constitution or other primary legal documents. Third, there must not have been any explicit challenges on the part of the military toward civilian authorities for an extended period of time. Last, the military must demonstrate its subordination by accepting willingly a major civilian decision that was previously refused by a politically active military.

Measuring and Classifying Contemporary Civil-Military Relations

Using a scale of several categories based on various criteria remains the commonly accepted practice for classifying the degree of military intervention into a state's political and civilian affairs, which allows us to place countries along a continuum. Although political scientists offer a variety of these continua describing the character of military intervention, all share a polarization between civilian governance, on one side, and military governance, on the other, and offer a gradation of different levels of military involvement in between. Although Liebenow notes that "levels of military involvement in domestic politics do not shift gradually between the points on a scale, such tools remain useful for comparative analyses."[19]

Of the various continua that have been outlined and used by scholars to indicate the range of civil-military relations, Fitch's scale suits our purpose best, but it needs some modification.[20] Fitch outlines five degrees of military intervention (or not): democratic control, conditional subordination, military tutelage, military control, and military regime. As with the definitions of civilian control or supremacy offered previously, the notion of democratic control insists that the military is fully subordinate and accountable to elected officials as well as to the general rule of law. Conditional subordination exists when the military enjoys greater institutional autonomy from the civilian government and, as such, reserves the (formal constitutional or merely historical) right to intervene and impress its preferences on the civilian regime—or even remove the civilian regime in a crisis situation. Military tutelage means that the armed forces enjoy autonomy from political control, exercise the oversight of civilian politicians in certain policy areas, and, again, retain the express right to intercede when a crisis is perceived. Countries are also classified as having the "equivalent to military tutelage" if they are autocracies led by a monarch, and the military is loyal to this monarch but not to civilian officials per se. Under military control, the armed forces direct most policy areas, and the civilian government is subordinate to and exists only at the tolerance of the military. Military control thus often involves a military body that oversees (and overrules) a civilian day-to-day cabinet, such as the Council for National Security in Thailand after its 2006 coup or the Supreme Council of the Armed Forces in Egypt from February 2011 to June 2012. Finally, military rule involves a literal military government having full control over state policy, with cabinet members being drawn from the officer corps of the armed forces, such as in Burma/Myanmar until recently.

Our continuum is presented in Table 2.1; Fitch's analysis is modified in particular by adding the category of **civilian supremacy**, which we have taken from Agüero as outlined earlier.[21] For our purposes, three key differences distinguish civilian control from civilian supremacy: (1) the civilians may lack (enough) expertise in military affairs, thus leaving the military largely with effective control over security policy; (2) the military is not seriously held to account for any past human rights violations; and (3) the military is basically in control of its own internal processes, including personnel matters. That said, both civilian supremacy and civilian control preclude any constitutionally entrenched military powers, military control over civilian positions, or any military sense of a "right" to intervene in times of crisis. Both also (normally) have a vertical command structure wherein a civilian-dominated defence ministry is below the head of government and above all military staff, and this ministry has full command over the military, including operational command. This arrangement is in contrast to a vertical command structure in which military personnel dominate the defence ministry or to a dual command structure in which the (civilian) defence ministry is not in charge of determining defence strategy and executing operational commands.[22]

Overall, it is important to stress (as Table 2.1 does) that, for our purposes, the first four categories—civilian supremacy, civilian control, conditional subordination, and military tutelage—are congruent with calling a country a democracy in the basic

TABLE 2.1 The Continuum of Civil-Military Relations

CIVIL-MILITARY RELATIONS	LIBERAL DEMOCRATIC		ELECTORAL DEMOCRATIC		AUTOCRATIC	
	Civilian Supremacy	**Civilian Control**	**Conditional Subordination**	**Military Tutelage**	**Military Control**	**Military Rule**
NUMERICAL SCORE	10	8	6	4	2	0
Military retains control over security policy	no (but minor influence)	maybe	maybe	yes	yes	yes
Military has control over other policy areas	no	no (but minor influence)	maybe	some	some/most	most/all
Military perceives a "right" to intervene in times of national crisis	no	no	usually	yes	n/a (de facto)	n/a
Head of government	civilian	civilian	civilian	civilian	caretaker; military or military-backed president; or, if civilian prime minister, then a figurehead or "front"	top
Vertical command structure, with a civilian-dominated defence ministry above the armed forces	yes	usually	no	no	no	no
Military defence minister	no	no	maybe	usually	usually	yes
Other military minister(s)	no	no	maybe	usually	usually	yes, a majority
Military has ability to appoint/ override civilian positions	no	no	maybe	some	most	most/all
Constitutionally entrenched military powers/prerogatives	no	no	maybe	yes	yes	yes
Military has "own resources"	no	maybe	some/many	some/many	many	many
Military is accountable for [past] human rights violations	yes	no	no	no	no	no
Military controls its own internal processes	no	yes	yes	yes	yes	yes

sense of a distinction between democracy and autocracy. However, to be deemed a **liberal democracy,** as that regime type will be defined in Chapter 3, a country must exhibit civilian supremacy or civilian control of the military. In other words, although the categories and concepts of conditional subordination and military tutelage are congruent with democracy, they also limit a country to being an **electoral democracy.** Granted, no current countries that we would place in the military tutelage category are electorally democratic, but for example, Brazil was when under military tutelage from 1985 to 1990. On the other side of the spectrum, the two categories of military rule and military control are both part of autocratic rule. Indeed, all of the countries that we would place in the last two categories are examples of **military authoritarianism**—a regime type that will be outlined in Chapter 9. Finally, having democratic civil-military relations is a necessary but not sufficient condition for being a democracy overall. Civilian supremacy or control can be found in many autocracies, such as China, North Korea, and Russia.

Table 2.2 lists the countries of the world as of late 2012 in terms of where they place on this continuum, with countries listed using the 10 to 0 score given under the categories of Table 2.1. Countries listed as "~4" have the "equivalent to military tutelage." One sees that most countries of the world now have either civilian supremacy or civilian control, although only a minority enjoy the highest category of civilian supremacy. Still, these rankings show a definite increase in average civilian control (and a corresponding decrease in average military control) compared with those of a generation ago. This positive trend is due not only to the "third wave of democratization" (see Chapter 10) but also to the fact that assorted new democracies have implemented the various techniques to increase civilian control over the military discussed previously. Indeed, today, there are just a dozen or so countries in which the military is dominant over the civilian authority (and these countries, by definition, are autocracies). Let us stress, however, that, in many countries, the military is subordinate only conditionally to civilian control, making these countries, at best, electoral democracies for the moment (even when democratic overall). Furthermore, in these democratic cases, the military, by definition, certainly could intervene and overthrow the civilian authority in a future crisis, as happened in recent crises in Thailand and Bangladesh. Both of these countries have since re-established democracy—but still with only the conditional subordination of the military.

The Meaning and Goals of Development

Scholars still debate what is meant by development. In part, this debate exists because some scholars argue for, or are criticized for having, a concept of development that is very much focused on the current features of developed Western countries. For them, development means "getting to Denmark," in Fukuyama's apt phrase—with "Denmark" not meaning literally Denmark but a developed country with effective state institutions and good outcomes.[23] For example, as Huntington notes,

TABLE 2.2 Ranking Nations on the Civil-Military Relations Continuum (October 2012)

Rank	Country			
10	Albania	Denmark	Korea, South	Singapore
	Antigua and Barbuda	Finland	Latvia	Slovakia
	Australia	France	Lithuania	Slovenia
	Austria	Germany	Luxembourg	South Africa
	Belgium	Greece	Malta	Spain
	Belize	Hungary	Netherlands	Sweden
	Canada	Iceland	New Zealand	Switzerland
	China	Ireland	Norway	Taiwan
	Costa Rica	Italy	Poland	Trinidad and Tobago
	Croatia	Japan	Portugal	United Kingdom
	Cyprus (Greek)	Jordan	Saint Kitts and Nevis	United States of America
	Czech Republic	Korea, North	San Marino	
8	Andorra	Ethiopia	Marshall Islands	São Tomé and Príncipe
	Argentina	Georgia	Mauritius	Senegal
	Armenia	Grenada	Micronesia	Serbia
	Azerbaijan	Guyana	Moldova	Seychelles
	Bahamas	Haiti	Monaco	Solomon Islands
	Bahrain	India	Mongolia	Tanzania
	Barbados	Iran	Montenegro	Timor-Leste (East Timor)
	Belarus	Iraq	Morocco	Tonga
	Bhutan	Israel	Mozambique	Tunisia
	Bosnia-Herzegovina	Ivory Coast	Namibia	Turkmenistan
	Botswana	Jamaica	Nauru	Tuvalu
	Brazil	Kazakhstan	Nepal	Ukraine
	Bulgaria	Kenya	Palau	United Arab Emirates
	Cameroon	Kiribati	Panama	Uruguay
	Cape Verde	Kyrgyzstan	Papua New Guinea	Uzbekistan
	Chile	Lebanon	Peru	Vanuatu
	Cuba	Lesotho	Philippines	Vietnam
	Djibouti	Libya	Romania	Yemen
	Dominica	Liechtenstein	Russia	Zambia
	Dominican Republic	Macedonia	Saint Lucia	
	Eritrea	Malaysia	Saint Vincent and the Grenadines	
	Estonia	Maldives	Samoa (Western)	
6	Afghanistan	Congo, DR (Kinshasa)	Indonesia	Paraguay
	Angola	Congo, R (Brazzaville)	Kosovo	Rwanda
	Bangladesh	Ecuador	Laos	Sierra Leone
	Benin	El Salvador	Liberia	South Sudan
	Bolivia	Equatorial Guinea	Madagascar	Suriname
	Burkina Faso	Fiji	Malawi	Syria
	Burundi	Gabon	Mauritania	Tajikistan
	Cambodia	Gambia	Mexico	Thailand
	Central African Republic	Ghana	Nicaragua	Turkey
	Chad	Guatemala	Niger	Uganda
	Colombia	Guinea	Nigeria	
	Comoros	Honduras	Pakistan	
4	Algeria	Sri Lanka	Venezuela	Zimbabwe
	Egypt	Togo		
-4	Brunei	Oman	Saudi Arabia	Swaziland
	Kuwait	Qatar		
2	Burma/Myanmar	Guinea-Bissau	Mali	Sudan
0	Somalia			

By the mid-1970s, substantial bodies of literature ... existed elaborating the importance of growth, equity, democracy, stability, and autonomy for developing societies and analyzing the ways in which those societies might best make progress toward those goals. Implicit in the widespread acceptance of these goals was also the acceptance of an image of the Good Society: wealthy, just, democratic, orderly, and in full control of its own affairs, a society, in short, very much like those found in Western Europe and North America. A backward society was poor, inequitable, repressive, violent, and dependent. Development was the process of moving from the latter to the former.[24]

This "modernization school" argument tended to produce three different debates, the first two within the school and the last one between the school and its critics. The first debate was whether all these goals were equally desirable. The second was whether all these goals were equally compatible or whether some had to be sacrificed (at least for a time) to achieve others. Thus, it was and is argued that democracy will impede economic development. The third debate was whether all these goals were still possible. That they were not was the critique of the "dependency school," whose proponents argued that the "core" nations of the North Atlantic had so structured the international economic and political order that it was next to impossible for "peripheral" nations to develop because these states were permanently stuck in a dependent situation. At a minimum, this critique implied that, without autonomy, the other goals of development would be difficult if not impossible to achieve.

Of these goals, the notions of wealth and egalitarianism are more socio-economic. To these could be added other economic and social aspects of modernity or modernization: e.g., high levels of education and literacy, a shift from agriculture to industry and services, urbanization, long life expectancy, and low infant mortality. Certainly, these features are part of any broader notion of development; as will be noted in the next chapter, wealth, life expectancy, and education are combined in the UN's Human Development Index (HDI). Yet none of these are explicitly political. What, then, is meant by **political development**? Huntington's list includes democracy, order, and autonomy, to which can be added the notion of institutionalization. Elsewhere, Huntington defines institutionalization generally as "the process by which organizations and procedures acquire value and stability" and thus become complex (with formal internal structures and hierarchies), adaptable, coherent, and autonomous from other institutions.[25] In terms of specifically political organizations, one means, of course, standard political institutions such as executives, legislatures, and judi-ciaries, which collectively both make and implement national laws and policies, as well as arm's length organizations such as electoral bodies. Above and beyond these, Huntington lays particular stress on the role of political parties in structuring politi-cal demands or "inputs" in modern societies with their consequent mass participa-tion in politics.[26]

The notion of order may sound somewhat "authoritarian," but what Huntington means here is political stability and the ability of governments to govern, which, in turn, he relates back to their level of **political institutionalization**. His classic work in this regard, *Political Order in Changing Societies,* is blunt in setting out the "prob-lem" here; although the book was written in the 1960s and political circumstances have changed (obviously, for example, the Soviet Union no longer exists), it is still worth quoting today because it distinguishes between countries not according to their form of government (their regime type) but instead according to their govern-ment's degree of legitimacy:

> The United States, Great Britain, and the Soviet Union have strong, adaptable, coher-ent political institutions: effective bureaucracies, well-organized political parties, a high degree of popular participation in public affairs, working systems of civilian control over the military, extensive activity by the government in the economy, and reasonably effective procedures for regulating succession and controlling political conflict. [They] command the loyalties of their citizens and thus have the capacity to tax resources, to conscript manpower, and to innovate and to execute policy. If the [Soviet] Politburo, the [British] Cabinet, or the [United States] President makes a decision, the probability is high that it will be implemented through the government machinery.
>
> [The situation is quite different] in many, if not most, of the modernizing countries of Asia, Africa, and Latin America. These countries ... suffer real shortages of food, liter-acy, education, wealth, income, health, and productivity.... [H]owever, there is a greater shortage: a shortage of political community and of effective, authoritative, legitimate government.... [I]n many cases, governments simply do not govern....
>
> In many modernizing countries governments are still unable to ... [control the gov-erned], much less ... [control themselves]. The primary problem is not liberty but the creation of a legitimate public order.... Authority has to exist before it can be limited, and it is authority that is in scarce supply.[27]

Obviously, Huntington is assuming here that government is a good in itself, a point rejected by anarchists. Yet, it is hard to see any goal of development being achieved in a state of anarchy. What is then, perhaps, actually controversial among the previous list of political goals is democracy. Many would argue that it is naïve to assume that everyone and every society wants to be democratic, much less will be. Writing in the 1960s, Rustow and Ward clearly stressed the "non-linkage" between democracy and modernization, even if they do note the linkage between egalitarianism and modernization:

> In the political sphere, it is advisable not to link the broad historical concept of modernization with any particular regime or ideology.... Democracy and representative government are not implied in our definition of modernization. Czar Peter of Russia [Peter the Great], Sultan Mahmud of Turkey, and Emperor Meiji of Japan were modernizers, but decidedly not democrats or conscious forerunners of democracy. Germany was more modern in the 1930s than in the 1880s, though its government was less representative and less liberal....
>
> There are nonetheless certain definite political characteristics that modernizing societies share. Commonly modernization ... proceeds toward some form of mass society—democratic or authoritarian. Under whatever regime, the hallmarks of the modern state are a vastly expanded set of functions and demands. Public services come to include education, social security, and public works while civic duties involve new forms of loyalty, tax payment and, in a world of warring states, military service. The very concepts of public service and civic duty, indeed, are among the vital prerequisites of modern politics.
>
> The tendency, moreover, is for services and obligations to become universal: schooling for all children, a road into every village, conscription for all men, and a tax out of every pay envelope. Hence political modernization clearly has egalitarian tendencies. The performance of all the new or expanded services usually means a vast increase in public employment, just as the more intensive interaction among citizens is accompanied by a vast expansion in the network of communications.[28]

Development and modernization thus involve increased state capacity, which, in turn, requires a change in bureaucratic structures. As Max Weber points out, in mediaeval Europe there was a "patrimonial" system of government in which the ruler was not only an all-powerful autocrat but also able to appoint and promote individuals to administrative positions personally and arbitrarily, based entirely on his (or rarely her) personal judgements. Likewise, the ruler arbitrarily modified these positions or responsibilities, which were thus fluid and without fixed limits or clear relations of authority (except to the ruler). The officials concerned often came from the personal household of the ruler and, in any case, had no particular technical qualifications. Finally, as an extension of the ruler, these officials may or may not have deigned to serve the public; usually a payment of tribute was required to get something done. In the modern (Western) state, these administrative patterns have been replaced by a permanent **bureaucracy**, which is based on a rational hierarchy of authority and which employs full-time civil servants who are hired by formal contracts and promoted based on training and experience, who have defined rights and duties and fixed salaries, and who serve the public neutrally and without using their positions for direct personal gain.[29]

Modernization without Democracy

Chinese political history provides a good illustration of the distinction between failed and successful modernization—separate from democracy.[30] The last imperial era in China was that of the Qing Dynasty, which, except for its prestigious merit-based bureaucracy, lacked modern institutions (for example, there was no national army, just regional ones). From the 1840s, the government could not protect the country from foreign encroachments. In 1911, a revolution toppled the longstanding Qing Dynasty, and a republic was proclaimed. A new provisional constitution was issued in 1912, and elections were held in 1912–13 for a new House of Representatives—the only relatively free national elections ever held in China. However, the leader of the party that won the most seats was assassinated before he could become premier, and the parliament was ultimately suppressed by the autocratic president. Various regional warlords soon replaced the weak authority of the state. Although many of these warlords were brought under control by the late 1920s, not all were, and the Nationalist government really only controlled the east of the country. Ultimately, China would descend into a civil war between the forces loyal to the government of the Republic of China led by the Kuomintang (the Nationalists) and the forces of the Communist Party of China. It is clear that, in the first half of the twentieth century, both legitimate government and political stability were absent in China. Political violence was commonplace. In contrast, after the communists came to power in 1949, they established effective control over mainland China. The communist institutions now function effectively and with regularity. For example, the National People's Congress is chosen every five years indirectly and with very limited competition. Leaders change regularly too, now every decade or so, most recently in 2012 from Hu Jintao to Xi Jinping, and these changes are planned out and occur reasonably smoothly. In short, China has clearly achieved political modernization, even though it is not at all democratic.

Nation Building

Of course, one can note that the challenges of modernization have been harder in China, given its huge size. The size of a country also leads to the issue of national identity—the first factor in the ideal sequence of political development. As Whittlesey notes, "a large state may be weaker than a less well-endowed smaller state because the material conditions of political unity function only in the presence of the emotion of nationality."[31] In other words, state building is easier when there is a clear national identity involved and perhaps easiest when there is complete ethnic homogeneity; both of these circumstances are more likely when a state does not cover a large geographic area. However, states with what amounts to an ethnically homogeneous population are very few in the world: Iceland, Japan, and North and South Korea stand out here, although the Scandinavian countries were also this way until postwar immigration. That said, immigration, if accompanied by some level of assimilation, will not lessen national identity provided this existed before. So perhaps a better way to phrase the issue is to assess the level of ethnic homogeneity at independence. Relating ethnicity to size, one sees that, indeed, the homogeneous nations mentioned are not huge, yet there are also many small countries with multiple ethnic groups— for example, Belgium, Bhutan, Bosnia-Herzegovina, Cameroon, Ghana, Moldova, Sierra Leone, Trinidad and Tobago, and the United Arab Emirates.

In any case, even if a country is ethnically diverse, national identity is facilitated if the country has a dominant ethnic core (provided it is tolerant of minorities). Thus, the national histories of many of the countries of Western Europe started with a core ethnic group (such as the English) or territory (such as the Île de France or the allied German-speaking cantons of Uri, Schwyz, and Unterwalden). Over the course of many centuries, other territories were added to these (sometimes willingly, sometimes not), until the creation of, respectively, today's United Kingdom, France, and Switzerland. This long time span meant that an initial state expanded into new territories, which, sooner or later, usually considered it legitimate—a much easier situation than that of much of Africa and Asia, where independence put multiple ethnic groups into new countries, and few of these ethnic groups could claim any historical dominance.[32] One exception, as Smith notes, is India, where national identity is centred on the Hindi-speaking Hindus of northern and central India.[33] As for Canada, one cannot forget its initial British majority. On the one hand, this majority accommodated the French minority through federalism and assimilated many subsequent waves of immigrants. On the other hand, for generations, this dominant ethnic group saw itself as "British"; *Canadian* identity would develop slowly.

Countries that, at independence, do not have a strong sense of national identity (even for the dominant group) have to establish this identity if they wish to facilitate the legitimacy of the state. This political development requires a conscious process of "nation building," some of which comes through state building, especially through the creation of standardized mass education. However, nation building also involves the creation (or strengthening) of an intangible national identity. As Smith stresses, "The 'nation' is not, as we see, built up only through the provision of 'infrastructures' and 'institutions,' as 'nation-building' theories assumed; but from the central fund of culture and symbolism and mythology provided by shared historical experiences."[34] "Shared historical experiences" is a broad category, and a vague one. The reality is that the creation of national identity involves differentiating one's nation from some *other* nation or nations, and thus the role of the *other* is crucial. Such differentiation, moreover, has come most strongly through war, at least in Western Europe where war not only "made the state," as noted previously, but also made or at least reinforced the nation. As Howard's study of Europe notes, "Self-identification as a Nation implies almost by definition alienation from other communities, and the most memorable incidents in the group-memory consisted in conflict with and triumph over other communities."[35]

A similar argument could be made for the United States, starting with its War of Independence, especially because those still loyal to Britain fled to Canada. But what if independence involves no struggle? In Africa, for example, only a few states (Angola, Guinea-Bissau, Mozambique, Namibia, and Zimbabwe) had to fight a war to gain independence.[36] Most Latin American countries technically fought wars, but these were so brief (Colombia's excepted) as to have little effect in terms of establishing a national identity. Consequently, Latin American countries overwhelmingly suffered from political instability and weak or even failed states during their first decades of independence. Exceptions were Brazil, which retained a monarchy until 1889, and Chile due to its military successes. As Valenzuela writes,

> It is doubtful that Chileans considered themselves a nation before independence.... However, the clear-cut [1839] military victory in the war against the Peru-Bolivia Confederation, a victory without parallel in Latin America, gave the small, divided nation a powerful new sense of confidence and purpose, creating tangible symbols of patriotism and nationality. These feelings were [later] reinforced with the [1883] victory of Chilean forces in the War of the Pacific, which led to the incorporation of large portions of Peruvian and Bolivian territory.[37]

Needless to say, it is not so much the fighting of a war but the actual winning of one that builds national identity. Winning at other more peaceful international events, such as the Olympics, also helps a people develop a national identity.

Sequencing Political Development

Ironically, even if there is some debate about whether to consider democracy the ultimate goal of political development, there has been for a long time a fair consensus among scholars regarding the ideal sequence by which political development should occur if one wishes to produce a stable, democratic state. This sequence of steps goes as follows:[38]

▶ First, there should be a national identity producing national unity. In Nordlinger's analysis, "a national identity may be said to exist when the great majority of the politically relevant actors accord the nation's central symbols and its political elite(s) greater loyalty than that which they maintain toward subnational units, such as tribes, castes, and classes, and toward political elite(s) residing outside the system's territory."[39] The resulting national unity thus ensures that people "have no doubt or mental reservations as to which political community they belong to."[40]

▶ Second, over time, state structures that are legitimate and effective are established and institutionalized, and penetrate throughout the country. These institutions are usually ultimately codified in a constitution.[41] At this point, after these first two steps, one can consider the country modernized in a basic sense.

▸ Third, the various elite groups engage in competition with each other, usually by forming rudimentary political parties. Even if these parties have small memberships and minimal organization, they can still become institutionalized over time. The "prize" for which they are competing may not be total power if the country still has a relevant monarch. Nevertheless, if successful, this stage of elite competition will produce alternations back and forth in power, leading elites to become tolerant of each other and to commit to the proto-democratic procedure of regular elections. Rustow calls this stage the "habituation phase," during which these new habits lead to the internalization of democratic norms.[42]

▸ Fourth, if responsible government does not already exist (as it does in republics), then it is created by monarchs and nobles giving up their political power to elected governments.

▸ Fifth and finally, voting rights slowly expand until there is universal suffrage.[43]

There are several reasons for this sequence. If a territory is without a national identity, any government institution will have great difficulty in getting its wishes followed—unless, of course, it uses coercion, which obviously will not increase the legitimacy of the state. State building should be a slow process because, whenever there is a large expansion of organizational structures, individuals tend to be more concerned with the competition for promotion than with the overall performance of the organization.[44] Moreover, any state structure that is new or rapidly expanding will be less coherent than an already institutionalized one; too many such expanding structures will be problematic. Time is also required for trust to develop between political competitors. Even if political competition is just among the elites, it will take some time for the more conservative to trust the more liberal and vice versa (that is, for each group to trust that the other will not go too far). Robert Dahl summarizes the historical path to this trust in successful polities:

> the rules, the practices, and the culture of competitive politics developed first among a small elite, and the critical transition from nonparty politics to party competition also occurred

TABLE 2.3 The Sequencing of Political Development in the Advanced Industrial States

Country	Decade of Party System Institutionalization	Year of Responsible Government	Year of Universal Male Suffrage
Australia	1900s	1901[a]	1902[c]
Austria	1890s	1918	1907
Belgium	1880s	1831	1919
Canada	1860s	1867[b]	1920[d]
Denmark	1870s	1901	1915
Finland	1860s	1917	1906
France	1900s	1875	1848
Germany	1860s	1918	1869[e]
Greece	1910s	1875	1844/1864
Iceland	(1910s)	1915	1920
Ireland	1920s	1921	1923
Italy	1910s	1861	1912/1919
Japan	1890s	1947	1925
Luxembourg	1900s	1919	1918
Netherlands	1880s	1848	1917
New Zealand	1890s	1854	1879
Norway	1880s	1884	1898
Portugal	1910s	1911	1918
Spain	1930s	1869	1869
Sweden	1880s	1917	1921
Switzerland	1890s	1848	1848
United Kingdom	1860s	1832	1918
United States	1820s	1789	1870

NOTE: Dates in brackets are pre-independence.
[a] 1856 in each colony.
[b] 1854 in the province of Canada.
[c] Before federation in each of the colonies, although full rights for aboriginal Australians not given until 1962.
[d] Full rights for indigenous peoples not given until 1960.
[e] 1849 in Prussia.

initially within the restricted group. Although ... party conflict was often harsh and bitter, the severity of conflict was restrained by ties of friendship, family [and] class ... that pervaded the restricted group of notables who dominated the political life of the country.[45]

A slow expansion of the franchise incorporates and socializes new groups bit by bit into an already existing political culture of tolerance and moderation. On the other hand, if there is no expansion to include new groups, the society is likely to become radicalized. Last but not least, if universal suffrage comes "too soon," for example, in the absence of established political parties and other strong institutions, this will likely either overwhelm the system or lead to a conservative reaction and ultimately to repression, as in Southern Europe. Table 2.3 gives the dates of party system institutionalization (defined here as stable competition between two or more parties, each with a clear voting base), responsible government, and universal male suffrage for the advanced industrial countries. Looking at the dates, one sees that, if universal male suffrage came last (with or without universal female suffrage at the same time), countries overwhelmingly underwent a stable and successful pattern of political development. If universal male suffrage came earlier or at the same time as the other factors, political development was unstable, with breakdowns in democracy.[46] Universal suffrage coming before responsible government led to the creation of mass "irresponsible" parties because these could not aspire to government, as was the case in Imperial Germany. Finally, if responsible government came first, or at least before institutionalized parties, the result was either governmental instability for a time as governments collapsed quickly (Belgium, France, New Zealand, United Kingdom, and for that matter some Canadian provinces) or heavy **clientelism** as governments "bought" legislative support or even rigged elections (Italy, Spain).

Although the United Kingdom is usually given as a country with stable political development, it did experience the violent breakaway of most of Ireland in 1916–22. If one wants to note ideal patterns of political development, it is really the three Scandinavian countries of Denmark, Norway, and Sweden that stand out. Norway, in particular, experienced a political development characterized by a cohesive national identity beginning in the ninth century and growing under the external control of first Denmark and then Sweden, very little violence (and none in achieving independence from Sweden in 1905), ever-increasing democracy, and a "remarkably stable and effective" democratic system[47] in a country with strong regional, cultural, and class divisions (or, as we shall call these later, "cleavages").[48]

Denmark, Norway, Sweden, and the United Kingdom all share the trait of being constitutional monarchies. As Lipset notes, most of the historically stable Western democracies are monarchies.[49] Monarchies seem most relevant in the fourth and fifth steps of political development because a monarch's support for or at least acceptance of these changes goes a long way to reassuring both traditional elites and the groups pressing for change. That is, "The preservation of the monarchy has apparently retained for these [Western] nations the loyalty of the aristocratic, traditionalist,

TABLE 2.4 Monarchies in the World Today

Country	Location (geographic subregion)	Ruling Dynasty	Since
FIGUREHEAD MONARCHIES			
Belgium	Western Europe	House of Belgium	1920
Denmark	Northern Europe	House of Glücksburg	1863
Japan	East Asia	Imperial House of Japan	539
Lesotho	Southern Africa	House of Moshesh	1822
Luxembourg	Western Europe	House of Nassau-Weilburg	1890
Netherlands	Western Europe	House of Orange-Nassau	1544
Norway	Northern Europe	House of Glücksburg	1905
Spain	Western Europe	House of Bourbon	1700/1975
Sweden	Northern Europe	House of Bernadotte	1818
United Kingdom	Western Europe	House of Windsor	1917
OTHER MONARCHIES			
Bahrain	Middle East	House of Khalifa	1783
Bhutan	South Asia	House of Wangchuck	1907
Brunei	South East Asia	House of Bolkiah	1485
Jordan	Middle East	House of Hashemite	1921
Kuwait	Middle East	House of Sabah	1718
Liechtenstein	Western Europe	House of Liechtenstein	1608
Monaco	Western Europe	House of Grimaldi	1297
Morocco	North Africa	House of Alaouite	1631
Oman	Middle East	House of Al Said	1744
Qatar	Middle East	House of Thani	1825
Saudi Arabia	Middle East	House of Saud	1744
Swaziland	Southern Africa	House of Dlamini	18th century
Thailand	South East Asia	House of Chakri	1782
Tonga	Polynesia	House of Tupou	16th century
United Arab Emirates	Middle East	*seven ruling families*	

and clerical sectors of the population which resented increased democratization and equalitarianism. And by accepting the lower strata and not resisting to the point where revolution might be necessary, the conservative orders won or retained the loyalty of the new 'citizens.'"[50] Such behaviour can be contrasted with that of monarchs in Imperial Russia or the Middle East. Of course, even though the general point about monarchies aiding political development still applies today in a theoretical sense, it is not much help if a country does not have a legitimate monarchy. Table 2.4

lists all the monarchies of the world today, distinguishing between those that are pure figureheads (in countries that have completed all five steps of political development) and other monarchies. As can be seen, there are no indigenous monarchies in the Americas, and many monarchies but no figurehead ones in the Middle East.[51]

At the opposite extreme of a country such as Norway, then, are many countries in Africa and Asia, which, when they became independent, had no national identity or viable political institutions nor did much to improve state capacity but which, nevertheless, in the spirit of the times, introduced elections with universal suffrage. It is no great surprise that democracy did not take root in these countries and that political instability and non-democratic rule have been quite common. Is this the fault of colonialism? Certainly the map of Africa in particular was drawn with little concern for traditional tribal identities. Yet perhaps the bigger issue is the nature of colonial rule. In countries that were British colonies, stable political institutions and competitive elections often predated independence. For example, Trinidad and Tobago had its first elections in 1925, decades before its independence in 1962. Granted, only some of the members of the Legislative Council were elected and the franchise was quite limited, but the elections were fair. In India as well there were elections before independence (although no completely free national ones), and the Indian National Congress Party dated back to 1885 and was highly organized. This institution is invariably argued to be one of the factors central to India's relative political and democratic stability. Another key factor contributing to the enduring and stable nature of Indian governance is the competent Indian Civil Service, which dates back to the early 1800s.[52] In contrast, other colonial powers, such as the Belgians or French, generally left their ex-colonies with little in the way of institutions or stable political patterns at the time of independence. Likewise, most of the new countries of Eastern and Central Europe that appeared as a result of the collapse of empires occasioned by World War I lacked any institutionalized administrative structures, in large part because non-ethnic majority bureaucrats left instead of staying around to work for the new states.[53]

Notes

1   Max Weber, *The Theory of Social and Economic Organization*, ed. Talcott Parsons, trans. A.M. Henderson and Talcott Parsons (New York, NY: The Free Press, 1964), 328ff.

2   Weber, *The Theory of Social and Economic Organization*, 363–64.

3   Max Weber, *Economy and Society,* Vol. 2, ed. Günther Roth and Claus Wittich (New York, NY: Bedminster Press, 1968), 928.

4   Muthiah Alagappa, "Investigating and Explaining Change: An Analytical Framework," in *Coercion and Governance: The Declining Political Role of the Military in Asia,* ed. Muthiah Alagappa, 29–66 (Stanford, CA: Stanford University Press, 2001), 47.

5   Samuel E. Finer, *The Man on Horseback: The Role of the Military in Politics,* 2nd rev. ed. (Boulder, CO: Westview Press, 1962), 78.

6   J. Samuel Fitch, *The Armed Forces and Democracy in Latin America* (Baltimore, MD: The Johns Hopkins University Press, 1998), 170, 140.

7   Finer, *The Man on Horseback,* 79–80.

8   Gerardo L. Munck, *Authoritarianism and Democratization: Soldiers and Workers in Argentina, 1976–1983* (University Park, PA: Pennsylvania State University Press, 1998), 26–31.

9   Finer, *The Man on Horseback,* 78.

10   Richard H. Kohn, "How Democracies Control the Military," *Journal of Democracy* 8, no. 4 (1997): 143–44.

11   Alagappa, "Investigating and Explaining Change," 29.

12   Kohn, "How Democracies Control the Military," 142.

13   Harold A. Trinkunas, "Crafting Civilian Control in Argentina and Venezuela," in *Civil–Military Relations in Latin America: New Analytical Perspectives,* ed. David Pion-Berlin, 161–93 (Chapel Hill, NC: The University of North Carolina Press, 2001), 163.

14   Felipe Agüero, *Soldiers, Civilians, and Democracy: Post-Franco Spain in Comparative Perspective* (Baltimore, MD: Johns Hopkins University Press, 1995), 19.

15   Agüero, *Soldiers, Civilians, and Democracy,* 19.

16   J. Gus Liebenow, *African Politics: Crises and Challenges* (Bloomington and Indianapolis, IN: Indiana University Press, 1986), 251; Kohn, "How Democracies Control the Military," 144–45.

17   Lyle N. McAlister, "The Military," in *Continuity and Change in Latin America,* ed. John J. Johnson, 136–60 (Stanford, CA: Stanford University Press, 1964), 144.

18   Agüero, *Soldiers, Civilians, and Democracy,* 21–22.

19   Liebenow, *African Politics,* 251.

20   J. Samuel Fitch, *The Armed Forces and Democracy in Latin America* (Baltimore, MD: The Johns Hopkins University Press, 1998), 39. For other continua, see Muthiah Alagappa, "Asian Civil–Military Relations: Key Developments, Explanations, and Trajectories," in *Coercion and Governance: The Declining Political Role of the Military in Asia,* ed. Muthiah Alagappa, 433–98 (Stanford, CA: Stanford University Press, 2001); Samuel E. Finer, *The Man on Horseback: The Role of the Military in Politics,* 2nd rev. ed. (Boulder, CO: Westview Press, 1962), 77–78; Liebenow, *African Politics,* 251–52; and Eric A. Nordlinger, *Soldiers in Politics: Military Coups and Governments* (Englewood Cliffs, NJ: Prentice-Hall, 1977), 22.

21   Agüero, *Soldiers, Civilians, and Democracy,* 19.

22   David Pion-Berlin, "Defense Organization and Civil-Military Relations in Latin America," *Armed Forces and Society* 35, no. 3 (April 2009): 562–586.

23   Francis Fukuyama, *The Origins of Political Order: From Prehuman Times to the French Revolution* (New York, NY: Farrar, Straus and Giroux, 2011), 14. The original use of Denmark as a generic successful state is found in Lant Pritchett and Michael Woolcock, "Solutions When *the* Solution

is the Problem: Arraying the Disarray in Development," *World Development*, 32, no. 2 (February 2004): 191–212, 192. Both Fukuyama and Pritchett and Woolcock emphasize that the institutions of "Denmark" cannot just be copied in the developing world, or at least not with any guarantee of similar success in a different context.

24 Samuel P. Huntington, "The Goals of Development," in *Understanding Political Development*, ed. Myron Weiner and Samuel P. Huntington, 3–32 (Glenview, IL: Scott, Foresman/Little, Brown, 1987), 6.

25 Samuel P. Huntington, *Political Order in Changing Societies* (New Haven, CT: Yale University Press, 1968), 12.

26 Huntington, *Political Order in Changing Societies*, 89.

27 Huntington, *Political Order in Changing Societies*, 1–8 passim.

28 Robert E. Ward and Dankwart A. Rustow, eds., *Political Modernization in Japan and Turkey* (Princeton, NJ: Princeton University Press, 1964), 4–5.

29 Max Weber, "The Theory of Social and Economic Organization," in *From Max Weber: Essays in Sociology*, eds. H.G. Gerth and C.W. Mills (New York, NY: Oxford University Press, 1946), 342–45.

30 On China's political development from the Qing period to today, see Jonathan D. Spence, *The Search for Modern China*, 2nd ed. (New York, NY: W.W. Norton, 1999).

31 Derwent Whittlesey, *The Earth and the State: A Study of Political Geography* (New York, NY: Henry Holt and Company, 1944), 23.

32 Anthony D. Smith, "State-Making and Nation-Building," in *States in History*, ed. John A. Hall, 228–63 (Oxford, UK: Basil Blackwell, 1986), 245–57 passim.

33 Smith, "State-Making," 255.

34 Smith, "State-Making," 258.

35 Michael Howard, *War and the Nation State* (Oxford, UK: Clarendon Press, 1978), 9.

36 Jeffrey Herbst, *States and Power in Africa: Comparative Lessons in Authority and Control* (Princeton, NJ: Princeton University Press, 2000), 128.

37 Arturo Valenzuela, "Chile: Origins and Consolidation of a Latin American Democracy," in *Democracy in Developing Countries: Latin America*, 2nd ed., ed. Larry Diamond, Jonathan Hartlyn, Juan J. Linz, and Seymour Martin Lipset, 191–247 (Boulder, CO: Lynne Rienner, 1999), 212–13.

38 The following draws from Eric A. Nordlinger, "Political Development: Time Sequences and Rates of Change," *World Politics* 20, no. 3 (April 1968): 494–520; Dankwart A. Rustow, "Transitions to Democracy: Toward a Dynamic Model," *Comparative Politics* 2, no. 3 (April 1970): 337–63; and Larry Diamond, Jonathan Hartlyn, and Juan J. Linz, "Introduction: Politics, Society, and Democracy in Latin America," in *Democracy in Developing Countries: Latin America*, 2nd ed., ed. Larry Diamond, Jonathan Hartlyn, Juan J. Linz, and Seymour Martin Lipset, 1–70 (Boulder, CO: Lynne Rienner, 1999), 13–15.

39 Nordlinger, "Political Development," 498.

40 Rustow, "Transitions," 350.

41 Table 1.1 gives the years of every contemporary state's first and current constitutions for reference.

42 Rustow, "Transitions," 360.

43 An alternative and traditional way of analysing political development is to view this process as a series of crises or challenges that all nations must meet to achieve democratic stability—these being crises of identity, authority/legitimacy, penetration, participation, and distribution. See Leonard

Binder, et al., *Crises and Sequences in Political Development* (Princeton, NJ: Princeton University Press, 1971).

44 Nordlinger, "Political Development," 513.

45 Robert A. Dahl, *Polyarchy: Participation and Opposition* (New Haven, CT: Yale University Press, 1971), 36.

46 It was certainly the case in Latin America that universal male suffrage came well after the creation of elected responsible governments. However, as we shall see, most of these systems lacked national unity and an effective state.

47 Harry Eckstein, *Division and Cohesion in Democracy: A Study of Norway* (Princeton, NJ: Princeton University Press, 1966), 11.

48 Nordlinger, "Political Development," 512; Eckstein, Chapter II and 119–20.

49 Seymour Martin Lipset, *Political Man: The Social Bases of Politics,* expanded ed. (Baltimore, MD: Johns Hopkins University Press, 1981), 65–66.

50 Lipset, *Political Man*, 66.

51 On the survival of the monarchies of the Middle East and North Africa, see Sean L. Yom and F. Gregory Gause III, "Resilient Royals: How Arab Monarchies Hang On," *Journal of Democracy* 23, no. 4 (October 2012): 74–88.

52 Huntington, *Political Order in Changing Societies*, 84.

53 The two exceptions here were Czechoslovakia and Finland. These countries also had decades of competitive elections before independence. Not coincidentally, they were the only two newly independent countries in the region whose democracies survived the interwar period.

CHAPTER THREE

State Effectiveness and Political Economy

IN THIS CHAPTER YOU WILL LEARN

► what the different types of states are (in terms of state effectiveness and penetration);

► what "building state capacity" means, and the geographic and demographic challenges in doing this;

► what is meant by the First, Second, and Third World; and

► how scholars and key international organizations classify states.

States as Institutions

There are four different types of states, that is, the bureaucratic structures of a regime. These are listed in Table 3.1. In the "default" type, which we shall call an **effective state**, the state controls the national territory and the borders and has sufficient domestic penetration to ensure that national laws and policies are in effect throughout the country. To this end, the state has a stable judicial system,[1] the bureaucracy is based on the Weberian principles noted in Chapter 2, and there is sufficient state capacity to raise tax revenues and (in the contemporary world) to provide at least primary education for the vast majority of children. Such an effective state is certainly not all-powerful, but it is legitimate both throughout the country and across the various social classes. In contrast, a **flawed state** is not as effective in terms of depth of penetration or legitimacy. This relative ineffectiveness can be seen in its lower levels of bureaucratic quality, its higher levels of corruption and of tax avoidance (especially when levels of tax avoidance are compared to those of other countries in its region),[2] and its problematic economic performance. As well, a flawed state will have more political riots and rebellions. Greece is a clear contemporary example of a flawed state and is known for its consequent economic difficulties.

Greece is estimated to have the largest shadow economy (as a percentage of the national economy) in the advanced industrial world.

A **weak state** is even less effective than a flawed state in that actual areas of the country are outside of government control. That is, it has problems not just of depth but also of breadth. A weak state is not able to impose national policies throughout the country; indeed, its effect may be limited to the capital and selected other areas, usually those adjacent to the capital. Elsewhere, it lacks a presence, or what presence it has is seen as illegitimate and ignored.[3] Within a weak state, individual state actors may well arbitrarily act to enrich themselves personally rather than follow any legal obligations. For this reason, Evans prefers the term "predatory state" to "weak state," at least for countries like Congo, DR.[4] In any case, a weak state will be inadequate for economic and social development. Often, a weak state arises because a country lacks a national identity (as discussed in Chapter 2).

As noted, a weak state will be in control of the national capital at least and able to impose most of its policies there. However, at the extreme, a state may simply cease to function. This is a **collapsed state**, in which there is truly no state authority but rather anarchy, multi-actor civil war, or fragmentation into various autonomous regional areas, often controlled by warlords. By "multi-actor civil war," we mean a civil war involving multiple actors, often including foreign ones, such as the recent wars in Iraq or Lebanon. However, a state in the throes of a civil war that divides the country in two along a frontline is not deemed to have collapsed, as long as it has a national government that still effectively controls "its" territory and adjacent national borders but not the "rebel" territory. (Examples would be Sri Lanka until recently or the United States during its civil war.) As Table 3.1 shows, only Somalia is currently a collapsed state (and it has been so for a couple of decades). However, several other countries—Afghanistan, Angola, Burundi, Democratic Republic of the Congo (Kinshasa), Iraq, Lebanon, Liberia, and Sierra Leone—have also seen their states collapse in the past decades, but states have since been re-established in these places. That said, there is a possibility of the Afghan state collapsing after the withdrawal of NATO troops. Yemen also seems to be risking collapse.

Of course, as "politics, like nature, abhors a vacuum," one may wonder why a neighbouring country does not take over a state that has collapsed or at least grab some choice territory. Historically, this was certainly the pattern in Europe and also in China when Japan took advantage of, first, the collapse of the Qing Dynasty and, later on, the volatile political situation in the Republic of China between the world

TABLE 3.1 Levels of State Strength (as of October 2012)

EFFECTIVE STATE

Andorra	Cuba	Italy	Monaco	Slovakia
Australia	Cyprus	Japan	Montenegro	Slovenia
Austria	Czech Republic	Korea, South	Netherlands	Spain
Bahamas	Denmark	Kuwait	New Zealand	Sweden
Barbados	Estonia	Latvia	Norway	Switzerland
Belgium	Finland	Liechtenstein	Oman	Taiwan
Botswana	France	Lithuania	Poland	Turkey
Canada	Germany	Luxembourg	Portugal	United Arab Emirates
Chile	Hungary	Macedonia	Qatar	United Kingdom
China	Iceland	Malaysia	San Marino	United States
Costa Rica	Ireland	Malta	Serbia	Vietnam
Croatia	Israel	Mauritius	Singapore	

FLAWED STATE

Albania	Burundi	Iran	Nicaragua	Suriname
Algeria	Cambodia	Jamaica	Palau	Swaziland
Angola	Cape Verde	Jordan	Panama	Syria
Antigua and Barbuda	Dominica	Kazakhstan	Paraguay	Tajikistan
Argentina	Dominican Republic	Kiribati	Peru	Tanzania
Armenia	Ecuador	Korea, North	Romania	Thailand
Azerbaijan	Egypt	Kyrgyzstan	Russia	Togo
Bahrain	Equatorial Guinea	Laos	Rwanda	Tonga
Belarus	Ethiopia	Malawi	Saint Kitts and Nevis	Trinidad and Tobago
Belize	Fiji	Maldives	Saint Lucia	Tunisia
Benin	Gabon	Marshall Islands	Saint Vincent and the Grenadines	Turkmenistan
Bhutan	Gambia	Mexico	Samoa (Western)	Tuvalu
Bolivia	Ghana	Micronesia	Saudi Arabia	Uganda
Bosnia-Herzegovina	Greece	Mongolia	Senegal	Ukraine
Brazil	Grenada	Morocco	Seychelles	Uruguay
Brunei	Guyana	Mozambique	Sierra Leone	Uzbekistan
Bulgaria	India	Namibia	South Africa	Vanuatu
Burkina Faso	Indonesia	Nauru	Sri Lanka	Zambia

WEAK STATE

Afghanistan	Djibouti	Iraq	Mali	Philippines
Bangladesh	El Salvador	Ivory Coast	Mauritania	São Tomé and Príncipe
Cameroon	Eritrea	Kenya	Moldova	Solomon Islands
Central African Republic	Georgia	Kosovo	Myanmar	South Sudan
Chad	Guatemala	Lebanon	Nepal	Sudan
Colombia	Guinea	Lesotho	Niger	Timor-Leste
Comoros	Guinea-Bissau	Liberia	Nigeria	Venezuela
Congo, DR	Haiti	Libya	Pakistan	Yemen
Congo, R	Honduras	Madagascar	Papua New Guinea	Zimbabwe

COLLAPSED STATE

Somalia

wars to seize large parts of Chinese territory in the 1930s. However, as was noted in the introduction, the postwar world has laid great stress on the inviolability of national borders. The international community thus tries to re-establish collapsed states and has never officially declared a state to have failed for good.

Perhaps a more common phrase than "collapsed state" is "failed state." Indeed, there is a "Failed States Index" produced by *Foreign Policy* magazine and the Fund for Peace. However, this index is problematic because many of its 12 measures of state failure (or, more precisely, of the risk of failure) are more evaluative of lack of socio-economic development or liberal democracy (see Chapter 5) than of state effectiveness. Thus, North Korea is consistently deemed by this index to be a "failed state," but it would be hard to argue that this regime does not control its people or its borders. A more useful, or at least more precise, view is that of the Crisis States Research Centre (CSRC) of the London School of Economics, which chooses to "define a 'failed state' as a condition of 'state collapse' [for example] a state that can no longer perform its basic security and development functions and that has no effective control over its territory and borders.... This term is used in very contradictory ways in the policy community (for instance, there is a tendency to label a 'poorly performing' state as 'failed'—a tendency we reject)." The CSRC also defines a "crisis state" as one in "danger of state collapse" and a "fragile state" as one "significantly susceptible to crisis."[5] The CSRC definitions of crisis and fragile states are compatible with our concept of weak states. In any case, beyond the failed states noted earlier, various other weak (or crisis) states have certainly come close to failure. For example, the Solomon Islands is generally seen as having been a "failing" state in the early part of the last decade, until matters were turned around—in large part due to Australian-led foreign intervention.

Last, one might expect the opposite of "weak states" to be "strong states," and Migdal has certainly used this term.[6] At first glance, communist states might appear to be strong. However, if by state *strength*, as opposed to merely adequate *effectiveness*, we mean a situation in which the state bureaucracy is highly autonomous from political actors and social interests, communist states are "merely" effective to their ends. The real example of a strong state—or a "super-effective" state—is one that has promoted capitalist development successfully and is thus called a *(capitalist) developmental state*. This term refers in particular to the East Asian cases of Japan, South Korea, and Taiwan, but it has also been used for France. In all of these countries, industrial development and planning have been central in the postwar era (and earlier, as well, in Japan).[7] Besides autonomy, the bureaucracy in the key economic ministries of developmental states is known for being highly meritocratic and highly respected, what Johnson summarizes as "a powerful, talented, and prestige-laden economic bureaucracy" when he describes the situation in Japan.[8] These bureaucracies attract and select the top students from the most elite universities and schools, such as the Tokyo University Law School and the École nationale d'administration in France. Such developmental states can only occur if the civil service has enormous prestige (not the case in North America); if the state is very centralized (not the case in federalism); if the bureaucracy is, in fact, small and skilled; and if economic development is the overriding national goal (even at the expense of consumers and the environment).

State Building

Consequently, we are unlikely to see many more developmental states. We may, however, see some weak states become effective. Shifting "upwards" in this regard—for example, from a weak state to an effective one or even establishing a weak state where no state existed—can be seen as the phenomenon of *building state capacity* or, in Mann's phrasing, developing the *infrastructural power* of the state.[9] As outlined earlier, creating or increasing such state capacity would seem to be both a part of political development and an aid to socio-economic development. So why do more states not do this? The answer relates, in part, to national attitudes to bureaucracy, as noted. However, it is also the case that, if a bureaucracy is autonomous, with its own recruitment procedures and qualifications, then it cannot be used for political patronage. As Geddes notes, the bureaucracy (and appointments to it) can be used to provide benefits to constituents, to other politicians whose support one needs, and to members of a supportive political party, or the bureaucracy can be used to develop and implement policies in the broad national interest—but these are alternatives, not a package of choices.[10] For politicians who are primarily focused on their own short-term political interests, the establishment of an autonomous, merit-based bureaucracy is hardly something to be supported. That said, modernization-related attitudinal change and public pressure may well lead to the realization and institutionalization of bureaucratic autonomy, such as happened with the creation in 1883 of the United States Civil Service Commission and the creation in 1908 of Canada's Civil Service Commission (now the Public Service Commission)—each based on the merit system.

However, the building of state capacity does not occur in a vacuum. It is easier or harder depending on a country's political geography, which facilitates control or penetration, and national identity, which facilitates legitimacy. In terms of political geography, Whittlesey argues that the ideal shape of the state is "chunky rather than elongate," with population density strongest in the centre and diminishing toward the borders and with these borders involving geographic barriers such as oceans, mountains, deserts, jungles, or other natural dividers.[11] There are obviously some trade-offs involved here. For example, Chile is bordered by the Pacific Ocean on the west, the Andes Mountains in the east, and the Atacama Desert in the north (which is good), but all this comes at the "price" of being very elongate. Poland (in its various incarnations) has always had a desirably chunky shape but few natural barriers between it and other countries, with the unfortunate result that it has been invaded often throughout its history. Small island states tend not to have these trade-offs. Of the larger states, Japan and Spain are good examples of countries with all of these various features, although they have been challenged by internal mountain ranges.

Although the shape of a state's territory is important, Whittlesey does not think that there is an ideal size for a state. Bigger is better in the sense that a large state will more likely have more, and more varied, natural resources. However, bigger states are also more likely to have multiple centres of population density and greater challenges in terms of communications. Consider the importance of railways and later air travel for integrating Canada or the United States. Prior to the introduction of these technologies, roads and rivers were the sole methods of non-ocean transport, but only roads can go most anywhere. Consequently, a dense and good-quality road network facilitates state capacity; think of the Roman Empire ("all roads lead to Rome"). As Whittlesey summarizes, "Efficient transportation consolidates political areas, whether the Roman Empire or the United States of America. The lack of ready means of circulation is a source of political weakness whatever the density of population, as the plight of [pre-communist modern] China proves."[12]

Thus, although the size of a state may well affect the challenge of establishing communications, *all* states except the tiniest are faced with the challenge of ensuring effective communications, especially roads, so as to facilitate the penetration of state authority. This point can be related to the weakness of many states in contemporary Africa. Herbst's recent comprehensive study points out that numerous sub-Saharan African states have an unfavourable or neutral geography in regard to population distribution and, moreover, that few such states have been willing or able to increase

TABLE 3.2 Size and Demography of Countries, 2011

Country	Population Total (thousands)	Area (sq. km)	Population Density (population per sq. km)	Urban Population %	Rural Population %	Median Age (years)
Afghanistan	32358.3	652230	49.6	22.9	77.1	16.7
Albania	3216.0	28748	111.9	52.9	47.1	30.5
Algeria	35980.2	2381741	15.1	67.1	32.9	26.6
Andorra	86.2	468	184.2	87.6	12.4	40.7
Angola	19618.4	1246700	15.7	59.4	40.6	16.7
Antigua and Barbuda	89.6	443	202.3	30.4	69.6	30.6
Argentina	40764.6	2780400	14.7	92.6	7.4	30.6
Armenia	3100.2	29743	104.2	64.3	35.7	32.3
Australia	22605.7	7741220	2.9	89.3	10.7	37.1
Austria	8413.4	83871	100.3	67.8	32.2	42.2
Azerbaijan	9306.0	86600	107.5	52.1	47.9	29.8
Bahamas	347.2	13880	25.0	84.3	15.7	31.3
Bahrain	1323.5	760	1741.4	88.7	11.3	30.7
Bangladesh	150493.7	143998	1045.1	28.6	71.4	24.6
Barbados	273.9	430	637.0	45.1	54.9	37.8
Belarus	9559.4	207600	46.0	75.2	24.8	38.4
Belgium	10754.1	30528	352.3	97.4	2.6	41.4
Belize	317.9	22966	13.8	52.7	47.3	22.1
Benin	9099.9	112622	80.8	42.5	57.5	18.0
Bhutan	738.3	38394	19.2	35.5	64.5	25.0
Bolivia	10088.1	1098581	9.2	67.0	33.0	21.9
Bosnia-Herzegovina	3752.2	51197	73.3	49.2	50.8	39.8
Botswana	2030.7	581730	3.5	61.8	38.2	23.1
Brazil	196655.0	8514877	23.1	86.9	13.1	29.5
Brunei	405.9	5765	70.4	76.1	23.9	29.2
Bulgaria	7446.1	110879	67.2	71.7	28.3	41.8
Burkina Faso	16967.8	274200	61.9	26.5	73.5	17.2
Burma/Myanmar	48336.8	676578	71.4	34.3	65.7	28.6
Burundi	8575.2	27830	308.1	11.3	88.7	20.4
Cambodia	14305.2	181035	79.0	20.4	79.6	23.3
Cameroon	20030.4	475440	42.1	59.2	40.8	19.4
Canada	34349.6	9984670	3.4	80.7	19.3	40.0
Cape Verde	500.6	4033	124.1	61.8	38.2	23.3
Central African Republic	4486.8	622984	7.2	39.2	60.8	19.6
Chad	11525.5	1284000	9.0	28.2	71.8	17.2
Chile	17269.5	756102	22.8	89.2	10.8	32.5
China	1324493.3	9596961	138.0	47.8	52.2	34.9
Colombia	46927.1	1138910	41.2	75.4	24.6	27.1
Comoros	753.9	2235	337.3	28.3	71.7	18.9
Congo, DR (Kinshasa)	67757.6	2344858	28.9	35.9	64.1	16.8
Congo, R (Brazzaville)	4139.7	342000	12.1	62.5	37.5	19.6
Costa Rica	4726.6	51100	92.5	64.9	35.1	28.9

Country	Population Total (thousands)	Area (sq. km)	Population Density (population per sq. km)	Urban Population %	Rural Population %	Median Age (years)
Croatia	4395.6	56594	77.7	58.0	42.0	41.7
Cuba	11253.7	110860	101.5	75.2	24.8	39.0
Cyprus (Greek)	1116.6	9251	120.7	70.5	29.5	34.5
Czech Republic	10534.3	78867	133.6	73.6	26.4	39.6
Denmark	5572.6	43094	129.3	87.1	12.9	40.7
Djibouti	905.6	23200	39.0	76.3	23.7	21.7
Dominica	67.7	751	90.1	67.4	32.6	31.1
Dominican Republic	10056.2	48670	206.6	69.8	30.2	25.4
Ecuador	14666.1	283561	51.7	67.6	32.4	25.9
Egypt	82536.8	1001450	82.4	43.5	56.5	24.7
El Salvador	6227.5	21041	296.0	64.8	35.2	23.5
Equatorial Guinea	720.2	28051	25.7	39.9	60.1	20.4
Eritrea	5415.3	117600	46.0	22.1	77.9	19.1
Estonia	1340.5	45228	29.6	69.5	30.5	39.8
Ethiopia	84734.3	1104300	76.7	16.8	83.2	19.0
Fiji	868.4	18274	47.5	52.3	47.7	26.7
Finland	5384.8	338145	15.9	85.4	14.6	42.1
France	63125.9	551500	114.5	85.9	14.1	40.1
Gabon	1534.3	267667	5.7	86.4	13.6	21.9
Gambia	1776.1	11295	157.2	58.9	41.1	17.9
Georgia	4329.0	69700	62.1	52.8	47.2	37.6
Germany	82162.5	357022	230.1	74.0	26.0	44.7
Ghana	24965.8	238533	104.7	52.2	47.8	20.6
Greece	11390.0	131957	86.3	61.7	38.3	41.7
Grenada	104.9	344	304.9	39.7	60.3	25.4
Guatemala	14757.3	108889	135.5	49.9	50.1	19.0
Guinea	10221.8	245857	41.6	35.9	64.1	18.4
Guinea-Bissau	1547.1	36125	42.8	30.2	69.8	19.2
Guyana	756.0	214969	3.5	28.7	71.3	24.1
Haiti	10123.8	27750	364.8	53.6	46.4	21.8
Honduras	7754.7	112090	69.2	52.2	47.8	21.3
Hungary	9966.1	93028	107.1	68.5	31.5	40.1
Iceland	324.4	103000	3.1	93.5	6.5	35.0
India	1241492.0	3287263	377.7	30.3	69.7	25.4
Indonesia	242325.6	1904569	127.2	44.6	55.4	28.1
Iran	74798.6	1648195	45.4	71.3	28.7	27.7
Iraq	32664.9	438317	74.5	66.1	33.9	18.4
Ireland	4525.8	70273	64.4	62.3	37.7	35.0
Israel	7562.2	20770	364.1	91.9	8.1	30.2
Italy	60788.7	301340	201.7	68.6	31.4	43.5
Ivory Coast	20152.9	322463	62.5	51.3	48.7	19.3
Jamaica	2751.3	10991	250.3	52.1	47.9	27.3
Japan	126497.2	377915	334.7	67.0	33.0	45.0
Jordan	6330.2	89342	70.9	78.6	21.4	21.2

Country	Population Total (thousands)	Area (sq. km)	Population Density (population per sq. km)	Urban Population %	Rural Population %	Median Age (years)
Kazakhstan	16206.8	2724900	5.9	58.8	41.2	29.2
Kenya	41609.7	580367	71.7	22.5	77.5	18.6
Kiribati	101.1	811	124.7	44.0	56.0	22.7
Korea, North	24451.3	120538	202.9	60.3	39.7	33.1
Korea, South	48391.3	99720	485.3	83.3	16.7	38.4
Kosovo	1733.9	10887	159.3	40.0	60.0	26.7
Kuwait	2818.0	17818	158.2	98.4	1.6	28.6
Kyrgyzstan	5392.6	199951	27.0	34.5	65.5	24.1
Laos	6288.0	236800	26.6	34.3	65.7	21.9
Latvia	2243.1	64589	34.7	67.7	32.3	40.3
Lebanon	4259.4	10400	409.6	87.4	12.6	29.5
Lesotho	2193.8	30355	72.3	27.6	72.4	20.5
Liberia	4128.6	111369	37.1	48.2	51.8	18.2
Libya	6422.8	1759540	3.7	78.1	21.9	26.0
Liechtenstein	36.3	160	226.9	14.3	85.7	42.0
Lithuania	3307.5	65300	50.7	67.1	32.9	39.5
Luxembourg	515.9	2586	199.5	85.4	14.6	39.0
Macedonia	2063.9	25713	80.3	59.4	40.6	36.3
Madagascar	21315.1	587041	36.3	30.6	69.4	18.3
Malawi	15380.9	118484	129.8	20.3	79.7	16.9
Malaysia	28859.2	329847	87.5	73.0	27.0	26.3
Maldives	320.1	298	1074.2	41.3	58.7	25.2
Mali	15839.5	1240192	12.8	36.6	63.4	16.4
Malta	417.9	316	1322.5	94.8	5.2	39.7
Marshall Islands	54.8	181	302.8	72.1	27.9	22.0
Mauritania	3541.5	1030700	3.4	41.7	58.3	19.9
Mauritius	1306.6	2040	640.5	41.9	58.1	32.8
Mexico	114793.3	1964375	58.4	78.1	21.9	27.0
Micronesia	111.5	702	158.8	22.8	77.2	21.0
Moldova	3544.9	33851	104.7	47.7	52.3	35.4
Monaco	35.4	2	17700.0	100.0	0.0	49.5
Mongolia	2800.1	1564116	1.8	62.5	37.5	25.8
Montenegro	632.3	13812	45.8	61.5	38.5	36.2
Morocco	32273.0	446550	72.3	58.8	41.2	26.7
Mozambique	23929.7	799380	29.9	39.2	60.8	17.9
Namibia	2324.0	824292	2.8	38.6	61.4	21.4
Nauru	10.3	21	490.5	100.0	0.0	24.4
Nepal	30485.8	147181	207.1	19.2	80.8	21.8
Netherlands	16664.7	41543	401.1	83.3	16.7	41.1
New Zealand	4414.5	267710	16.5	86.2	13.8	36.7
Nicaragua	5869.9	130370	45.0	57.6	42.4	22.4
Niger	16069.0	1267000	12.7	17.2	82.8	15.5
Nigeria	162470.7	923768	175.9	50.5	49.5	18.5
Norway	4924.8	323802	15.2	79.8	20.2	39.0

Country	Population Total (thousands)	Area (sq. km)	Population Density (population per sq. km)	Urban Population %	Rural Population %	Median Age (years)
Oman	2846.1	309500	9.2	73.3	26.7	26.5
Pakistan	176745.4	796095	222.0	36.2	63.8	22.0
Palau	20.6	459	44.9	84.3	15.7	32.8
Panama	3571.2	75420	47.4	75.5	24.5	27.6
Papua New Guinea	7013.8	462840	15.2	12.6	87.4	20.6
Paraguay	6568.3	406752	16.1	62.1	37.9	23.3
Peru	29399.8	1285216	22.9	77.3	22.7	25.9
Philippines	94852.0	300000	316.2	49.1	50.9	22.4
Poland	38298.9	312685	122.5	60.9	39.1	38.3
Portugal	10689.7	92090	116.1	61.3	38.7	41.4
Qatar	1870.0	11586	161.4	95.9	4.1	32.1
Romania	21436.5	238391	89.9	58.0	42.0	38.8
Russia	142835.6	17098242	8.4	73.2	26.8	38.1
Rwanda	10943.0	26338	415.5	19.2	80.8	18.6
Saint Kitts and Nevis	53.1	261	203.4	32.6	67.4	32.3
Saint Lucia	176.0	616	285.7	28.1	71.9	27.8
Saint Vincent and the Grenadines	109.4	389	281.2	49.8	50.2	28.2
Samoa (Western)	183.9	2831	65.0	20.1	79.9	21.0
San Marino	31.7	61	519.7	94.1	5.9	42.7
São Tomé and Príncipe	168.5	964	174.8	63.0	37.0	19.5
Saudi Arabia	28082.5	2149690	13.1	82.3	17.7	26.2
Senegal	12767.6	196722	64.9	42.7	57.3	18.0
Serbia	7120.7	77474	91.9	56.4	43.6	37.8
Seychelles	86.9	455	191.0	55.9	44.1	32.8
Sierra Leone	5997.5	71740	83.6	38.8	61.2	18.4
Singapore	5187.9	697	7443.2	100.0	0.0	38.1
Slovakia	5471.5	49035	111.6	54.9	45.1	37.3
Slovenia	2035.0	20273	100.4	49.5	50.5	42.0
Solomon Islands	552.3	28896	19.1	18.9	81.1	20.1
Somalia	9556.9	637657	15.0	37.9	62.1	17.5
South Africa	50460.0	1219090	41.4	62.2	37.8	25.1
South Sudan	8260.0	644329	12.8	17.0	83.0	20.2
Spain	46454.9	505370	91.9	77.6	22.4	40.5
Sri Lanka	21045.4	65610	320.8	14.3	85.7	31.0
Sudan	36372.4	1861484	19.5	40.8	59.2	19.9
Suriname	529.4	163820	3.2	69.8	30.2	27.9
Swaziland	1203.3	17364	69.3	21.3	78.7	19.7
Sweden	9440.7	450295	21.0	84.8	15.2	40.8
Switzerland	7701.7	41277	186.6	73.7	26.3	41.8
Syria	20766.0	185180	112.1	56.2	43.8	21.5
Taiwan	23072.0	35980	641.2	82.0	18.0	37.9
Tajikistan	6977.0	143100	48.8	26.4	73.6	20.6
Tanzania	46218.5	947300	48.8	26.9	73.1	17.5
Thailand	69518.6	513120	135.5	34.4	65.6	34.6

Country	Population Total (thousands)	Area (sq. km)	Population Density (population per sq. km)	Urban Population %	Rural Population %	Median Age (years)
Timor-Leste (East Timor)	1153.8	14874	77.6	28.6	71.4	16.8
Togo	6154.8	56785	108.4	44.1	55.9	19.9
Tonga	104.5	747	139.9	23.5	76.5	21.3
Trinidad and Tobago	1346.4	5128	262.6	14.2	85.8	31.2
Tunisia	10594.1	163610	64.8	67.7	32.3	29.4
Turkey	73639.6	783562	94.0	70.1	29.9	28.7
Turkmenistan	5105.3	488100	10.5	50.0	50.0	24.9
Tuvalu	9.8	26	376.9	50.9	49.1	24.3
Uganda	34509.2	241038	143.2	13.5	86.5	15.8
Ukraine	45190.2	603550	74.9	69.1	30.9	39.4
United Arab Emirates	7890.9	83600	94.4	84.4	15.6	30.8
United Kingdom	62417.4	243610	256.2	79.8	20.2	39.9
United States	313085.4	9528960	32.9	82.6	17.4	37.0
Uruguay	3380.0	176215	19.2	92.6	7.4	33.9
Uzbekistan	27760.3	447400	62.0	36.3	63.7	24.6
Vanuatu	245.6	12189	20.1	26.0	74.0	20.8
Venezuela	29436.9	912050	32.3	93.6	6.4	26.4
Vietnam	88792.0	331210	268.1	31.0	69.0	28.7
Yemen	24799.9	527968	47.0	32.4	67.6	17.6
Zambia	13475.0	752618	17.9	35.9	64.1	16.6
Zimbabwe	12754.4	390757	32.6	38.8	61.2	19.7

SOURCES: Central Intelligence Agency, *The World Factbook* (Washington, DC: CIA, 2012), accessed October 2012, https://www.cia.gov/library/publications/the-world-factbook/; United Nations, Department of Economic and Social Affairs, Population Division, *World Population Prospects: The 2010 Revision* (New York: United Nations, May 2011), accessed October 2012, http://esa.un.org/unpd/wpp/index.htm; United Nations estimates; author's calculations and estimates.

their road densities greatly. Indeed, in a couple of African countries there are fewer kilometres of roads today than there were at independence![13]

Size and Demography of Countries

Countries vary tremendously in their size. Table 3.2 gives the population, area (excluding coastal waters), and population density of the countries of our analysis. Does size matter for state control? Today, the very largest countries by area—Russia, Canada, China, the United States, Brazil, and Australia—are all bigger than the Roman Empire at its peak. However, Russia, historically, has been seen as "too big" or, at least, "too sparse" for Western-style development. As Lynch notes, "Russia's immense spaces have constituted a significant burden on the country's ability to govern itself, not to mention to modernize effectively."[14] Of course, countries can control greater areas today than they could historically due to modern communications. That said, governing an ever-larger area does work against effective central control. If one puts the categories of state strength outlined in Table 3.1 into a 0 to 3 scale (with an effective state being 3), one finds a significant negative correlation (r = –0.163) between the level of state strength and the logged area of the country. (The correlation with logged population is only half this, r = –0.084, as population density facilitates state control.) However, there is a much stronger negative correlation between the level of state strength and the rural share of the population in 2011 (r = –0.495), confirming that weak states are most likely to be found in more rural (and thus less "modern") societies, where the population is harder to reach from the centre.[15] There is an even stronger positive correlation between the level of state strength and the median age of the population in 2010 (r = 0.722), indicating that countries with older populations are more effectively controlled and more stable politically.[16] Table 3.2 provides the urban and rural shares of population and the median age of the population for all countries.

Political and Economic Classifications of States

When scholars categorized states according to their political and economic differences, the most common method throughout much of the postwar period was to use a threefold grouping into the First World, the Second World, and the Third World. The key features of these categories are clearly summarized by Harris, Moore, and Schmitz in Table 3.3.[17] The First World comprised the developed capitalist economies of the United States, Canada, Western Europe, Japan, Australia, and New Zealand, which were and are still often referred to as simply the "West." The Second World comprised the Soviet Union and Eastern Europe (broadly defined), or what was often called the "East." These countries were seen as developed, but they followed a communist economic and political system. Thus, the distinction between the First World and the Second World was primarily a political one. Finally, the Third World included everywhere else: African, Asian, Latin American, and Caribbean countries that were generally non-aligned but, more crucially, that were seen as less developed. As Spero points out, the Western system of First World countries has involved many dense patterns of *interdependence,* with reasonable symmetry among the countries concerned. In contrast, the North–South system between the First and Third Worlds

TABLE 3.3 First, Second, and Third Worlds after World War II

TYPICAL "INTERNAL" FEATURES	FIRST WORLD (developed)	SECOND WORLD	THIRD WORLD (developing)
Political system	Liberal democratic	Communist; single party	Mixed; rarely democratic
Economic system	Market oriented (but usually with large welfare states)	Centrally planned	Variable
Income level	High	Mixed; generally medium	Low

TYPICAL "EXTERNAL" FEATURES	FIRST WORLD (developed)	SECOND WORLD	THIRD WORLD (developing)
Main trading partners	Other First World countries	Other Second World countries	First World countries
Geopolitical relationships	Competitor of the Second World	Competitor of the First World	Area of geopolitical competition between the First and Second World
Aid and power relationships	Former colonial power dominating Third World; still aid donor to this world and dominant over most of its countries	Aid donor to and influential in parts of the Third World	Aid recipient; subordinate
Influence in international economic institutions	High	Low	Low

SOURCE: Adapted from Dan Harris, Mick Moore, and Hubert Schmitz, *Country Classifications for a Changing World*, IDS Working Paper 326 (Brighton: Institute of Development Studies, University of Sussex, May 2009), 11 (their Table 2.1). Used with permission.

also involved much interaction, but these dealings were between unequal actors with the Third World in a situation of *dependence*; that is, Third World countries were dependent on those of the First World for market access, investment, and finance and the reverse was not true. Finally, Second World economies were closely tied to each other in terms of economic planning and trade, but, as a group, they interacted very little with the rest of the world. So Spero characterized the East–West system as one of *independence*.[18] That said, for the purposes of comparative politics and economics, almost every country fell into one of these three groupings. (Countries such as Israel, South Africa, and China were, in various ways, borderline cases.)

With the fall of the Berlin Wall, the Second World no longer exists even if there are still some communist political regimes remaining. However, it would be a leap to put many Eastern European and especially Soviet successor states into the First World. How, then, does one determine today whether a state is part of the advanced industrial world? To avoid crude geographical distinctions, one can look at whether a state possesses some of the several features shown in Table 3.4. First, there is having a high income of $20,000 or more per capita, which is the definition of an advanced economy given by Spence.[19] Second, there is being classified as an innovation-driven economy by the World Economic Forum, a categorization that combines GDP per capita and a control as to whether exports overwhelmingly consist of factor-driven raw materials.[20] Third, there is being a member of the Organisation for Economic Co-operation and Development (OECD). Membership in the OECD is effectively restricted to developed capitalist economies as the organization conceives this. Fourth, there is being a country that draws in migrants, presumably from less developed areas. This factor is measured by determining whether international migrants are over 10 per cent of the population as of 2010. Fifth, there is having a highly educated population, which is measured according to whether at least 25 per cent of a country's 25- to 64-year-old population has received tertiary education as of 2009. Sixth, there is having a high technological base. Significant spending on research and development, at least 1.0 per cent or more of GDP as of 2009, is the measure for this. (Israel leads all countries here at 4.2 per cent of GDP.) Seventh and last, there is whether a country has a positive net international investment position, meaning its foreign assets exceed its foreign liabilities. The difference must measure at least +1.0 per cent of GDP for the most recent data.[21] Table 3.4 lists all 47 countries with at least two of these features, arranging countries in descending order according to how many factors they possess. We would argue that at least four or five features are needed for a country to be considered part of the "core" of the advanced industrial or developed world. Indeed, Germany, Luxembourg, the Netherlands, Norway, and Switzerland have *all* of these features. Various non-Western countries do make this list, led by oil-rich Bahrain and the United Arab Emirates. China is also on this list. (Five OECD members—Chile, Hungary, Mexico, Poland, and Turkey—are not on this list, as they have no other features.)

Many countries on this list of advanced industrial economies would not have been here a generation ago; however, they are today due to rapid growth and structural change. Table 3.5 gives a list of the dozen postwar high-growth economies; it uses the common definition of a high-growth economy—national income growing at a rate of at least 7 per cent a year or more (thus doubling every decade) for at least 25 years.[22] As can be seen, most of these economies are in Asia—including the high-growth territory of Hong Kong. Moreover, of these economies, only Hong Kong, Japan, South Korea, Singapore, and Taiwan have actually caught up with Western countries in terms of income per capita; no non-Asian high-growth economy has. Other developing countries, even initially high-growth ones, usually get stuck in what is called the "middle-income trap": they reach middle-income status but are unable to transition their economy from labour-intensive to capital- and knowledge-intensive industries,

TABLE 3.4 The Most Developed Nations, 2007–2012

	2010 GNI per capita = $20,000 or more	Innovation-driven economy	OECD member	International migrants = 10% of population or more	High tertiary education	High research & development spending	Positive international investment position	Total factors
Germany	1	1	1	1	1	1	1	7
Luxembourg	1	1	1	1	1	1	1	7
Netherlands	1	1	1	1	1	1	1	7
Norway	1	1	1	1	1	1	1	7
Switzerland	1	1	1	1	1	1	1	7
Australia	1	1	1	1	1	1		6
Belgium	1	1	1		1	1	1	6
Canada	1	1	1	1	1	1		6
Denmark	1	1	1		1	1	1	6
Finland	1	1	1		1	1	1	6
France	1	1	1	1	1	1		6
Iceland	1	1	1	1	1	1		6
Ireland	1	1	1	1	1	1		6
Israel	1	1	1		1	1	1	6
Japan	1	1	1		1	1	1	6
New Zealand	1	1	1	1	1	1		6
Singapore	1	1		1	1	1	1	6
Spain	1	1	1	1	1	1		6
Sweden	1	1	1	1	1	1		6
United Kingdom	1	1	1	1	1	1		6
United States	1	1	1	1	1	1		6
Austria	1	1	1		1	1		5
Cyprus (Greek)	1	1		1	1		1	5
Korea, South	1	1	1		1	1		5
Taiwan	1	1			1	1	1	5
Bahrain	1	1		1			1	4
Estonia			1	1	1	1		4
Italy	1	1	1			1		4
Liechtenstein	1	1		1			1	4
Portugal	1	1	1			1		4
Slovenia	1	1				1		4
United Arab Emirates	1	1		1			1	4
Andorra	1	1		1				3
Brunei	1			1			1	3
Czech Republic		1	1			1		3
Greece	1	1	1					3
Kuwait	1			1			1	3
Monaco	1			1				3
Qatar	1			1			1	3
San Marino	1	1		1				3

	2010 GNI per capita = $20,000 or more	Innovation-driven economy	OECD member	International migrants = 10% of population or more	High tertiary education	High research & development spending	Positive international investment position	Total factors
China						1	1	2
Latvia				1	1			2
Libya				1			1	2
Malta		1					1	2
Oman				1			1	2
Saudi Arabia				1			1	2
Slovakia	1	1						2

SOURCES: OECD, List of Member Countries, http://www.oecd.org/general/listofecdmembercountries-ratificationoftheconventionontheoecd. htm; World Economic Forum, *The Global Competitiveness Report, 2012–2013* (Geneva: World Economic Forum, 2012); World Bank, *World Development Indicators 2012* (Washington, DC: The World Bank, 2012), Table 1.1, 20–22; Philip R. Lane and Gian Maria Milesi-Ferretti, "The External Wealth of Nations Mark II: Revised and Extended Estimates of Foreign Assets and Liabilities, 1970–2004," *Journal of International Economics*, 73, no. 2 (November 2007): 223–250.

so they do not reach advanced industrial status and its related per capita wealth.[23] Whether China will be able to escape this middle-income trap is a central question for the next couple of decades in the world economy, but that China will seems quite probable.[24] Indeed, based on his cut-off for establishing high-income status, Felipe sees this happening quite soon.[25]

Although advanced industrial states have various structural features in common, they differ in terms of ideologies and resulting policies. There are four main types in this regard. First, there is a northern European type of industrial state, such as in Austria, Germany, and Sweden, which is characterized by high taxes and high welfare spending, powerful but cooperative and integrated labour unions, a highly skilled work force, and flexible labour markets. Second, there is a southern European type, as in Greece, Italy, and Spain, which has medium to high taxes and similar welfare spending but also inflexible labour markets. Their lack of competitiveness with northern Europe has proven unsustainable, at least in the context of a common European currency. Third, there is an Anglo-Saxon type, as in the United States, Canada, and the United Kingdom. These states have low to medium taxes, similarly low to medium welfare spending, weak labour unions, flexible labour markets, and relatively high income inequality. Last, there is an East Asian type of industrial state, as in Japan, Singapore, and South Korea. This type has a strong export focus, low taxation, low welfare spending, weak or co-opted labour unions, but relatively low income inequality due to land reforms (often imposed externally) and high-quality

TABLE 3.5: List of High-Growth Economies through 2012

Country	Location (geographic subregion)	Start Year	End Year
Botswana	Southern Africa	1966	2004
Brazil	South America	1950	1980
China	East Asia	1977	ongoing
*Hong Kong**	*East Asia*	*1960*	*1997*
Indonesia	South East Asia	1968	1997
Japan	East Asia	1946	1973
Korea, South	East Asia	1963	1997
Malaysia	South East Asia	1967	1997
Oman	Middle East	1962	1997
Singapore	South East Asia	1965	2000
Taiwan	East Asia	1947	2000
Thailand	South East Asia	1959	1996

*Data for Hong Kong are in italics as this region is not a sovereign state.

SOURCE: Based on calculations from the data set of the late Angus Maddison, with updates. See the data under the heading "Historical Statistics," http://www.ggdc.net/maddison/oriindex.htm. This data set updated by his colleagues at the *Maddison Project*, http://www.ggdc.net/maddison/maddison-project/home.htm.

universal education. As noted previously, these East Asian countries are often called capitalist development states.

Furthermore, if, as noted earlier, there is no longer a grouping called the Second World, then it obviously does not make much sense to still use the term *Third* World. Two alternatives are common these days. The first is to call African, Asian, Caribbean, Latin American, and Middle Eastern countries "developing states" or "less-developed states" in contrast to the developed states of the First World. The second, more geographic, approach is to refer to the "South" versus the "North" because Third World countries generally are geographically to the south of the First World (Australia and New Zealand excepted, of course).[26] However, the increasing heterogeneity of the "developing world," which now includes countries at varying levels of development, makes one question whether *any* single category can cover all the "South," that is, all of Africa, Asia, the Caribbean, Latin America, and the Middle East.

Table 3.6 outlines various alternative measures of development and how countries are classified today. The World Bank puts countries into four groupings based on per capita income: "low," "lower middle," "upper middle," and "high." The United Nations assesses development more broadly in its **Human Development Index (HDI)**. The HDI combines three factors: (1) life expectancy, (2) years of schooling, and (3) gross national income per capita, which is corrected for variations in purchasing power and is adjusted by being logged.[27] These combined factors lead to a standardized score in which higher values indicate higher levels of development. Based on the HDI, the UN then groups countries into "low," "medium," "high," and "very high" human development. Next we can contrast countries in terms of their fertility rates, that is, births per woman in her childbearing years (estimates for 2010–2015). Countries are classified into one of five categories: very high fertility (5.00 or more), high fertility (3.50 to 4.99), medium fertility (2.11 to 3.49), low fertility (1.51 to 2.10), and very low fertility (1.50 or below). These last two categories are, in a sense, "too low" as, at these levels, national populations will shrink absent any immigration.

Finally, Table 3.6 also gives a more specific and contemporary sense of development: Internet users as a percentage of the population, which measures the level of global communications access. In a country where a significant number of people access the Internet, both literacy and technology can be seen as broadly diffused—as opposed to being restricted to the elite. Here we divide countries into the following five categories based on 2011 values (or on those of the most recent year): very low Internet usage (less than 10 per cent of the population), low Internet usage (from 10 to 29 per cent), medium Internet usage (from 30 to 49 per cent), high Internet usage (from 50 to 69 per cent), and very high Internet usage (70 per cent or more). With 95 per cent of its population using the Internet, Iceland is thus the world leader.

One aspect in the relationship between developed and developing countries is foreign aid. In fact, measuring whether countries are donors or recipients is another means of classifying countries in terms of development, as is done in Table 3.7. Here countries are divided into three groups: those that are major donors of foreign aid (giving $50 or more per capita); those that are major recipients (receiving $50 or more per capita); and, the largest group, those that either give or receive minor amounts (less than $50 per capita) or, in some cases, that both receive aid from some and give aid to others. The major donors can be categorized as either core economies or oil-rich economies.

The Least Developed Countries

As noted, many countries that in the early postwar period used to be quite underdeveloped are now moderately or even (in East Asia) highly developed. However, other

TABLE 3.6 Alternate Classifications of Development: Countries of the World after 2010

Country	World Bank (Per Capita) Income Group Category for 2010	United Nations Human Development Index Category for 2011	Fertility Rate 2010 to 2015	Level of Global Communications Access 2011 (Internet usage as a percentage of the population)
Afghanistan	low	low	very high	very low
Albania	upper middle	high	low	medium
Algeria	upper middle	medium	medium	low
Andorra	high	very high	very low	very high
Angola	lower middle	low	very high	low
Antigua and Barbuda	upper middle	high	low	very high
Argentina	upper middle	very high	medium	medium
Armenia	lower middle	high	low	low
Australia	high	very high	low	very high
Austria	high	very high	very low	very high
Azerbaijan	upper middle	high	medium	high
Bahamas	high	high	low	high
Bahrain	high	very high	medium	very high
Bangladesh	low	low	medium	very low
Barbados	high	very high	low	very high
Belarus	upper middle	high	very low	medium
Belgium	high	very high	low	very high
Belize	lower middle	high	medium	low
Benin	low	low	very high	very low
Bhutan	lower middle	medium	medium	low
Bolivia	lower middle	medium	medium	medium
Bosnia-Herzegovina	upper middle	high	very low	high
Botswana	upper middle	medium	medium	very low
Brazil	upper middle	high	low	medium
Brunei	high	very high	low	high
Bulgaria	upper middle	high	low	high
Burkina Faso	low	low	very high	very low
Burma/Myanmar	low	low	low	very low
Burundi	low	low	high	very low
Cambodia	low	medium	medium	very low
Cameroon	lower middle	low	high	very low
Canada	high	very high	low	very high
Cape Verde	lower middle	medium	medium	medium
Central African Republic	low	low	high	very low
Chad	low	low	very high	very low
Chile	upper middle	very high	low	high
China	upper middle	medium	low	medium
Colombia	upper middle	high	medium	medium
Comoros	low	low	high	very low
Congo, DR (Kinshasha)	low	low	very high	very low
Congo, R (Brazzaville)	lower middle	medium	high	very low
Costa Rica	upper middle	high	low	medium

Country	World Bank (Per Capita) Income Group Category for 2010	United Nations Human Development Index Category for 2011	Fertility Rate 2010 to 2015	Level of Global Communications Access 2011 (Internet usage as a percentage of the population)
Croatia	high	very high	very low	very high
Cuba	upper middle	high	very low	low
Cyprus (Greek)	high	very high	low	high
Czech Republic	high	very high	very low	very high
Denmark	high	very high	low	very high
Djibouti	lower middle	low	high	very low
Dominica	upper middle	high	low	high
Dominican Republic	upper middle	medium	medium	medium
Ecuador	upper middle	high	medium	medium
Egypt	lower middle	medium	medium	medium
El Salvador	lower middle	medium	medium	low
Equatorial Guinea	high	medium	very high	very low
Eritrea	low	low	high	very low
Estonia	high	very high	low	very high
Ethiopia	low	low	high	very low
Fiji	lower middle	medium	medium	low
Finland	high	very high	low	very high
France	high	very high	low	very high
Gabon	upper middle	medium	medium	very low
Gambia	low	low	high	low
Georgia	lower middle	high	very low	medium
Germany	high	very high	very low	very high
Ghana	lower middle	medium	high	low
Greece	high	very high	very low	high
Grenada	upper middle	high	medium	medium
Guatemala	lower middle	medium	high	low
Guinea	low	low	very high	very low
Guinea-Bissau	low	low	high	very low
Guyana	lower middle	medium	medium	medium
Haiti	low	low	medium	very low
Honduras	lower middle	medium	medium	low
Hungary	high	very high	very low	high
Iceland	high	very high	low	very high
India	lower middle	medium	medium	low
Indonesia	lower middle	medium	medium	low
Iran	upper middle	high	low	low
Iraq	lower middle	medium	high	very low
Ireland	high	very high	low	very high
Israel	high	very high	medium	very high
Italy	high	very high	very low	high
Ivory Coast	lower middle	low	high	very low
Jamaica	upper middle	high	medium	medium
Japan	high	very high	very low	very high

Country	World Bank (Per Capita) Income Group Category for 2010	United Nations Human Development Index Category for 2011	Fertility Rate 2010 to 2015	Level of Global Communications Access 2011 (Internet usage as a percentage of the population)
Jordan	upper middle	medium	medium	medium
Kazakhstan	upper middle	high	medium	medium
Kenya	low	low	high	low
Kiribati	lower middle	medium	medium	low
Korea, North	low	. .	low	very low
Korea, South	high	very high	very low	very high
Kosovo	lower middle	. .	medium	medium
Kuwait	high	high	medium	very high
Kyrgyzstan	low	medium	medium	low
Laos	lower middle	medium	medium	very low
Latvia	upper middle	very high	very low	very high
Lebanon	upper middle	high	low	high
Lesotho	lower middle	low	medium	very low
Liberia	low	low	very high	very low
Libya	upper middle	high	medium	low
Liechtenstein	high	very high	low	very high
Lithuania	upper middle	very high	very low	high
Luxembourg	high	very high	low	very high
Macedonia	upper middle	high	very low	high
Madagascar	low	low	high	very low
Malawi	low	low	very high	very low
Malaysia	upper middle	high	medium	high
Maldives	upper middle	medium	low	medium
Mali	low	low	very high	very low
Malta	high	very high	very low	high
Marshall Islands	lower middle	. .	high	very low
Mauritania	lower middle	low	high	very low
Mauritius	upper middle	high	low	medium
Mexico	upper middle	high	medium	medium
Micronesia	lower middle	medium	medium	low
Moldova	lower middle	medium	very low	medium
Monaco	high	. .	low	very high
Mongolia	lower middle	medium	medium	low
Montenegro	upper middle	high	low	medium
Morocco	lower middle	medium	medium	high
Mozambique	low	low	high	very low
Namibia	upper middle	medium	medium	low
Nauru	. .	. .	medium	very low
Nepal	low	low	medium	very low
Netherlands	high	very high	low	very high
New Zealand	high	very high	low	very high
Nicaragua	lower middle	medium	medium	low
Niger	low	low	very high	very low

Country	World Bank (Per Capita) Income Group Category for 2010	United Nations Human Development Index Category for 2011	Fertility Rate 2010 to 2015	Level of Global Communications Access 2011 (Internet usage as a percentage of the population)
Nigeria	lower middle	low	very high	low
Norway	high	very high	low	very high
Oman	high	high	medium	high
Pakistan	lower middle	low	medium	very low
Palau	upper middle	high	low	low
Panama	upper middle	high	medium	medium
Papua New Guinea	lower middle	low	high	very low
Paraguay	lower middle	medium	medium	low
Peru	upper middle	high	medium	medium
Philippines	lower middle	medium	medium	low
Poland	high	very high	very low	high
Portugal	high	very high	very low	high
Qatar	high	very high	medium	very high
Romania	upper middle	high	very low	medium
Russia	upper middle	high	very low	medium
Rwanda	low	low	very high	very low
Saint Kitts and Nevis	upper middle	high	low	very high
Saint Lucia	upper middle	high	low	medium
Saint Vincent and the Grenadines	upper middle	high	low	medium
Samoa (Western)	lower middle	medium	high	very low
San Marino	high	..	very low	high
São Tomé and Príncipe	lower middle	low	high	low
Saudi Arabia	high	high	medium	medium
Senegal	lower middle	low	high	low
Serbia	upper middle	high	low	medium
Seychelles	upper middle	high	low	medium
Sierra Leone	low	low	high	very low
Singapore	high	very high	very low	very high
Slovakia	high	very high	very low	very high
Slovenia	high	very high	very low	very high
Solomon Islands	lower middle	low	high	very low
Somalia	low	..	very high	very low
South Africa	upper middle	medium	medium	low
South Sudan	..	..	high	very low
Spain	high	very high	very low	high
Sri Lanka	lower middle	medium	medium	low
Sudan	lower middle	low	high	low
Suriname	upper middle	medium	medium	medium
Swaziland	lower middle	medium	medium	low
Sweden	high	very high	low	very high
Switzerland	high	very high	very low	very high
Syria	lower middle	medium	medium	low
Taiwan	high	..	very low	very high
Tajikistan	low	medium	medium	low

Country	World Bank (Per Capita) Income Group Category for 2010	United Nations Human Development Index Category for 2011	Fertility Rate 2010 to 2015	Level of Global Communications Access 2011 (Internet usage as a percentage of the population)
Tanzania	low	low	very high	low
Thailand	upper middle	medium	low	low
Timor-Leste (East Timor)	lower middle	low	very high	very low
Togo	low	low	high	very low
Tonga	lower middle	high	high	low
Trinidad and Tobago	high	high	low	high
Tunisia	upper middle	high	low	medium
Turkey	upper middle	high	low	medium
Turkmenistan	lower middle	medium	medium	very low
Tuvalu	lower middle	. .	medium	medium
Uganda	low	low	very high	low
Ukraine	lower middle	high	very low	medium
United Arab Emirates	high	very high	low	very high
United Kingdom	high	very high	low	very high
United States	high	very high	low	very high
Uruguay	upper middle	high	low	high
Uzbekistan	lower middle	medium	medium	medium
Vanuatu	lower middle	medium	high	very low
Venezuela	upper middle	high	medium	medium
Vietnam	lower middle	medium	low	medium
Yemen	lower middle	low	high	low
Zambia	lower middle	low	very high	low
Zimbabwe	low	low	medium	low

SOURCES: World Bank, *World Development Indicators*, http://data.worldbank.org/data-catalog/world-development-indicators; United Nations, *Human Development Index (HDI)–2011 Rankings*, http://hdr.undp.org/en/statistics/; CIA, "Country Comparison: Total Fertility Rate," in *The World Factbook*, accessed October 2012, https://www.cia.gov/library/publications/the-world-factbook/rankorder/2127rank.html; International Telecommunication Union, "Percentage of Individuals Using the Internet, 2000–2011," *ICT Indicators Database*, http://www.itu.int/ITU-D/ict/publications/world/world.html.

countries remain quite underdeveloped—especially those in sub-Saharan Africa and south Asia. The most underdeveloped countries are shown in Table 3.8, which ranks countries as to how many of the following features they currently have (assuming they have at least two): (1) a "permanent" (since 1950) situation of being low income, thus being in what economists call a "low-level equilibrium trap";[28] (2) a significant share of the population (25 per cent or more) in abject poverty (living on less than $1.25 a day); (3) a high infant mortality rate (100 or more deaths per 1,000 live births); (4) a lack of literacy (defined as less than 75 per cent of the population being literate); and (5) a high share of the labour force (50 per cent or more) still in agriculture. In addition, the countries in this list have very low or low income. Also, although India is at least developing in a dynamic sense, most of the countries on

TABLE 3.7 Foreign Aid Donors and Recipients, 2008

MAJOR DONOR (giving $50 or more per capita)

Australia	Germany	Luxembourg	Spain
Belgium	Iceland	Netherlands	Sweden
Canada	Ireland	New Zealand	Switzerland
Denmark	Italy	Norway	United Arab Emirates
Finland	Japan	Portugal	United Kingdom
France	Kuwait	Saudi Arabia	United States

MINOR DONOR, MINOR RECIPIENT, OR BOTH

Algeria	Czech Republic	Latvia	Russia
Andorra	Dominican Republic	Libya	San Marino
Angola	Ecuador	Liechtenstein	Singapore
Argentina	Egypt	Lithuania	Slovakia
Austria	El Salvador	Madagascar	Slovenia
Azerbaijan	Eritrea	Malaysia	South Africa
Bahamas	Estonia	Malta	Sri Lanka
Bahrain	Ethiopia	Mexico	Syria
Bangladesh	Fiji	Moldova	Taiwan
Barbados	Gabon	Monaco	Tajikistan
Belarus	Greece	Morocco	Thailand
Brazil	Guatemala	Nauru	Trinidad and Tobago
Brunei	Guinea	Nepal	Tunisia
Bulgaria	Hungary	Niger	Turkey
Burma/Myanmar	India	Nigeria	Turkmenistan
Cameroon	Indonesia	Oman	Tuvalu
Chad	Iran	Pakistan	Ukraine
Chile	Israel	Panama	Uruguay
China	Ivory Coast	Papua New Guinea	Uzbekistan
Colombia	Jamaica	Paraguay	Venezuela
Congo, DR (Kinshasa)	Kazakhstan	Peru	Vietnam
Costa Rica	Kenya	Philippines	Yemen
Croatia	Korea, North	Poland	Zimbabwe
Cyprus	Korea, South	Romania	
Cuba	Kosovo	Qatar	

MAJOR RECIPIENT (receiving $50 or more per capita)

Afghanistan	Equatorial Guinea	Malawi	Senegal
Albania	Gambia	Maldives	Serbia
Antigua and Barbuda	Georgia	Mali	Seychelles
Armenia	Ghana	Marshall Islands	Sierra Leone
Belize	Grenada	Mauritania	Solomon Islands
Benin	Guinea-Bissau	Mauritius	Somalia
Bhutan	Guyana	Micronesia	South Sudan
Bolivia	Haiti	Mongolia	Sudan
Bosnia-Herzegovina	Honduras	Montenegro	Suriname
Botswana	Iraq	Mozambique	Swaziland
Burkina Faso	Jordan	Namibia	Tanzania
Burundi	Kiribati	Nicaragua	Timor-Leste (East Timor)
Cambodia	Kyrgyzstan	Palau	Togo
Cape Verde	Laos	Rwanda	Tonga
Central African Republic	Lebanon	Saint Kitts and Nevis	Uganda
Comoros	Lesotho	Saint Lucia	Vanuatu
Congo, R (Brazzaville)	Liberia	Saint Vincent and the Grenadines	Zambia
Djibouti	Macedonia	Samoa	
Dominica		São Tomé and Príncipe	

SOURCE: World Bank, *Atlas of Global Development*, 3rd ed. (Washington, DC: The World Bank, 2011), 94–95.

TABLE 3.8 The Most Underdeveloped Nations

	Always a low-income country	25% or more of population in abject poverty	Infant mortality rate = 100 or more	Literacy rate below 75%	50% or more of labour force in agriculture	Total factors
Afghanistan	1	1	1	1	1	5
Angola	1	1	1	1	1	5
Burkina Faso	1	1	1	1	1	5
Burundi	1	1	1	1	1	5
Central African Republic	1	1	1	1	1	5
Chad	1	1	1	1	1	5
Comoros	1	1	1	1	1	5
Congo, DR (Kinshasa)	1	1	1	1	1	5
Ethiopia	1	1	1	1	1	5
Gambia	1	1	1	1	1	5
Guinea	1	1	1	1	1	5
Guinea-Bissau	1	1	1	1	1	5
Haiti	1	1	1	1	1	5
Laos	1	1	1	1	1	5
Liberia	1	1	1	1	1	5
Madagascar	1	1	1	1	1	5
Malawi	1	1	1	1	1	5
Mali	1	1	1	1	1	5
Niger	1	1	1	1	1	5
Nigeria	1	1	1	1	1	5
Rwanda	1	1	1	1	1	5
Senegal	1	1	1	1	1	5
Sierra Leone	1	1	1	1	1	5
Somalia	1	1	1	1	1	5
South Sudan	1	1	1	1	1	5
Sudan	1	1	1	1	1	5
Tanzania	1	1	1	1	1	5
Togo	1	1	1	1	1	5
Uganda	1	1	1	1	1	5
Zambia	1	1	1	1	1	5
Bangladesh	1	1	1	1		4
Benin	1	1	1	1		4
Cameroon	1		1	1	1	4
Ghana	1	1		1	1	4
Lesotho	1	1	1		1	4
Mozambique		1	1	1	1	4
Nepal	1	1		1	1	4
Cambodia		1	1		1	3
Eritrea	1			1	1	3
India		1		1	1	3
Ivory Coast			1	1	1	3

	Always a low-income country	25% or more of population in abject poverty	Infant mortality rate = 100 or more	Literacy rate below 75%	50% or more of labour force in agriculture	Total factors
Kenya	1		1		1	3
Mauritania	1		1	1		3
Papua New Guinea		1		1	1	3
Timor-Leste (East Timor)		1		1	1	3
Zimbabwe	1	1			1	3
Bhutan		1		1		2
Burma/Myanmar		1			1	2
Congo, R (Brazzaville)		1	1			2
Djibouti			1	1		2
Pakistan			1	1		2
São Tomé and Príncipe		1	1			2
Swaziland		1	1			2
Yemen			1	1		2

SOURCES: Author's calculations based on data from Jesus Felipe, *Tracking the Middle Income Trap (Part 1)*, ABD Economics Working Paper No. 306 (Manila, Philippines: Asian Development Bank, March 2012); Jesus Felipe, *Tracking the Middle Income Trap (Part 2)*, ABD Economics Working Paper No. 307 (Manila, Philippines: Asian Development Bank, March 2012); United Nations, *Human Development Report 2011* (New York: Oxford University Press, 2012); CIA, *The World Factbook*, accessed October 2012, https://www.cia.gov/library/publications/the-world-factbook/; United Nations Conference on Trade and Development, *Statistics*, accessed October 2012, http://unctad.org/en/Pages/Statistics.aspx.

this list are stagnating. As Paul Collier notes, countries failing to develop (what he calls the "bottom billion" of the world's population) are burdened by various hard-to-solve and usually interrelated "traps": repeated internal conflicts (civil wars), an over-reliance on natural resources, being landlocked with bad neighbours, and having bad governance.[29] Conversely, as noted, China—where the population in abject poverty has declined by several hundred million in a generation—is not on this list and does not have these "traps."

Overall, though, the majority of the world's population lives neither in the least developed countries nor in the most developed countries, but rather in intermediate nations such as Brazil, China, Indonesia, and Russia (to note some of the most populous ones). Crucially, even if stuck in the "middle-income trap," these intermediate nations all have some sort of middle class, not in the Western sense but certainly in terms of people with some resources living above the poverty line—thus, potentially, making them more critical citizens in terms of demanding accountability and good government performance. That said, it is important to note the regional variations within the developing world, in particular the strong growth in the Asian middle class since 1990 and the still-small middle class in sub-Saharan Africa.[30]

Notes

1 The notion of including a stable judicial system as one of the components of an effective state comes from J. G. Merquior, "Patterns of State-Building in Argentina and Brazil," *States in History,* ed. John A. Hall, 264–88 (Oxford, UK: Basil Blackwell, 1986), 276.

2 Friedrich Schneider, "Shadow Economies Around the World: What Do We Really Know?" *European Journal of Political Economy* 21, no. 3 (September 2005): 598–642. For the size of the shadow economy in OECD countries, see Table 3.8, p. 611 of this article. On the contrast between the neighbouring flawed state of Argentina and the effective state of Chile in terms of tax compliance, see Marcelo Bergman, *Tax Evasion and the Rule of Law in Latin America: The Political Culture of Cheating and Compliance in Argentina and Chile* (University Park, PA: The Pennsylvania State University Press, 2009).

3 In some weak states, the state presence may be not just ignored but, indeed, physically opposed. Rotberg thus uses the term "failed state" to refer to those states experiencing civil war or insurrections combined with—or indeed resulting from—the failure of the state to deliver socioeconomic "goods" (security, public services, economic growth) in the areas it does control. He lists Afghanistan, Angola, Burundi, the Democratic Republic of the Congo, Liberia, Sierra Leone, and Sudan as the failed states of this decade, with Somalia as a collapsed state. Robert I. Rotberg, "The New Nature of Nation-State Failure," *The Washington Quarterly* 25, no. 3 (Summer 2002): 85–96.

4 Peter Evans, *Embedded Autonomy: States and Industrial Transformation* (Princeton, NJ: Princeton University Press, 1995), 44–45.

5 "Crisis, Fragile and Failed States: Definitions used by the CSRC." Crisis States Research Centre, London, 2006, http://www2.lse.ac.uk/internationalDevelopment/research/crisisStates/download/drc/FailedState.pdf

6 Joel S. Migdal, *Strong Societies and Weak States: State-Society Relations and State Capabilities in the Third World* (Princeton, NJ: Princeton University Press, 1988).

7 See Chalmers Johnson, *MITI and the Japanese Miracle: The Growth of Industrial Policy, 1925–1975* (Stanford, CA: Stanford University Press, 1982); Robert Wade, *Governing the Market: Economic Theory and the Role of Government in East Asian Industrialization* (Princeton, NJ: Princeton University Press, 1990); and, more generally, Meredith Woo-Cumings, ed., *The Developmental State* (Ithaca, NY: Cornell University Press, 1999).

8 Johnson, *MITI*, 21.

9 Michael Mann, "The Autonomous Power of the State: Its Origins, Mechanisms and Results," *States in History,* ed. John A. Hall, 109–36 (Oxford, UK: Basil Blackwell, 1986), 113.

10 Barbara Geddes, *Politician's Dilemma: Building State Capacity in Latin America* (Berkeley and Los Angeles, CA: University of California Press, 1994), 134–39.

11 Derwent Whittlesey, *The Earth and the State: A Study of Political Geography* (New York, NY: Henry Holt and Company, 1944), 23.

12 Whittlesey, *The Earth and the State*, 11.

13 Jeffrey Herbst, *States and Power in Africa* (Princeton, NJ: Princeton University Press, 2000), see Chapter Five on "National Design and the Broadcasting of Power," 139–72.

14 Allen C. Lynch, *How Russia Is Not Ruled: Reflections on Russian Political Development* (Cambridge, UK: Cambridge University Press, 2005), 26.

15   On the central historical role of rural civil society in keeping the state weak in Guinea-Bissau, see Joshua B. Forrest, *Lineages of State Fragility: Rural Civil Society in Guinea-Bissau* (Athens, OH: Ohio University Press, 2003).

16   On the "youth bulge" and political violence, see Henrik Urdal, "A Clash of Generations? Youth Bulges and Political Violence," *International Studies Quarterly* 50, no. 3 (September 2006): 607–629.

17   Dan Harris, Mick Moore, and Hubert Schmitz, *Country Classifications for a Changing World*, IDS Working Paper 326 (Brighton, UK: Institute of Development Studies, University of Sussex, May 2009), 10–11.

18   Joan Edelman Spero, *The Politics of International Economic Relations*, 4th ed. (New York, NY: St. Martin's Press, 1990), 11–15.

19   Michael Spence, *The Next Convergence: The Future of Economic Growth in a Multispeed World* (New York, NY: Farrar, Straus and Giroux, 2011), 19.

20   World Economic Forum, *Global Competitiveness Report 2012–2013* (Geneva: World Economic Forum, 2012).

21   The central source here is the updated and extended version of the dataset constructed by Lane and Milesi-Ferretti (2007): Philip R. Lane and Gian Maria Milesi-Ferretti, "The External Wealth of Nations Mark II: Revised and Extended Estimates of Foreign Assets and Liabilities, 1970–2004," *Journal of International Economics* 73, no. 2 (November 2007): 223–50.

22   Spence, *The Next Convergence*, 19, 53.

23   Spence, *The Next Convergence*, 100–102.

24   Spence, *The Next Convergence*, 103, 195; World Bank, *China 2030: Building a Modern, Harmonious, and Creative High-Income Society* (Washington, DC: The World Bank, 2012), 12.

25   Jesus Felipe, *Tracking the Middle-Income Trap: What is It, Who is in It, and Why? Part 1*, ADB Economics Working Paper Series 306 (Manila: Asian Development Bank, March 2012), 25.

26   For a visual illustration of this dividing line, see Andrew Webster, *Introduction to the Sociology of Development*, 2nd ed. (Basingstoke, UK: Macmillan, 1990), 5 [Map 1.1].

27   That is, the HDI compresses the effects of increased per capita income by logging this data because it is felt that "the transformation function from income to capabilities is likely to be concave." *United Nations Human Development Report 2011*, 168. Logging is used, for example, in the Richter scale for earthquakes and, more generally, when extreme values throw off the average. With the standard base 10 logarithm, when the number goes up by 1, the effect goes up by 10.

28   The source here is Felipe, *Tracking the Middle-Income Trap*, and his cut-off for low income is GDP per capita in 1990 PPP (purchasing power parity) dollars continuously below $2,000 from 1950 (even if then a colony) through 2010. Additional countries added from the data set of the late Angus Maddison. See the data under the heading "Historical Statistics," http://www.ggdc.net/maddison/oriindex.htm.

29   Paul Collier, *The Bottom Billion: Why the Poorest Countries are Failing and What Can Be Done About It* (New York, NY: Oxford University Press, 2007).

30   Martin Ravallion, "The Developing World's Bulging (but Vulnerable) Middle Class," *World Development*, Volume 38, no. 4 (April 2010): 445–54. On Asia specifically, see also the Asian Development Bank, "The Rise of Asia's Middle Class," in *Key Indicators for Asia and the Pacific 2010*, 2–57 (Manila: Asian Development Bank, August 2010).

CHAPTER FOUR

Electoral Democracies, Liberal Democracies, and Autocracies

IN THIS CHAPTER YOU WILL LEARN

► what the minimal factors needed for an electoral democracy are;
► what the "fallacy of electoralism" means;
► what the five specific aspects of liberal democracy are, and how these developed historically;
► what a semi-liberal autocracy is;
► what a closed autocracy is;
► what the differences are between liberal democracy, electoral democracy, semi-liberal autocracy, and closed autocracy;
► where each country in the world fits into this typology; and
► what critiques have been made of and improvements suggested for liberal democracies.

Democracy and the *Demos*

Democracy is a difficult concept to define, or at least one that is hard to define succinctly. The word has its root in the Greek term *demos,* meaning "the people," combined with the suffix "-cracy" from the Greek *kratos,* meaning "power" or "strength." Thus, the people are clearly part of a democracy. But in what way or ways? In his Gettysburg Address of 1863, Abraham Lincoln eloquently spoke of "government of the people, by the people, and for the people." Yet each of these aspects is problematic at some level. Government "of the people" refers to the people being the actual decision makers. But rarely in the world does a national legislature, for example, exactly mirror its society in terms of age (parliamentarians are, on average, older than their nation's mean age), gender (every democratic national parliament has a male majority except for tiny Andorra, although the extent of this gender imbalance varies greatly), education (parliamentarians tend to be better educated than the average citizen, and many would defend this reality), or occupational background (politicians, at least in North America, overwhelmingly come from legal backgrounds). The issue here may be simply the possibility of an "average person" holding office, however average may be defined.

Government "by the people" implies that the people are somehow participating in the process. Participation could mean voting, speaking out publicly on an issue, or contacting a government official. Yet, outside of Switzerland, where it is the constitutional and political reality that most issues will be dealt with ultimately through public initiatives or referenda, rarely do the people in any democracy actually take decisions on policies. (An *initiative* is a citizen-sponsored or "bottom-up" proposal for a policy change, whereas a *referendum* is a vote whereby the population has the final say on proposed government legislation or constitutional changes.[1]) Democracies are essentially delegative rather than direct, although political analysts like Robert A. Dahl (discussed later in this chapter) argue that they should be more direct to be truly democratic. Certainly in Canada, it has been a political convention since the Charlottetown Accord (although not a formal constitutional requirement) that major constitutional changes will require approval in a national referendum.

Finally, government "for the people" could mean government in the public interest or, more simply, "good government." But a benevolent dictator could rule "for the people," and certainly many dictators claim to be acting in the national interest. The issue is who decides whether the government or a specific policy is a good one. Rousseau wrote of the "general will," but this theoretical concept does not seem to exist naturally. There must be some *political* process for determining what the people want. And investigating this process will lead us shortly into the realm of elections. It is worth noting here that some people may not understand a proposed policy, or, even if they understand it, they may not have a strong opinion on it as long as it is still theoretical. Consequently, people tend to have clearer opinions on *actual* policies and *actual* governments. Because people are thus generally able to decide whether what they have had for, say, the last four years has been "good government," they are able to decide whether they want "more of the same."

Elections and Accountability

And if the people do not like what they have had? Presumably, then, they would remove the current government at the next election. Indeed, one rare succinct definition of democracy is Przeworski's: "Democracy is a system in which parties lose elections."[2] In fact, this simple statement carries some important assumptions: first, there is someone else to vote for; second, the governing party or president will actually hand over power; and third, elections are not just *a way* but *the only acceptable way* to remove governments. Each of these points is understood to be part of democracy. Moreover, as Przeworski further notes, elections occur under set rules (an institutional framework) that structure the competition.[3] In a sense, then, the role of the people in a democracy, at a minimum, involves choosing between the electoral alternatives on offer. Mirroring this point is another: being chosen by the voters—directly or indirectly—is the only way one acquires a democratic right to govern. This point is, essentially, the definition of democracy offered several decades ago by Schumpeter: "the democratic method is that institutional arrangement for arriving at political decisions in which individuals acquire the power to decide by means of a competitive struggle for the people's vote."[4] Thus, democracy involves *competition;* if there is only one party or choice on the ballot, there cannot be democracy. Competition and elections also provide for vertical *accountability*, that is, accountability of the government party or parties to the voters. Even if this accountability is admittedly after the fact, the desire to be re-elected should produce "good government," or at least better government than if there were no accountability at all.

Conversely, if a political system has no competition and no true accountability, then those in power will presumably stay there indefinitely, regardless of the wishes of the people. Such a political system we call an **autocracy**. The Greek root *auto* means "self," and, thus, an autocracy is literally the absolute rule by one individual (the autocrat). However, for our purposes, autocracy also applies to rule by a group as long as this group is unaccountable to the *demos* as a whole. Autocracies do have great variations within them, but, for now, the key point is that an autocracy is the opposite of a democracy.

Electoral Democracy versus Liberal Democracy

Schumpeter's definition of democracy can certainly be called minimalist. He does not even assume that political competition will be perfectly fair; instead, he draws a parallel with business competition in the marketplace, which he notes is hardly ever perfect.[5] Business competition can involve fraud, false advertising, and the general attempt of bigger firms to squeeze out smaller ones. Sometimes, established firms can collude to keep control over a market. Ideally, though, procedures are in place to prevent such restraints on business competition. It is the same for political competition: this involves not just two or more parties or candidates competing, but also procedures to ensure the fairness of the competition, such as laws against bribery or coercion. In political competition, the key test is usually whether an opposition party or candidate has a reasonable opportunity to defeat the incumbent party or candidate; failure to do so must be because the voters, in fact, prefer "more of the same" to any of the alternatives, rather than because of fraud or coercion. For the population to assess opposition proposals fairly, they must have access to them and at least relatively unbiased commentary on them. Although Schumpeter does not equate democracy with freedom per se, he does note that a situation in which everyone is free to run for office (though few may have the resources to do so) is likely to lead to "a considerable amount of freedom of discussion *for all*" and likewise "a considerable amount of freedom of the press."[6] In summary, then, Schumpeter sees democracy as involving sufficient if imperfect competition for political office in the context of some civil liberties. At the time he wrote, this definition of democracy seemed acceptable, inasmuch as the countries that had competitive elections were rarely "flawed" on other matters. However, today, most political systems have elections with at least some degree of competition, if only because of international pressure to hold elections. Furthermore, inevitably, elections are relatively rare events (held usually every four or five years),[7] whereas democracy is ideally an ongoing process.

Consequently, to equate elections with democracy is to commit what Terry Lynn Karl and others call the "fallacy of electoralism," the assumption that an election, just by being held, will produce representative yet competitive parties or candidates, effective and accepted political institutions, and a legitimate government that is then able to govern. As Karl notes, electoralism as an ideology "elevates elections over all other dimensions of democracy."[8] Certainly, having an elected and thus downwardly accountable government is a key difference between a democracy and an autocracy, but full democracy needs more. Indeed, a non-competitive, non-democratic election, which is no rarity in the world, may produce citizens who are cynical of elections even if these do become or had earlier been somewhat free and fair. Russians today under Putin appear to fit this description.

Even if an election is basically free and fair, it is nevertheless crucial to distinguish between the minimal nature of an **electoral democracy** and a full-fledged **liberal democracy**. The recent work of Larry Diamond is very clear on this regard:

> *Electoral* democracy is a civilian, constitutional system in which the legislative and chief executive offices are filled through regular, competitive, multiparty elections with universal suffrage [thus producing the vertical accountability of responsible government].
>
> ... In addition to the elements of electoral democracy, [*liberal* democracy] ... requires, first, the absence of reserved domains of power for the military or other actors not accountable to the electorate, directly or indirectly. Second, in addition to the vertical accountability of rulers to the ruled (secured mainly through elections), it requires the horizontal accountability of officeholders to one another; this constrains executive power and so helps protect constitutionalism, legality, and the deliberative process. Third, it encompasses extensive provisions for political and civil pluralism as well as for individual and group freedoms, so that contending interests and values may be expressed and compete through ongoing processes of articulation and representation, beyond periodic elections.
>
> Freedom and pluralism, in turn, can be secured only through a "rule of law," in which legal rules are applied fairly, consistently, and predictably across equivalent cases, irrespective of the class, status, or power of those subject to the rules.[9]

Consequently, one should note that, whereas an electoral democracy is not a liberal democracy, a liberal democracy is an electoral democracy—and then some. In other words, we can group together liberal democracies and electoral democracies into a complete list of electoral democracies, if that is our only concern or threshold. For example, the Freedom House organization, which divides the world's countries and territories into the often-cited categories of "free," "partly free," and "not free," also now makes a separate list of electoral democracies. This list includes all of its "free" countries but not all of its "partly free" ones.

The Five Elements of Liberal Democracy

For our purposes, liberal democracy involves no less than five separate elements, as outlined in Table 4.1. First there is **responsible government,** a concept with which many students of political science have some trouble. Responsible government does not mean only that the government is responsible to the people, in the sense of accountability "downwards," but that the government is *only* responsible to the people and not to any other political actor who may be "pulling the strings," perhaps behind the scenes. Potentially, two political "string pullers" are (1) a monarch and (2) the military. At one extreme, one could argue that a monarch is, by definition, an affront to democracy, because a monarch is neither elected nor accountable. A more moderate distinction, though, and the one used in Chapter 2, is to ask whether the monarch exercises any real political power or is merely a symbolic figurehead. Only in the former case does a monarch violate—to a partial or complete degree—the principle of responsible government. As for the military, it must be under civilian control for there to be a liberal democracy. Conversely, if the military controls the civilian government, then the government is not accountable "downwards" to the people, and accountability is undemocratic. As noted in Chapter 2, military intervention in recent decades has been most common in Latin America and Africa, but has occurred also in parts of Asia and even in Southern Europe.

The struggle for responsible government was and is central to the struggle for democracy. Power being finite, the issue is whether it is concentrated in the hands of democratically chosen politicians or non-democratic actors. It is not enough to have an elected "government" if it is not the *real* government: responsible government includes the "explicit criterion that the elected government must to a reasonable degree have effective power to rule."[10] In this vein, J. Samuel Valenzuela has emphasized the problematic factor of "nondemocratically generated *tutelary powers,*" which

attempt to exercise broad oversight of the government and its policy decisions while claiming to represent vaguely formulated fundamental and enduring interests of the nation-state. A regime cannot be considered a consolidated democracy if those who win government-forming elections are placed in state power and policymaking positions that are subordinate in this manner to those of nonelected elites.... Part of the process of building European democracies in the nineteenth and early twentieth centuries was to eliminate the tutelary power held by monarchs, making cabinets and prime ministers

TABLE 4.1 Definitional Features of Liberal Democracy (five factors)

1. RESPONSIBLE GOVERNMENT

► Political decisions are taken in a reasonably transparent way by elected officials (or those under their authority) who are thus directly accountable to the electorate or, ultimately, accountable via an elected parliament, and are not accountable to a tutelary monarch or military.

► Governments are thus never overthrown nor deposed by such tutelary actors nor, indeed, forced out of office by any non-constitutional means, such as public protests.

► Horizontal accountability exists via checks and balances on the executive and especially by oversight bodies.

► A non-accountable head of state (such as a monarch) has at most a minimal political role and no power over policy.

► There is full civilian executive control over the military.

2. FREE AND FAIR COMPETITION FOR POLITICAL OFFICE

► Elected officials are chosen and peacefully removed in free, fair, and relatively frequent elections with minimal or ideally no coercion of the voters.

► Political parties can freely form and compete in elections (note that in some countries antidemocratic parties are banned).

3. FULL AND EQUAL RIGHTS OF POLITICAL PARTICIPATION

► Practically all adults have the right to vote.

► There is only one vote per person.

► Likewise, most adults have the right to run for office.

4. FULL CIVIL LIBERTIES

► There is freedom of expression including online commentary, and including the right to criticize public officials and governmental policies.

► There is freedom of the press; as part of this freedom, various alternative, non-governmental sources of information exist, as well as unblocked access to the Internet.

► There is freedom of organization (into autonomous groups).

► There is freedom of religion.

5. A LEGALLY BASED, WELL-FUNCTIONING STATE, WITH EFFECTIVE AND FAIR GOVERNANCE

► The state, that is, the political-bureaucratic system, penetrates effectively and more or less evenly throughout the country.

► The rule of law clearly exists and is upheld by an independent, unbiased judiciary.

► Political and bureaucratic corruption is minimal or, ideally, non-existent.

accountable only to elected parliaments, and armies subordinate to decisions taken by the government rather than the crown. In recent transition settings, the military have often sought to place themselves in such a tutelary role.[11]

In fact, such a tutelary role has a long tradition in most Latin American militaries.

In contrast, in a liberal democracy, it is not only acceptable but indeed necessary for bureaucrats and political executives to be supervised by "oversight bodies" so as to prevent or at least minimize abuse of power. The first type of these bodies is the office of a parliamentary ombudsman (in some countries called a people's defender or public defender), which was first created in Sweden in 1809. This office is focused on overseeing the bureaucracy, not elected politicians. The second type is a supreme audit institution, often called an auditor general or comptroller general, to aid in fiscal and managerial accountability. Auditing bodies and individuals date back to mediaeval times, but the first modern ones were set up in the nineteenth century, such as the one established by William Gladstone (then chancellor of the exchequer) in the United Kingdom in 1866. Beyond these bodies are the more general checks and balances on the executive of the legislature and the courts.

Moreover, it should be stressed in our analysis of responsible government that we are assuming that there *is* a government and, furthermore, that it presides over a sovereign, autonomous, existing state. Consequently, liberal democracy—or indeed democracy generally—cannot exist in a colony because political authority ultimately rests with the non-accountable imperial power.[12] That said, colonies can certainly have some liberal democratic elements, which would facilitate them becoming liberal democracies at independence (see "The Cultural-Historical Legacy" in Chapter 5 for more on democracy and colonialism.) Equally, democracy cannot exist in a **collapsed state** as no authoritative decisions are actually taken or effectively implemented. For example, this was the situation of Iraq with its elected "government" of May 2006 (based on what was a free and fair election in December 2005). In contrast, the Iraqi government of December 2010 is a real government, albeit presiding over a weak state. Last, democracy is also not possible under a foreign military occupation that seeks to impose its preferred government independent of public opinion. For example, in Hungary in November 1945, the Independent Smallholders Party won a clear majority of seats with 57 per cent of the vote. However, the occupying Soviets forced the Smallholders into a coalition government—specifically, one in which the Communists controlled the Interior Ministry (and thus the police) and other portfolios, which then allowed the Communists to threaten and marginalize their political opponents.[13]

Note also that accountability is down to the electorate, that is, the people expressing themselves via the democratic process of elections. Accountability is much more dubious when "the people" (in reality only some of them) effect the removal of an elected government via mass public protests, which have often led to the fall of presidents in countries such as Argentina, Bolivia, and Ecuador. The reality of a liberal democracy is that, unless recall provisions are in place, voters have to wait, perhaps impatiently, until the next election to legitimately remove a government. Obviously, though, more patience is likely required in countries with fixed terms for governments, which is the case in presidential systems, for example.

Second, a liberal democracy also requires *free and fair competition* or, alternatively, the holding of free and fair elections. The terms "free" and "fair" have some overlap, but the basic distinction is as follows. "Free" refers to the opportunities and rights of individuals not just to run for office (or to form political parties and run for office as party candidates) but also to be able to campaign publicly and access the media. Freedom in this context is thus the ability to participate. "Fair" refers to the electoral process, which must be unbiased with regard to the various candidates and parties and transparent in its procedures. Harassment of opposition candidates; bribery, vote buying, or, alternatively, coercion and intimidation of voters; obstruction of opposition supporters' access to the polls, including having significantly fewer polling stations in opposition areas; manipulating voters' lists, for example, by removing opposition supporters or padding the lists with dead or non-existent "government supporters"; stuffing individual ballot boxes; "premarking" ballots; and the manipulation of vote totals are all examples of unfair or biased electoral practices.[14] In a liberal democracy, elections are normally unaffected by such flaws, being carried out in a highly professional if not, indeed, "squeaky clean" manner in terms of the actual voting on election day and the subsequent official vote tabulations, which are transparent and thus can be monitored by the competing candidates or parties. In contrast, electoral democracies may experience localized voting irregularities. However, these irregularities do not affect who is the overall winner and thus do not thwart the voters' wishes. In contrast, autocratic elections are characterized by widespread and systematic election fraud or pro-regime bias in the election campaign.

Assuming it exists, election freedom thus essentially occurs during the campaign. Election fairness, however, occurs during the campaign, on election day (or the election days), and, indeed, afterwards in terms of certification of the results. Spain in 1936 under its Second Republic provided an interesting example of an election that was largely free and fair up through the election day. Thereafter, though, the victorious Popular Front coalition did not feel that its narrow majority (based on very close vote results) provided a sufficient quorum for the quick passage of legislation. Consequently, the coalition set out to "improve" its position, taking advantage of a very non-neutral electoral process. As Payne notes,

Under the Republican system, the first major task of a new parliament was to elect a *comisión de actas* (electoral commission) to review the electoral results and determine if they should be cancelled or reversed in any district on account of fraud or other improprieties. This meant in effect that the victors in each election had the power to sit in judgment on the losers and determine if their parliamentary representation should be reduced still further. This power had been exercised with moderation by the center-right in 1933, but the [leftist] Popular Front, consistent with its intention to eliminate all political opposition it could, intended to conduct a sweeping review of all the districts won by the center-right in 1936. The extreme left demanded cancellation of nearly all rightist victories, judging, as *El Socialista* put it on 20 March, that "not a single deputy of the right can say that he won his seat fairly." Membership of the commission was voted on 17 March with a heavy leftist majority.[15]

In the end, the extreme left certainly did not get its wish, but still dozens of seats were reassigned or annulled, and the subsequent elections held were under unfair and fraudulent conditions. Although, overall, some seats were given to the centre and one to the right, these concessions were essentially for show, as the vast majority of seats that changed hands went to the left, which, in turn, lost not a single one. Election irregularities that had benefited the Popular Front were, not surprisingly, mostly ignored. As Payne concludes, "Electoral fraud had been frequent in the history of parliamentary government in Spain, but this explicit and highly formalized reassignment of voting results was without precedent."[16]

A necessary but not sufficient component of a fair election is a secret ballot,[17] whose introduction represented a key historical step in election fairness. The use of a secret ballot began in Australia—more specifically, in South Australia in 1856—and then spread out to other countries. (Indeed, for a time in the United States, the secret ballot was known simply as the "Australian ballot.") In Canada, the central role of ensuring the fairness of federal elections is played by the chief electoral officer (who personally cannot vote) and the Chief Electoral Office, which dates back to 1920. The number of analogous offices worldwide has expanded greatly in the past two decades as a means of removing the administration of elections from the government of the day.[18] One key country, however, that lacks such an office is the United States, and this deficiency has led to such problems and controversy as occurred in its 2000 presidential elections. Finally, it must be stressed that, in rare circumstances, elections may still be free and fair without responsible government, but they will not be "relevant" in the sense of determining the government. Recent parliamentary elections in Morocco are examples of this phenomenon. So too have been all elections in Monaco.

The third element a liberal democracy requires is *full and equal rights of political participation.* (Of course, it is unlikely that absolutely everyone will use such rights, but that is the nature of any right.) "Full" here refers to having universal adult suffrage, as opposed to excluding women, the poor, the illiterate, aboriginals, and so on, all of whom have been excluded at times historically throughout the world. After World War I, universal (white) male suffrage was common, and, in almost all Protestant nations, universal (white) female suffrage was also granted. In nations where other religions were prominent, universal female suffrage was generally not granted until after World War II. Yet even granting women the vote did not necessarily bring full suffrage, as literacy requirements continued in many nations, especially in Latin America. Indeed, voting rights for illiterates were not granted until the late 1970s in Ecuador and Peru, and not until 1988 in Brazil. It should also be stressed that, today, "adulthood" for voting purposes is set at 18 years in the vast majority of countries,[19] but still ranges from 16 in such countries as Austria and Brazil to 20 or 21 in some East and South East Asian countries. A cut-off of 21, the Western norm until the 1970s, is still a clear drop from the minimum age for suffrage in nineteenth-century Europe, which was as high as 30 years (Denmark) and often 25. Moreover, those higher age thresholds in the nineteenth century occurred in the context of much shorter lives: in 1900, the average life expectancy in Western Europe was 46 and only 35 in Spain![20] Also, because countries were at a lower level of socio-economic development, there was much greater variation of life expectancy across social classes. Consequently, high minimum ages for suffrage produced an indirect (but probably intentional) class bias in the electorate independent of any wealth requirements. The same point can be made for literacy tests, although these were often directed more at aboriginals, in South America, for example, or at blacks in the United States South.[21]

"Equal" political participation in this context refers to each voter having but one vote or, more generally, the same number of votes. Some electoral systems, e.g., in Germany and New Zealand, give everyone two votes (see Chapter 7). Historically, however, countries such as Belgium, Prussia (Germany), and the United Kingdom not only restricted who could vote but effectively or in fact gave extra or additional votes to certain voters based on a *régime censitaire,* that is, based on property or income (tax payments) or business ownership; a *principe capacitaire,* that is, based on education level; and even male head of household status. "One person one vote"—and no more—was not fully established in the United Kingdom until 1948, for example.[22]

Moreover, the assumption here is that legislative elections determine the entire legislature; in the modern world, a partly elected legislature does not meet democratic
standards. So, for example, although in 2010 the Tongan Legislative Assembly had
17 out of 26 seats elected by the voters and filled by peoples' representatives, nobles
elected 9 seats. These nobles' representatives were decisive in determining the government after the 2010 elections—helping to elect a noble as prime minister rather
than the leader of the party that had, in fact, won a clear majority of the 17 popularly elected seats.

The fourth characteristic of a liberal democracy is that its citizens enjoy *full
civil liberties.* Civil liberties are often constitutionally enumerated and entrenched,
such as in the Canadian Charter of Rights and Freedoms. One can note that the
Schumpeterian definition of democracy does not assume full civil liberties. However,
two decades after Schumpeter's book, the political scientist Robert A. Dahl argues
that civil liberties are part of the necessary institutional guarantees of or requirements for proper political competition and participation.[23] Since that time, civil liberties have been seen as central to democracy—at times perhaps a bit too central,
as some politicians, especially in the United States, seem to equate democracy with
freedom. In fact, one can have a reasonable amount of civil liberty without responsible government or even elections, if, for example, one lives under an autocratic but
tolerant monarch. One of the virtues of the annual surveys of freedom by the New
York–based Freedom House organization is that these give separate scores for political rights and for civil liberties, allowing one to see how these diverge.

The fifth and final element of a liberal democracy is the need for *a legally based
and well-functioning state, with effective and fair governance.* Civil liberties cannot
truly exist in the absence of a general rule of law (as Diamond notes), and the rule
of law requires an independent and unbiased judiciary as a separate component of
the state. The rule of law must apply to everyone, including members of the state
itself. This point goes back to the traditional German notion of a **Rechtsstaat**, that is,
a "state subject to law." The law protects the citizens against the power of the state,
specifically the abuse (defined as the arbitrary use) of this power. More precisely, in
the classic analysis of Carl Schmitt,

> A state may be termed a *Rechtsstaat* only when all administrative authority—especially
> that of the police—is subject to the conditions and procedure of law, and when interven-
> tion into the sphere of individual freedom is permissible solely on the basis of a law. Its

identifying characteristic is the lawlike nature of the administration. The guarantee of its citizens' freedom lies in the law.[24]

Indeed, citizens in a *Rechtsstaat* have more than legally based civil liberties and free-doms: they can use the courts—and now in most liberal democracies an ombudsman or equivalent—to seek restitution from any abuse, neglect, or unfairness by state officials. It is worth stressing that the creation of a *Rechtsstaat* was an achievement of nineteenth-century liberals (especially but not exclusively in Europe), paralleling their initiation of responsible government. Yet, because universal suffrage or even universal male suffrage came often much later, the emergence of a *Rechtsstaat* in the West came long before full democratization.[25]

A country cannot be considered a liberal democracy if it lacks a *Rechtsstaat*. Nor can the state be weak in the sense discussed in Chapter 3 because, if it is, the geographic areas outside of its effective control are not subject to the rule of law, and, indeed, all democratic rules are not properly enforceable throughout its realm. Colombia has been a paradigmatic example of this problem. Finally, it is not just elections that must be fair, but the whole determination and implementation of government policies. A liberal democracy cannot be said to exist if politicians or bureaucrats exhibit endemic corruption. Political corruption has received increasing analysis over the past decade or so, in particular by the Berlin-based Transparency International organization, which produces annual rankings of countries in terms of their level of corruption or lack of it.[26] Similar to the point that a liberal democratic state must have full civil liberties, the notion that it must also be a well-functioning state was not dealt with by political analysts several decades ago, or perhaps meeting this standard was just assumed to have occurred, especially as the focus was often on Western countries only. But this aspect is now assessed in many international comparisons of democracy.

Finally, let us stress again that, of the five elements of liberal democracy, the first three—responsible government, free and fair competition, and full and equal rights of political participation—are needed in the contemporary world for a state to be considered an electoral democracy as opposed to an autocracy. One of the main international texts laying out these factors is the 1990 Copenhagen Document of the Conference on Security and Co-operation in Europe.[27] The last section of this chapter gives in full the key article of this document as a detailed "check list" of the components of electoral democracy. That said, historically, all electoral democracies in the sense of regimes with responsible government and free and fair competition would have lacked the universal and equal suffrage aspect considered a requirement of democracy today. Consequently, in Chapter 10, we shall introduce the qualified notion of a "moderately inclusive electoral democracy."

Political Regimes in the World Today (October 2012)

Even if most, if not all, of the five elements of liberal democracy tend to go together, they are conceptually and empirically separate. In particular, we have noted that civil liberties can exist under autocracy. Thus, just as we can distinguish liberal democracies from electoral democracies, we can distinguish what we shall call *semi-liberal autocracies* from *closed autocracies*. A semi-liberal autocracy has a political opposition of some elected significance—that is, say, 15 per cent or more of the seats held by national parties opposed to the regime[28]—and some genuine civil liberties. A closed aristocracy tolerates no or next to no political opposition and has no civil liberties or next to none.[29] The term "semi-liberal" as opposed to simply "liberal" is used to connote the fact that, in semi-liberal autocracies, we are talking about fewer civil liberties than in a liberal democracy or, indeed, in most electoral democracies.

Table 4.2 outlines four regime types, each with decreasing levels of democracy from left to right. Consequently, a liberal democracy is the most democratic regime type, and a closed autocracy is the least; a closed autocracy is thus the antithesis of a liberal democracy. Electoral democracies and semi-liberal autocracies fall between these two extremes, having some to most civil liberties but lacking both the full civil liberties and, in particular, the strong rule of law found in liberal democracies. Again, though, the key distinction between an electoral democracy and a semi-liberal autocracy is that, in the former, the government can be voted out and thereby replaced whereas, in the latter, it effectively cannot. The concept of a semi-liberal autocracy parallels Ottaway's description of a "semi-authoritarian regime":

The most important characteristic of semi-authoritarian regimes is the existence and persistence of mechanisms that effectively prevent the transfer of power through elections from the hands of the incumbent leaders or party to a new political elite or organization. It is the existence of such mechanisms that makes the term *semi-authoritarian* more appropriate than any that contains the word *democracy*—if power cannot be

TABLE 4.2 Democracies and Autocracies as Regime Types

	Liberal Democracy	Electoral Democracy	Semi-liberal Autocracy	Closed Autocracy
Political Parties and Elections and Overall Political Opposition	Free and fair competition involving two or more parties; citizens can change their government through elections; an open and usually strong political opposition.	Two or more parties exist; open political opposition; citizens can change their government through elections, but elections are sometimes not completely free and fair.	Usually more than one party; limited political pluralism and consequent political opposition; however, national elections are not free and fair enough to actually change the government (or do not determine the government).	Either one official party or all parties are forbidden, although political independents can sometimes be elected if they are not openly anti-regime.
Socio-economic Pluralism	Many autonomous actors in economy and broader society (of course, not all have equal political influence).	Often quite extensive social and economic pluralism.	Some social and economic pluralism, perhaps predating the autocratic regime.	No significant social pluralism; usually some economic and religious pluralism.
Civil Liberties	Full civil liberties.	Civil liberties are usually incomplete if not limited.	Civil liberties are limited or at best incomplete.	No or next to no civil liberties.
Ideology	Emphasis on civilian authority, the rule of law, individualism, and minority rights.	Usually no formal guiding ideology.	No formal guiding ideology; at best distinctive tendencies.	No formal guiding ideology unless totalitarian; usually nationalistic.
Mobilization	Participation largely generated autonomously by civil society and by competing parties.	Participation largely generated autonomously by civil society and by competing parties.	Participation largely generated autonomously by civil society, but with some restrictions.	Emphasis on demobilization, except at some historical points.
Legitimacy of Authority	Legitimacy comes from legal-rational authority, even if some leaders may be aided by their personal charisma.	Legitimacy usually comes from legal-rational authority, although the processes are imperfect.	Wide range of legitimizing factors, including the illusion of legal-rational authority.	Legitimacy comes from tradition and claims of acting in the national interest.
Constraints on Authority	Clearly constrained by the constitution, the courts and the rule of law, a professional bureaucracy, and socio-political pluralism.	Clearly constrained by the constitution; only somewhat constrained by the courts and the rule of law, the bureaucracy, and socio-political pluralism.	Constrained only somewhat (if at all) by the constitution, courts, the rule of law, and the bureaucracy; constrained more by socio-political pluralism, especially the independent media.	A leader or perhaps a small group enjoys legally undefined limits but, in fact, is somewhat constrained by the bureaucracy, the military, and economic actors.
Political Accountability to Population	Definite political accountability to the voters at elections and to society in an ongoing sense.	General political accountability to the voters at elections and to society in an ongoing sense.	No true political accountability.	No political accountability.
Leadership Duration	Leaders must subject themselves to periodic free and fair elections; transitions are legitimate and smooth.	Certain political leaders must subject themselves to periodic elections; tutelary actors shielded from this.	Individual leaders may well be of limited duration; often, elections "confirm" new leader, however produced.	Leadership usually for life unless overthrown.
Transition to (Liberal) Democracy		Usually a gradual removal of selected remaining barriers.	A variety of scenarios; however, a stable negotiated transition can occur in competitive autocratic regimes with developed civil societies.	Needs to go first through a semi-liberal autocratic phase with some socio-political pluralism, unless defeated in war and occupied by a foreign power willing to democratize.

Source: Based, in part, on concepts in Juan J. Linz and Alfred Stepan, *Problems of Democratic Transition and Consolidation: Southern Europe, South America, and Post-Communist Europe* (Baltimore, MD: The Johns Hopkins University Press, 1996), Table 3.1 and 4.2, with modifications.

transferred by elections, there is little point in describing a country as democratic, even with qualifiers. These mechanisms for blocking power transfers function despite the existence of formally democratic institutions and the degree of political freedom granted to the citizens of the country. Semi-authoritarian states [semi-liberal autocracies] may have a reasonably free press. The regime may leave space for autonomous organizations of civil society to operate, for private businesses to grow and thus for new economic elites to arise. The regime may hold fairly open elections for local or regional governments or even allow backbenchers from the government party to be defeated in elections.... [However,] there is no way to challenge [successfully] the power of the incumbents. At the center, competition is a fiction; even if elections are held, outsiders are not allowed to truly challenge the power of the incumbents. Elections are not the source of the government's power [even if they are claimed as such for the purposes of legitimization], and thus voters cannot transfer power to a new leadership.[30]

Table 4.3 classifies all of the countries of the world into the four regime types listed in Table 4.2, based on each country's situation in October 2012. We find 54 cases of liberal democracy. Within this group is a subset of countries in which political and bureaucratic corruption is clearly minimal and, conversely, in which state personnel have very high levels of integrity. This subset is based on largely impressionistic distinctions, however, and is thus presented for interest rather than as a definitional aspect. Next, 59 countries are electoral democracies without being liberal democracies. Elections are still central for determining who has power, but these countries lack full civil liberties or a clear rule of law. A few of these electoral democracies (for example, Guatemala and Pakistan) also have incomplete civilian control over their militaries—see Chapter 2. Liechtenstein is classified here due to the continuing real political power of its Grand Duke, a fact made explicit in its constitutional revision of 2003 and effectively accepted by the voters when its referendum of 2012 was unsuccessful. Next are 47 semi-liberal autocracies. These include Singapore, which will be discussed in Chapter 9. Singapore is known for its efficient, incorrupt bureaucracy, but the country remains dominated by a People's Action Party (PAP) that maintains power, in part, by harassing and intimidating what political opposition exists. Another semi-liberal autocracy, Monaco (where the government—led by a French national civil servant—is accountable to the prince but not to the freely and fairly elected legislature) is worth noting for its "liberal" extension of civil liberties to citizens, who certainly enjoy these to a greater extent than in almost all electoral

TABLE 4.3 Democracies and Autocracies as of October 2012 (total regimes = 195)

LIBERAL DEMOCRACIES (N = 54) with very high integrity of state personnel where a " + "

Andorra +	Dominica	Malta	Saint Vincent and the Grenadines
Australia +	Estonia	Marshall Islands	Samoa (Western)
Austria +	Finland +	Mauritius	San Marino
Bahamas +	France +	Micronesia	Slovakia
Barbados +	Germany +	Nauru	Slovenia
Belgium +	Grenada	Netherlands +	Spain
Belize	Iceland +	New Zealand +	Sweden +
Canada +	Ireland +	Norway +	Switzerland +
Cape Verde	Italy	Palau	Taiwan
Chile +	Japan +	Poland	Tuvalu
Costa Rica	Korea, South	Portugal	United Kingdom +
Cyprus (Greek)	Latvia	Saint Kitts and Nevis	United States +
Czech Republic	Lithuania	Saint Lucia +	Uruguay +
Denmark +	Luxembourg +		

ELECTORAL DEMOCRACIES (N = 59) with very high integrity of state personnel where a " + "

Antigua and Barbuda	Greece	Liechtenstein +	Romania
Argentina	Guatemala	Macedonia	São Tomé and Príncipe
Bangladesh	Guyana	Mexico	Senegal
Benin	Honduras	Moldova	Serbia
Bolivia	Hungary	Mongolia	Sierra Leone
Botswana	India	Montenegro	South Africa
Brazil	Indonesia	Namibia	Suriname
Bulgaria	Iraq	Niger	Thailand
Colombia	Israel	Nigeria	Timor-Leste (East Timor)
Comoros	Ivory Coast	Pakistan	Trinidad and Tobago
Croatia	Jamaica	Panama	Tunisia
Dominican Republic	Kiribati	Papua New Guinea	Turkey
Ecuador	Kyrgyzstan	Paraguay	Vanuatu
El Salvador	Lesotho	Peru	Zambia
Ghana	Liberia	Philippines	

SEMI-LIBERAL AUTOCRACIES (N = 47) with very high integrity of state personnel where a " + "

Albania	Congo, DR (Kinshasa)	Kosovo	Morocco	Tanzania
Algeria	Egypt	Kuwait	Mozambique	Togo
Angola	Fiji	Lebanon	Nepal	Tonga
Armenia	Gabon	Libya	Nicaragua	Uganda
Bhutan	Georgia	Madagascar	Russia	Ukraine
Bosnia-Herzegovina	Guinea	Malawi	Seychelles	Venezuela
Burkina Faso	Guinea-Bissau	Malaysia	Singapore +	Yemen
Burundi	Haiti	Maldives	Solomon Islands	Zimbabwe
Cambodia	Jordan	Mali	Sri Lanka	
Central African Republic	Kenya	Monaco		

CLOSED AUTOCRACIES (N = 35) with very high integrity of state personnel where a " + "

Afghanistan	Chad	Ethiopia	Oman	Swaziland
Azerbaijan	China	Gambia	Qatar +	Syria
Bahrain	Congo, R (Brazzaville)	Iran	Rwanda	Tajikistan
Belarus	Cuba	Kazakhstan	Saudi Arabia	Turkmenistan
Brunei	Djibouti	Korea, North	Somalia	United Arab Emirates
Burma/Myanmar	Equatorial Guinea	Laos	South Sudan	Uzbekistan
Cameroon	Eritrea	Mauritania	Sudan	Vietnam

democracies. A similar point can be made for Tonga. Finally, 35 countries are closed autocracies. Of these closed autocracies, several have no popular national elections at all (Brunei, China, Eritrea, Qatar, and Saudi Arabia) or very restricted suffrage (United Arab Emirates); the rest are one-party systems or hegemonic party systems that allow very little opposition, elected or otherwise. Overall, the first two categories combined give us 113 of the world's 195 regimes, or 58 per cent. This is an encouraging breadth of democratization. On the other hand, only a little more than a quarter of the world's regimes are liberal democracies, and the prospect of a vast increase in their number seems remote. Moreover, the category with the most growth in recent years has been that of semi-liberal autocracies. (Chapter 11 will analyse the prospects for more, or fewer, democracies in the world.)

To repeat, this list is the way the countries line up as of October 2012. Obviously, if one went back in time, such a list would be somewhat different. For example, South Africa was a semi-liberal, racially based autocracy before 1994 and its transition to democracy. Mexico was also a semi-liberal autocracy through the early 1990s, inasmuch as national elections were clearly not free and fair. They got "better" starting in the 1970s, but, even as late as the 1988 presidential election, most independent observers assume that votes and vote totals were doctored to produce a win for Carlos Salinas, the candidate of the ruling Institutional Revolutionary Party (PRI). However, by the 1990s—in part due to an independent electoral commission established by constitutional reform in 1990 and made fully autonomous from the executive in 1996—Mexican elections were increasingly free and fair, a change that culminated in the victory of Vincente Fox of the opposition PAN in the 2000 presidential election. The PRI returned to power in 2012, but in a free and fair election. On the other hand, both Iran and Zimbabwe were semi-liberal autocracies in the late 1990s, but, in both, the regime cut back on political openness and eliminated civil liberties, transforming the countries to closed autocracies as of the early 2000s. They still are today.

Beyond Liberal Democracy?

Despite the fact that only a minority of regimes worldwide are liberal democracies, one can argue (especially if one lives in such a system) that political systems can still do better in some ways. We have already noted that democracies function indirectly in that elected representatives make the decisions. So one way in which a system could go beyond liberal democracy is to have a more *direct democracy*, in which the population as a whole makes decisions on specific issues. Switzerland, in fact, decides most controversial issues this way. Deciding policy by ballot also happens at the state level in parts of the United States, especially in its western states (most notably Oregon and California). However, because direct democracy is rarely combined with compulsory voting, the "population as a whole" actually boils down to whomever shows up to vote, and, in Switzerland, this is normally less than 50 per cent of eligible voters, basically the better off and more educated ones. Moreover, referenda on policy issues often involve large sums of money being spent to sway the voters, and it is no surprise that, most of the time, the side with more money is the victorious one.

A more substantive but still hardly universal critique of liberal democracy is that it is focused on political *procedures* and not *policy outcomes*; in other words, it may involve accountable, competitive, and procedurally fair government, but there is no guarantee that the policies produced by such a government are substantively equal to everybody, for example, in providing equal access to health care and education.[31] In this vein, Huber, Rueschemeyer, and Stephens distinguish between formal and social democracy; the latter involves high levels of political participation across all social categories (what they call separately participatory democracy) and "increasing equality in social and economic outcomes." For them, the key factors leading from formal democracy to social democracy are working-class organization in terms of political parties, trade unions, and peasant leagues, as well as an effective state that is autonomous from the dominant socio-economic interests. These combine to produce the welfare state policies that are central to social democracy.[32] Of course, a list of such social democracies would be rather brief and largely drawn from Northern Europe—in short, a tiny subset of all democracies or even of all liberal democracies.

The Copenhagen Document

The Organization for Security and Co-operation in Europe (OSCE), previously the Conference on Security and Co-operation in Europe (CSCE), groups together the countries of Europe, post-Soviet Central Asia, and Canada and the United States. On 29 June 1990, the member states adopted the Document of the Copenhagen Meeting of the Conference on the Human Dimension of the CSCE, more commonly known simply as the Copenhagen Document. Within this document are wide-ranging commitments to democratic practices, including commitments to hold genuinely free and fair elections and to invite CSCE (now OSCE) observers to scrutinize one's own elections so as to enhance democratic electoral processes. Although not phrased for the purpose of defining democracy, this document speaks thoroughly to the concept of electoral democracy and outlines various of its aspects. Parts of Articles 5 and 6 and especially Article 7 are the most definitional:

(5.4)   [An essential element of justice is] a clear separation between the State and political parties; in particular, political parties will not be merged with the State....

(6)   The participating States declare that the will of the people, freely and fairly expressed through periodic and genuine elections, is the basis of the authority and legitimacy of all government....

(7)   To ensure that the will of the people serves as the basis of the authority of government, the participating States will

(7.1)   hold free elections at reasonable intervals, as established by law;

(7.2)   permit all seats in at least one chamber of the national legislature to be freely contested in a popular vote;

(7.3)   guarantee universal and equal suffrage to adult citizens;

(7.4)   ensure that votes are cast by secret ballot or by equivalent free voting procedure and that they are counted and reported honestly with the official results made public;

(7.5)   respect the rights of citizens to seek political or public office, individually or as representatives of political parties or organizations, without discrimination;

(7.6)   respect the right of individuals and groups to establish, in full freedom, their own political parties or other political organizations and provide such political parties and organizations with the necessary legal guarantees to enable them to compete with each other on a basis of equal treatment before the law and by the authorities;

(7.7)   ensure that law and public policy work to permit political campaigning to be conducted in a fair and free atmosphere in which neither administrative action, violence nor intimidation bars the parties and the candidates from freely presenting their views and qualifications, or prevents the voters from learning and discussing them or from casting their vote free of fear of retribution;

(7.8) provide that no legal or administrative obstacle stands in the way of unimpeded access to the media on a non-discriminatory basis for all political groupings and individuals wishing to participate in the electoral process;

(7.9) ensure that candidates who obtain the necessary number of votes required by law are duly installed in office and are permitted to remain in office until their term expires or is otherwise brought to an end in a manner that is regulated by law in conformity with democratic parliamentary and constitutional procedures.

Notes

1   On direct democracy in Switzerland, see Wolf Linder, *Swiss Democracy: Possible Solutions to Conflict in Multicultural Societies,* 2nd ed. (Basingstoke, UK: Macmillan, 1998), Chapter 3. More generally, see David Butler and Austin Ranney, *Referendums around the World: The Growing Use of Direct Democracy* (Washington, DC: American Enterprise Institute, 1994).

2   Adam Przeworski, *Democracy and the Market: Political and Economic Reforms in Eastern Europe and Latin America* (New York, NY: Cambridge University Press, 1991), 10.

3   Przeworski, *Democracy and the Market*, 10.

4   Joseph A. Schumpeter, *Capitalism, Socialism, and Democracy,* 3rd ed. (New York, NY: Harper and Brothers, 1950), 269.

5   Schumpeter, *Capitalism*, 271.

6   Schumpeter, *Capitalism*, 271–72.

7   There are some exceptions here. The Micronesian Congress (constituency members) and the United States House of Representatives are elected every two years, and national elections in Australia, Nauru, New Zealand, and Taiwan must be held at least every three years. On the other hand, some Latin American presidents are, or have been, elected for six-year terms.

8   Terry Lynn Karl, "Electoralism," *International Encyclopedia of Elections,* ed. Richard Rose (Washington, DC: CQ Press, 2000), 95. See also Philippe C. Schmitter and Terry Lynn Karl, "What Democracy Is … and Is Not," *Journal of Democracy* 2, no. 3 (1991): 75–88, see page 78; Terry Lynn Karl, "The Hybrid Regimes of Central America," *Journal of Democracy* 6, no. 3 (1995): 72–86.

9   Larry Diamond, *Developing Democracy: Toward Consolidation* (Baltimore, MD: Johns Hopkins University Press, 1999), 10–11.

10   David Collier and Steven Levitsky, "Democracy with Adjectives: Conceptual Innovation in Comparative Research," *World Politics* 49, no. 3 (April 1997): 430–51, see page 443.

11 J. Samuel Valenzuela, "Democratic Consolidation in Post-Transitional Settings: Notion, Process, and Facilitating Conditions," in *Issues in Democratic Consolidation: The New South American Democracies in Comparative Perspective,* ed. Scott Mainwaring, Guillermo O'Donnell, and J. Samuel Valenzuela, 57–104 (Notre Dame, IN: University of Notre Dame Press, 1992), 62–63.

12 Juan J. Linz and Alfred Stepan, "Toward Consolidated Democracies," *Journal of Democracy* 7, no. 2 (April 1996): 14–33, see pages 17–19.

13 Mária Palasik, *Chess Game for Democracy: Hungary between East and West, 1944–1947,* translated by Mario Fenyo (Montreal, QC and Kingston, ON: McGill-Queens University Press, 2011).

14 On the various practices of electoral manipulation and fraud, see Andreas Schedler, "Elections Without Democracy: The Menu of Manipulation," *Journal of Democracy* 13, no. 2 (April 2002): 36–50; and Sarah Birch, *Electoral Malpractice* (New York, NY: Oxford University Press, 2011).

15 Stanley G. Payne, *The Collapse of the Spanish Republic, 1933–1936: Origins of the Civil War* (New Haven, CT and London, UK: Yale University Press, 2006), 210.

16 Payne, *The Collapse,* 212.

17 Jørgen Elklit and Palle Svensson, "What Makes Elections Free and Fair?," *Journal of Democracy* 8, no. 3 (July 1997): 35–37.

18 Rafael López-Pintor, *Electoral Management Bodies as Institutions of Governance* (New York, NY: Bureau for Development Policy, United Nations Development Program, 2000).

19 André Blais, Louis Massicotte, and Antoine Yoshinaka, "Deciding Who Has the Right to Vote: A Comparative Analysis of Election Laws," *Electoral Studies* 20, no. 1 (2001): 41–62, see pages 43–51.

20 Angus Maddison, *The World Economy: A Millennial Perspective* (Paris, FR: OECD, 2001), 30.

21 Richard S. Katz, *Democracy and Elections* (New York, NY: Oxford University Press, 1997), 231.

22 Stein Rokkan, *Citizens, Elections, Parties: Approaches to the Comparative Study of the Processes of Development* (New York, NY: David McKay and Oslo: Universitetsforlaget, 1970), 148–49.

23 Robert A. Dahl, *Polyarchy: Participation and Opposition* (New Haven, CT: Yale University Press, 1971), 2–4.

24 Carl Schmitt, *Verfassungslehre* (1928; Berlin: Duncker and Humblot, 1970), 130, as translated by and quoted in Rune Slagstad, "Liberal Constitutionalism and its Critics: Carl Schmitt and Max Weber," in *Constitutionalism and Democracy,* ed. Jon Elster and Rune Slagstad, 103–30 (Cambridge, UK: Cambridge University Press and Oslo: Norwegian University Press, 1988), 106.

25 Linz and Stepan, "Toward Consolidated," 19.

26 To be more precise, Transparency International ranks countries in terms of *perceived* levels of corruption.

27 The Conference on Security and Co-operation in Europe changed its name to the Organization for Security and Co-operation in 1995, after the collapse of the Soviet Union required it to adopt a new role.

28 The most significant elected opposition in a semi-liberal autocracy is in Malaysia. In its 2008 elections, parties opposed to the government won 37 per cent of the seats and 5 of the 13 state assemblies.

29 Levitsky and Way call this last group "full authoritarian" regimes, which they note either (1) lack national-level multi-party elections or (2) are hegemonic in that they exclude major opposition parties or candidates from national elections, engage in large-scale vote fraud, or imprison or drive

underground or into exile much of the political opposition to the regime—thus reducing elections to a facade. Steven Levitsky and Lucan A. Way, *Competitive Authoritarianism: Hybrid Regimes After the Cold War* (New York, NY: Cambridge University Press, 2010), 6–7, 365.

30   Marina Ottaway, *Democracy Challenged: The Rise of Semi-Authoritarianism* (Washington, DC: Carnegie Endowment for International Peace, 2003), 15; italics in original.

31   Howard Handelman, *The Challenge of Third World Development*, 3rd ed. (Upper Saddle River, NJ: Prentice Hall, 2003), 28.

32   Evelyne Huber, Dietrich Rueschemeyer, and John D. Stephens, "The Paradoxes of Contemporary Democracy: Formal, Participatory, and Social Dimensions," *Comparative Politics* 29, no. 3 (April 1997): 323–42, see page 324.

CHAPTER FIVE

Factors Conducive to Democracy

IN THIS CHAPTER YOU WILL LEARN

► what factors facilitate democracy as opposed to autocracy;

► where quantifiable, the current differences between democracies and autocracies on these factors;

► which factors collectively matter most in terms of where countries rank on the four-category scale of liberal democracy, electoral democracy, semi-liberal autocracy, and closed autocracy; and

► which countries are thus the most "logical" extremes of this scale.

Overview

Our discussion of military intervention in Chapter 2 noted a key role for national political culture. Indeed, this point can be broadened to a general discussion of the factors that facilitate democracy. Consequently, in this chapter, we build on the classifications of Chapter 4 to assess why some countries are more democratic than others based on various independent variables, that is, historical, socio-economic, cultural, and demographic causal factors. (Note that we cannot assess why a country is in one category or another based on the political factors used to *define* the categories; to do so would be to commit a tautology.) Our first overall distinction is that between democracies, be they liberal or electoral, and autocracies, be they semi-liberal or closed. In other words, we are collapsing into two categories—democracy and autocracy—the four categories defined in Chapter 4. Our second overall distinction of interest is that between liberal democracies and electoral democracies.

Political Development and Democratization

In Chapter 2, we discussed historical sequences, in particular Dahl's argument about the advantages of establishing free and fair competition before universal male suffrage. This distinction does seem relevant for prewar developments. Table 5.1 lists the 72 sovereign states that existed at the start of 1938, that is, just before Nazi Germany's territorial expansion. These are grouped into two categories: democracies and autocracies. Of the countries that were democracies at that time, the vast majority developed according to Dahl's recommended route. The only major exception was France. Austria, Italy, and Uruguay stand out as the only places that established, or at least attempted to establish, free and fair competition before full male participation and yet still wound up as autocracies. Besides those three, various other countries in the second category did have periods of electoral democracy prior to 1938, but in none did free and fair competition precede universal male suffrage; instead, participation came before (Germany, Greece) or at the same time as (Argentina, Estonia, Japan, Latvia, Lithuania, Poland, Spain) competition. So, in summary, although having competition come before participation in the prewar era was neither completely necessary nor completely sufficient to maintain democracy, it certainly made it likely. Conversely, taking an alternate route—France excepted—was associated with subsequent democratic failure.

However, as Dix shows, in the postwar era the pattern is less clear.[1] Certainly, many places—mostly former British colonies—became sovereign electoral democracies at independence after having had political competition when they were colonies, without or before full participation. Dix lists India, Trinidad and Tobago, Jamaica, and Mauritius,[2] to which one could add other places in the Caribbean. However, other countries that followed this route, such as Burma/Myanmar, Lebanon, and the Philippines, could not maintain democracy. Democracy also broke down in Chile in 1973, even though it had taken the competition-preceding-participation route and had had decades of competition. Conversely, the establishment and maintenance of democracy was not fatally hindered by having participation come at the same time as competition in countries such as Israel (1948) and Papua New Guinea (1975). More critically, as Dix points out, by the 1970s, the most common pattern for new democracies was neither competition preceding participation nor the direct opposite, but what he calls an "interrupted" pattern. This pattern involved an *earlier* period of some level of competition, which preceded full participation, then a shift to autocracy that was followed by a new attempt at democratization.[3] Various countries in

TABLE 5.1 The World at the Start of 1938

DEMOCRACIES (liberal and electoral) N = 21

Australia	Czechoslovakia	Iceland	Netherlands	Sweden
Belgium*	Denmark	Ireland	New Zealand	Switzerland*
Canada	Finland	Liechtenstein*	Norway	United Kingdom
Chile*	France*	Luxembourg	South Africa**	United States**
Costa Rica*				

AUTOCRACIES N = 51

Afghanistan	Dominican Republic	Hungary	Mongolia	Romania
Albania	Ecuador	Iran	Nepal	San Marino
Argentina	Egypt	Iraq	Newfoundland	Saudi Arabia
Austria	El Salvador	Italy	Nicaragua	Soviet Union
Bhutan	Estonia	Japan	North Yemen	Spain
Bolivia	Germany	Latvia	Panama	Thailand
Brazil	Greece	Liberia	Paraguay	Turkey
Bulgaria	Guatemala	Lithuania	Peru	Uruguay
China	Haiti	Mexico	Poland	Venezuela
Colombia	Honduras	Monaco	Portugal	Yugoslavia
Cuba				

* suffrage restricted by gender
** suffrage restricted by race

Southern Europe, post-communist Central and Eastern Europe, and Latin America fit here. Moreover, many of these places also became democracies after the collapse or overthrow of the old autocratic regime rather than through the slow, evolutionary process that Dahl saw as most favourable.[4] Dahl did not deal with interrupted patterns, but they hardly seemed implied in his model. Thus, the competition-preceding-participation "advantage" does seem less crucial in the modern era, as does the slow-inauguration "advantage." Finally, competition preceding participation is also a route that is practically impossible today, inasmuch as many autocracies have granted universal suffrage despite or in many cases because of the lack of competition and the potential to rig elections. Indeed, of today's democracies, the last one to follow the competition-preceding-participation route was South Africa, where suffrage was restricted based on race. Of course, by the 1960s, South Africa was being condemned, not praised, for restricting the expansion of its suffrage.

In this context, we can also note the concept of getting "democratization backwards," by which is meant that Western countries had most civil liberties and the rule of law in place before full participation and often before any competition. In contrast, many countries today have competition and participation without having first established the rule of law—Romania, for example.[5] The rule of law may be one of the hardest parts of a liberal democracy to create, so perhaps the West was "lucky" to have developed it early on. Of course, we should not necessarily assume the Western sequence to have been anything like a conscious strategy. Moreover, it is not clear that the rule of law itself is easier to establish if suffrage is restricted rather than universal. Thus, the notion of getting "democratization backwards" may be more an issue of whether the "hardest part" of democracy was established early on or still remains to be done.

Contemporary Factors

Returning to the contemporary classifications outlined in Chapter 4, we can ask why some countries are more democratic than others. The reasons advanced can be divided into eight areas: (1) political culture and political leadership, (2) the military, (3) the level of development, (4) the nature of the economic system, (5) the cultural-historical legacy, (6) the extent of homogeneity or mitigating factors, (7) population size, and (8) regional factors. Tables 5.2 through 5.4 will provide data on various differences, first between democracies and autocracies and then between liberal democracies and electoral democracies.

Let us stress in advance that no single one of these factors is sufficient to ensure a democracy, nor does any one of these prove to be absolutely necessary, as exceptions exist for each factor. Consequently, the most crucial factors explaining why one specific country is a democracy or autocracy may differ from those that explain another country's regime.[6] Furthermore, to use words such as "preconditions," "prerequisites," or "requirements" for democracy is incorrect; indeed, the strongest term most social scientists would use is "requisites." However, this term still implies that various factors are necessary for maintaining democracy, just not that these factors are needed in advance of establishing the democratic regime. Because there do seem to be exceptions for each of the following factors, we use the more cautious term "conducive factors."

Political Culture and Political Leadership

We will begin with the self-evident fact that the more political leaders and the people believe in democracy, its institutions, and its values, the more likely a country is to be democratic.[7] In other words, a democratic political culture—that is, one stressing civility, tolerance for opposing views, moderation, pragmatism, and a willingness to compromise—is conducive to democracy, whereas a non-democratic or indifferent political culture makes democracy less likely, both in an immediate context and over the long term.[8] What appears to be particularly crucial is the political culture of a society's political leaders and activists, because they are more likely than the average person to have a clearly developed set of political beliefs, to be actually guided in their actions by their beliefs, and to have a greater influence on political events.[9] It is not a gross oversimplification to note that democracies are usually led by people who believe in democracy and who may well expound on their beliefs, whereas autocracies are led by people who do not believe in democracy and whose actions and words aim to keep their countries autocratic. Thus, what is crucial in individual cases is the nature of political leadership, particularly the post-independence or post-democratization leadership. Where this leadership has been respectful of democratic principles—even at the price of policy goals—and competent, democracy has been more likely to survive. India is a classic example, inasmuch as

> a major reason for India's democratic development was that elites reached out to mass society to raise political consciousness, develop democratic practices, and mobilize participation—both in electoral politics and in a wide range of voluntary organizations. Political leadership and [democratic] ideology were crucial in this process, particularly in the person of Mahatma Gandhi, who emphasized the values of liberty, nonviolent and consensual resolution of conflict, and continuous incorporation of excluded groups.[10]

Gandhi's successor, Jawaharlal Nehru, Costa Rica's José Figueres, and South Africa's Nelson Mandela are other classic examples of leaders who demonstrated effectively their democratic values at a crucial point in their country's development. Figueres, for example, held free and fair elections for a Constituent Assembly after winning the 1948 civil war, accepted the defeat both of his newly drafted constitution and of his candidates for the assembly, and handed power over to his opponents. Conversely, if a country has a monarch unwilling to give up power fully—such as those contemporary non-figurehead monarchs noted in Chapter 2—then its leadership would tend to favour a traditional autocracy.

The Military

As Chapter 2 notes, the military has been a political actor at some time or another in many nations, and it remains a potential threat to democracy in most of Africa and Latin America. So to "do something" about the military would definitely be conducive to preserving democracy. Basically, three successful options have been followed. (These are in no way mutually exclusive.) First, the armed forces of a country may be so small as to have what Dahl calls "virtual insignificance" in a political sense.[11] At the extreme, this insignificance means literally having no armed forces. Iceland, for example, has never had any armed forces of its own (even though it is a NATO member). Costa Rica abolished its army in 1948–49, and Panama did likewise in 1994. Of the world's larger countries, the key example of one without an official military is Japan; after World War II, the United States effectively imposed on it a constitution that forbade Japan from maintaining land, sea, or air forces. Japan has since created a small "self-defence force," but it is both militarily and politically insignificant, most certainly in comparison with the strength and influence of the military in prewar Japan. More generally, even if one's armed forces are large enough to deter what few enemies one has, they can still be small or "insignificant" enough as a share of the population that they could not effectively take over, occupy, and administer the country in the face of civilian opposition or even lack of cooperation. Canada's small armed forces (now numbering 66,000 in a country of 34 million) are an obvious example here. In fact, the peacetime armed forces of both the United Kingdom and the United States prior to World War II were never significant in a numerical sense. Moreover, to the end of the nineteenth century, the armed forces of the United States were essentially local militias, lacking any central control. Central control is needed for a military regime. Citizen militias also played a decentralizing role in the modern histories of other countries, such as Canada, the United Kingdom, and Switzerland.[12]

However, many countries have or have had significant armed forces for security reasons, especially since the rise of large standing armies in eighteenth-century Europe. Consequently, if the first option of an insignificant army is not chosen, and would be foolish to choose given hostile enemies, then the maintenance of democracy requires ensuring that the armed forces are not individually and psychologically apart from and feeling superior to the rest of society. One way to achieve this condition—and the second option overall—is to have an armed force composed of the "population as a whole." This scenario involves calling all or random citizens into the armed forces, normally through either universal or male conscription. These citizens serve a term in the military and may (as in Switzerland) go back annually for manoeuvres, but, throughout their lives, they are definitely citizens and not professional soldiers. The proto-democracy of ancient Athens was certainly facilitated by having such a citizen militia from the seventh century B.C. onwards. In contrast, nineteenth-century continental Europe tended to create professional armies with less democratic consequences—a pattern that remains to this day in much of Latin America. Finally, if the armed forces are in fact an organization of lifetime professionals "cut off" socially from the rest of society, then democracy requires providing them with a democratic indoctrination. This indoctrination can be accomplished as part of military training that inculcates loyalty to the constitution and civilian authorities—something that, in their own way, communist countries were and are highly successful in doing. Conversely, as we saw in Chapter 2, if the constitution establishes the armed forces as the ultimate political "umpire" (as has been the case in Latin America), then such indoctrination is next to impossible; instead, an opposite antidemocratic indoctrination is likely to occur. And, as we saw, even if military intervention is not a constitutional "duty," when a professional military is a separate social order that feels superior to civilian authorities (in part due to their very professionalism), then the armed forces may resist civilian control and claim a "right" to intervene, as in Pakistan, Thailand, and much of Africa.[13] Therefore, an antecedent factor in facilitating democracy is a democratic political culture, especially attitudes in favour of civilian rule and democracy, held by political elites and activists. Such beliefs may have little to do with the level of a country's socio-economic development (and thus are a separate factor), although they may arise from historical patterns.[14]

Empirically, we can measure the "military participation ratio" of a country, that is, the size of armed forces per 1,000 population. The most recent global figures that can be calculated are for 2011 (using data on the size of armed forces from *The Military Balance*).[15] As in shown in Table 5.2, the mean military participation ratio for all democracies is 2.813, whereas, for all autocracies, it is 5.505—essentially double. A *t*-test here, with equal variances not assumed, yields a value of –3.084; this measure is significant at the .003 level. Thus, autocracies are found to be significantly more militarized than democracies. However, in terms of levels of militarization, no significant distinction exists between liberal democracies and electoral democracies.

The Level of Development

Looking at Table 4.3 in Chapter 4, we see that perhaps the most obvious distinction between democracies and autocracies is that democracies tend to be wealthier. For decades, a link between wealth and democracy has been made by social scientists,

TABLE 5.2 Differences in Explanatory Factors between Categories (as of October 2012)

1. ALL DEMOCRACIES VERSUS ALL AUTOCRACIES

	Total N	Mean for all autocracies	Mean for all democracies	t-test	Significance level (2-tailed)
Military participation ratio per 1,000 population, 2011	195	5.505	2.813	−3.084	0.003
GNI per capita, 2011 (US$ at PPPs)	185	9178	15149	2.583	0.011
HDI value, 2011	185	0.579	0.721	5.964	0.000
Life expectancy, 2011 (years)	195	65.451	72.713	5.450	0.000
Mean years of schooling (population 25 and above), 2011	195	6.254	8.624	5.837	0.000
Median age of population, 2010	195	24.529	30.501	5.400	0.000
Urbanization, 2011 (percentage)	195	49.717	60.787	3.316	0.001
Internet users per 100 population, 2011	195	30.452	39.154	2.064	0.041
Cell phones per 100 population, 2011	195	78.009	97.620	3.083	0.002
Ethnic fractionalization (Fearon data)	156	0.545	0.417	−3.154	0.002
Linguistic diversity (*Ethnologue*)	190	0.541	0.394	−3.382	0.001
Total population, 2011 (logged)	195	0.901	0.616	−2.185	0.030
Equivalent in millions		7.962	4.130		

2. LIBERAL DEMOCRACIES VERSUS ELECTORAL DEMOCRACIES

	Total N	Mean for all electoral democracies	Mean for all liberal democracies	t-test	Significance level (2-tailed)
Military participation ratio per 1,000 population, 2011	113	2.889	2.729	−0.265	0.792
GNI per capita, 2011 (US$ at PPPs)	108	8286	23413	6.532	0.000
HDI value, 2011	108	0.632	0.827	8.863	0.000
Life expectancy, 2011 (years)	113	67.992	77.872	8.134	0.000
Mean years of schooling (population 25 and above), 2011	113	7.200	10.180	7.450	0.000
Median age of population, 2010	113	25.988	35.431	7.188	0.000
Urbanization, 2011 (percentage)	113	51.858	70.543	5.073	0.000
Internet users per 100 population, 2011	113	34.390	44.359	1.908	0.059
Cell phones per 100 population, 2011	113	94.261	101.291	0.975	0.332
Ethnic fractionalization (Fearon data)	84	0.510	0.280	−4.784	0.000
Linguistic diversity (*Ethnologue*)	112	0.499	0.277	−4.190	0.000
Total population, 2011 (logged)	113	0.892	0.314	−2.946	0.004
Equivalent in millions		7.796	2.063		

SOURCES: International Institute for Strategic Studies, *The Military Balance 2011* (Washington, DC: International Institute for Strategic Studies, 2011); United Nations, *Human Development Report 2011* (New York: Oxford University Press, 2012); United Nations, Department of Economic and Social Affairs, Population Division, *World Population Prospects: The 2010 Revision* (New York: United Nations, May 2011), accessed October 2012, http://esa.un.org/unpd/wpp/index.htm; International Telecommunication Union, "Core indicators on access to and use of ICT by households and individuals, 2000–2011" *ICT Data and Statistics*, http://www.itu.int/ITU-D/ict/statistics/.

especially Seymour Martin Lipset.[16] Moreover, the causal link is clearly from wealth to democracy, not the other way around.[17] Autocracies can often deliver economic growth just as well as democracies can, and sometimes better (think of China in recent decades). However, the significance of wealth to democracy really involves not just wealth per se but broader, related aspects of development: industrialization, urbanization, and related economic diversity; literacy and advanced education; and low infant mortality and the subsequently long life expectancy. These various factors produce a society that is not just developed but also *dynamic* (in the sense of having economic growth and social mobility) and *pluralist* (in the sense of having many groups and independent organizations, especially in the economy).[18] However, such dynamism and pluralism will not flow from development if a wealthy country has its wealth concentrated in a few hands; the oil-rich nations of the Middle East that belong to the Organization of Petroleum Exporting Countries (OPEC) are the clearest examples of this qualification. Nor does such pluralism exist under a communist economic system in which individuals and most groups lack independent economic resources.

These various factors of development lead to a broad distribution (as opposed to a concentration) of what Tatu Vanhanen calls "**power resources**." These are the economic, intellectual, and organizational resources that an individual or group can bring to bear in the struggle for political power.[19] In social terms, broadly distributed power resources means a society with a large middle class rather than with a sharp divide between a small elite and the impoverished masses—in Barrington Moore's classic phrase, "no bourgeois, no democracy."[20] Developed societies with deconcentrated power resources are conducive to democracy for two reasons. First, this diversity of power resources means that more people and groups can demand a say in the system, resist domination by others, and engage in competition and bargaining with other groups—all while having the resources to do such things effectively.[21] Likewise, it is that much harder for an individual or a small group to suppress its competitors and establish an autocracy. As Vanhanen summarizes, "The concentration of power resources leads to autocratic political structures, whereas the wide distribution of the same resources makes the sharing of power and democracy possible."[22] Second, in developed societies, the greater equality of conditions and socioeconomic opportunities fosters the existence of ideologies of equality (rather than of hierarchy and deference) and positive-sum rather than zero-sum behaviour. In turn, these beliefs and behaviours make it more likely that most people will be willing to share power with others and able to see the point of cooperation—to have, in other words, a predisposition toward the previously mentioned notions of a democratic political culture.[23] Generally, as noted in Chapter 2, those with the most power (the traditional elites) have to feel that they will not lose everything in a more open system; such a feeling is more likely if most of the rest of society consists of people with something to lose and with moderate attitudes rather than with nothing to lose and radical or revolutionary attitudes.

Although this diversity of power resources is most likely to occur in urban industrial societies, it is still possible in more rural ones. The central economic issue here is the pattern of land ownership. When a society is still predominantly rural and most land is owned by relatively few large landowners, then the power resources are too concentrated to favour democracy; autocratic rule is more likely to exist. If the pattern of land ownership is such that most land is held by independent family farmers rather than by large landowners, then a large middle class and, consequently, the diversification of economic resources can arise. Democratic development was facilitated by this typical "family farmer" pattern of land ownership in the British settler societies of Australia, Canada, New Zealand, and the United States, as well as in some of the smaller Western European countries (those of Scandinavia and Switzerland, to be specific).[24] In contrast, land ownership was highly concentrated in most of nineteenth-century Europe, with consequent antidemocratic effects; consider, for example, the role of the Junkers in Prussia and Imperial Germany. A similar concentration of land ownership has been the norm in most of the developing world, with rare exceptions (Costa Rica is one). It is worth stressing that, besides demilitarizing postwar Japan, the United States also effected a major land reform there.

As mentioned, Table 5.2 summarizes the statistical differences between, first, democracies and autocracies and, second, liberal democracies and electoral democracies. These two sets of groupings are compared in terms of eight different measures of socio-economic development. First is GNI (gross national income) per capita in 2011 at purchasing power parities. The calculations show significant differences between the values for all democracies and all autocracies and highly significant differences between those for liberal democracies and electoral democracies. In short, wealth is related to democracy, but especially to liberal democracy. (Electoral democracies are actually a bit poorer, on average, than autocracies.) However, a broader and thus presumably better measure of development is the United Nations Human Development Index (HDI), which, as noted in Chapter 3, adds to GNI measures of life expectancy and years of education (both the current level for the population 25 and above and the expected level for a child now starting school).[25] Table 5.2 shows that, for the 185 countries with scores, the difference between the average HDI values for all democracies and for all autocracies is highly significant, as is the difference between these values for liberal democracies and for electoral democracies. We can also assess the political effects of some of the other component measures of HDI here, specifically life expectancy and mean years of schooling for the population 25 and above.[26] Years of schooling data are missing for a few countries. However, as estimates, we can use the values for specific neighbouring countries.[27] For measures of both life expectancy and mean years of schooling, the differences are highly significant, across all comparisons. These findings confirm the overall relationship between human development and regime type—and for all 195 countries, not just for the 185 countries for which HDI scores are available. Years of schooling is also a superior measure to literacy, although the latter is also used in studies of democratization.[28] Literacy can be considered a problematic measure for two reasons. First, we are talking about basic reading and writing ability, not the complex expression of ideas. Second, and more crucially, because literacy is defined as a basic concept in many societies, essentially everyone is deemed to be literate; that is, in many countries a value of 99 per cent is given—though one doubts that all are equally literate.

Last, we can assess a couple of the demographic variables mentioned in Chapter 3. Note that the difference in the median age of the population for all democracies and all autocracies is highly significant, as is the difference between the means for liberal democracies versus electoral democracies. Next, look at the measure of urbanization, that is, the percentage of the population living in urban areas. There is a highly significant difference between the urbanization values for all democracies and all autocracies and between those for liberal democracies and electoral democracies.

The last two socio-economic variables measure communications access. The first measures the level of Internet access (per 100 people as of 2011). (A broader assessment of Internet access was reported in Chapter 3; see Table 3.6.) This variable is interesting because, in theory, it speaks to the effects of national education (educated people are more likely to use the Internet) and national wealth and income distribution (more affluent individuals are more likely to have a computer or at least to have access to one). However, as Table 5.2 shows, the statistical relationship between the number of Internet users per 100 people in all democracies and that number in all autocracies is not as significant as for other variables, and the difference between the values for liberal democracies and for electoral democracies is not statistically

significant. The other variable here is the number of cell phones, which is an important measure because cell phones facilitate communication, especially outside of government control. The difference between values for democracies and for autocracies
is certainly significant, but it is not at all significant when liberal democracies and
electoral democracies are compared.

Finally, one should note that the eight variables in Table 5.2 in varying ways tap
into the same matter: the level of socio-economic development. It is not surprising
that almost all of these variables are statistically intercorrelated (the one bivariate
exception is GNI per capita and cell phone usage). Of these, the two variables that
seem most central in both comparisons are the overall HDI score and the mean
years of schooling (which, again, is half of one of the three components of the HDI).
However, as HDI values are missing for ten countries, it is better to use the mean
years of schooling as the central socio-economic variable explaining regime type.
Doing so also makes theoretical sense, in that ever more schooling (rather than just
basic literacy) should tend to make people more knowledgeable, efficacious, and
politically engaged rather than apathetic. Education improves both understanding
and communication and thus people's ability to interact with each other in a cooperative, peaceful, and informed way—behaviour that is central to a functioning democracy. In many countries, education also indoctrinates students to be civic-minded and
to participate in politics.[29]

In terms of measuring socio-economic equality, most data on family farms is not
up to date enough to make a credible cross-national analysis across regime types.
However, an alternative measure of equality—and one more crucial for urbanized
societies—is the GINI index, which measures income distribution in a country. This
ranges from 0 to 1, where 0 indicates a completely equal distribution of income
across households and 1 indicates a single household having the entire national
wealth and everyone else having absolutely nothing. However, although earlier
cross-national analyses have shown a link between (relative) economic equality and
democracy, there does not seem to be a global pattern any longer. The mean GINI
index for democracies is 41.621, which is, in fact, slightly worse (more unequal) than
that for autocracies (40.157). (These values are based on the most recent year of data
available in 2012.) Of course, these data are available for only 128 countries, just
two-thirds of all countries. Two different conclusions are possible here. The first is
that there is no direct relationship between equality and democracy.[30] The second
is that the relationship is a more long-term one between equality and democratic

survival.[31] In this sense, many contemporary democracies could well be risking breakdown if they remain highly inegalitarian. It should also be noted that liberal democracies are clearly more statistically egalitarian than electoral democracies.

The link between development and democracy may be strong, but it is neither completely perfect nor fully deterministic. India is the classic example of a long-standing electoral democracy that is underdeveloped in various socio-economic ways. Newer examples of such "outliers" are the Ivory Coast, Papua New Guinea, and Timor-Leste. In contrast, both Kuwait and Singapore have a high level of socio-economic development, and Malaysia has a moderately high one, but all are still semi-liberal autocracies. More generally, if we contrast the list of the least developed nations (Table 3.8) with the list of countries according to regime type (Table 4.3), we see that not only India but also Bangladesh, Benin, Comoros, Ghana, Lesotho, Liberia, Niger, Nigeria, Senegal, and Sierra Leone currently combine a very low level of development with being an electoral democracy. Conversely, although most of the nations categorized as core economies are democracies, Bahrain, Brunei, Kuwait, Monaco, Qatar, Singapore, and the United Arab Emirates are not (compare Table 3.4 and Table 4.3).

The Nature of the Economic System

Classical liberalism was as much about securing property rights, free markets, and free trade as it was about securing political freedoms and responsible government—and it was certainly more interested in promoting these goals than in advocating universal suffrage. To the extent that democracy involves freedom, and freedom has both political and economic dimensions, then we would expect democracies to have market economies. However, autocracies can have market economies as well; a market economy allows an autocratic elite to enrich itself.[32] Such an economic system presumably would be more likely to lead ultimately to democracy than a statist economic system in which economic resources are controlled by the state.

To test this hypothesis, we can measure the role of the state in contemporary economies in terms of the public sector share of GDP, state-owned enterprises as a share of total industry (industrial production or investment), combined government and state-owned industry employment as a share of total employment, and the extent of government regulation of the economy. Data on such variables are not always available for every country, and sometimes there are differences in assessment, but,

generally, most analyses agree in terms of basic national classifications and comparative patterns.[33] Consequently, we shall use here not a single continuous variable but
rather two different dummy variables reflecting three categories. The first dummy
variable, that of a capitalist market economy, is for economies with a predominance
of private ownership and low-to-moderate government regulation of the economy.
No exclusion is made for having a large welfare state. There are currently 52 countries that are deemed to have capitalist market economies. The contrasting dummy
variable is for a statist economy, that is, an economy with significant levels of government ownership, regulation, or overall control of the economy. Of the contemporary
world economies, only 27 are clearly statist. All of the remaining economies—the
majority—fall in between these extremes, having a mixed capitalist-statist economy
or being in transition away from a statist economy, as is true in most post-communist
countries. They form a residual category.

The patterns are quite striking. Of the 52 capitalist market economies, 46 are
democracies and 42, almost all, are liberal democracies. Only 6 are autocracies, and
only 3 of these are closed autocracies. Of the 27 statist economies, 23 are autocracies, and only 4 are democracies (all are electoral democracies). In each case, a statistical test (chi-square) confirms the significance of the dummy variable. In contrast,
the residual economies divide more or less evenly: 63 are democracies and 53 are
autocracies.

The Cultural-Historical Legacy

It has been argued that British colonialism was more favourable for later democratic
development than being a colony of other imperial powers. For example, seeking
to explain the strength and durability of liberal democracy in the Commonwealth
Caribbean, Sutton argues that "[t]he Westminster model, which was bequeathed
to all Caribbean countries on independence, has taken root in the Caribbean and
enjoyed widespread support. Its persistence is the single most important explanation for the comparative success of democracy in the region."[34] By the "Westminster
model," Sutton does not mean the executive-dominated parliamentary systems to
be outlined in Chapter 8 (although these are also the "norm" in the Caribbean) but
the democratic principles of constitutionalism, limited government, civilian supremacy, competitive elections (which began before independence), and civil liberties.[35]
British colonialism generally left behind such features and much greater political

institutionalization than was the case for the former colonies of other European powers. France comes second in this regard, followed by the Netherlands; at the other extreme, Belgium and Portugal were "the worst" in terms of their imperial legacies. We shall assess this point by looking at the entire list of colonies and protectorates that became independent after 1945, that is, all countries outside of continental Europe that gained their independence from 1945 onwards. Information about these countries and when they became independent can be found in Table 1.1.[36] The total here is 103 countries. We have divided these into former British colonies or protectorates and all other places. Table 5.3 first compares the current regime of all former British colonies and protectorates that became independent since 1945 with that of all the former dependencies of other imperial powers that became independent since that date. In fact, the relationship here between having been a British dependency and becoming democratic is weak: only half of the former British colonies and protectorates are now democratic, a ratio not much more than that for the other places that have become independent since 1945. This difference is not at all statistically significant. Sutton's specific point about the Westminster model "taking root" is thus crucial: British colonialism planted more democratic roots (including pre-independence legislatures and other institutions) first in the white settler countries of Australia, Canada, New Zealand, and the United States, and then later on in the Caribbean and Pacific, than it did in most of Africa and Asia. These earlier settled areas inherited the true British colonial legacy. Dag Anckar has emphasized this point; he makes a distinction between "long-time" and "short-time" British colonies—"long-time" means having been under British control for 100 years or more at the time of independence.[37] Consequently, the second part of Table 5.3 groups the countries into three categories: former longstanding British colonies and protectorates, other former British colonies and protectorates, and all other former colonies and protectorates. It shows that the relationship between having been a longstanding British colony or protectorate and being a democracy is highly significant statistically, in contrast to the insignificant results gained in the first modelling of the data.

Another aspect of culture that is argued to affect whether countries become democracies or autocracies is their religious heritage. The key factor appears to be the extent to which a religion is hierarchical and dogmatic, traits that do not lend themselves to questioning authority or demanding participation. Certainly, future Canadian prime minister Pierre Trudeau thought in the 1950s that the hierarchical

TABLE 5.3 Colonial Legacy and Democracy versus Autocracy for Former Colonies and Protectorates Gaining Independence since 1945 (as of October 2012)

MODEL ONE

Colonial Legacy	Total Democracies	Total Autocracies	Total Ex-Colonies
British	25	25	50
Other	22	31	53
TOTALS	47	56	103

Pearson chi-square is 0.748 (significance level of 0.387).

MODEL TWO

Colonial Legacy	Total Democracies	Total Autocracies	Total Ex-Colonies
Longstanding British	19	4	23
Other British	6	21	27
Other	22	31	53
TOTALS	47	56	103

Pearson chi-square is 19.003 (significance level of 0.000).

nature of Catholicism was part of the reason Quebec, up until that time, was less democratic than other parts of Canada. As he wrote then,

> French Canadians are Catholics; and Catholics have not always been ardent supporters of democracy. They are authoritarian in spiritual matters; and since the dividing line between the spiritual and the temporal may be very fine or even confused, they are often disinclined to seek truth in temporal affairs through the mere counting of heads. If this be true in general, it is particularly so in the case of the clergy and laity of Quebec, influenced as they were by the Catholicism of nineteenth-century France, which largely rejected democracy as the daughter of the [French] Revolution.[38]

In contrast, Protestantism, some argue, is a much more individualistic religion, and thus Protestant countries are more likely to be democratic. As is the case with theories about the historical sequences of democratization, this point was certainly once empirically valid. Looking again at the democracies and autocracies listed in Table 5.1, we see that, of the various democracies at the start of 1938, almost two-thirds were either Protestant or mixed Protestant-Catholic (usually with the Protestants politically dominant). There were seven Catholic democracies then— Belgium, Chile, Costa Rica, France, Ireland, Liechtenstein, and Luxembourg— although most of these had not yet granted women the vote (nor, for its part, had Switzerland), and, in Chile, the suffrage was quite restricted. In any case, there were many more than seven Catholic autocracies of the time. In contrast, only three of the 1938 autocracies were dominated by Protestants—Estonia, Germany, and Latvia. It is still the case today that almost all countries in which Protestantism dominates are democracies (except for Malawi, Swaziland, and Tonga), and most are liberal democracies. However, the list of liberal and electoral democracies today contains many Catholic, Orthodox, and non-Christian countries. Certainly, it no longer seems the case that Catholicism tends to work against democracy, in large part due to changes in the Catholic Church in the 1960s that made it much more sympathetic to the poor and oppressed. Religious distinctions now centre more on Islam, because the vast majority of today's 48 majority-Islamic states are either semi-liberal or closed autocracies. Some, however, are electoral democracies: Bangladesh, Comoros, Indonesia, Iraq, Kyrgyzstan, Niger, Pakistan, Senegal, Sierra Leone, Tunisia, and Turkey.

Some scholars focus on developmental aspects rather than on religion as an explanation for the number of Islamic-dominated autocracies, noting that Muslim societies are generally either underdeveloped or have highly concentrated oil-based wealth—neither of which are socio-economic situations favouring democracy.[39] Yet socio-economic factors only explain part of the story in terms of the correlation between Muslim societies and autocracy.[40] Moreover, the relationship is much clearer for Arab countries than for all Muslim ones.[41] Why? Eric Chaney has contributed an important observation: Muslim democracies tend to be at the geographic edges of the Muslim world, and they adopted Islam by choice. In contrast, the countries at the geographic core of the Muslim world were conquered by the early caliphs and had Islam imposed on them. More crucial was the imposition of political institutions, especially of Islamic laws that compelled power sharing between the military and religious leaders, both committed to maintaining the political status quo to the exclusion of all other potential centres of political power, such as a merchant class. The state was thus highly centralized, with slave armies, and civil society was weak. Where these patterns lasted, autocracy became well entrenched. Specifically, Chaney defines the area of "Arab conquest" as those countries that had at least half of their current landmass conquered by Arab armies by 1100 A.D. and were thus ruled for centuries by Muslim dynasties. His other criterion is that these dynasties had to still rule in both 1500 A.D. and 1900 A.D. (Spain, therefore, is excluded because its Muslim political institutions vanished centuries ago.) Chaney's "persistent boundaries of the Islamic world" from 1100 A.D. today comprises 29 countries wherein democracy was quite rare as of 2010.[42]

Ethnic Homogeneity and Political Polarization

All other things being equal, it is reasonable to assume that the agreements and compromises needed to make democracy work and survive are easier if the society is not sharply divided, with each side feeling that the other threatens its goals and underlying values. Although such polarization can be conceived of in class terms, it is important to remember that many economic issues can be dealt with by "splitting the difference," that is, by setting program spending, tax levels, or specific tariffs at the halfway level between what two opposing groups want. Compromise can be achieved if there is a collective will. In contrast, one cannot split the difference in terms of the number of official languages or religions in a country. Consequently, when a society is very heterogeneous in ethnocultural terms, we expect democracy to be less likely to survive. To investigate this hypothesis, we first must make a basic distinction between homogeneous and heterogeneous societies, with the former being defined as one in which the dominant ethnolinguistic group is at least 70 per cent of the total population and all other groups are each below 10 per cent of the total population. Defined as such, homogeneous countries number 77 currently and heterogeneous ones 118. The 77 homogenous countries are largely democratic (56 versus 21 autocracies), whereas the heterogeneous countries are evenly split (58 democracies, 60 autocracies). If one prefers a continuous rather than a dichotomous measure, Fearon has provided values on ethnic fragmentation for 156 countries.[43] These fractionalization scores range from 0.000 (perfect ethnic homogeneity) to 1.000 (complete ethnic fragmentation) for each country. As Table 5.2 shows, the mean ethnic fragmentation scores for all democracies is 0.417, whereas, for all autocracies, it is 0.545, a statistically significant difference. The difference is even greater statistically between the scores for liberal democracies and electoral democracies, with the liberal democracies, on average, having low ethnic fragmentation. More complete country coverage is available using the linguistic diversity measure from the *Ethnologue* encyclopaedia, which includes 190 of our countries.[44] As shown in Table 5.2, the patterns are confirmed with the almost-complete country set: democracies are less diverse linguistically than autocracies, and liberal democracies are clearly less diverse than electoral ones. Phrasing these patterns the reverse way, one sees that autocracies are more heterogeneous than democracies, and electoral democracies are even more heterogeneous when compared to liberal democracies. Of course, the relationship is far from perfect. There are certainly many "homogeneous autocracies"; for example, one cannot get much more homogeneous than North Korea. Conversely, one can find various cases of heterogeneous democracies, such as Canada.

It is important to note here that there are ways to mitigate ethnocultural pluralism, if the political elites (including the constitution drafters) are willing to do so. The most comprehensive way has been argued to be a system of **consociational democracy** (or consociationalism). This political system is based on power sharing as opposed to majoritarianism, and it involves four aspects: (1) rule by a grand (broad) coalition; (2) mutual and thus minority vetoes on all sensitive issues; (3) proportionality not just in the cabinet but also in the civil service and official agencies and boards; and (4) local autonomy, including ultimately federalism where the various groups are geographically concentrated.[45] The classic cases of consociationalism are the small but divided European countries of Austria, Belgium, the Netherlands, and Switzerland, all of which reached their "high point" of consociational development in the late 1950s.[46] Key aspects of consociationalism still exist today in Belgium and Switzerland, but Austria and the Netherlands have become much more homogeneous as previous "cleavages" or divisions have lessened or even vanished. Arend Lijphart argues that there are many elements of consociationalism in India, which helps to explain the survival of democracy in that diverse, continental country.[47] Even if complete consociational democracy is not implemented, the use of some of its more flexible aspects—such as federalism, or at least some form of regional government where the minorities form a local majority—can accommodate ethnocultural divisions.

Conversely, the political elites may not be willing to accommodate ethnolinguistic differences. They may even exacerbate them in a country. And even an ethnically homogeneous society can be sharply divided over public policies—even if it finds splitting the differences easier. At the extreme are polarized societies in which political conflicts become violent, up to and including civil war. The likelihood of this sort of conflict is assessed for most of the developing countries based on their "conflict intensity" scores in the Bertelsmann Transformation Index since 2006.[48] Using this index measure, we can create a dummy variable for countries that are polarized societies with violent political conflict. There are 46 such countries, and, indeed, democracy is rare in these countries—existing in only 15, none of which is a liberal democracy. One should note that there is a strong but not perfect overlap between having a polarized society with violent political conflict and being a heterogeneous society, in that 42 of these countries are heterogeneous. Yet most heterogeneous countries (the other 76) lack such violent polarization, so polarization leading to conflict does not follow heterogeneity automatically. There are also 4 countries that are polarized societies with violent political conflict but that are fairly ethnically homogeneous (homogeneity, again, is defined as the dominant ethnolinguistic group having at least 70 per cent of the total population and all other groups each having less than 10 per cent of the total population). These countries are Bangladesh, Georgia, Haiti, and Uzbekistan. For example, Bangladesh is relatively homogeneous, but the two central political parties there are extremely polarized and antagonistic, and the political culture is intolerant and conflictual, leading to frequent political violence.[49]

Population Size and Island Status

One factor relating to democracy that social scientists did not emphasize much early in the postwar era but that they have stressed in recent decades is population size. Many countries that became independent in the 1970s and 1980s are small, and democracy has survived in most of these. Smallness is normally defined by population size, as opposed to area. Still, scholars differ somewhat on what is meant by a small population. The most common procedure is to use a population cut-off of 1 million, as Anckar does.[50] However, Ott uses a cut-off of 1.5 million.[51] For his part, Diamond uses both 1 million and 0.5 million, but finds "most striking" the frequency of democracy and, indeed, liberal democracy in the "microstates" of less than half a million people.[52] Diamond appears correct to use multiple cut-offs, as the likelihood of democracy is even greater with a very small cut-off, a point Ott also notes.[53] Empirically, using the current distribution of regimes and 2011 populations (from Table 3.2), there appear to be break-points—in decreasing order—at 5 million, 1.5 million, and 0.5 million. Specifically, the 79 countries with fewer than 5 million people divide into 52 democracies and 27 autocracies (almost a 2:1 ratio); the 46 countries with fewer than 1.5 million people divide into 34 democracies and 12 autocracies (a 2.8:1 ratio), and, most sharply, the 28 tiny countries with fewer than 0.5 million people divide into 23 democracies and 5 autocracies (a 4.6:1 ratio). Conversely, there also appears to be an autocracy break-point at 15 million people: the 66 countries with a population of 15 million or more divide exactly evenly into 33 democracies and 33 autocracies. Yet this last point is deceptive because, counting down from the most populous countries, after China there are several democracies— that said, these are all federal (see Chapter 6).

Still, one can assess actual population as well as a given break-point of small-ness. However, because national population levels are so skewed, in Table 5.2, we log the population values (in millions) for 2011. The average logged population for all democracies is 0.616, whereas the average logged population for all autocracies is 0.901. As noted in the table, the equivalent "real" numbers are averages of 4.130 million people for all democracies and 7.962 million people for all autocracies; thus, autocracies have, on average, almost double the population of democracies. The *t*-test of the logged population, with equal variances not assumed, shows that this difference in size between democracies and autocracies is statistically significant. This statistical relationship between the average logged population size of all liberal democracies and all electoral democracies is much more significant, though: liberal democracies have an average logged population of 0.314 (that is, 2.063 million people), whereas electoral democracies have an average logged population of 0.892 (that is, 7.796 million people). In summary, democracies, but, more specifically, liberal democracies, tend to have small if not indeed tiny populations.

The relationship of size to democracy has been demonstrated to exist regardless of income (except, presumably, at the very highest income levels, where all countries are democracies). In other words, if there are two countries at the same level of income or development but with a clear difference in size, then the smaller one is more likely to be democratic and to maintain democracy.[54] Moreover, Ott's analysis stresses that, separately, "island countries were found to be far more likely to be democratic than non-island countries."[55] Because many island countries are also small, this finding might indicate a reinforcing relationship; that is, democracy may be particularly likely in small island states.

A state having a small population or being a small island is seen to favour democratization for four reasons, some of which are antecedent factors of previous points. First, there is the assumption that small island states and small countries are more likely to be homogeneous than other countries. This assumption is basically true: the 77 homogeneous countries are smaller, on average, than the 118 heterogeneous ones (with mean logged populations of 0.578 and 0.839 respectively). However, this difference is not statistically significant. Of course, this pattern of distinctive homogeneity may exist only for small *island* states. Yet there are also some small heterogeneous island states, such as Fiji, Mauritius, and Trinidad and Tobago,[56] and, certainly, ethnic heterogeneity in Fiji is at the centre of its inability to maintain democracy. Second, in small states people have a greater chance of reaching and influencing decision makers, so they develop feelings of political efficacy and participation in politics more. (Although this is not the central explanatory factor for voter turn-out, turnout in elections is indeed higher in smaller countries than in larger ones.) Political leaders, in turn, are more attentive to individual citizens in small states.[57] For this reason, Diamond stresses political decentralization in large states as a desirable policy in and of itself, although Ott is more sceptical here.[58] Third, elites in small states are more likely to be cooperative than confrontational.[59] This behaviour occurs, in part, because the smaller number of elites makes it likely that all know each other and, in part, because the country does not want to appear vulnerable to outsiders. Indeed, small size is one of the factors seen to facilitate consociational-ism.[60] Fourth, and finally, small island states have no direct neighbours and thus no hostile neighbours; therefore, they can spend less on defence and undertake more easily one of the options for taming military coercion. With the exception of Fiji, no small island state has experienced a military coup. Beyond this, even if a small country is not an island, it may see little point in military spending because it cannot defend itself against a hostile enemy without help (or, to put this point more charita-bly, it will be unlikely to have an aggressive military posture vis-à-vis its neighbours). The assumption here is that there will be less militarization in small states regardless of whether they are islands.[61] In fact, a correlation between population size (logged) and military participation ratios for 2011 yields a statistically insignificant value of 0.139, so there is no statistically significant relationship between population size and the lack of militarization. To repeat, then: in today's world, small size alone does not relate directly to either ethnic homogeneity or having a proportionally small military, so these other factors remain as separate explanations for the level of democracy.

Indeed, Diamond argues that the greater frequency of both electoral and liberal democracy in former Anglo-American colonies is a spurious result of the fact that these are more likely to be smaller than the former colonies of other powers. As noted earlier, he argues that small countries and especially microstates are likely to be democracies—whether they are former Anglo-American colonies or not (that is, the ratios are basically the same).[62] These points are confirmed in this analysis. The 23 longstanding British colonies noted earlier are heavily skewed to tiny countries—in terms of population, the median country is Guyana, with 756,000 people. The feature of being a longstanding British colony is not a statistically significant predictor of regime type once this factor is controlled for a population threshold—be this 0.5, 1.0, or 1.5 million. It is, of course, doubtful that the British made a special effort to colonize tiny places, but it does make sense that their tiny colonies would wait longer for independence. Indeed, the remaining dozen or so British Overseas Territories today all have populations of less than 100,000 (the largest is Bermuda at 69,000).

Regional Factors

A final observation from Table 4.3 is that the countries that are autocracies tend to be surrounded largely, if not wholly, by other autocracies. Consequently, they can avoid pressure to democratize both from their neighbours and from their own people, who, especially in a semi-liberal autocracy, could well be aware of the situation in neighbouring countries. (Access to information, of course, is easier today with the spread of communications such as satellite dishes and the Internet).[63] Conversely, there have been "positive regional outliers"—that is, democracies that are more or less surrounded by autocracies, such as India and Israel today (although India is big enough not to be affected easily by its neighbours) or Czechoslovakia in the late 1930s.

If the countries of an area establish an organized regional association *and* if most members of this body are democratic, then they may use the regional organization to try to encourage the spread of democracy or at least to discourage attempts to overthrow current democracies in the region. We see this pattern today on two continents: Europe, via the Council of Europe and the Organization for Security and Co-operation in Europe, and Latin America, via the Organization of American States (OAS). The OAS, along with the United States and others, intervened to neutralize coups in both Guatemala in 1993 and Paraguay in 1996.[64] Even in Africa, two coups in São Tomé and Príncipe—in 1995 and 2003—each fizzled out after about a week due to opposition from neighbouring West African countries.

A stronger type of regional pro-democracy effect has been the foreign pressure or influence of the European Union (EU) on would-be members. EU membership is, in theory, conditional on a country being a liberal democracy—not that the EU uses this precise phrase, but that is what the stated membership criteria comprise, even if the standard of a well-functioning state is not always followed when it comes to minimizing corruption in particular. This membership requirement has acted as a pro-democratic incentive to EU neighbours wishing to join (but only if they thought they had a reasonable chance of admission). However, it seems to have little effect once a country is a member—given that EU members such as Hungary have fallen from liberal to electoral democracy status.[65]

TABLE 5.4 Multiple Regressions on the Key Factors Collectively Explaining Regime Type (measured on a 1 to 4 scale from liberal democracy to closed autocracy)

MODEL ONE	b	Std. Error	t	Significance Level
Non-figurehead monarch (dummy)	1.250	0.191	6.557	0.000
Military participation ratio, 2011	0.040	0.010	4.154	0.000
Polarized society with violent political conflicts (dummy)	0.389	0.129	3.029	0.003
Mean years of schooling, 2011	−0.051	0.021	−2.394	0.018
Capitalist market economy (dummy)	−0.905	0.137	−6.607	0.000
Statist economy (dummy)	0.639	0.156	4.105	0.000
Population below 0.5 million, 2011 (dummy)	−0.483	0.150	−3.232	0.001
Constant	2.589	0.174	14.914	0.000

N = 195
adjusted r-square = 0.584

MODEL TWO	b	Std. Error	t	Significance Level
Non-figurehead monarch (dummy)	1.014	0.194	5.236	0.000
Military participation ratio, 2011	0.035	0.009	3.861	0.000
Polarized society with violent political conflicts (dummy)	0.295	0.124	2.370	0.019
Mean years of schooling, 2011	−0.059	0.021	−2.842	0.005
Capitalist market economy (dummy)	−0.807	0.133	−6.079	0.000
Statist economy (dummy)	0.577	0.149	3.876	0.000
Population below 0.5 million, 2011 (dummy)	−0.398	0.144	−2.768	0.006
In area of Arab conquest (dummy)	0.423	0.148	2.854	0.005
ASEAN member / SCO member / Belarus (dummy)	0.669	0.172	3.881	0.000
Constant	2.554	0.167	15.255	0.000

N = 195
adjusted r-square = 0.623

In contrast to regional organizations that promote democracy or, at least, electoral democracy are those that tolerate or even bolster autocracy. The first such organization is the now 10-member Association of Southeast Asian Nations (ASEAN),[66] which has always emphasized the sovereignty of its members and the parallel doctrine of non-interference in internal affairs, although there has been some modest lessening of this doctrine with regards to Burma/Myanmar.[67] The second such organization is the Shanghai Cooperation Organisation (SCO) comprising China, Russia, and four of the ex-Soviet Central Asian states (Kazakhstan, Kyrgyzstan, Tajikistan, and Uzbekistan). As Ambrosio argues, this organization emphasizes stability over regime change, opposes external democracy promotion in Central Asia, and, indeed, argues that each country is entitled to its own path of political development. Although this "Shanghai Spirit" does not explicitly forbid democracy in the standard sense of the term (Kyrgyzstan is currently an electoral democracy, for example), it crucially allows all sorts of "models" of democracy that have nothing to do with or that even counteract the definitional features of liberal democracy presented in Table 4.1.[68] Belarus is only a dialogue partner here, as it is a purely European rather than Asian country, but given Russia's support for authoritarianism in Belarus[69] and the Customs Union of Belarus, Kazakhstan, and Russia, Belarus can effectively be viewed to share the spirit of the SCO and is included in terms of showing this effect.

A Multivariate Analysis

To keep the analysis simple (or at least simpler), we have focused so far on dichotomies, first between all democracies and all autocracies and then between liberal democracies and electoral democracies. We have also generally looked at the variables in turn without too much focus on the ones that matter most. However, by classifying the categories used in Table 4.3 into a four-point scale (with liberal democracy as "1," electoral democracy as "2," semi-liberal autocracy as "3," and closed autocracy as "4"), we can make a multiple regression analysis of all the quantifiable and dummy variables, which allows us to consider how significant various factors are in collectively explaining regime type—as opposed to the individual factors in Table 5.2. The results are reported in two ways in Table 5.4. Model One assesses just domestic or internal factors. The following seven such variables are key: (1) the existence of a non-figurehead monarch dummy variable, (2) the military participation ratio (armed forces per 1,000 population), (3) the polarized society with violent political conflicts dummy variable, (4) the mean years of schooling in the population aged 25 and above, (5) the capitalist market economy dummy variable, (6) the statist market economy dummy variable, and (7) the tiny population (below 500,000) dummy variable. These seven variables explain almost 60 per cent of the variance in the level of democracy versus autocracy across our four categories. (See the adjusted r-square for Model One, which is 0.584.) Also, each variable is individually significant, even allowing for the others.

Model Two then adds two further dummy variables to reflect regional factors and assesses the statistical significance of being in these groups on regime type. The first

TABLE 5.5 Country Values for Key Variables Relevant to Regime Type, 2012 (or most recent year)

Country	Regime Category (late 2012)*	Non-Figurehead Monarch (dummy)	Military Participation Ratio, 2011 (per 1,000 population)	Polarized Society with Violent Political Conflicts (dummy)	Mean Years of Schooling, Population 25 and Above, 2011	Capitalist Market Economy (dummy)	Statist Economy (dummy)	Tiny Population (below 0.5 million), 2011 (dummy)	In Area of Long-standing Arab Conquest (dummy)	ASEAN Member / SCO Member / Belarus (dummy)
Afghanistan	3	0	5.28	1	3.3	0	0	0	1	0
Albania	3	0	4.43	0	10.4	0	0	0	0	0
Algeria	3	0	3.61	1	7.0	0	0	0	1	0
Andorra	1	0	0.00	0	10.4	1	0	1	0	0
Angola	3	0	5.45	0	4.4	0	1	0	0	0
Antigua and Barbuda	2	0	1.90	0	8.9	0	0	1	0	0
Argentina	2	0	1.79	0	9.3	0	0	0	0	0
Armenia	3	0	15.75	0	10.8	0	0	0	0	0
Australia	1	0	2.50	0	12.0	1	0	0	0	0
Austria	1	0	3.06	0	10.8	1	0	0	0	0
Azerbaijan	4	0	7.19	0	8.6	0	0	0	1	0
Bahamas	1	0	2.48	0	8.5	1	0	1	0	0
Bahrain	4	1	6.20	1	9.4	1	0	0	1	0
Bangladesh	2	0	1.04	1	4.8	0	0	0	0	0
Barbados	1	0	2.23	0	9.3	1	0	1	0	0
Belarus	4	0	7.63	0	9.3	0	1	0	0	1
Belgium	1	0	3.19	0	10.9	1	0	0	0	0
Belize	1	0	3.30	0	8.0	0	0	1	0	0
Benin	2	0	0.52	0	3.3	0	0	0	0	0
Bhutan	3	1	0.00	0	2.3	0	0	0	0	0
Bolivia	2	0	4.57	1	9.2	0	0	0	0	0
Bosnia/Herzegovina	3	0	2.82	1	8.7	0	0	0	0	0
Botswana	2	0	4.43	0	8.9	1	0	0	0	0
Brazil	2	0	1.62	0	7.2	0	0	0	0	0
Brunei	4	1	17.25	0	8.6	0	0	1	0	1
Bulgaria	2	0	4.21	0	10.6	0	0	0	0	0
Burkina Faso	3	0	0.66	0	1.3	0	0	0	0	0
Burma/Myanmar	4	0	8.40	1	4.0	0	1	0	0	1
Burundi	3	0	2.33	1	2.7	0	0	0	0	0
Cambodia	3	0	8.69	0	5.8	0	0	0	0	1
Cameroon	4	0	0.71	1	5.9	0	0	0	0	0
Canada	1	0	1.91	0	12.1	1	0	0	0	0
Cape Verde	1	0	2.40	0	3.5	0	0	0	0	0
Central African Republic	3	0	0.48	1	3.5	0	1	0	0	0
Chad	4	0	2.20	1	1.5	0	1	0	1	0
Chile	1	0	3.42	0	9.7	1	0	0	0	0
China	4	0	1.73	0	7.5	0	0	0	0	1
Colombia	2	0	6.03	1	7.3	0	0	0	0	0
Comoros	2	0	0.66	0	2.8	0	1	0	0	0

Country	Regime Category (late 2012)*	Non-Figurehead Monarch (dummy)	Military Participation Ratio, 2011 (per 1,000 population)	Polarized Society with Violent Political Conflicts (dummy)	Mean Years of Schooling, Population 25 and Above, 2011	Capitalist Market Economy (dummy)	Statist Economy (dummy)	Tiny Population (below 0.5 million), 2011 (dummy)	In Area of Long-standing Arab Conquest (dummy)	ASEAN Member / SCO Member / Belarus (dummy)
Congo, DR (Kinshasa)	3	0	2.35	1	3.5	0	1	0	0	0
Congo, R (Brazzaville)	4	0	2.42	1	5.9	0	1	0	0	0
Costa Rica	1	0	0.00	0	8.3	0	0	0	0	0
Croatia	2	0	4.23	0	9.8	0	0	0	0	0
Cuba	4	0	4.35	0	9.9	0	1	0	0	0
Cyprus (Greek)	1	0	10.75	0	9.8	1	0	0	0	0
Czech Republic	1	0	2.41	0	12.3	1	0	0	0	0
Denmark	1	0	3.34	0	11.4	1	0	0	0	0
Djibouti	4	0	11.54	0	3.8	0	0	0	0	0
Dominica	1	0	0.00	0	7.7	0	0	1	0	0
Dominican Republic	2	0	2.44	0	7.2	0	0	0	0	0
Ecuador	2	0	3.99	0	7.6	0	1	0	0	0
Egypt	3	0	5.31	0	6.4	0	0	0	1	0
El Salvador	2	0	2.49	0	7.5	0	0	0	0	0
Equatorial Guinea	4	0	1.83	0	5.4	0	1	0	0	0
Eritrea	4	0	37.26	0	3.4	0	1	0	0	0
Estonia	1	0	4.29	0	12.0	1	0	0	0	0
Ethiopia	4	0	1.63	1	1.5	0	0	0	0	0
Fiji	3	0	4.03	1	10.7	0	0	0	0	0
Finland	1	0	4.10	0	10.3	1	0	0	0	0
France	1	0	3.78	0	10.6	1	0	0	0	0
Gabon	3	0	3.06	0	7.5	0	0	0	0	0
Gambia	4	0	0.45	0	2.8	0	0	0	0	0
Georgia	3	0	4.77	1	12.1	1	0	0	0	0
Germany	1	0	3.06	0	12.2	1	0	0	0	0
Ghana	2	0	0.62	0	7.1	0	0	0	0	0
Greece	2	0	12.79	0	10.1	0	0	0	0	0
Grenada	1	0	0.00	0	8.6	0	0	1	0	0
Guatemala	2	0	1.03	1	4.1	0	0	0	0	0
Guinea	3	0	1.20	1	1.6	0	0	0	0	0
Guinea-Bissau	3	0	2.88	0	2.3	0	1	0	0	0
Guyana	2	0	1.46	1	8.0	0	0	0	0	0
Haiti	3	0	0.00	1	4.9	0	1	0	0	0
Honduras	2	0	1.55	0	6.5	0	0	0	0	0
Hungary	2	0	2.27	0	11.1	1	0	0	0	0
Iceland	1	0	0.00	0	10.4	1	0	1	0	0
India	2	0	1.07	0	4.4	0	0	0	0	0
Indonesia	2	0	1.25	1	5.8	0	0	0	0	1
Iran	4	0	6.99	1	7.3	0	1	0	1	0

Country	Regime Category (late 2012)*	Non-Figurehead Monarch (dummy)	Military Participation Ratio, 2011 (per 1,000 population)	Polarized Society with Violent Political Conflicts (dummy)	Mean Years of Schooling, Population 25 and Above, 2011	Capitalist Market Economy (dummy)	Statist Economy (dummy)	Tiny Population (below 0.5 million), 2011 (dummy)	In Area of Long-standing Arab Conquest (dummy)	ASEAN Member / SCO Member / Belarus (dummy)
Iraq	2	0	8.31	1	5.6	0	1	0	1	0
Ireland	1	0	2.13	0	11.6	1	0	0	0	0
Israel	2	0	23.34	0	11.9	1	0	0	0	0
Italy	1	0	3.04	0	10.1	1	0	0	0	0
Ivory Coast	2	0	1.98	1	3.3	0	0	0	0	0
Jamaica	2	0	1.03	0	9.6	0	0	0	0	0
Japan	1	0	1.96	0	11.6	1	0	0	0	0
Jordan	3	1	15.88	0	8.6	1	0	0	1	0
Kazakhstan	4	0	3.02	0	10.4	0	0	0	0	1
Kenya	3	0	0.58	1	7.0	0	0	0	0	0
Kiribati	2	0	0.00	0	7.8	0	0	1	0	0
Korea, North	4	0	48.67	0	7.5	0	1	0	0	0
Korea, South	1	0	13.54	0	11.6	1	0	0	0	0
Kosovo	3	0	1.44	0	10.2	0	0	0	0	0
Kuwait	3	1	5.50	0	6.1	0	0	0	1	0
Kyrgyzstan	2	0	2.02	0	9.3	0	0	0	0	1
Laos	4	0	4.63	0	4.6	0	1	0	0	1
Latvia	1	0	2.05	0	11.5	1	0	0	0	0
Lebanon	3	0	13.88	1	7.9	0	0	0	1	0
Lesotho	2	0	0.91	0	5.9	0	0	0	0	0
Liberia	2	0	0.50	1	3.9	0	0	0	0	0
Libya	3	0	2.65	0	7.3	0	1	0	1	0
Liechtenstein	2	1	0.00	0	10.3	1	0	1	0	0
Lithuania	1	0	3.22	0	10.9	1	0	0	0	0
Luxembourg	1	0	1.74	0	10.1	1	0	0	0	0
Macedonia	2	0	3.88	0	8.2	0	0	0	0	0
Madagascar	3	0	0.63	0	5.2	0	0	0	0	0
Malawi	3	0	0.34	0	4.2	0	0	0	0	0
Malaysia	3	0	3.78	0	9.5	0	0	0	0	1
Maldives	3	0	3.12	0	5.8	0	0	1	0	0
Mali	3	0	0.46	0	2.0	0	0	0	1	0
Malta	1	0	4.68	0	9.9	1	0	1	0	0
Marshall Islands	1	0	0.00	0	9.8	0	0	1	0	0
Mauritania	4	0	4.48	1	3.7	0	0	0	1	0
Mauritius	1	0	0.00	0	7.2	1	0	0	0	0
Mexico	2	0	2.44	0	8.5	0	0	0	0	0
Micronesia	1	0	0.00	0	8.8	0	0	1	0	0
Moldova	2	0	1.51	0	9.7	0	0	0	0	0
Monaco	3	1	0.00	0	10.6	0	0	1	0	0
Mongolia	2	0	3.57	0	8.3	0	0	0	0	0

Country	Regime Category (late 2012)*	Non-Figurehead Monarch (dummy)	Military Participation Ratio, 2011 (per 1,000 population)	Polarized Society with Violent Political Conflicts (dummy)	Mean Years of Schooling, Population 25 and Above, 2011	Capitalist Market Economy (dummy)	Statist Economy (dummy)	Tiny Population (below 0.5 million), 2011 (dummy)	In Area of Long-standing Arab Conquest (dummy)	ASEAN Member / SCO Member / Belarus (dummy)
Montenegro	2	0	4.72	0	10.6	0	0	0	0	0
Morocco	3	1	6.07	0	4.4	0	0	0	1	0
Mozambique	3	0	0.47	0	1.2	0	0	0	0	0
Namibia	2	0	3.96	0	7.4	0	0	0	0	0
Nauru	1	0	0.00	0	7.8	0	0	1	0	0
Nepal	3	0	3.14	1	3.2	0	1	0	0	0
Netherlands	1	0	2.24	0	11.6	1	0	0	0	0
New Zealand	1	0	2.19	0	12.5	1	0	0	0	0
Nicaragua	3	0	2.04	0	5.8	0	0	0	0	0
Niger	2	0	0.33	0	1.4	0	0	0	1	0
Nigeria	2	0	0.49	1	5.0	0	0	0	0	0
Norway	1	0	4.96	0	12.6	1	0	0	0	0
Oman	4	1	14.97	0	5.5	0	0	0	1	0
Pakistan	2	0	3.63	1	4.9	0	0	0	1	0
Palau	1	0	0.00	0	12.1	0	0	1	0	0
Panama	2	0	0.00	0	9.4	0	0	0	0	0
Papua New Guinea	2	0	0.44	1	4.3	0	0	0	0	0
Paraguay	2	0	1.62	0	7.7	0	0	0	0	0
Peru	2	0	3.91	0	8.7	0	0	0	0	0
Philippines	2	0	1.32	1	8.9	0	0	0	0	1
Poland	1	0	2.61	0	10.0	0	0	0	0	0
Portugal	1	0	3.99	0	7.7	1	0	0	0	0
Qatar	4	1	6.31	0	7.3	1	0	0	1	0
Romania	2	0	3.45	0	10.4	0	0	0	0	0
Russia	3	0	6.69	0	9.8	0	0	0	0	1
Rwanda	4	0	3.02	1	3.3	0	0	0	0	0
Saint Kitts and Nevis	1	0	0.00	0	8.4	1	0	1	0	0
Saint Lucia	1	0	0.00	0	8.3	1	0	1	0	0
Saint Vincent and the Grenadines	1	0	0.00	0	8.6	1	0	1	0	0
Samoa (Western)	1	0	0.00	0	10.3	0	0	1	0	0
San Marino	1	0	0.00	0	10.1	1	0	1	0	0
São Tomé and Príncipe	2	0	3.56	0	4.2	0	0	1	0	0
Saudi Arabia	4	1	8.31	0	7.8	0	0	0	1	0
Senegal	2	0	1.07	0	4.5	0	0	0	0	0
Serbia	2	0	4.05	0	10.2	0	0	0	0	0
Seychelles	3	0	2.30	0	9.4	0	0	1	0	0
Sierra Leone	2	0	1.75	0	2.9	0	1	0	0	0
Singapore	3	0	13.97	0	8.8	1	0	0	0	1
Slovakia	1	0	2.89	0	11.6	1	0	0	0	0
Slovenia	1	0	3.73	0	11.6	1	0	0	0	0

Country	Regime Category (late 2012)*	Non-Figurehead Monarch (dummy)	Military Participation Ratio, 2011 (per 1,000 population)	Polarized Society with Violent Political Conflicts (dummy)	Mean Years of Schooling, Population 25 and Above, 2011	Capitalist Market Economy (dummy)	Statist Economy (dummy)	Tiny Population (below 0.5 million), 2011 (dummy)	In Area of Long-standing Arab Conquest (dummy)	ASEAN Member / SCO Member / Belarus (dummy)
Solomon Islands	3	0	0.00	1	4.5	0	0	0	0	0
Somalia	4	0	0.21	1	1.5	0	0	0	1	0
South Africa	2	0	1.23	1	8.5	0	0	0	0	0
South Sudan	4	0	16.95	0	3.1	0	0	0	0	0
Spain	1	0	3.08	0	10.4	1	0	0	0	0
Sri Lanka	3	0	7.65	1	8.2	0	0	0	0	0
Sudan	4	0	3.01	1	3.1	0	0	0	0	0
Suriname	2	0	3.48	0	7.2	0	0	0	0	0
Swaziland	4	1	2.49	0	7.1	0	0	0	0	0
Sweden	1	0	2.16	0	11.7	1	0	0	0	0
Switzerland	1	0	3.28	0	11.0	1	0	0	0	0
Syria	4	0	14.21	0	5.7	0	1	0	1	0
Taiwan	1	0	12.57	0	11.0	1	0	0	0	0
Tajikistan	4	0	1.26	1	9.8	0	0	0	1	1
Tanzania	3	0	0.58	0	5.1	0	0	0	0	0
Thailand	2	1	4.40	1	6.6	0	0	0	0	1
Timor-Leste (East Timor)	2	0	1.15	0	2.8	0	0	0	0	0
Togo	3	0	1.39	0	5.3	0	1	0	0	0
Tonga	3	1	4.78	0	10.3	0	0	1	0	0
Trinidad and Tobago	2	0	3.02	0	9.2	0	0	0	0	0
Tunisia	2	0	3.38	0	6.5	0	0	0	1	0
Turkey	2	0	6.93	0	6.5	0	0	0	1	0
Turkmenistan	4	0	4.31	0	9.9	0	1	0	1	0
Tuvalu	1	0	0.00	0	10.3	0	0	1	0	0
Uganda	3	0	1.30	1	4.7	0	0	0	0	0
Ukraine	3	0	2.88	0	11.3	0	0	0	0	0
United Arab Emirates	4	1	6.46	0	9.3	1	0	0	1	0
United Kingdom	1	0	2.79	0	9.3	1	0	0	0	0
United States	1	0	5.01	0	12.4	1	0	0	0	0
Uruguay	1	0	7.28	0	8.5	1	0	0	0	0
Uzbekistan	4	0	2.41	1	10.0	0	1	0	1	1
Vanuatu	2	0	0.00	0	6.7	0	0	1	0	0
Venezuela	3	0	3.91	0	7.6	0	1	0	0	0
Vietnam	4	0	5.43	0	5.5	0	0	0	0	1
Yemen	3	0	2.69	1	2.5	0	0	0	1	0
Zambia	2	0	1.12	0	6.5	0	0	0	0	0
Zimbabwe	4	0	2.27	1	7.2	0	1	0	0	0
MEAN			4.42		7.6					

* Liberal Democracy = 1   Electoral Democracy = 2   Semi-liberal Autocracy = 3   Closed Autocracy = 4

dummy variable identifies the countries being from the area of longstanding Arab conquest, a concept discussed earlier. The second dummy variable groups together the countries that are members of ASEAN or the Shanghai Cooperation Organisation (SCO) and Belarus, as discussed earlier. These dummy variables increase the variance explained in the type of regime from 58.4 to 62.3 per cent, with each individual variable remaining significant. (See the adjusted r-square for Model Two, which is 0.623.) So Model Two is offered as a more thorough explanation for differing political regimes. Table 5.5 provides, for reference, the actual values for each of these aforementioned variables for all countries. In both models, the capitalist market economy dummy is the most significant variable.

These several variables explaining regime type help us see, for example, that all of the Nordic countries are "logical liberal democracies" given their figurehead monarchs (in Scandinavia), their limited militarization, their lack of polarized societies and violent political conflict, their well-educated populations, and their capitalist market economies. Even more logically, both models predict Andorra and Iceland—each of which has a tiny population—to be the most democratic countries. On the other hand, Saudi Arabia can serve as a "logical closed autocracy" given its monarchy, which actually rules the country; its high level of militarization; its statist economy; and its being in the area of longstanding Arab conquest. So too can Chad, given its polarized society with violent political conflicts, its very low level of education, and its statist economy. So too can Uzbekistan, given its polarized society with violent political conflicts, its statist economy, and its membership in the SCO. In an overlapping way, so can North Korea, given especially its extreme militarization (the highest in the world) and its statist economy. Both models, in fact, predict North Korea to be the most autocratic country.

Of course, some countries are surprising in terms of their regime. India is a democracy despite its huge population and limited development (the models predict it to be a bit below an electoral democracy). However, India also has some of the other factors noted in this chapter—a very pro-democratic political leadership, especially at independence, and a favourable longstanding British colonial legacy, with key institutions in place before independence—as well as a strong national identity.[70] Given the models, some other "surprising" democracies are Indonesia, Iraq, Kyrgyzstan, Pakistan, the Philippines, and Thailand—although, in each of these countries, the current democracy is new, and there is no guarantee of it continuing (more on this issue in Chapter 11).

Notes

1   Robert H. Dix, "History and Democracy Revisited," *Comparative Politics* 27, no. 1 (October 1994): 91–105.

2   Dix, "History and Democracy," 94.

3   Dix, "History and Democracy," 95.

4   Dix, "History and Democracy," 96–98.

5   Richard Rose and Doh Chull Shin, "Democratization Backwards: The Problem of Third-Wave Democracies," *British Journal of Political Science* 31, no. 2 (April 2001): 331–54.

6   Samuel P. Huntington, *The Third Wave: Democratization in the Late Twentieth Century* (Norman, OK: University of Oklahoma Press, 1991), 38.

7   Robert A. Dahl, *Democracy and its Critics* (New Haven, CT: Yale University Press, 1989), 262.

8   Larry Diamond, Juan J. Linz, and Seymour Martin Lipset, "Introduction: What Makes for Democracy?," in *Politics in Developing Countries: Comparing Experiences with Democracy*, 2nd ed., ed. Larry Diamond, Jonathan Hartlyn, and Juan J. Linz, 1–70 (Boulder, CO: Lynne Rienner, 1995), 19.

9   Robert A. Dahl, *Polyarchy: Participation and Opposition* (New Haven, CT: Yale University Press, 1971), 126–28.

10   Diamond, Linz, and Lipset, "Introduction," 20.

11   Dahl, *Democracy and its Critics*, 248.

12   Dahl, *Democracy and its Critics*, 248–49.

13   Dahl, *Democracy and its Critics*, 246–50.

14   Dahl, *Democracy and its Critics*, 260–62.

15   International Institute for Strategic Studies, *The Military Balance 2011* (Washington, DC: Inernational Institute for Strategic Studies, 2011).

16   Seymour Martin Lipset, "Some Social Requisites of Democracy: Economic Development and Political Legitimacy," *American Political Science Review* 53, no. 1 (March 1959): 69–105; Seymour Martin Lipset, "The Social Requisites of Democracy Revisited," *American Sociological Review* 59, no. 1 (February 1994): 1–22.

17   On this causal sequence, see Adam Przeworski and Fernando Limongi, "Modernization: Theories and Facts," *World Politics* 49 (1997): 155–83.

18   Dahl, *Democracy and its Critics*, 251.

19   Tatu Vanhanen, *The Process of Democratization: A Comparative Study of 147 States, 1980–88* (New York, NY: Crane Russak, 1990), 50–65.

20   Barrington Moore, *Social Origins of Dictatorship and Democracy: Lord and Peasant in the Making of the Modern World* (Boston, MA: Beacon Press, 1966), 418.

21   Dahl, *Democracy and its Critics*, 252.

22   Vanhanen, *The Process of Democratization*, 50.

23   Dahl, *Democracy and its Critics*, 252.

24   Dahl, *Democracy and its Critics*, 253–54.

25 On the superior utility of using the HDI as opposed to just per capita wealth as a causal explanation for democracy, see Larry Diamond, "Economic Development and Democracy Reconsidered," *American Behavioral Scientist* 35, no. 4–5 (March/June 1992): 450–99, see 457–60.

26 For an analysis of levels of democracy (using Freedom House scores), which includes average years of schooling as a variable, see Henry S. Rowen, "The Tide Underneath the 'Third Wave,'" *Journal of Democracy* 6, no. 1 (January 1995): 52–64.

27 The seven missing countries and the specific country values used as estimates are as follows: Monaco (the value of France is used), Nauru (Kiribati), North Korea (China), San Marino (Italy), Somalia (Ethiopia), South Sudan (Sudan), and Tuvalu (Samoa or Tonga, which have the same value).

28 Axel Hadenius has argued that literacy is the most central factor in explaining the differing levels of democracy in developing countries. Axel Hadenius, *Democracy and Development* (Cambridge, UK: Cambridge University Press, 1992), 86–91.

29 Edward L. Glaeser, Giacomo A. M. Ponzetto, and Andrei Shleifer, "Why Does Democracy Need Education?," *Journal of Economic Growth* 12, no. 2 (June 2007): 77–99, see 82–83.

30 This lack of relationship may be so even though both equality and democracy are related to wealth, as wealthier countries generally have less inequality. For the available data (128 countries), the correlation between GNI per capita and the GINI index is –0.297, which is indeed significantly negative (significant at the .001 level).

31 See for example Edward N. Muller, "Democracy, Economic Development, and Income Inequality," *American Sociological Review* 53, no. 11 (February 1988): 50–68. Specifically, Muller found that, of countries that were democracies as of 1961 and for which inequality data existed, those with high levels of income inequality all failed to maintain stable democracy through 1980. In contrast, most of the sample countries with intermediate levels of income inequality maintained stable democracy, as did all of the countries with low levels of income inequality (Muller 63).

32 Charles E. Lindblom, *Politics and Markets: The World's Political-Economic Systems* (New York, NY: Basic Books, 1977), 164–65.

33 The analyses used for these purposes are primarily those of the Heritage Foundation (its Index of Economic Freedom), the Fraser Institute (its Economic Freedom of the World Index), and the United States Department of State (its Country Commercial Guides).

34 Paul Sutton, "Democracy in the Commonwealth Caribbean," *Democratization* 6, no. 1 (Spring 1999): 67–86, see page 68.

35 Sutton, "Democracy in the Commonwealth," 68–69.

36 The Mediterranean countries of Cyprus and Malta are considered to be outside of continental Europe in this analysis.

37 Dag Anckar, "Democracy as a Westminster Heritage," *Taiwan Journal of Democracy* 7, no. 1 (July 2011): 47–71, see 66.

38 Pierre Elliott Trudeau, "Some Obstacles to Democracy in Quebec," *The Canadian Journal of Economics and Political Science* 24, no. 3 (August 1958): 297–311, see 300.

39 Adrian Karatnycky, "The 2001 Freedom House Survey: Muslim Countries and the Democracy Gap," *Journal of Democracy* 13, no. 1 (January 2002): 99–112.

40 M. Steven Fish, *Are Muslims Distinctive? A Look at the Evidence* (New York, NY: Oxford University Press, 2011), 249.

41   Alfred Stepan with Graeme B. Robertson, "An 'Arab' More Than a 'Muslim' Democracy Gap," *Journal of Democracy* 14, no. 3 (July 2003): 30–44.

42   Eric Chaney, "Democratic Change in the Arab World, Past and Present" (paper prepared for the Brookings Panel on Economic Activity, March 2012). Chaney, in fact, assesses only 28 such countries, due to a lack of data for Afghanistan, which, however, is clearly in the area of Arab conquest.

43   James D. Fearon, "Ethnic and Cultural Diversity by Country," *Journal of Economic Growth* 8 (2003): 195–222.

44   M. Paul Lewis, ed., *Ethnologue: Languages of the World*, 16th ed. (Dallas, TX: SIL International, 2009), http://www.ethnologue.com.

45   Dahl, *Democracy and its Critics*, 256–57; Arend Lijphart, *Democracy in Plural Societies: A Comparative Exploration* (New Haven, CT: Yale University Press, 1977).

46   Lijphart, *Democracy in Plural Societies*, 1–2.

47   Arend Lijphart, "The Puzzle of Indian Democracy: A Consociational Reinterpretation," *American Political Science Review* 90, no. 2 (1996): 258–68.

48   Bertelsmann Stiftung, "BTI Scores 2003–2012 [Data file]," *Bertelsmann Transformation Index*, http://www.bti-project.org/index/: Data used were from 2006, 2008, 2010, and 2012.

49   M. Moniruzzaman, "Party Politics and Political Violence in Bangladesh: Issues, Manifestation and Consequences," *South Asian Survey* 16, no. 1 (March 2009): 81–99.

50   For example, Dag Anckar, "Democratic Standard and Performance in Twelve Pacific Micro-states," *Pacific Affairs* 75:2 (Summer 2002): 207–25, see page 208.

51   Dana Ott, *Small is Democratic: An Examination of State Size and Democratic Development* (New York, NY, and London, UK: Garland Publishing, 2000).

52   Diamond, *Developing Democracy*, 117–18.

53   Diamond, *Developing Democracy*, 117–19; Ott, *Small is Democratic*, 209, note 1.

54   Ott, *Small is Democratic*, 197.

55   Ott, *Small is Democratic*, 200.

56   H.E. Chehabi, "Small Island States," *The Encyclopedia of Democracy*, ed. Seymour Martin Lipset (Washington, DC: Congressional Quarterly, 1995), 1136.

57   Ott, *Small is Democratic*, 203.

58   Diamond, *Developing Democracy*, 119ff.; Ott, *Small is Democratic*, 208.

59   Ott, *Small is Democratic*, 203.

60   Lijphart, *Democracy in Plural Societies*, 65–68.

61   See Lijphart, *Democracy in Plural Societies*, 69–70.

62   Diamond, *Developing Democracy*, 118–19.

63   Note the regional domino effect of democratization in the 1980s and 1990s and also of the democratic breakdowns in the 1930s (in East-Central Europe) and in the 1960s (in Latin America).

64   Morton H. Halperin and Kristen Lomasney, "Guaranteeing Democracy: A Review of the Record," *Journal of Democracy* 9, no. 2 (April 1998): 134–47, see 137–39.

65   Erin K. Jenne and Cas Mudde, "Hungary's Illiberal Turn: Can Outsiders Help?," *Journal of Democracy* 23, no. 3 (July 2012): 147–155.

66   Brunei, Burma/Myanmar, Cambodia, Indonesia, Laos, Malaysia, Philippines, Singapore, Thailand, and Vietnam are the members.

67   Erik Martinez Kuhonta, "Walking a Tightrope: Democracy Versus Sovereignty in ASEAN's Illiberal Peace," *The Pacific Review* 19, no. 3 (September 2006): 337–358.

68   Thomas Ambrosio, *Authoritarian Backlash: Russian Resistance to Democratization in the Former Soviet Union* (Farnham, Surrey, UK: Ashgate, 2009); and more generally on autocratic diffusion Thomas Ambrosio, "Constructing a Framework of Authoritarian Diffusion: Concepts, Dynamics, and Future Research," *International Studies Perspectives* 11, no. 4 (November 2010): 375–392.

69   Ambrosio, *Authoritarian Backlash*, Chapter 6.

70   Sumit Ganguly, "Six Decades of Independence," *Journal of Democracy* 18, no. 2 (April 2007): 30–40, in the section on "India's Unlikely Democracy"; Alfred Stepan, Juan J. Linz, and Yogendra Yadav, *Crafting State-Nations: India and Other Multinational Democracies* (Baltimore, MD: Johns Hopkins University Press, 2011), Chapter 2. For a comparison of India and Pakistan, see Philip Oldenburg, *India, Pakistan, and Democracy: Solving the Puzzle of Divergent Paths* (New York, NY: Routledge, 2010).

CHAPTER SIX

Institutional Variations of Democracies

IN THIS CHAPTER YOU WILL LEARN

► the precise definition of a presidential system and a parliamentary system;

► the strengths and weaknesses of each of these systems, and how these weaknesses might be mitigated;

► why democratic systems can be neither fully presidential nor fully parliamentary but rather "mixed";

► what the differing types of heads of state in parliamentary systems are;

► the reasons for bicameralism;

► how lower houses and upper houses differ;

► the precise definition of federalism in terms of both interstate and intrastate factors; and

► how federalism differs from other spatially based political structures.

As outlined in Chapter 4, today, 113 of the world's independent countries are democracies, either liberal or electoral democracies. This chapter will outline how these democracies vary in terms of their institutional features. First, we make a distinction between presidential and parliamentary systems. Then we note some variations in the roles and natures of legislatures. Finally, we outline what is meant by federalism and look at its alternatives. Note that the following analysis applies only to the liberal and electoral democracies in the world, so, for example, although many non-democracies are run by presidents, they are not our concern here.

Presidential and Parliamentary Systems

Although students undoubtedly have a "gut" understanding of these variations, the full definitions need to be noted. Let us start with a **presidential system**. There are five aspects to such a system:

▶ the positions of head of government (the one who runs the country) and head of state (the symbolic national head) are fused in the single office of the president;

▶ the presidency is a one-person executive office that cannot be shared, thus making it a "winner-take-all" position;

▶ the president is chosen separately from the legislature (even if on the same day), making the president independent from the legislature in terms of political survival (and vice versa);

▶ the president is elected for a fixed term of a specified number of years, as are legislators for their own fixed terms; and

▶ the head of government (the president) is elected directly by the voters or possibly by an **electoral college**, which is itself directly elected for this specific purpose and no other (so it is not an ongoing body).

In short, this system provides a definite stability for the position of president. Table 6.1 lists the 30 current democracies that meet these criteria. Of these 30, 15 are in Latin America and 10 in Africa. Presidentialism is thus clearly the most common institutional system in Latin America. In the political systems of these 30 countries, the length of the presidential terms varies from four to seven years, but terms longer than five years are now rare. Analyses have linked a shorter term to greater political stability because six years is a long time to wait for a head of government to leave office or face the voters again. However, not all presidents will or even can face the voters again, because almost all presidential systems (Cyprus being the one exception) place a limit on the number of consecutive terms one individual can serve as president—and some presidential systems go further by limiting individuals to one term only, so a president cannot *ever* run for re-election.[1] This hard constraint has been particularly common historically in Latin America, although, as of 2012, it continues to exist in only Guatemala, Honduras, Mexico, and Paraguay. Although this rule obviously prevents someone being in office too long, it also lessens the incentive to do a good job to the extent that this is driven by a desire for re-election. Of course, even if a president can serve two consecutive terms—the most common pattern for presidencies[2]—he or she will still be a "lame duck" in the second or final term.[3]

TABLE 6.1 Data on the Presidential Systems of Liberal and Electoral Democracies (2012)

Country	Length of Presidential Term (years)	Maximum Consecutive Terms	Minimum Age to Serve	Electoral Formula	Vice President	Legislative Elections (lower house)
Argentina	4	2	30	plurality of 45%, otherwise runoff *	yes	concurrent, but with midterm elections for half the seats
Benin	5	2	40	absolute majority, otherwise runoff	no	non-concurrent (normally in different years)
Bolivia	5	2	30	absolute majority, otherwise runoff *	yes	concurrent
Brazil	4	2	35	absolute majority, otherwise runoff	yes	concurrent
Chile	4	1	40	absolute majority, otherwise runoff	no	concurrent
Colombia	4	2	30	absolute majority, otherwise runoff	yes	non-concurrent (two months earlier than presidential elections)
Comoros[1]	4	1	none	simple plurality	no	non-concurrent (normally in different years)
Costa Rica	4	1	30	plurality of 40%, otherwise runoff	yes	concurrent
Cyprus (Greek)	5	unlimited	35	absolute majority, otherwise runoff	yes (but permanently vacant)	non-concurrent (normally in different years)
Dominican Republic	4	1	30	absolute majority, otherwise runoff	yes	concurrent from 2016
Ecuador	4	2	40	absolute majority, otherwise runoff **	no	concurrent
El Salvador	5	1	30	absolute majority, otherwise runoff	yes	non-concurrent (normally in different years)
Ghana	4	2	40	absolute majority, otherwise runoff	yes	concurrent
Guatemala	4	1	40	absolute majority, otherwise runoff	yes	concurrent
Honduras	4	1	30	simple plurality	yes	concurrent
Indonesia	5	2	35	absolute majority, otherwise runoff (plus provincial minimums)	yes	non-concurrent (three months earlier than presidential elections)
Ivory Coast	5	2	40	absolute majority, otherwise runoff	no	non-concurrent (normally in different years)
Liberia	6	2	35	absolute majority, otherwise runoff	yes	concurrent
Mexico	6	1	35	simple plurality	no	concurrent, but with midterm elections
Niger	5	2	40	absolute majority, otherwise runoff	no	concurrent
Nigeria	4	2	35	simple plurality plus regional minimums, otherwise runoff	yes	basically concurrent (same month)
Palau	4	2	35	consequential absolute majority ***	yes	concurrent

Country	Length of Presidential Term (years)	Maximum Consecutive Terms	Minimum Age to Serve	Electoral Formula	Vice President	Legislative Elections (lower house)
Panama	5	1	35	simple plurality	yes	concurrent
Paraguay	5	1	35	simple plurality	yes	concurrent
Philippines	6	1	40	simple plurality	yes	concurrent, but with midterm elections
Senegal	7	2	35	absolute majority, otherwise runoff	no	non-concurrent (normally in different years)
Sierra Leone	5	2	40	qualified majority of 55%, otherwise runoff	yes	concurrent
United States	4	2	35	absolute majority in electoral college, otherwise election by House of Representatives	yes	concurrent, but with midterm elections
Uruguay	5	1	35	absolute majority, otherwise runoff	yes	concurrent
Zambia	5	2	35	simple plurality	yes	concurrent

NOTE: In a given election, the president is selected from candidates representing only one of the three islands of the Comoros, and the presidency thus rotates amongst these islands.

* In Argentina and Bolivia, 40 per cent is sufficient to win outright on the first ballot if this result is also at least 10 per cent above that of the second-place candidate.

** In Ecuador, 45 per cent is sufficient to win outright on the first ballot if this result is also at least 10 percent above that of the second-place candidate.

*** In Palau, if there are more than two presidential candidates, a national primary—open to all registered voters—is held a few weeks before, and then the top two candidates from this contest go on to the actual presidential election.

‡ In Cyprus, the vice president must be a Turkish Cypriot.

Likewise, most but not all presidential systems have a minimum age requirement for presidents (from 30 to 40, well above the voting age).

The most common method of electing a president is requiring someone to win an absolute majority of the votes on the first ballot; otherwise, there is a runoff election of the top two candidates. Several presidents, however, are elected by simple plurality; that is, there is only one ballot and the candidate with the most votes wins. Of course, under any plurality system, there is no guarantee of high let alone majority support if there are multiple candidates. In 1970, under such a system, the leftist Salvador Allende won the presidency of Chile with only 36 per cent of the vote. Three years later, just over halfway into his term, he was overthrown in a military coup.[4] Some countries have qualified this plurality method by insisting that a candidate win a certain percentage of the vote, even if that percentage is less than an absolute majority—otherwise, there will be a runoff election. The United States uses a very unique system to elect its president, one based not on the total popular vote (as, most recently, the 2000 election showed) but on candidates winning votes in an electoral college that is determined state by state.[5]

There is much less variation in presidential powers across these democracies. All of these presidents handpick their cabinets and make a range of other appointments (in both cases, presidential selections may be subject to confirmation by the legislature). They all chair the cabinet meetings and thus set the agenda, are in charge of foreign policy, and have a veto on legislation (but thresholds vary in regards to overturning presidential vetoes). Of course, a legislative veto is a negative power; it stops or delays change. In terms of bringing forth new legislation, most presidents must rely on their political skills to sell initiatives to their legislatures. Only a very few presidents (those in Argentina, Brazil, and Chile) have decree powers whereby they can effectively proclaim something to take effect unless or until there is actual legislation on the issue.

Many presidential systems, but hardly all, also have a vice president, who is usually elected on the same ballot or "ticket" simultaneously with the president. However, in the Philippines, these offices are decided through separate ballots, so at times—most recently in 2010—the victorious president and vice president have been from different parties because of vote splitting. Palau also had separate ballots until 2008. In Zambia, the winning president then appoints a vice president. Vice presidents have, at best, a minimal role in terms of legislation and policy, and they mainly serve a succession function: they are next in line if something should happen to the president.[6] In the United States prior to the 25th Amendment of 1967, the government was without a serving vice president on many occasions, often for some years at a time. With respect to the legislature of these 30 democracies, lower house elections are sometimes fully concurrent with those for the president, meaning they are held on the same day and have the same term lengths. Concurrent elections maximize the likelihood of the president's party also controlling the lower (or single) house for the term. Non-concurrent terms and midterm legislative elections, on the other hand, have a check-and-balance effect.

A **parliamentary system** can also be viewed as having five aspects, listed here so as to provide a point-by-point contrast with a presidential system:

▶ the key day-to-day political position is that of the head of government (prime minister or equivalent), but this person is not the head of state; instead, there is almost always a separate head of state;

- ▸ the cabinet is much more of a collegial body than in presidential systems, making parliamentary cabinets amenable to coalition governments (and thus parliamentary governments not necessarily winner take all);

- ▸ the government is continually dependent for its survival on maintaining the confidence, or at least the acquiescence, of the parliament;

- ▸ consequently, the government can fall at any time during parliamentary sessions through a motion of non-confidence; and

- ▸ the head of government is not chosen directly by the voters but is ultimately selected by the legislature (in effect by its partisan composition, which is arrived at through elections).

Because of non-confidence motions, a parliamentary head of government does not have any constitutionally fixed minimum term of office, so, in some cases, people have lasted as prime minister for only a matter of days or weeks. Another variation involves how the head of government is selected. Following Arend Lijphart, we use the broad term "selected" because of a key difference between two methods.[7] In some parliamentary systems, there is a formal vote by the parliament on a would-be prime minister or cabinet. Winning this vote of investiture is necessary in order to assume office. Such a procedure is called *positive parliamentarianism* because it requires a positive endorsement of a new or continuing government (even if the voters have apparently already given this endorsement). In contrast, under *negative parliamentarianism*, there is no vote of investiture or "election" by the parliament that one must win. A prime minister and government are simply appointed, and they are assumed to be acceptable (they receive "negative" confirmation) unless or until there is a successful motion of non-confidence. When no party wins a majority, positive parliamentarianism is likely to lead to a majority coalition (so the government has the votes to be invested)[8] whereas negative parliamentarianism is likely to lead to a minority government of the largest party in the legislature. Because of this variation, it is also generally the case that it takes longer to form a government under positive parliamentarianism,[9] usually a month and sometimes several months. Broadly speaking, positive parliamentarianism is the more common version globally; however, the United Kingdom, Canada, and most other former British colonies use negative parliamentarianism, as do Austria, France, Portugal, and most Nordic countries.[10] Of course, majority coalitions *can* occur under negative parliamentarianism, such as happened in the United Kingdom in 2010.

Parliamentary systems obviously vary in terms of the strength of their heads of government. However, such variations relate more to contextual factors, such as whether the head of government is a party leader, how many seats the government has, and how many parties are in the government. In a coalition government of two or more parties, key policies and cabinet positions are worked out beforehand, leaving the head of government much less freedom to change policies or shuffle ministers than in a one-party government. These contextual variations can be shaped by institutions, such as positive versus negative parliamentarianism, but the key antecedent institution is probably the electoral system—which we shall get to later.

We can now note the various strengths and weaknesses of presidential and parliamentary systems, strengths and weaknesses that tend to be the mirror image of each other. Parliamentary systems can be unstable, with governments collapsing or changing frequently (as happened in Weimar Germany or Italy after World War II). However, if a parliamentary government has both a majority and policy consensus within this majority, then it is quite likely to get its legislation passed. In contrast, presidential systems are stable in the sense of the individual president remaining in office, but there is no guarantee of any desired legislation being passed if the president's party has little strength in the legislature. Thus, presidential systems are prone to a gridlock, which has no parliamentary equivalent. Indeed, a president may not even be able to count on members of her or his own party. In a parliamentary system, deputies almost never vote against a government of their own party because doing so could bring down this government; however, in a presidential system, there is no such constraint.

That said, within each system, various procedures can mitigate the likelihood of dysfunctional outcomes. In a parliamentary system, one effective procedure is to require a "constructive vote of non-confidence" so that, in order for a prime minister or government to be removed, there must be majority support for a designated alternative, which then takes over. Given its interwar parliamentary instability, postwar Germany chose this system, and there has been only one successful non-confidence vote in Germany after World War II (in 1982). Similar requirements for a "constructive vote of non-confidence" now exist in Belgium, Hungary, Lesotho, Poland, Slovenia, and Spain. A weaker but still useful variant of this procedure occurs in Portugal and Sweden, where an absolute majority of all deputies (not merely those

FIGURE 6.1 Liberal and Electoral Democracies, Systems of Government

PARLIAMENTARY (dual executive, with head of government accountable to legislature)				
MONARCHY		REPUBLIC		
parliamentary system with indigenous monarch	parliamentary system with governor general	parliamentary system with a figurehead president	parliamentary system with a presidential corrective	parliamentary system with presidential dominance

PRESIDENTIAL (single executive, not accountable to legislature)

MIXED

MIXED 1: dual executive, with prime minister directly elected (Israel 1996 to 2001)

MIXED 2: dual executive, with prime minister not accountable (Guyana, South Korea)

MIXED 3: single executive, accountable to legislature (Botswana, Kiribati, Marshall Islands, Nauru, South Africa)

MIXED 4: single executive, chosen by but not accountable to legislature (Micronesia, Suriname, Switzerland)

MIXED 5: co-executives, chosen by but not accountable to legislature (San Marino)

NOTE: All mixed systems are republics.

present and voting) is needed for a successful non-confidence motion. In a presidential system, in order to increase the president's support in the legislature, scholars have argued for having the entire legislature elected at the same time as the president, so as to maximize the president's "coat-tails effect," and for the same length of term—what we call a "concurrent" election. Certainly, having the legislature elected at a different time than the president tends to weaken the showing of the president's party in elections. For example, in the United States, the president's party almost always loses support in midterm Congressional elections.

Mixed Systems

Currently, the world's liberal and electoral democracies consist of some 71 pure parliamentary systems. Before subdividing these further, let us note the several systems that are neither presidential nor parliamentary but that we call "mixed." Figure 6.1 lists these. The first type has a dual executive, but the prime minister is elected directly using a popular vote separate from that for the legislature. This was the situation in Israel from 1996 through 2001, and it was also seriously discussed in the Netherlands in the 1960s and 1970s. Such a system is meant to counteract the instability that comes from a fragmented multi-party system. However, in Israel, if anything, this system exacerbated party fragmentation because people no longer had to vote for one of the larger parties in the hope that its leader would become prime minister. The second type has a dual executive but is effectively presidential because neither the president nor the prime minister is accountable to the legislature, and the president has the usual range of presidential powers. In countries with these systems (Guyana and South Korea), the prime minister is more of a "house leader" for the president, aiming to get legislation passed, than an independent political leader. The third and fourth types of mixed systems have a single executive and might, at first glance, seem fully presidential. However, in countries with the third type (Botswana, Kiribati, the Marshall Islands, Nauru, and South Africa), the president is accountable to the legislature and can be removed by a simple vote of non-confidence—as was the president of Nauru in 2004. Thus, they are more parliamentary than presidential. With the exception of Kiribati, these presidents are chosen by the legislatures and not directly by the voters—and, even in Kiribati, presidential candidates are picked by and from the House of Assembly.[11] In the fourth type of mixed system, the single executive president is chosen by the legislature but thereafter is not accountable to it. These systems enjoy presidential-like stability, but their presidents lack the legitimacy of direct election. Such a system is found in Micronesia, Suriname, and Switzerland (although Swiss presidents serve only a one-year rotating term). Finally, San Marino's mixed system is analogous to Switzerland's in that it has a rotating executive. However, San Marino has a leadership term of only six months, and there are *two* joint "captains-regent" (one each representing the city and the countryside). As noted in Figure 6.1, all mixed systems are republics.

Heads of State in Parliamentary Systems

Two key distinctions can be made concerning the heads of state in parliamentary systems. As Figure 6.1 demonstrates, the first involves the nature of the position: Is the head of state a monarch or a president? The second involves the position's power: Is the head of state a figurehead or a relevant actor? In a relatively small group of 12 parliamentary democracies, largely in Western and Northern Europe, there is an indigenous monarch as head of state (Belgium, Denmark, Japan, Lesotho, Liechtenstein, Luxembourg, the Netherlands, Norway, Spain, Sweden, Thailand, and the United Kingdom). Although, as Table 2.4 shows, the monarchs of two of these democracies (Liechtenstein and Thailand) are exceptions, these democratic monarchs have basically no political power; they "reign but do not rule" as figureheads.

As of October 2012, the 14 Commonwealth democracies that recognize the British monarch as head of state are also formally constitutional monarchies: Antigua and Barbuda, Australia, Bahamas, Barbados, Belize, Canada, Grenada, Jamaica, New Zealand, Papua New Guinea, Saint Kitts and Nevis, Saint Lucia, Saint Vincent and the Grenadines, and Tuvalu. In each of these Commonwealth realms, a local governor general (appointed for a fixed term) serves as the British monarch's representative and can be argued to be the country's effective head of state. However, those who wish to "cut the British link" want an indigenous president as head of state, as is the case in the remaining Commonwealth countries.[12]

The other parliamentary liberal and electoral democracies are all republics with a president as head of state. Some of these presidents are popularly elected by the voters; others are chosen by the national legislature or by the national legislature and regional politicians combined. These presidents, especially when elected, may exercise political power. These individual powers could be the same as those exercised by presidents in presidential systems plus the power to dissolve the legislature, which does not exist in pure presidential systems. Obviously, the more power exercised by the president as head of state, the less available to the head of government (the prime minister or equivalent), which weakens this office. Many scholars refer to parliamentary systems with strong presidents, such those in France and Russia (when Russia was democratic, anyway), as being "semipresidential," which is normally defined as having a directly elected president with various political powers but also a prime minister and cabinet accountable to the legislature (as well as to the president). This term is problematic, however, because such systems retain the most central feature of parliamentary democracy: the ability to remove the prime minister and cabinet through a vote of non-confidence. Thus, these systems can all be considered parliamentary, albeit with qualifications relating to the role and power of the head of state (our second key distinction for parliamentary democracies). Consequently, a threefold distinction is offered here,[13] as shown in Figure 6.1. First, there are 26 parliamentary systems with a president who is purely or effectively a figurehead, who normally plays only a symbolic role analogous to the one played by monarchs or governors general or who has maybe one modest or occasional power. These countries are Austria, Bangladesh, the Czech Republic, Dominica, Estonia, Finland since its 2000 constitution, Germany, Greece, Hungary, Iceland, India, Iraq, Israel once again after its "mixed-system" period, Italy, Latvia, Malta, Mauritius, Moldova, Montenegro, Pakistan, Samoa, Serbia, Slovakia, Slovenia, Trinidad and Tobago, and Vanuatu.[14] Six of these presidents are directly elected by the voters (those of Austria, Iceland, Montenegro, Serbia, Slovakia, and Slovenia), as will be the case in the Czech Republic from 2013.

However, in other parliamentary systems, the president does have political powers and usually can do some combination but not all of the following: make discretionary appointments, shape the cabinet in terms of including or excluding specific parties, chair cabinet meetings, veto legislation or send it to a referendum, issue emergency decreees, dissolve the legislature, and play the central role in foreign policy. These systems can be called "parliamentary systems with a presidential corrective," inasmuch as the president is able to intervene politically from time to time or control selected areas of governance or policy.[15] There are now 13 countries with this system, largely in Europe: Bulgaria, Croatia, Ireland, Kyrgyzstan, Lithuania, Macedonia, Mongolia, Poland, Portugal, Romania, Taiwan, Timor-Leste, and Turkey. In all these countries, presidents are directly elected or will be soon (Turkey's first presidential election will be in 2014).[16]

Finally, despite the apparent contradiction, there are parliamentary systems in which coalition governments, motions of non-confidence, and the like are possible but the president exercises most of the executive branch's political power; in other words, doing most if not all of the items listed above. These can be called "parliamentary systems with presidential dominance," but we should not forget that they are, ultimately, parliamentary, and, if parties hostile to the president gain control of the legislature, the president will be "demoted" to a corrective role. Currently, only six of these systems are liberal or electoral democracies: Cape Verde, Comoros, France, Namibia, Peru, and São Tomé and Príncipe. Note also that both Finland and Portugal had this system but then changed to ones with a weaker president. For their part, Russia and Ukraine have this system but are no longer democratic, and several other African countries (former colonies of France or Portugal) had this system but likewise have seen democracy break down. Consequently, France should be seen as the main stable example of this system in a democracy—and, in 2002, it changed its presidential and parliamentary election timing to minimize conflict between the president and the National Assembly.

Comparing Legislatures: Structural Distinctions

Let us now turn to variations across democratic legislatures. Table 6.2 provides information on these for all liberal and electoral democracies. In terms of more formal variations across legislatures, the first structural distinction to note is whether the legislature can exert independent policymaking, normally through a system of numerous standing committees that match government departments and that assess or can introduce legislation early on in the process. Such powerful committees are standard in presidential systems but exist in only a minority of parliamentary systems, such as those of most of continental Western Europe and of Japan. In contrast, the parliaments of the United Kingdom and its former colonies, as well as those of France after 1958 under the Fifth Republic, are known for weak committees and for legislatures that are more focused on debating and "grandstanding" than on policy details. In these parliaments, it is rare for any legislation to be changed greatly from the wishes of the cabinet.

Another structural distinction regarding legislatures, and a central one for us, is whether the legislature is *unicameral* (has one chamber) or *bicameral* (has two chambers). Most of the current liberal and electoral democracies are unicameral, but 46 (40 per cent) are bicameral. It is extremely rare for a country to add a new upper house to a unicameral legislature, although South Africa did this when it adopted a fully democratic constitution in 1994. Newly democratic Indonesia likewise added an upper house in 2004. In contrast, several democratic countries have abolished their upper houses: Denmark (in 1953), New Zealand (in 1951), Sri Lanka (in 1971), Sweden (in 1971), and Venezuela (in 2000).[17] Because bicameral systems are in the minority, we should ask the question "why bicameralism?" rather than "why unicameralism?" Two reasons can be offered. First, upper houses can provide a vehicle for regional interests, especially those of less populated regions that would be outvoted in the lower house. Second, upper houses can act as a counterbalance to the lower house, independent of any regional concerns. This counterbalancing has taken differing forms. Historically, upper houses were composed of nobles or of people elected on a more restricted franchise than the lower house. These upper houses served as a conservative "check" on the popularly elected lower houses. Today, such a rationale would be seen as unacceptably undemocratic. So the issue has become not so much that a lower house produces excessively radical legislation as that the lower house may produce hasty or ill-considered legislation that needs modification. Hence the expression in Canada that the Senate is the chamber of "sober second thought."

An alternative way of looking at the continued existence of bicameralism is to note which types of countries have bicameral systems. Two factors are relevant.

TABLE 6.2 Data on the National Legislatures of Liberal and Electoral Democracies (2012)

Country	Lower House Name	Number of Members*	Term (years)	Upper House Name	Number of Members*	Term (years)	Upper House Appointed or Directly or Indirectly Elected
Andorra	General Council	28	4	n/a	n/a	n/a	n/a
Antigua and Barbuda	House of Representatives	19	5	Senate	17	5	appointed
Argentina	Chamber of Deputies	257	4	Senate	72	6	directly elected
Australia	House of Representatives	150	3	Senate	76	6	directly elected
Austria	National Council	183	5	Federal Council	62	4 to 6	indirectly elected
Bahamas	House of Assembly	38	5	Senate	16	5	appointed
Bangladesh	National Parliament	350	5	n/a	n/a	n/a	n/a
Barbados	House of Assembly	30	5	Senate	21	5	appointed
Belgium	House of Representatives	150	4	Senate	71	4	40 directly / 21 appointed / 10 co-opted
Belize	House of Representatives	32	5	Senate	12	5	appointed
Benin	National Assembly	83	4	n/a	n/a	n/a	n/a
Bolivia	Chamber of Deputies	130	5	Chamber of Senators	36	5	directly elected
Botswana	National Assembly	63	5	n/a	n/a	n/a	n/a
Brazil	Chamber of Deputies	513	4	Federal Senate	81	8	directly elected
Bulgaria	National Assembly	240	4	n/a	n/a	n/a	n/a
Canada	House of Commons	308	5	Senate	105	until age 75	appointed
Cape Verde	National People's Assembly	72	5	n/a	n/a	n/a	n/a
Chile	Chamber of Deputies	120	4	Senate of the Republic	38	8	directly elected
Colombia	Chamber of Representatives	166	4·	Senate of the Republic	102	4	directly elected
Comoros	Assembly of the Union	33	5	n/a	n/a	n/a	n/a
Costa Rica	Legislative Assembly	57	4	n/a	n/a	n/a	n/a
Croatia	House of Representatives	151	4	n/a	n/a	n/a	n/a
Cyprus (Greek)	House of Representatives	80	5	n/a	n/a	n/a	n/a
Czech Republic	Chamber of Deputies	200	4	Senate	81	6	directly elected

Country	Lower House Name	Number of Members*	Term (years)	Upper House Name	Number of Members*	Term (years)	Upper House Appointed or Directly or Indirectly Elected
Denmark	Parliament	179	4	n/a	n/a	n/a	n/a
Dominica	Chamber of Assembly	31	5	n/a	n/a	n/a	n/a
Dominican Republic	House of Deputies	183	4	n/a	n/a	n/a	n/a
Ecuador	Chamber of Representatives	124	4	n/a	n/a	n/a	n/a
El Salvador	Legislative Assembly	84	3	n/a	n/a	n/a	n/a
Estonia	State Assembly	101	4	n/a	n/a	n/a	n/a
Finland	Parliament	200	4	n/a	n/a	n/a	n/a
France	National Assembly	577	5	Senate	348	6	indirectly elected
Germany	Federal Diet	598	4	Federal Council	69	varies	appointed by state governments
Ghana	National Assembly	230	4	n/a	n/a	n/a	n/a
Greece	Parliament	300	4	n/a	n/a	n/a	n/a
Grenada	House of Representatives	15	5	Senate	13	5	appointed
Guatemala	Congress of the Republic	158	4	n/a	n/a	n/a	n/a
Guyana	National Assembly	65	5	n/a	n/a	n/a	n/a
Honduras	National Congress	128	4	n/a	n/a	n/a	n/a
Hungary	National Assembly	386	4	n/a	n/a	n/a	n/a
Iceland	Althing (Parliament)	63	4	n/a	n/a	n/a	n/a
India	House of the People	543	5	Council of States	245	6	233 indirectly elected / 12 appointed
Indonesia	People's Representative Council	560	5	Regional Representative Council	132	5	directly elected
Iraq	Council of Representatives	325	4	n/a	n/a	n/a	n/a
Ireland	House of Representatives	166	5	Senate	60	5	49 elected / 11 appointed
Israel	Assembly of the Republic	120	4	n/a	n/a	n/a	n/a
Italy	Chamber of Deputies	630	5	Senate of the Republic	322	5	315 elected / 5 appointed / 2 ex-officio
Ivory Coast	National Assembly	255	5	n/a	n/a	n/a	n/a
Jamaica	House of Representatives	63	5	Senate	21	5	appointed
Japan	House of Representatives	480	4	House of Councillors	242	6	directly elected

Country	Lower House Name	Number of Members*	Term (years)	Upper House Name	Number of Members*	Term (years)	Upper House Appointed or Directly or Indirectly Elected
Kiribati	House of Assembly	45	4	n/a	n/a	n/a	n/a
Korea, South	National Assembly	300	4	n/a	n/a	n/a	n/a
Kyrgyzstan	Supreme Council	120	5	n/a	n/a	n/a	n/a
Latvia	Parliament	100	4	n/a	n/a	n/a	n/a
Lesotho	National Assembly	120	5	Senate	33	5	hereditary and appointed
Liberia	House of Representatives	73	6	Senate	30	9	directly elected
Liechtenstein	Diet	25	4	n/a	n/a	n/a	n/a
Lithuania	Parliament	141	4	n/a	n/a	n/a	n/a
Luxembourg	Chamber of Deputies	60	5	n/a	n/a	n/a	n/a
Macedonia	Assembly	123	4	n/a	n/a	n/a	n/a
Malta	House of Representatives	65	5	n/a	n/a	n/a	n/a
Marshall Islands	House of Representatives	33	4	n/a	n/a	n/a	n/a
Mauritius	National Assembly	62	5	n/a	n/a	n/a	n/a .
Mexico	Chamber of Deputies	500	3	House of Senators	128	6	directly elected
Micronesia	Congress	14	2	n/a	n/a	n/a	n/a
Moldova	Parliament	101	4	n/a	n/a	n/a	n/a
Mongolia	State Great Hural	76	4	n/a	n/a	n/a	n/a
Montenegro	Parliament	81	4	n/a	n/a	n/a	n/a
Namibia	National Assembly	72	5	National Council	26	6	indirectly elected
Nauru	Parliament	18	3	n/a	n/a	n/a	n/a
Netherlands	First Chamber	150	4	Second Chamber	75	4	indirectly elected
New Zealand	House of Representatives	120	3	n/a	n/a	n/a	n/a
Niger	National Assembly	113	5	n/a	n/a	n/a	n/a
Nigeria	House of Representatives	360	4	Senate	109	4	directly elected
Norway	Parliament	169	4	n/a	n/a	n/a	n/a
Pakistan	National Assembly	342	5	Senate	104	6	indirectly elected
Palau	House of Delegates	16	4	Senate	9	4	directly elected
Panama	Legislative Assembly	71	5	n/a	n/a	n/a	n/a
Papua New Guinea	National Parliament	111	5	n/a	n/a	n/a	n/a

Country	Lower House Name	Number of Members*	Term (years)	Upper House Name	Number of Members*	Term (years)	Upper House Appointed or Directly or Indirectly Elected
Paraguay	House of Deputies	80	5	House of Senators	45	5	directly elected
Peru	Congress of the Republic	130	5	n/a	n/a	n/a	n/a
Philippines	House of Representatives	286	3	Senate	24	6	directly elected
Poland	Chamber of Deputies	460	4	Senate	100	4	directly elected
Portugal	Assembly of the Republic	230	4	n/a	n/a	n/a	n/a
Romania	Chamber of Deputies	333	4	Senate	137	4	directly elected
Saint Kitts and Nevis	National Assembly	15	5	n/a	n/a	n/a	n/a
Saint Lucia	House of Assembly	18	5	Senate	11	5	appointed
Saint Vincent and the Grenadines	House of Assembly	22	5	n/a	n/a	n/a	n/a
Samoa (Western)	Legislative Assembly	49	5	n/a	n/a	n/a	n/a
San Marino	Grand General Council	60	5	n/a	n/a	n/a	n/a
São Tomé and Príncipe	National Assembly	55	4	n/a	n/a	n/a	n/a
Senegal	National Assembly	150	5	Senate	100	5	65 appointed / 35 indirectly elected
Serbia	National Assembly	250	4	n/a	n/a	n/a	n/a
Sierra Leone	Parliament	124	5	n/a	n/a	n/a	n/a
Slovakia	National Council	150	4	n/a	n/a	n/a	n/a
Slovenia	National Assembly	90	4	National Council	40	5	elected by interest organizations
South Africa	National Assembly	400	5	National Council of Provinces	90	5	indirectly elected
Spain	Congress of Deputies	350	4	Senate	266	4	208 directly elected / 58 appointed
Suriname	National Assembly	51	5	n/a	n/a	n/a	n/a
Sweden	Riksdagen (Parliament)	349	4	n/a	n/a	n/a	n/a
Switzerland	National Council	200	4	Council of States	46	4	directly elected
Taiwan	Legislative Yuan	113	4	n/a	n/a	n/a	n/a
Thailand	House of Representatives	500	4	Senate	150	6	77 directly / 73 indirectly elected
Timor-Leste (East Timor)	National Parliament	65	5	n/a	n/a	n/a	n/a

Country	Lower House Name	Number of Members*	Term (years)	Upper House Name	Number of Members*	Term (years)	Upper House Appointed or Directly or Indirectly Elected
Trinidad and Tobago	House of Representatives	41	5	Senate	31	5	appointed
Tunisia**	National Constituent Assembly	217	1	n/a	n/a	n/a	n/a
Turkey	Grand National Assembly	550	5	n/a	n/a	n/a	n/a
Tuvalu	Parliament	15	4	n/a	n/a	n/a	n/a
United Kingdom	House of Commons	650	5	House of Lords	827	life	appointed / hereditary ex-officio
United States	House of Representatives	435	2	Senate	100	6	directly elected
Uruguay	Chamber of Representatives	99	5	House of the Senate	31	5	directly elected
Vanuatu	Parliament	52	4	n/a	n/a	n/a	n/a
Zambia	National Assembly	158	5	n/a	n/a	n/a	n/a

* The values for number of members are for the base number of members, not the actual number of current members.

** To be replaced by a new parliament once a new constitution is approved.

SOURCE: Inter-Parliamentary Union, PARLINE Database on National Parliaments, accessed October 2012, http://www.ipu.org/parline-e/ParliamentsAtaGlance.asp.

The first is size: small countries having fewer citizens tend to be unicameral, larger and presumably more diverse countries, bicameral. Indeed, the upper houses in larger countries generally have a fixed regional composition. The second factor is federalism; as we shall see, federal systems are invariably bicameral. One factor that might seem relevant here is whether a country has a presidential system and its logic of "checks and balances"—not so. Of the 30 presidential systems in Table 6.1, only 6 are federal, which hardly indicates a pronounced relationship between bicameralism and presidentialism.

Variations across the Two Chambers

What variations occur between the lower and upper houses in bicameral liberal and electoral democracies? Five main differences are worth noting. The first difference is chamber size: lower houses are almost always larger than their corresponding upper houses. Only in the United Kingdom is this not the case (in fact, its House of Lords used to be even bigger until most of the hereditary lords were removed from it). The second difference is length of term; these are normally longer for upper houses. For example, United States senators serve terms of six years, three times the two-year term of House members. Canadian senators used to be appointed for life; now they must resign at age 75, but they certainly have job security. However, one should not be too biased by these North American figures; in many countries, the term length is the same for both houses (for example, in Bolivia, Colombia, Ireland, Poland, and Switzerland). The third difference is selection procedure; members of the lower house are invariably directly elected, but one gets to be a member of an upper house through a variety of ways: direct election, indirect election by a regional assembly (itself directly elected), appointment, and, in some cases, by gaining or inheriting ex-officio member status (as do the royal children in Belgium). Where indirect election occurs, often the regional assemblies will select some of their own for this additional job. The fourth difference is that, at least for the elected upper houses, these elections tend to be staggered so that only some individuals are elected at any one time (in any one year).[18] Staggered elections are extremely rare in lower houses, existing only in Argentina, where one-half of the Chamber of Deputies is elected every two years for a four-year term. (The Luxembourg Chamber of Deputies also had staggered elections until 1954.) At best, elections may be spread over a couple of weeks, as in India, Papua New Guinea, or nineteenth-century Canada; however, this staggering is a matter of logistics and not a "check and balance."

The fifth and final difference is that upper houses are normally weaker than lower houses in two senses—government formation and legislative power. The normal process of government formation in parliamentary systems is that only the lower house selects the government, so only lower house elections matter for coming to office. (Italy is an exception to this situation; there, the government must maintain the confidence of both houses.) Of course, in bicameral presidential systems, neither house plays this role in government formation. The second point is that, whereas lower houses have to pass legislation for it to become law, the consent of the upper house is not always required. Objections or modifications to legislation by the upper house can often be overcome by the lower house passing the legislation again after a set period of time. This is the pattern in the United Kingdom, for example. Obviously, then, an upper house that cannot actually stop or modify any legislation significantly is much weaker than one that can.

Arend Lijphart argues that, for bicameralism to be **strong bicameralism**, in which the upper house truly matters, three factors must be present.[19] First, both houses must be equal or relatively equal in terms of legislative powers. Second, the upper house must have the legitimacy to use its powers. Legitimacy normally comes from direct elections, but it could also involve, as in Germany, the upper house representing elected regional governments. In any case, Canada's appointed Senate is a perfect counter-example here. Finally, the upper house must be composed or selected in a different way from the lower house; most commonly, this difference involves changing the allocation of members to benefit less-populated regions, but it may also involve a unique electoral system for each chamber or even having the two chambers elected at different times (assuming the upper house is elected). If the upper house is chosen in more or less the same way as the lower house and at the same time, it should be no surprise that its partisan composition will look the same; thus, one party or a coalition would presumably control both houses. Chile, Romania, and Uruguay are the main examples of this "duplicate" pattern.[20] In short, relatively few democracies—Argentina, Australia, Brazil, Colombia, Germany, Italy, Mexico, the Philippines, Switzerland, and the United States—meet these three criteria of strong bicameralism. Note that a majority of these are presidential systems. Yet, in a parliamentary system with strong bicameralism and different parties or alliances controlling the lower and upper houses, the government, which is based in the lower house, may be stable but will often find it very difficult to get legislation through. In Australia, when legislation fails to get through the upper house twice, the prime minister may dissolve both houses. Of course, the resulting "*double dissolution*" election puts the government—and the prime minister's job—on the line. Should such an Australian government be re-elected yet still be unable to get the legislation through the new Senate, then a *joint sitting* of the House of Representatives and the Senate takes place, and the numerical superiority of the House is usually decisive in passing the legislation.[21] In Germany, a "double dissolution" and a consequent joint sitting are not options because the German upper house is indirectly elected, so the Germans have taken to using the term *Reformstau* ("political gridlock") to describe a situation of differing partisan control of the chambers.

Comparing Legislatures: Gender Variations

Legislatures also vary in terms of the dominant demographic characteristics of their members: age, education, gender, and occupational background. Consequently, as noted in Chapter 4, we can assess a legislature's demographic patterns in comparison to those in the broader society as a whole. Of these characteristics, the one most thoroughly studied in a global sense is gender: To what extent is a legislature relatively balanced between men and women?[22] Again, as noted, women comprise exactly half the legislature in Andorra but less than half of the deputies in every other democratic national parliament in the world. At the extreme, as of October 2012, there were no women in the parliaments of some democracies in Oceania: Micronesia, Nauru, and Palau. Besides looking at the extremes, we can also dichotomize the world's legislatures in terms of whether the female minority nevertheless amounts to a **critical mass** of around 30 per cent—the scholarly consensus suggests that, when women reach such a critical mass, they will have a clear effect on a legislature in terms of both its general behaviour, which will become less antagonistic, its policy priorities, and the resulting policies. Looking at the legislatures of the world's democracies or, more precisely, looking only at the lower chambers in the bicameral systems because, as noted, these are almost always the more important chambers, we see that, as of October 2012, such a critical mass of female deputies exists in only 21 of the 113 liberal and electoral democracies. In descending order of female percentages, these democracies are Andorra, Sweden, Finland, South Africa, the Netherlands, Iceland, Norway, Denmark, Costa Rica, Belgium, Argentina, Spain, Taiwan, Germany, Serbia, Ecuador, Timor-Leste, New Zealand, Slovenia, Guyana, and Macedonia. Note that almost all of these countries use proportional representation, and the others in this list do so in part (see Chapter 7). They generally also exhibit political leftism or progressivism—both as a broader national ideology and in terms of the strength of leftist parties—combined with non-traditional cultural values.

Federalism

The previous discussion of upper houses leads us to an analysis of federalism. Nearly every liberal democracy or electoral democracy, unless it is very tiny, has local governments: e.g., governments for townships, counties, communes, and municipalities. These need not be elected, and, even if they are, such governments are not constitutionally guaranteed. In any case, the real issue is the number of levels of government that come between the national and the local one. At one extreme is the unitary state, which has no regional governments, merely a national government with most of the

TABLE 6.3 Liberal and Electoral Democracies, Federal Systems (2012)

Country	Federal Since	Key Constituent Parts Today	Origins of Federalism**
Argentina	1853	23 provinces and 1 autonomous city (federal capital)	coming together
Australia	1901	6 states, 1 territory, and 1 capital territory	coming together
Austria	1918	9 Lander (provinces)	coming together
Belgium	1993	3 regions and 3 cultural communities (overlapping)	holding together
Brazil	1891	26 states and 1 federal capital district	mixed
Canada	1867	10 provinces and 3 territories	mixed
Germany	1871/1919/1949	16 Lander (states)	mixed
India	1950	28 states, 6 union territories, and 1 national capital territory	holding together
Indonesia*	2004	29 provinces, 9 special regions, and 1 special capital region	holding together
Iraq*	2005	18 governorates (provinces), 3 of which comprise the Iraqi Kurdistan region	holding together
Mexico	1917	31 states and 1 federal district	holding together
Micronesia	1986	4 states	coming together
Nigeria	1947	36 states and 1 federal capital territory	holding together
Pakistan	1947/1973	4 provinces, 2 autonomous territories, federally administered tribal areas, and 1 federal capital territory	holding together
South Africa*	1994	9 provinces	holding together
Spain*	1978	17 autonomous communities and 2 autonomous cities	holding together
Switzerland	1848	26 cantons	coming together
United States	1789	50 states and 1 federal district	coming together

* borderline cases of federalism
** Alfred Stepan's categories of how federalism evolves are used here.

SOURCES: Forum of Federations, *Handbook of Federal Countries 2005*, ed. Ann L. Griffiths (Montreal, QC and Kingston, ON: McGill-Queen's University Press, 2005); Alfred Stepan, "Toward a New Comparative Politics of Federalism, (Multi) Nationalism, and Democracy: Beyond Rikerian Federalism," in *Arguing Comparative Politics*, 315–62 (New York, NY: Oxford University Press, 2001); author's additions.

power and all of the sovereignty, and usually some local governments. **Federalism** goes well beyond: a federal state (1) has regional governments and (2) gives these regional governments constitutionally entrenched powers and some sort of national role. In other words, federalism involves a combination of "elements of *shared-rule* through common institutions and *regional self-rule* for the governments of the constituent units."[23] Table 6.3 gives the 18 liberal or electoral democracies that are constitutionally federal or effectively federal. Note that these form a very small percentage of all liberal and electoral democracies. In short, federalism is a rare political phenomenon. Considered as a group, these countries tend to be large in area or culturally diverse or both; again, this diversity is usually regionally concentrated.

A full definition of federalism has no fewer than five features:

► two autonomous levels of government—central (federal) and regional—with each being directly elected and accountable;

► a formal division of authority specifying the powers and sources of revenue held by each level of government (each level thus, in some ways, acts directly on the citizens), as well as the level that holds the residual powers;

► a written constitution that, among other things, sets out the respective powers of each level of government and that can be changed only with some difficulty or with broad agreement;

► a supreme court to, among other things, arbitrate between the central and regional governments when there are disputes over whether one level of government may act in a certain way; and

► a bicameral legislature in which the lower house represents the people as a whole but the upper house represents the regions or the people in each region. Normally, the composition of the upper house will be weighted to a lesser or greater extent in favour of the less populous regions, whereas that of the lower house is based more purely on population, which is obviously to the advantage of the more populous regions.[24]

The first four of these features speak to what is called *interstate federalism,* that is, the divisions and relations *between* the two levels of government. The last feature, in contrast, speaks to what is called *intrastate federalism,* that is, the role of the regions or regional governments *within* the national political institutions (or, if one prefers, their role in the national capital). If we view federalism in terms of these component parts, then strong interstate federalism means that the regions "matter" as regions in terms of policy areas, taxing and spending, and generally having an effect on the lives of those who live in them. In contrast, strong intrastate federalism means that the regions, especially the smaller ones, are important in a powerful upper house that produces national policy outcomes different from those one would get if power rested solely on the population-based lower house. Figure 6.2 gives a crude attempt to situate the federal systems considering these two dimensions. Thus, in Canada, for example, the provinces as provinces matter within their borders, but provincial voters are unable to use an effective Senate to counteract the weight of the two most populous provinces, Ontario and Quebec, in the House of Commons. This "incompleteness" is also found in some other systems. However, the most common subgroup of federalism consists of those systems that feature both relevant regional governments and strong bicameralism (to use the earlier term) in which the upper house is weighted toward the less populous areas. The government of the United States is the standard example here. The least common pattern is found in Argentina and Mexico, which have strong bicameralism but weak regional governments—the polar opposite to Canadian federalism. Of course, Mexico is a relatively recent electoral democracy, so its situation may well evolve. Finally, it is worth noting that the countries that are stronger on intrastate federalism tend to be more homogeneous than those that are weaker. This is perhaps because, in more heterogeneous societies, the emphasis has been on regional autonomy, which is often asymmetrically granted in favour of the more "distinct" regions, rather than on checking and balancing the national government.

Alfred Stepan has noted that federalism evolved in three different ways, which he calls "coming together," "holding together," and "putting together" federations.[25] Under "coming together" federalism, which incorrectly has often been seen as the only way to achieve this political system, various distinct parts—which may be sovereign entities or simply separate colonies—more or less freely agree to form a single political entity. This formation involves some sort of conference or convention at which the "founding fathers" of the country work out details. Because unanimity is required, even the smallest component parts will have a lot of say in the initial set-up. The United States is the classic example of this route to a federal structure, but it also occurred in various other countries (see Table 6.3). The second variant, "holding together" federalism, begins with a sovereign, unitary state. However, centrifugal tendencies and demands from certain regions for autonomy (if not outright independence) push the system toward federalism as an alternative to the breakup of the country or the loss of some of its territory. Thus, federalism is a means to "hold together" a polity, hence the term. Obviously, regional demands must not only exist but also reach a certain undefined level for the centre to "give in" and agree to this change. Both the amount of time for the change and the amount of time the country spent as a unitary state beforehand can vary. Belgium is a good example of

FIGURE 6.2 Liberal and Electoral Democracies, Comparative Federal Systems

INTRASTATE FEDERALISM
(regions, especially the smaller ones, are
important via a strong upper house)

	LESS SO	**MORE SO**
MORE SO	Canada India Micronesia Spain	Australia Brazil Germany Switzerland United States
LESS SO	Austria Belgium Indonesia Iraq Nigeria Pakistan South Africa	Argentina Mexico

INTERSTATE FEDERALISM
(regional governments have
policy importance, especially
re. taxing and spending)

the slowness of these processes. Changes toward federalism began in 1971 but were not completed until its constitutional accord of 1993. Yet, for a century and a half before 1970 (from 1830 onwards, to be precise), Belgium existed as a centralized unitary state. On the other hand, federalism in India arose only three years after its independence and was created more because of the foresight of its national leaders. Finally, "putting together" federalism is the non-democratic variant: sovereign entities are conquered or forced into a theoretically federal entity. The creation in 1922 of the Union of Soviet Socialist Republics, to use its full name, is Stepan's standard example here. Of course, as Stepan notes, countries can combine some or all of these routes; for example, elements of all three existed in Canada from the conquest of Quebec in 1759 through 1867.

Alternatives to Federalism

Federalism is but one of many forms of multilevel political organization. As Figure 6.3 shows, the nine different types of multilevel political organization relate to each other on two different dimensions. The first involves centralization versus decentralization

FIGURE 6.3 Federalism and Its Alternatives

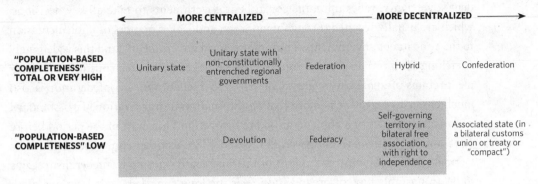

NOTE: Everything within the shaded area involves only one sovereign polity.

and is fairly self-evident in Figure 6.3. However, there is a second dimension, which we call "population-based completeness," that is, the extent to which the specific political organization applies on all levels to the entire population.

Let us start by looking at situations in which this "completeness" is perfect or close to it. We have already distinguished between a *federation,* with its two levels of government and related features, and a *unitary state,* with but one level of government above the local one. Examples of unitary states are Estonia, Greece, Iceland, and New Zealand—all rather small places. In between a federation and a unitary state, though, are countries with regional governments and, indeed, with regional governments that are elected, as they are in a federation. However, in these states, regional governments and their powers are not "protected" by being entrenched in the constitution. Consequently, these regions could be abolished, merged, or have their powers reduced, and they have no legal right to prevent such changes. Of course, central governments might rarely choose to do such things so as to avoid annoying the public, but they could. Countries with this type of political organization are Bolivia, Colombia, France, Italy, Japan, Peru, Poland, Slovakia, and Sweden. In Sweden, regional governments have existed for centuries; in the other cases, they are much more recent. In fact, Italy seems to be moving somewhat toward full federalism, but it is not there yet.

Moving away from a federation toward the most decentralized system with "population-based completeness" brings us to a **confederation**. A confederation is a group of sovereign entities forming a common government for specific and limited purposes, such as defence or economics. This common government has no independent sovereignty; relies upon the constituent governments to take all key decisions, which are usually reached through unanimity; and leaves matters of implementation to the constituent governments. Thus, the "central government" (and this is definitely stretching the term) does not act directly on the citizens, and each constituent government retains ultimate sovereignty. Compared to a federation, a confederation is also much easier to leave—it is more like an international organization. Two standard historical examples of a confederation are Switzerland for most of the period before 1848 and the United States between 1776 and 1789. Another confederation was the German Zollverein (customs union) of the nineteenth century. Confederalism seems to be an unstable type of organization over the long run, and confederations often evolve into federations, as did the previously mentioned examples, or they dissolve. Two recent examples of confederal dissolution are Senegambia in 1989 and Serbia and Montenegro in 2006. The European Union (EU) is often called a confederation, although this classification does not seem appropriate, especially since the Maastricht Treaty of 1993, if not, indeed, earlier. On the other hand, the EU is clearly not yet a federation (and there is strong debate on this goal), and its component countries still retain considerable sovereignty even if they have "pooled" their sovereign rights in an ever-increasing number of areas. The EU is best thought of as a sort of *hybrid* between confederation and federation, as indicated in Figure 6.3.

We turn now to situations of low "population-based completeness." The first variant is currently called *devolution* in the United Kingdom, but, until the 1920s, it was known as "home rule." Historically, devolution involved demands by the Celtic peripheral areas—Ireland especially but also Scotland and Wales—for their own assemblies so they would not be so dependent on the English-dominated government in London. The creation of the Irish Free State in 1922, after decades of the British government trying to find a "solution" to Irish demands, largely pushed this issue off the table, although Northern Ireland retained its own assembly from 1921 until 1972. In the latter year, the government in London first prorogued the Northern Irish Assembly (seeing it as contributing to the local political violence) and then abolished it, something that obviously could not occur under true federalism. In the 1970s, demands for local assemblies resurfaced, although now these were stronger in Scotland and Wales. In 1978, referenda on devolution were held in those two areas but were unsuccessful. Further demands were largely resisted, however, by the Conservative governments of Margaret Thatcher (1979–90) and John Major (1990–97). Still, by the end of the

1990s, an elected Scottish parliament and elected Welsh and Northern Irish assemblies were established or re-established under a Labour government. These bodies, though, especially in Wales and Northern Ireland, are quite weak compared to, say, a provincial legislature in Canada. Devolution also exists in the Philippines with respect to the Autonomous Region in Muslim Mindanao.

Where is the low "population-based completeness" in all of this? One should remember that, under federalism, every citizen also lives in a constituent part of the federation. For example, all Canadians live in either a province or a territory. Likewise, each and every constituent part (1) has its own legislature *and* (2) is represented in the national legislature. These patterns are also true for the polities with non-constitutionally entrenched regional governments everywhere. Under devolution, however, the "main part" normally does not have its own, separate legislature. There is no separate assembly or parliament for England the way there is for Scotland, Wales, and Northern Ireland, for example. Consequently, over 80 per cent of the United Kingdom's population is not represented by any regional government. (This figure leaves aside the elected Greater London Assembly, but, even if one generously calls this a regional parliament, the rest of England—some 70 per cent of the total UK population—has only the national government and local government.)

The next variation of political organization is called a *federacy*. This type also involves a smaller region (at least in the sense of population) but one with considerable constitutionally entrenched autonomy from the larger unitary state of which it is a part. The relationship can be changed only by mutual agreement between the federacy and the central government. So what a federacy amounts to is a federal-like arrangement for a specific territory within a unitary state. This territory is normally geographically separate from the main part of the country and is linguistically different or unique in some other way. It may even have cultural-historical ties to a neighbouring state. Thus, a federacy is an asymmetrical unit of government with "special status" that still keeps the territory part of the country—and avoids full federalism.[26] Examples of federacies are the Faroe Islands within Denmark, the Åland Islands within Finland, the five "regions of special statute" within Italy,[27] the Azores and Madeira within Portugal, and Bougainville within Papua New Guinea. All of these territories have very small populations. Although some consider Puerto Rico a federacy of the United States, this designation is not quite correct. First of all, the United States is a federal, not a unitary, system. Second, Puerto Rico is not a constituent part of the United States. Consequently, Puerto Rico has only a single commissioner in the

United States House of Representatives (who is free to speak but can only vote and introduce legislation). Moreover, its residents—though United States citizens—cannot vote for the president unless they move to the United States mainland.[28]

Even more autonomy can be granted to a small region by giving it the right to determine its own future, including independence if and when it wishes. Such a territory is self-governing (except for in matters of defence, foreign affairs, and usually some other areas), but it is not sovereign. In Figure 6.3, we call a political entity in this situation "a self-governing territory in bilateral free association, with a right to independence." Some sort of treaty or equivalent will define this association. Most eastern Caribbean islands went through this stage prior to independence from the United Kingdom. Current examples are the Cook Islands with New Zealand (since 1965), Niue Island with New Zealand (since 1974), and Aruba with the Netherlands (since 1986). Greenland, which was a federacy like the Faroe Islands, now has this status vis-à-vis Denmark as of the 2009 Act on Greenland Self-Government (following a 2008 referendum in Greenland). In theory, Jammu and Kashmir is self-governing in association with India; however, India has never recognized that region's right to self-determination, merely granting it special autonomy as a state. Finally, the 1998 Nouméa Accord established an ongoing transition to a similar state of affairs for New Caledonia with respect to France, created a New Caledonian citizenship, and provided for a referendum on independence to be held sometime between 2014 and 2019.

Last, a small sovereign country may wish to have formal links with a larger country; e.g., to have the larger country take care of its defence or to use the currency of the larger country. The "larger country" may or may not have been the colonial power formerly ruling the smaller one. This small sovereign territory becomes an *associated state* of the larger country. The two countries will have a formal bilateral treaty—or a customs union if their relationship is merely economic. Formal sovereignty is retained by each part, and either can end the relationship (as in a confederation). However, the relationship is clearly asymmetrical in that one speaks of the smaller country being associated with the larger country, never the other way around. Given this asymmetry, the relationship is effectively one of low "population-based completeness." Long-lasting examples of associated states are Bhutan with India (associated since 1949), Liechtenstein with Switzerland (associated since 1923), Monaco with France (associated since 1919), and San Marino with Italy (associated since 1862). Interestingly, neither Bhutan nor Monaco is a democracy, although of course India and France, respectively, are. More recent examples of associated states are the Marshall Islands and Micronesia, each of which signed a Compact of Free Association with the United States to define their post-independence relationship. These "compacts" took effect in 1986. A similar compact was reached with Palau in 1993. Their main benefit to the United States is the maintenance of military bases in these countries; in return, the associate states each receive substantial funds.[29]

Notes

1   In a weaker version of restrictions on re-election, the president has to spend a term out of office before being able to run again. Chile, the Dominican Republic, and Uruguay are examples here. In Panama and now in Costa Rica, two terms must elapse before a former president can run again. The change in Costa Rica thus allowed Óscar Arias Sánchez, the president from 1986 to 1990 (during which time he won the Nobel Peace Prize), to return to office in the 2006 presidential election.

2   This pattern did not become common in Latin America until the 1990s, when Argentina, Brazil, and Venezuela all changed their respective constitutions to permit immediate re-election to a second term. Colombia did the same in 2005. Autocratic Venezuela would later abolish term limits.

3   An equivalent "lame duck" status also applies to a second-term prime minister in the parliamentary system of Andorra and Thailand, the prime ministers of which are constitutionally limited to two consecutive complete terms.

4   As Table 6.1 shows, since re-democratization in Chile, one requires an absolute majority to be elected president.

5   Until 1994, Argentina also picked its president via an electoral college.

6   Jody C. Baumgartner and Rhonda Evans Case, "Constitutional Design of the Executive: Vice Presidencies in Comparative Perspective," *Congress and the Presidency* 36, no. 2 (2009): 148–163.

7   Arend Lijphart, *Patterns of Democracy: Government Forms and Performance in Thirty-Six Countries* (New Haven, CT: Yale University Press, 1999), 117.

8   A majority coalition is certainly likely if an absolute majority of deputies must vote in favour of a new government for it to win the vote of investiture.

9   Torbjörn Bergman, "Constitutional Design and Government Formation: The Expected Consequences of Negative Parliamentarianism," *Scandinavian Political Studies* 16, no. 4 (December 1993): 285–304, see 287–89.

10 Some clarification is needed here on Portugal and Sweden. Formally, both appear to involve positive parliamentarianism in that there is an actual vote of investiture. However, in each case, the government does not have to "win" the vote in the sense of having more votes in favour than against; it merely has to ensure or hope that there is not an absolute majority of votes (of the eligible deputies) against it. In other words, both formal abstentions and absences count on the government side. For example, in Sweden in 1981, a government was invested with 102 votes in favour, 174 votes against, 62 abstentions, and 11 absences (of the 349 deputies). See Bergman, "Constitutional Design," 297.

Consequently, then, both Portugal and Sweden should be considered to have negative parliamentarianism *in effect*. In contrast, Luxembourg and the Netherlands do not formally require a vote of investiture, but each normally undertakes such a vote, so, effectively, they have positive parliamentarianism. Likewise in India, the convention is that there is a vote of investiture, but the president may not require this if it is obvious that the new government has a clear majority of support.

11   Despite the worldwide recognition of Nelson Mandela, he was never directly elected by South African voters (although he would have won). Mandela was elected unopposed by the National Assembly in 1994 and so was his successor as president, Thabo Mbeki, in both 1999 and 2004. That said, in 2008, Mbeki would resign after having lost the support of his party—also a parliamentary, not a presidential, outcome. (Since 2008, elections of the South African president by the National Assembly have involved a contested vote with an opposition candidate.) Certainly for the third type of mixed system, parliamentary elections and support are what ultimately determine the single-person executive. However, the real-world cases assigned to this category are complicated by the relatively unusual natures of their party systems (see the next chapter). On the one hand, Botswana and South Africa each have had one and only one dominant party in power since independence and democratization respectively. On the other hand, Kiribati, the Marshall Islands, and Nauru all lack political parties.

12   Australia held a referendum on making such a change in 1999, but it was unsuccessful.

13   Taken from Alan Siaroff, "Comparative Presidencies: The Inadequacy of the Presidential, Semi-Presidential, and Parliamentary Distinction," *European Journal of Political Research* 42, no. 3 (May 2003): 287–312.

14   Effectively, Andorra also fits here, even though it has *two* figurehead heads of state, representing, respectively, the president of France and the Bishop of Seo de Urgell in Spain.

15   The term corrective has a positive normative connotation, and that is the standard reality—but not always. In Weimar Germany, the corrective powers of the preseident were used when needed by the first president, Friedrich Ebert, but in ways that supported the democratic order and party government. The second president, Paul von Hindenburg, alsu used these powers reasonably in his first term. However, once re-elected in 1932, the aged Hindenburg quickly and repeatedly abused the presidential powers of appointing and dismissing chancellors and dissolving the parliament, greatly contributing to the breakdown of Weimar democracy. On the Weimar president, see Gordon Smith, *Democracy in Western Germany: Parties and Politics in the Federal Republic*, 3rd ed. (New York, NY: Holmes and meier, 1986), 19–21, 27–29.

16   Constitutional changes approved in a 2007 referendum mean that future Turkish presidents will be popularly elected for a five-year term. However, the seven-year presidential term of current President Gül runs until 2014, so the first presidential election will not be until then.

17   Though not democratic now, each of Sri Lanka and Venezuela were democratic at the time of this change.

18   Lijphart, *Patterns of Democracy*, 205.

19   Lijphart, *Patterns of Democracy*, 211.

20   This "duplicate pattern" used to be the situation in Italy, but elections to the House of Representatives (the lower house) now involve a large national bonus given to the leading coalition so that it will enjoy a clear majority, whereas elections to the Senate (the upper house) involve only smaller,

regional bonuses. Thus, in Italy's 2006 election, the Olive Tree coalition won a comfortable majority in the lower house but only a one-seat majority in the upper house.

21   Joint sittings also occur in the weak bicameralism of India, requiring only one rejection of specific legislation by the upper house and no intervening election.

22   The Inter-Parliamentary Union is an invaluable source of data and analysis on this issue: see http://www.ipu.org/.

23   Ronald L. Watts, *Comparing Federal Systems*, 2nd ed. (Montreal, QC, and Kingston, ON: McGill-Queen's University Press, 1999), 7.

24   The Federated States of Micronesia fits the spirit if not strictly the letter of this feature. That is, the Congress in Micronesia is unicameral but functions in various ways more like a bicameral system. First of all, two different types of members are elected: one at-large member from each state (thus four of these) and ten local constituency members. These ten local congressional districts are allocated based on population, although each state must have at least one. (Currently, the allocations from biggest to smallest state are 5, 3, 1, and 1.) Moreover, the "state-at-large" members are elected for four years, whereas the local constituency members are elected for only two years. This arrangement parallels the pattern of upper house members serving longer terms than lower house members. Then, in terms of passing legislation, two readings are required: first, a bill must pass in the Congress overall (by a two-thirds vote), and then, in a final reading on a later day, each state delegation casts one block vote (again, with two-thirds needed to pass). Likewise, presidential vetoes are overridden by congress members voting as state delegations; each delegation casts one vote, and at least three of the four delegations are needed to override the veto.

25   Alfred Stepan, "Toward a New Comparative Politics of Federalism, (Multi) Nationalism, and Democracy: Beyond Rikerian Federalism," in *Arguing Comparative Politics*, 315–62 (New York, NY: Oxford University Press, 2001), 320–23.

26   Alfred Stepan, Juan J. Linz, and Yogendra Yadav, *Crafting State-Nations: India and Other Multinational Democracies* (Baltimore, MD: Johns Hopkins University Press, 2011), Chapter Seven: "Federacy: A Formula for Democratically Managing Multinational Societies in Unitary States." They also provide the following ideal-type definition of federacy (p. 204): "A federacy is a political-administrative unit in an independent unitary state with exclusive power in certain areas, including some legislative power, constitutionally or quasi-constitutionally embedded, that cannot be changed unilaterally and whose inhabitants have full citizenship rights in the otherwise unitary state."

27   Three of these are linguistically distinct: German-speaking South Tyrol, French-speaking Valle d'Aosta, and largely Slovene-speaking Friuli-Venezia Giulia; the other two are islands off the mainland: Sicily and Sardinia.

28   On the relationship between Puerto Rico and the United States, see David A. Rezvani, "The Basis of Puerto Rico's Constitutional Status: Colony, Compact, or 'Federacy'?" *Political Science Quarterly* 122, no. 1 (Spring 2007): 115–140. Note that he uses federacy in a less restrictive sense than we do, not requiring representation in the national government.

29   Note that some scholars use the term "associated state" to apply to the last two categories; however, we wish to make a distinction based on the key difference of sovereignty, so we reserve the term for the last category.

CHAPTER SEVEN

Electoral Systems, Party Systems, and Government Formation in Democracies

IN THIS CHAPTER YOU WILL LEARN

- ▶ what the components of an electoral system are;
- ▶ what the various electoral systems used in the world's democracies are, and how their individual mechanics differ;
- ▶ how electoral systems vary in terms of proportionality and its inverse, disproportionality—the latter being what scholars actually calculate in terms of an election;
- ▶ what some precise ways of measuring party system fragmentation are;
- ▶ what the six main types of party systems defined in terms of fragmentation and competition are and the differences between them;
- ▶ what the differences between more and less institutionalized party systems are, and how democracies divide in terms of this distinction;
- ▶ how and why party system institutionalization matters for democratic performance and stability;
- ▶ what the variations in government formation rules and conventions are; and
- ▶ what the alternatives to a formal cabinet coalition are.

Electoral Systems

Regardless of the institutional distinctions outlined in the previous chapter, all democracies have legislatures elected in more or less free and fair elections. But how, exactly, are these legislatures elected? In the first part of this chapter, we examine the various electoral systems used to elect the lower house or single chamber in all the liberal and electoral democracies in the world. Electoral systems have enormous consequences for what government is formed, or at least for which party dominates the chamber in a presidential system. However, it is incorrect, or at least too broad, to consider an electoral system to be the method of electing a *government*. Rather, an **electoral system** determines the partisan composition of the legislature by establishing, in the words of Farrell, "*the means by which votes are translated into seats in the process of electing politicians into office.*"[1]

Four aspects of an electoral system are useful for analytical purposes: district magnitude, electoral formula, ballot structure, and total size of the legislature. The first three are the most central.[2] By **district magnitude**, we mean the number of seats to be filled in an electoral district. At one extreme, Israel, Kyrgyzstan, Moldova, the Netherlands, Serbia, and Slovakia elect their parliaments in a single national calculation; thus, they each have only one district. Everywhere else, however, the country is divided into various electoral districts or constituencies.[3] For each district in a country, then, we need to know how many members are being elected—this is the district magnitude. In the United Kingdom, each of its 650 constituencies elects one member to the House of Commons; thus, the district magnitude is one, as it is in Canada and the United States. Conversely, in Israel, the district magnitude is 120 (the size of the *Knesset*). The district magnitude is likewise equal to the number of seats in the legislature or chamber in Moldova at 104, in the Netherlands and Slovakia at 150, and in Serbia at 250. As long as elections are not decided by a winner-take-all electoral formula, then, the larger the district magnitude, the greater the proportionality.[4] Finally, a country with multiple districts does not have to have the same district magnitude in each district; indeed, this will not be the case if the districts vary in population. The *electoral formula* is the precise calculation within each district and, sometimes, regionally or nationally that allocates the seats amongst the competing candidates and parties. Although, in theory, an infinite number of such formulae could exist, in reality only a few do. *Ballot structure* involves whether the voter makes one choice or alternatively ranks a list of competing candidates. Some scholars note a fourth aspect of an electoral system—the total size of the legislature.[5] Very small legislatures, in particular, tend to be less proportional regardless of the electoral formula.

Table 7.1 classifies the various electoral systems in today's liberal and electoral democracies, grouped into three main categories based on their overall national effects. First are *majoritarian* electoral systems, so named because of their tendency to give a majority of seats to one party. To repeat, this is a tendency, not a "guarantee." Such a majority of seats will often occur even if the party does not win a majority of the popular vote, a circumstance known as a **manufactured majority**

TABLE 7.1 Types of Electoral Systems (2012)

MAJORITARIAN SYSTEMS

single-member plurality	Antigua and Barbuda	Grenada	Papua New Guinea
	Bahamas	India	Saint Kitts and Nevis
	Bangladesh	Jamaica	Saint Lucia
	Barbados	Lesotho	Saint Vincent and the Grenadines
	Belize	Liberia	Sierra Leone
	Botswana	Micronesia	Trinidad and Tobago
	Canada	Nigeria	United Kingdom
	Dominica	Pakistan	United States
	Ghana	Palau	Zambia
single-member majority runoff	Comoros		
single-member majority-plurality	France		
single-member majority (alternative vote)	Australia	Kiribati	
mixture of single-member, dual-member, and/or multi-member plurality	Ivory Coast Marshall Islands	Mauritius* Nauru^	Samoa Tuvalu
single non-transferable vote	Vanuatu		

PROPORTIONAL SYSTEMS

single transferable vote	Ireland	Malta**	
party list proportional representation	Argentina	Guinea-Bissau	Paraguay
	Austria	Guyana	Peru
	Belgium	Honduras	Poland
	Benin	Iceland	Portugal
	Brazil	Indonesia	Romania*
	Cape Verde	Iraq*	San Marino
	Chile	Israel	São Tomé and Príncipe
	Colombia	Italy***	Serbia
	Costa Rica	Kyrgyzstan	Slovakia
	Croatia*	Latvia	Slovenia
	Cyprus	Liechtenstein	South Africa
	Czech Republic	Luxembourg	Spain
	Denmark	Macedonia	Suriname
	Dominican Republic	Moldova	Sweden
	Ecuador	Montenegro	Switzerland
	El Salvador	Namibia	Tunisia
	Estonia	Netherlands	Turkey
	Finland	Niger*	Uruguay
	Greece***	Norway	
mixed member proportional (fully compensatory)	Bolivia Germany	Lesotho	New Zealand

IN-BETWEEN SYSTEMS

parallel	Andorra	Korea, South	Senegal
	Bulgaria	Lithuania	Taiwan
	Guatemala	Mongolia	Thailand
	Japan	Panama	Timor-Leste
mixed member semi-compensatory	Hungary	Mexico	Philippines

^ With preferential voting in Nauru.

* Includes some single-member constituencies for ethnic minorities.

** In Malta, extra seats may be given to one of the top two parties to make the results proportional between them, while maintaining an odd number of deputies in total.

*** In Greece, 50 extra seats are given to the largest party; in Italy, extra seats are given to the largest coalition sufficient to give it a clear majority of about 54 per cent of the seats.

because the majority in the legislature has been "manufactured" by the electoral system. (Sometimes this manufactured majority is "spurious" in that it does not even go to the party leading in the popular vote but rather to the second-place party in terms of national votes. Such a "spurious majority" occurred, for example, in the United States House of Representatives in 2012 and has occurred in various Canadian provincial elections.)[6] In these majoritarian electoral systems, there is no conscious attempt to make the final percentage of seats match the overall percentage of the vote won by each party. Very rarely in majoritarian electoral systems, the legislature's composition is very close to the distribution of the votes—the Canadian federal election of 1925 is one exceptional example—but this proportionality is a "fluke" rather than anything automatic. Indeed, even if there is a **hung parliament** in which no one party has a majority, a majoritarian system normally produces a bias in favour of the largest party or parties. Table 7.2 shows this pattern clearly for the United Kingdom election of 2010, contrasting this with the "exceptional" Canadian election of 1925.

Proportional electoral systems, the second category, have proportionality as an explicit goal. They try to match the share of seats won with the share of votes won, except, perhaps, when it comes to the representation of very tiny parties. Consequently, in these systems, a single party should not win a majority of seats unless it has won a majority of the popular vote or something very close. The third category includes systems that combine elements of each of the first two types to produce a pattern somewhat in between, that is, with some elements of proportionality but not the clear overall pattern found in the second category.

Far and away the most common type of majoritarian system is the single-member plurality (SMP) electoral system, which is used in the United Kingdom and many former British colonies, including Canada and the United States. In this system, the district magnitude is one: a single member is elected at a time in each district. To win the seat, a candidate needs to have more votes than any other candidate; all that is required is a plurality of votes, not necessarily a majority. Of course, some victors will have won a majority of the votes in their constituencies, but, again, winning a majority is not required. Indeed, *no* specific share of the vote is required to win under SMP; the winning share will vary with the number and strength of the candidates. Consequently, the frequently used description of these elections as "first-past-the-post" races is incorrect and inappropriate: there is no actual "post." (A more accurate analogy would be the kind of set-time race in which whoever is leading when time

TABLE 7.2 Comparing Two Hung Parliaments in History and Their Disproportionality

A.

UNITED KINGDOM May 2010 (total of 650 seats)	VOTE %	SEATS	SEAT %	PERCENTAGE DIFFERENCE
Conservative Party	36.05	306	47.08	11.03
Labour Party	28.99	258	39.69	10.70
Liberal Democrats	23.03	57	8.77	−14.26
United Kingdom Independence Party	3.10	0	0.00	−3.10
British National Party	1.90	0	0.00	−1.90
Scottish National Party	1.66	6	0.92	−0.74
Green Party of England and Wales	0.89	1	0.15	−0.74
Plaid Cymru (The Party of Wales)	0.56	3	0.46	−0.10
Main Northern Irish Parties				
Sinn Fein	0.58	5	0.77	0.19
Democratic Unionist Party	0.57	8	1.23	0.66
Social Democratic and Labour Party	0.37	3	0.46	0.09
Ulster Conservatives and Unionists	0.34	0	0.00	−0.34
Alliance	0.14	1	0.15	0.01
Others and independents	1.82	2	0.31	−1.51

NOTE: Total disproportionality (based on individual parties) was 22.68. As shown, each of the two largest parties received a significant seat bonus, as did the two largest parties in Northern Ireland—which has its own party system.

B.

CANADA October 1925 (total of 245 seats)	VOTE %	SEATS	SEAT %	PERCENTAGE DIFFERENCE
Conservatives	46.48	116	47.35	0.87
Liberals	39.87	99	40.41	0.54
Progressives	8.95	24	9.80	0.85
Others and independents	4.70	6	2.45	−2.25

NOTE: Total disproportionality was only 2.25. As shown, the seat bonus for the leading party was only 0.87. Ironically, a party with 46 per cent of the vote would normally win a manufactured majority under such a national vote distribution.

runs out is declared the winner.) Under SMP, the election is a series of individual races in however many districts there are. No link exists between overall votes won and overall seats won, nor is any consolation prize given for coming second in a constituency. Indeed, a party that comes second everywhere wins the same number of seats—zero!—as a party that comes, say, last everywhere.

One criticism of such a system is that the winning candidate in a district may have won only a minority of the vote; in other words, most people did not vote for her or him. One solution to this "problem" could be to have a run-off vote between the top two candidates. In fact, although various presidential elections have run-off votes (see Chapter 6), the only democracies that actually do this at the legislative level are

Comoros and, for its single-member seats, Lithuania. The French National Assembly, which uses a single-member electoral system, follows a related procedure: a run-off election in every constituency in which nobody wins a majority on the first ballot. However, rather than restricting the run-off to the top two candidates, the rules allow any candidate who gets 12.5 per cent of the constituency's electorate—that is, of the total potential vote—to contest the run-off. Candidates above this threshold are not *obliged* to contest the run-off, and parties will often make deals between the ballots (if not before) that involve candidates who clear the threshold withdrawing in favour of other, stronger candidates of allied parties. Such strategic withdrawal is necessary because only a plurality is needed to win the run-off, and a plurality may be all that is achieved when there are more than two candidates. Consequently, the French system is categorized as a "single-member majority-plurality."

The Australian House of Representatives requires that candidates achieve overall majority support. These elections (and also now those of Kiribati and Papua New Guinea) use the alternative vote, namely, a *preferential ballot* to determine the ultimate winner. So, rather than just indicating one preferred choice, each voter ranks all the candidates: 1, 2, 3, and so on. Then a calculation is made of each candidate's "first preferences"—their number of "1"s. If one candidate receives a majority, the counting stops. However, if no candidate has a majority of first preferences, then the candidate with the least number of first preferences is dropped, and the second preferences of her or his voters are distributed. If this does not push anyone over the 50 per cent level, then the next least popular candidate is dropped, and so on. Of course, if a voter has unpopular tastes, it may be that her vote keeps being recounted until she is using, say, her fifth preference! Nevertheless, at some point, a candidate will win a majority of preferences—even if the win requires getting down to two final choices. In Papua New Guinea, where the alternative vote has been in use since 2007, voters are restricted to a maximum of three preferences; hence the more specific description of the Papua New Guinea system as a "limited preferential" vote (LPV). Under such a limited preferential system candidates are still eliminated until someone has a majority—invariably so in a count involving only two candidates; however, in actual Papua New Guinea elections, which have up to dozens of candidates per constituency, many voters do not express any preference concerning either of the candidates that make it to the final two. Consequently, their ballots are deemed "exhausted," and the "majority" winning candidate only has a majority of those votes still under count.

To repeat, all of these systems use single-member districts (district magnitudes of one). However, also classified as majoritarian systems are those that use a combination of SMP, dual-member plurality, and multi-member plurality. Here we emphasize the plurality aspect, that is, the electoral formula. In such systems, the voter gets as many votes as there are members to be elected in the constituency, and the parties normally also run that number of candidates. Assuming that voters vote for each and every candidate of their preferred party, then one party will win all the seats in the constituency with each of their candidates getting (basically) the same number of votes—but not necessarily a plurality. Of course, a voter may "mix and match" candidates across parties, but doing so is rare, or at least rare enough that it is seldom the case that candidates of more than one party are elected. Although this pattern of plurality voting in districts of varying magnitude (but none very large) exists today only in Mauritius and three Pacific islands (see Table 7.1), it should be stressed that it was used historically in some Canadian provinces.

The final type of majoritarian electoral system is called a single non-transferable vote (SNTV). As in the previous examples, deputies are elected in multi-member districts. However, the voter is given only *one* vote that must be cast for a specific candidate. A plurality electoral formula is used so that, if it is a five-member district, then the top five candidates all get elected. As voters get only one vote, they have to choose among the candidates of their preferred party, assuming that there are more than one of these. A voter cannot vote for all the candidates of a given party (because each voter only has one vote), nor can a voter rank the candidates, as in a preferential ballot. Consequently, multiple candidates of the same party have to compete against each other (on something other than party label, obviously). Also, larger parties have to decide strategically how many candidates to run in a district: too many and they will divide the vote excessively, too few and an extra seat that could have been won will be lost. Generally, a party with overall majority support in a district will run, say, three candidates in a five-member district and hope to elect all three. Conversely, small parties will run only one candidate in a district and hope to get about one-fifth (or whatever) of the vote to win one seat. Although SNTV is now used only in Vanuatu, from 1947 through 1993 it was the system used in Japanese lower-house elections.

All of these majoritarian electoral systems can lead to manufactured majorities; even if this phenomenon does not occur, the system generally creates an imbalance between the percentage of votes won and the percentage of seats won by individual parties. This imbalance amounts to a deviation from pure proportionality (wherein the seat percentage exactly equals the vote percentage for every party) and is more commonly phrased in terms of how *dis*proportional the election results are. Mathematically, we measure the disproportionality of elections (under all electoral systems) by the Loosemore-Hanby **index of disproportionality**, which sums the absolute value of each party's vote share to seat share difference and then divides this total by two (because some party's excessively high percentage of seats must be balanced by some other party's excessive low percentage) to get a value between zero and 100— the higher the number, the greater the disproportionality.[7] For example, for the countries that use SMP and for which there is relevant data, the average disproportionality value is 14.6; for all countries using majoritarian electoral systems and with relevant data, the average disproportionality value is 15.5 (calculated from Table 7.4). In such majoritarian systems, parties whose support is broad geographically but not very deep locally (such as the federal Progressive Conservatives in Canada in 1993) will come up short with most of their votes "wasted" (not electing the desired candidate). Yet, it is also the case that parties who are extremely popular locally (such as the Canadian federal Conservatives in Alberta) will have candidates winning with well over half the vote; all of these "surplus" votes are also wasted.[8] Thus, by definition any single-member system is disproportional; so too are multi-member plurality systems.

Electoral systems that are proportional in their philosophy avoid both of these features: that is, they use multi-member rather than single-member districts, and they use a non-plurality electoral formula. One type of proportional system is that of the single transferable vote (STV). The STV electoral system has the moderate district magnitude (usually three to five) and the single vote of the SNTV system; however, it not only allows but often requires voters to indicate their preferences (1, 2, 3, etc.) across all the candidates of all the parties. This preferential ballot structure is the same as that of the alternative vote, but in an alternative vote only one person gets elected. Under STV, a few people will get elected in each constituency. The key mechanism is the establishment of an electoral quota, known as the "Droop quota," which is one more than the total number of valid votes divided by the total number of district seats plus one. This quota is thus the smallest share of the vote needed to elect a full number of candidates, but no more. Consequently (in rounded-up terms), for a five-member district the quota is 17 per cent, for a four-member district the quota is 21 per cent, and for a three-member district the quota is 26 per cent. Indeed, for a single-member district the quota is 51 per cent, which is the definition of single-member *majority* systems such as that of the Australian lower house.[9] As is the case with the alternative vote, unpopular candidates get dropped from the ballot, and the second (and subsequent) preferences of their voters get transferred. Even more multiple rounds of counting take place to elect all the candidates. However, what is really different from the alternative vote (and SMP too, of course) is that, under STV, one can never win "too many" votes. Whenever a candidate reaches or exceeds the quota—be this on the first or a subsequent count—that candidate is declared elected. At this stage, any preferences the elected candidate has that are above the quota are then redistributed as a share of the next preferences of *all* that candidate's voters. These subsequent preferences will, presumably, help to elect someone else of the same party. And, although parties do run only a reasonable number of candidates given their size, unlike in SNTV systems, parties operating under an STV electoral formula do not run the same danger of splitting their vote if they run an excessive number of candidates because surplus preferences transfer.

Although the electoral formula used in STV systems is certainly proportional, the small district magnitude tends to prevent this system from achieving full proportionality. That is, although a quota of 17 per cent or 21 per cent is certainly better for smaller parties than 51 per cent or even being the plurality candidate, 17 per cent may still be too high for small parties. They would not win any seats in a given constituency; conversely, another party (usually the largest) will win, say, one seat too many given the voters' first preferences. Such a problem is less the greater the district magnitude; however, because voters can or must rank multiple candidates of various parties and because the more candidates to be elected, the more rounds of counting are involved, for practical purposes, STV is not normally used with a district magnitude of more than five or six. Indeed, in Ireland, many constituencies have a district magnitude of only three or four. (However, in Malta, all districts have a magnitude of five.) On the other hand, the modest district magnitudes and constituency sizes mean that all deputies have clear local ties.

These patterns are essentially inverted in the main form of proportional representation, the party list system. Indeed, party list proportional representation is the single most common type of electoral system in the world's democracies due to its dominance in continental Europe and Latin America (see Table 7.1). We have already noted that Israel, Moldova, the Netherlands, Serbia, and Slovakia each has only one electoral district, and parties offer only national lists. However, the usual pattern for party list proportional representation is to divide the country into a few districts (normally the provinces or equivalents if there are regional governments), each of which elects perhaps 10 or 20 or 40 members who are no more locally based than at this regional level. Spain is an exception in that some of its districts have magnitudes as low as three. Under party list proportional representation, some seats may also be allocated at the national level to "correct" any imperfections that are a consequence of regional level calculations, as is the case in Sweden. Voters normally vote for the party list as a whole, although, as we shall see, some systems allow (or, in Finland, require) the voter to express a preference within the list. Still, unlike in the STV system, the voter in party list proportional representation does not rank everyone or express a series of preferences. Thus, the basic electoral formula is quite simple: a party that wins, say, 10 per cent of the votes gets 10 per cent of the seats. Of course, parties usually win fractional amounts of votes whereas seat numbers are integers, so varying formulae exist to determine which party gets the last unclaimed seat (some formulae favour larger parties, some favour smaller ones). There is no quota per se, as in the STV system. However, what matters usually is a legal threshold of support that a party must meet in order to win any proportional seats at all. This threshold is often 4 or 5 per cent of the national vote, but it may be established regionally instead. The real-world highest value here is the legal threshold of 10 per cent of the national vote found in Turkey, which, in its 2002 election, eliminated all but two parties. The real-world lowest value here is the legal threshold of 2 per cent of the national vote found in Denmark and, since 2006, in Israel, which eliminates only very marginal parties.[10] Yet, even where no legal thresholds are in place, an effective threshold based on the size of the legislature exists. For example, the Dutch lower house has 150 members, so a party that cannot win 1/150th of the vote (0.667 per cent) is out of luck.

Indeed, party list proportional representation only truly lives up to its "name" consistently—by providing near-perfect proportionality—when the legal threshold is low or non-existent and when the average district magnitude is medium or high, such as in Denmark (current disproportionality of only 1.3), the Netherlands (2.5), South Africa (1.1), and Sweden (2.2). Conversely, a high threshold (as in Turkey, most extremely) and small district magnitudes (as in Peru outside of Lima)[11] do not normally result in very proportional representation. Overall, the average disproportionality for party list proportional representation systems is 9.5—clearly lower than that for majoritarian systems but far from zero. Lack of a proportional outcome despite the use of party list proportional representation is particularly common in new democracies, where often, huge numbers of parties compete and voters are not

TABLE 7.3 Party List Proportional Representation and Ballot Structure (2012)

CLOSED LIST

Argentina	Guinea-Bissau	Namibia	Serbia
Benin	Guyana	Niger	Sierra Leone
Cape Verde	Honduras	Paraguay	South Africa
Costa Rica	Israel	Portugal	Spain
Croatia	Kyrgyzstan	Romania	Tunisia
Dominican Republic	Moldova	São Tomé and Príncipe	Turkey
El Salvador	Montenegro		

OPEN LIST

Austria	Greece	Netherlands	Slovakia
Belgium	Iceland	Norway	Slovenia
Cyprus	Indonesia	Panama	Suriname
Czech Republic	Iraq	Peru	Sweden
Denmark	Latvia	Poland	Uruguay
Estonia	Liechtenstein	San Marino	

OPEN AND COMPLETELY DECISIVE LIST

Brazil	Chile	Colombia	Finland

OPEN, FREE, AND COMPLETELY DECISIVE LIST (voter has multiple votes and is free to combine these across parties)

Ecuador	Luxembourg	Switzerland

clear about which parties are likely to be successful or, conversely, fringe. In this situation, large numbers of "wasted" votes go to parties that fail to clear the threshold. The recent initial elections in newly democratic Kyrgyzstan (with 29 parties running) and Tunisia (with about 100 parties [!] running) are clear illustrations, with disproportionality values of 32.1 and 24.6 respectively (see Table 7.4).

Given that party list proportional representation, as its very name indicates, involves lists of candidates, which individual candidates of a party actually get elected? A continuum of ballot structures and, thus, outcomes exists, from the structure giving parties the most control over the process to the one giving voters the most flexibility. These are detailed for specific countries in Table 7.3. A closed list system gives each political party the power to determine the order of its candidates on the list, and the voters cannot change this ranking. Consequently, if a party wins, say, four seats, the top four candidates named on that party's list are elected. In contrast, an open list allows voters to indicate their preferences in terms of the individual candidates on a party list. With enough preferences, a candidate will "move up" the list and conceivably become one of those elected. That said, what it takes to move up the list and, thus, the likelihood of a candidate's election varies greatly from specific system to system. Moreover, the party still draws up the initial list, so starting at the top, even if no guarantee, gives a candidate a better chance to be elected. In some countries, though, the list is what we call "open and completely decisive"—that is, the party does not rank candidates but provides instead an alphabetical list. Voters must vote specifically for an individual party candidate, and, although these votes collectively determine how many seats a party wins, the individual preference votes decide entirely which candidate or candidates are elected. Finally, some countries using an open and completely decisive list go further and make the list "free" by giving the voters multiple votes, which can be not only assigned within a given party in terms of its candidates but also spread across the lists of differing parties (a process known as *panachage*). These "open, free, and completely decisive" lists thus provide the greatest flexibility for the voter—and conversely the least control for the parties.

One attempt to combine party list proportional representation with at least partial local constituency representation is called mixed member proportional (MMP) representation. This system has been used in Germany since its first postwar election in 1949 and has also been adopted in Bolivia, Lesotho, and New Zealand—in the case of New Zealand, as a conscious change away from an SMP system. Under MMP representation, a certain number of deputies (half in Germany) are elected in local constituencies using SMP voting. Thus, everyone can be said to have a local member of parliament, although this matters more in New Zealand than it ever has in Germany. The other deputies are elected from regional party lists. Voters have separate votes for the local candidate and for the party list, and they can engage in "ticket-splitting." Of these two votes, the party list one is by far the more important because the goal of the system is to make the final outcome of seats as proportionally close as possible to the party list share of the vote for all those parties above the legal threshold. So if a party gets 40 per cent of the party list vote, it should, at the end of the process, have 40 per cent of the total seats in the parliament. How many seats it gets from the party lists will vary inversely with how many it wins in the single-member constituencies. For example, if the constituency to list seat ratio is 50:50 and a given party won 20 per cent of the list vote but only 10 per cent of the constituency seats—and thus only 5 per cent of the overall seats from the constituency part—it would "need" another 15 per cent overall for proportionality. Consequently, it would receive 30 per cent of the list seats. Of course, all of the usual biases of the SMP system apply to the local seats, so smaller parties, such as the Greens in Germany or New Zealand, may *never* win a local seat and will get all of their seats from the party lists. Yet, as long as sufficient numbers of seats are available in the list portion (as is the case under the German 50:50 ratio), the overall result will be quite proportional. Consequently, the MMP system can be said to be *fully compensatory*, in that the party list seats should fully compensate any party above the threshold that won too few seats in the local constituencies. Hence, this electoral system is clearly in the proportional category. Indeed, the average index of disproportionality for the four MMP systems is 4.6, well below the average for the party list proportional representation systems.

The final category of electoral systems comprises those that are neither fully majoritarian nor fully proportional; instead, they fall in between as a compromise (or perhaps because of an internal contradiction). The more common variant is usually called a parallel system. In these, local deputies are elected (usually using an SMP formula), as are deputies from regional or national lists. Voters usually have two separate votes. However, each component's electoral formula remains totally independent; that is, only the calculation of party list seats is proportional to the party list vote, regardless of how well a party did in the local, single-member constituencies. Because the seats determined by the locally elected constituencies invariably will be disproportional and because the party list seats in no way compensate for this disproportionality, the overall result will not be fully proportional. However, results should be more proportional than if, say, all the seats were elected using an SMP formula. Consequently, the ratio of locally elected seats to party list seats is crucial: if the system is heavily weighted toward the locally elected seats (as in South Korea), the result will be more disproportional than if the ratio is 50:50, all other things being equal. Overall, though, the average index of disproportionality for all parallel systems is 16.3, a bit higher than even that for all majoritarian systems.

Finally, the three cases of what we call mixed-member semi-compensatory electoral systems fall basically between the parallel systems and the pure proportional representation ones, at least conceptually if not always in terms of their index of disproportionality (for which the average is 12.3). These semi-compensatory systems do take into account the results of the single-member constituencies when allocating the party list seats, but not to the extent of aiming to achieve full proportionality. Instead, some compensation is achieved, normally by "capping" the leading party. For example, in Mexico, this is done so that said party does not get an overall seat percentage more than 8 per cent above its party list vote percentage.

Party Systems

A **party system** involves the relationship amongst the various political parties in a territory, that is, their total number, relative size, competitiveness, and so on. (In some countries, the concept may make more sense in terms of blocs of parties.) For a party system to exist, a country must have at least two parties; one party by itself does not interact with any other party. Almost every democracy has a party system; the exceptions are six island states in Oceania (Kiribati, the Marshall Islands, Micronesia, Nauru, Palau, and Tuvalu), which do not have formal political parties for cultural-traditional reasons.[12] (Similarly, there are no parties in the Northwest Territories or Nunavut.) To be clear, party-like alliances may form in the legislatures of these six democracies, but everyone is elected as an independent. (In contrast, if political parties did not exist because they were banned, then a system would not be democratic.)

Party systems can be assessed and compared in three ways. The two traditional ways are in terms of fragmentation and polarization.[13] By *fragmentation*, we mean how many parties there are, both in an absolute sense and allowing for relative size. By *polarization*, we mean the ideological spread amongst parties, between the two most extreme parties, or perhaps between the two largest parties. Polarization is, however, very difficult to measure and compare globally, and we do not attempt to do so in this analysis. Note, too, that the ending of communism in Eastern Europe and the decline of the far left have meant that left–right ideological gaps in most of the world are not what they were a generation ago.[14] The newest way in which scholars look at party systems is in terms of institutionalization. By *party system institutionalization*, we mean the extent to which individual parties are well organized, have stable and deep roots in society or in segments of society, are consistent in their ideological positions vis-à-vis each other, and experience relatively stable interparty competition; also included in this concept is the extent to which political parties and elections have high legitimacy.[15] Scholarly concern with the organizational structure and capacity of individual parties goes back to the 1960s, but it originally focused more on party institutionalization than on broader party *system* institutionalization.[16]

Measuring party system fragmentation is essentially objective because it involves tabulating the "hard" numbers of votes and seats for various parties. Table 7.4 provides a range of data on the most recent elections (as of November 2012) in the world's democracies. These data are mostly based on the distribution of parliamentary seats although a few are based on vote share. The actual measure of party system fragmentation (PFRG) used by scholars weights the parties by size, as is done for the effective number of parties (ENPP). However, the calculation of party system fragmentation is different from the calculation of an "effective number," which was explained in Chapter 1. In the calculation of party system fragmentation, the sum of the squared decimal values of all parties is subtracted from 1.000 rather than taking its inverse, as in the calculation of an "effective number." Consequently, party system fragmentation ranges from zero (0.000), when a single party has all the seats, to one (1.000), when no party has any seat. This latter situation cannot exist, of course, as long as political parties are being elected, so a value of 1.000 would occur only in those countries without political parties. As Table 7.4 shows, the most fragmented democracies with parties—Vanuatu and Papua New Guinea—have parliamentary fragmentation values of 0.924 and 0.907, respectively. (Perhaps the following scenario is more illustrative: in a 100-seat legislature, if 100 different parties each win one seat, then the fragmentation value is 0.990.)

Another way of looking at party system fragmentation is to count the effective number of parties, which, as noted, weights parties by size (as does PFRG) but expresses this measurement differently, on a scale with a minimum of 1 and no absolute maximum value. Finally, one can simply count all the parties without weighting them to give an integer value. However, should we consider a party with only one or two seats as being relevant? To measure the number of empirically relevant parties, we use a cut-off of at least 2 per cent of the seats because, as noted, that is now the minimum legal threshold found in actual proportional representation (PR) systems. Although the maximum number of parties here could be 50 (100 per cent divided by 2 per cent, if that is the threshold), the real-world maximum at the moment is in Brazil, which has 13 relevant parties. Brazil is followed by Israel (12 parties) and Vanuatu (11 parties). Though the most fragmented overall, Vanuatu does not lead in terms of P2%S because several of its parties have only one seat.[17]

Table 7.4 presents various measures of looking at the top party or the top two parties. Of central concern is whether any one party has won a majority of seats, which would give it control of the legislature and, outside of presidential systems, the government. Alternatively, if no one party has a majority, the **hung parliament** necessitates legislative compromise and will likely produce a coalition government, again, assuming we are discussing parliamentary rather than presidential systems. As of November 2012, there are 41 cases of single-party majorities in the world's 107 democracies with political parties—clearly fewer than the 66 hung parliaments. The subsequent issue is whether those majority governments are **earned majorities**. Has a political party "earned" a majority of seats by winning a majority of the popular vote, or was the majority "manufactured" by the electoral system? Of the 41 majorities, only 22 are earned whereas 19 are manufactured. Interestingly, although the 19 manufactured majorities include SMP systems such as those in Canada and the United States, manufactured majorities also occur in party list proportional representation systems (e.g., in Liechtenstein, Slovakia, and Turkey, with Turkey's electoral system uniqueness having been noted) and in in-between systems (e.g., in Japan). Thus a majoritarian electoral system is hardly the only type to have a manufactured majority. What is largely eponymous about majoritarian electoral systems is the fact that, leaving aside those without political parties, around two-thirds currently have single-party majorities. Some of these are manufactured; the rest are, by definition, earned. And although the earned majorities could involve only a modest "seat bonus" for the largest party (as has normally been the case in the United States, for example), it is often the case that a party with 50-something per cent of the vote gets around 80 per cent of the seats (as in many Caribbean systems). So, we return to the general high level of disproportionality in majoritarian electoral systems. For (comparative) information, the last column of Table 7.4 gives the index of disproportionality wherever possible for each democracy.

The previous descriptions of party systems have involved either a continuum (for example, more to less fragmentation) or a dichotomy (for example, a single-party majority or not). That said, we can also group the various party systems of democracies into a few types based on long-term patterns of the number of relevant parties (P2%S) and on certain key relative sizes. Arguably, there are six of these types:

1. A *competitive two-party system* has two relevant parties, which alternate in power at various times. In any given election, or at least in most of them, each of the two parties has a reasonable chance of winning. The US party system is a clear example, although more for its Senate than its House of Representatives (which has been less competitive for long periods of time).[18] Even better examples of competitive two-party systems are Malta and most of the former British colonies of the Caribbean.

2. An *imbalanced two-party system* also has only two relevant parties, but one party is in power for a very long time, and the other has little chance of winning

TABLE 7.4 Data on the Most Recent Elections for All Liberal and Electoral Democracies (as of November 2012)

YEAR: Year of Elections

PFRG: Parliamentary Fragmentation

ENPP: Effective Number of Parliamentary Parties

P2%S: Number of Parties with Two Per Cent or More of the Seats

2PSC: Two-Party Seat Concentration (combined seat percentage of the top two parties in terms of seats)

2PVC: Two-Party Vote Concentration (combined vote percentage of the top two parties in terms of seats)

1PSC: One-Party Seat Concentration (seat percentage of the top party in terms of seats)

1PVC: One-Party Vote Concentration (vote percentage of the top party in terms of seats)

ED: Electoral Decisiveness (EM = earned majority, MM = manufactured majority, HP = hung parliament)

SR 1:2: Ratio of Seats between the Top Party and the Second-Largest Party

SR 2:3: Ratio of Seats between the Second-Largest Party and the Third-Largest Party

TVOL: Total Volatility (vote shares) between the Given Election and the Previous One [Pedersen Index]

DISP: Disproportionality between Seat Percentages and Vote Percentages (for all parties) [Loosemore-Hanby Index]

	YEAR	PFRG	ENPP	P2%S	2PSC	2PVC	1PSC	1PVC	ED	SR 1:2	SR 2:3	TVOL	DISP
Andorra	2011	0.337	1.51	2	100.0	90.0	78.6	55.2	EM	3.67	∞	23.1	23.4
Antigua and Barbuda	2009	0.547	2.21	3	94.1	98.1	52.9	51.1	EM	1.29	7.00	5.5	6.6
Argentina (total parliament)	2011	0.679	3.12	6	67.3		51.0		MM	3.12	2.00		
Australia	2010	0.603	2.52	3	88.0	75.3	48.0	38.0	HP	1.20	5.00	5.9	15.2
Austria	2008	0.766	4.27	5	59.0	55.3	31.1	29.3	HP	1.12	1.50	15.0	6.1
Bahamas	2012	0.361	1.57	2	100.0	90.7	76.3	48.6	MM	3.22	∞	10.2	27.7
Bangladesh	2008	0.394	1.65	3	86.7	82.2	76.7	49.0	MM	7.67	1.11		30.7
Barbados	2008	0.444	1.80	2	100.0	99.7	66.7	53.2	EM	2.00	∞	9.3	13.5
Belgium	2010	0.881	8.42	10	35.3	31.3	18.0	17.3	HP	1.04	1.44	15.8	8.3
Belize	2012	0.495	1.98	2	100.0	98.9	54.8	50.7	EM	1.21	∞	7.1	4.1
Benin	2007	0.743	3.89	9	66.3		42.2		HP	1.75	2.00		
Bolivia	2009	0.460	1.85	3	96.2	90.7	67.7	64.2	EM	2.38	12.33		5.5
Botswana	2009	0.360	1.56	3	89.5	75.2	78.9	53.3	EM	7.50	1.50	4.6	25.7
Brazil	2010	0.802	5.06	13	32.2	29.7	17.0	16.8	HP	1.12	1.47	12.0	5.8
Bulgaria	2009	0.700	3.34	6	65.0	57.4	48.3	39.7	HP	2.90	1.05	46.8	10.0
Canada	2011	0.585	2.41	3	87.3	70.2	53.9	39.6	MM	1.61	3.03	14.4	17.1
Cape Verde	2011	0.523	2.10	3	97.2	94.6	52.8	52.2	EM	1.19	16.00	1.7	2.6
Chile	2009	0.823	5.66	8	46.7	37.5	30.8	23.3	HP	1.95	1.06	12.9	12.4
Colombia	2010	0.798	4.95	6	51.8	47.3	28.7	25.9	HP	1.24	1.03	27.7	9.8
Comoros *	2009	0.278	1.38	2	100.0		83.3		MM	5.00	∞		
Costa Rica	2010	0.753	4.05	5	59.6	54.8	40.4	37.2	HP	2.09	1.10		10.3
Croatia	2011	0.718	3.55	5	72.8		41.7		HP	1.34	3.92	9.6	18.7
Cyprus	2011	0.722	3.60	5	69.6	67.0	35.7	34.3	HP	1.05	2.11	5.8	2.9
Czech Republic	2010	0.778	4.51	5	54.5	42.3	28.0	22.1	HP	1.06	1.29	33.6	18.8
Denmark	2011	0.822	5.61	8	52.0	51.6	26.9	26.7	HP	1.07	2.00	11.6	1.3
Dominica	2009	0.245	1.32	2	100.0	96.2	85.7	61.4	EM	6.00	∞	9.5	24.3
Dominican Republic	2010	0.503	2.01	2	98.4	80.0	57.4	41.6	MM	1.40	25.00		18.4
Ecuador	2009	0.733	3.75	9	62.9	60.7	47.6	45.8	HP	3.11	1.73		13.6
El Salvador	2012	0.685	3.18	4	76.2	76.5	39.3	39.8	HP	1.06	2.82	12.6	4.8
Estonia	2011	0.740	3.84	4	58.4	51.9	32.7	28.6	HP	1.27	1.13	11.1	10.5

	YEAR	PFRG	ENPP	P2%S	2PSC	2PVC	1PSC	1PVC	ED	SR 1:2	SR 2:3	TVOL	DISP
Finland	2011	0.828	5.83	8	43.0	39.5	22.0	20.4	HP	1.05	1.08	14.9	6.0
France	2012	0.647	2.83	5	82.1	56.5	48.5	29.4	HP	1.44	8.82	21.6	26.5
Germany	2009	0.748	3.97	5	61.9	56.8	38.4	33.8	HP	1.64	1.57	12.6	6.0
Ghana	2008	0.529	2.12	2	96.9		50.2		MM	1.07	53.50		
Greece	2012	0.734	3.76	7	66.7	56.6	43.0	29.7	HP	1.82	2.15	21.1	13.3
Grenada	2008	0.391	1.64	2	100.0	99.1	73.3	51.2	EM	2.75	∞	6.0	22.2
Guatemala	2011	0.759	4.14	6	65.8	49.2	35.4	26.6	HP	1.17	3.43	37.1	16.6
Guyana	2011	0.586	2.42	3	89.2	89.4	49.2	48.6	HP	1.23	3.71	7.3	1.1
Honduras	2009	0.566	2.30	5	90.6	87.2	55.5	53.9	EM	1.58	9.00		3.4
Hungary	2010	0.496	1.98	4	83.4	72.0	68.1	52.7	EM	4.46	1.26	32.7	15.4
Iceland	2009	0.761	4.18	5	57.1	53.5	31.7	29.8	HP	1.25	1.14	20.7	4.2
India	2009	0.800	5.01	10	59.3	47.5	37.9	28.6	HP	1.78	5.04		
Indonesia	2009	0.838	6.18	9	45.7	35.3	26.4	20.8	HP	1.37	1.16	23.8	19.7
Iraq	2010	0.781	4.57	5	55.4	49.2	28.0	24.9	HP	1.02	1.27		9.5
Ireland	2011	0.719	3.56	4	68.1	55.5	45.8	36.1	HP	2.05	1.85	29.8	12.8
Israel	2009	0.852	6.77	12	45.8	44.1	23.3	22.5	HP	1.04	1.80	17.0	4.2
Italy	2008	0.675	3.08	5	78.3	70.6	43.8	37.4	HP	1.27	3.62	11.4	9.7
Ivory Coast	2011	0.657	2.91	3	80.3		50.0		HP	1.65	11.00		
Jamaica	2011	0.444	1.80	2	100.0	99.9	66.7	53.3	EM	2.00	∞	3.5	13.4
Japan	2009	0.524	2.10	3	89.0	69.1	64.2	42.4	MM	2.59	5.67	14.8	21.8
Kiribati	2011	1.000					No Parties						
Korea, South	2012	0.562	2.28	3	93.0	79.3	50.7	42.8	MM	1.20	9.77	16.1	13.7
Kyrgyzstan	2010	0.796	4.90	5	45.0	30.7	23.3	16.1	HP	1.08	1.04		32.1
Latvia	2011	0.779	4.52	5	53.0	49.2	31.0	28.4	HP	1.41	1.10	29.4	5.9
Lesotho	2012	0.728	3.67	5	65.0	64.8	40.0	39.6	HP	1.60	1.15		2.9
Liberia	2011	0.844	6.41	8	47.9	32.8	32.9	19.0	HP	2.18	1.57		23.3
Liechtenstein	2009	0.534	2.15	3	96.0	91.1	52.0	47.6	MM	1.18	11.00	9.4	4.9
Lithuania	2012	0.811	5.28	7	50.7	33.5	27.1	18.4	HP	1.15	1.14	28.2	18.7
Luxembourg	2009	0.724	3.63	5	65.0	59.6	43.3	38.0	HP	2.00	1.44	4.8	5.4
Macedonia	2011	0.657	2.91	4	79.7	71.8	45.5	39.0	HP	1.33	2.80	16.3	10.5
Malta	2008	0.500	2.00	2	100.0	98.1	50.7	49.3	MM	1.03	∞	2.5	1.9
Marshall Islands	2011	1.000					No Parties						
Mauritius	2010	0.465	1.87	3	95.2	90.8	67.7	49.3	MM	2.47	8.50		20.2
Mexico	2012	0.728	3.68	7	64.6	57.8	41.4	31.9	HP	1.78	1.17	8.1	11.4
Micronesia	2011	1.000					No Parties						
Moldova	2010	0.691	3.23	4	73.3	68.7	41.6	39.3	HP	1.31	2.13	15.3	8.6
Mongolia	2012	0.666	3.00	4	78.9	66.6	40.8	35.3	HP	1.07	2.64		12.3
Montenegro	2012	0.686	3.18	5	72.8	69.5	48.1	46.3	HP	1.95	2.22	16.7	4.6
Namibia	2009	0.422	1.73	5	86.1	85.5	75.0	74.3	EM	6.75	4.00		3.2
Nauru	2010	1.000					No Parties						
Netherlands	2012	0.825	5.70	9	52.7	51.2	27.3	26.5	HP	1.08	2.53	15.4	2.5
New Zealand	2011	0.665	2.98	5	76.9	74.8	48.8	47.3	HP	1.74	2.43	10.3	3.9
Niger	2011	0.778	4.51	7	55.8	53.6	32.7	33.0	HP	1.42	1.04		4.8

	YEAR	PFRG	ENPP	P2%S	2PSC	2PVC	1PSC	1PVC	ED	SR 1:2	SR 2:3	TVOL	DISP
Nigeria	2011	0.625	2.66	5	76.1		57.4		EM	3.06	1.89		9.3
Norway	2009	0.754	4.07	6	62.1	58.3	37.9	35.4	HP	1.56	1.37	6.6	5.4
Pakistan	2008	0.771	4.36	6	62.2	50.2	35.9	30.6	HP	1.37	1.69		13.7
Palau	2012	1.000					No Parties						
Panama	2009	0.732	3.73	5	67.6	57.9	36.6	35.7	HP	1.18	1.69		10.1
Papua New Guinea	2012	0.907	10.74	9	35.1		24.3		HP	2.25	1.50		
Paraguay	2008	0.708	3.42	5	71.3	61.3	37.5	33.0	HP	1.11	1.80		11.2
Peru	2011	0.748	3.97	6	64.6	48.2	36.2	25.3	HP	1.27	1.76		17.7
Philippines	2010	0.721	3.58	5	64.6	57.9	46.3	38.2	HP	2.52	1.35		10.1
Poland	2011	0.666	3.00	5	79.1	69.1	45.0	39.2	HP	1.32	3.93	10.0	10.0
Portugal	2011	0.659	2.93	5	79.1	66.8	47.0	38.7	HP	1.46	3.08	13.1	12.3
Romania	2008	0.723	3.60	4	68.6	65.5	34.4	32.4	HP	1.01	1.75	20.2	6.1
Saint Kitts and Nevis	2010	0.628	2.69	4	72.7	58.0	54.5	47.0	MM	3.00	2.00	5.0	14.7
Saint Lucia	2011	0.457	1.84	2	100.0	98.0	64.7	51.0	EM	1.83	∞	4.4	13.7
Saint Vincent and the Grenadines	2010	0.498	1.99	2	100.0	99.8	53.3	51.1	EM	1.14	∞	4.2	2.2
Samoa	2011	0.390	1.64	2	100.0	80.3	73.5	55.6	EM	2.77	∞		19.7
San Marino	2012	0.809	5.23	8	51.7	43.8	35.0	29.5	HP	2.10	1.43	27.4	8.2
São Tomé and Príncipe	2010	0.614	2.59	3	85.5	75.9	47.3	43.1	HP	1.24	3.00		9.6
Senegal	2012	0.362	1.57	4	87.3	68.3	79.3	53.1	EM	9.92	3.00		26.3
Serbia	2012	0.790	4.77	6	56.4	46.3	29.2	24.0	HP	1.07	1.51	16.4	16.9
Sierra Leone	2012	0.474	1.90	2	100.0	91.9	61.5	53.7	EM	1.32	∞	15.6	7.8
Slovakia	2012	0.653	2.88	6	66.0	53.2	55.3	44.4	MM	5.19	1.00	18.5	19.3
Slovenia	2011	0.788	4.73	7	60.0	54.8	31.1	28.5	HP	1.08	2.60	40.0	8.5
South Africa	2009	0.528	2.12	4	82.8	82.6	66.0	65.9	EM	3.94	2.23	11.9	1.1
Spain	2011	0.615	2.60	5	84.6	73.3	53.1	44.6	MM	1.69	6.88	15.4	12.5
Suriname	2010	0.688	3.21	4	72.5	71.9	45.1	40.2	HP	1.64	2.00	32.3	13.9
Sweden	2010	0.777	4.48	8	63.0	60.9	32.4	30.9	HP	1.06	4.28	8.6	2.2
Switzerland	2011	0.821	5.57	7	50.0	45.3	27.0	26.6	HP	1.17	1.53	10.1	7.3
Taiwan *	2012	0.482	1.93	2	99.1	95.0	61.1	51.5	EM	1.60	43.00	0.9	9.6
Thailand	2011	0.611	2.57	4	84.8	83.6	53.0	48.4	MM	1.67	4.68		9.3
Timor-Leste	2012	0.623	2.65	4	84.6	66.5	46.2	36.7	HP	1.20	3.13	15.1	20.1
Trinidad and Tobago	2010	0.414	1.71	2	100.0	99.7	70.7	60.0	EM	2.42	∞	7.5	10.7
Tunisia	2011	0.784	4.62	7	54.4	48.6	41.0	39.4	HP	3.07	1.12		24.6
Turkey	2011	0.573	2.34	4	84.0	75.8	59.5	49.8	MM	2.42	2.55	9.7	9.7
Tuvalu	2010	1.000					No Parties						
United Kingdom	2010	0.611	2.57	3	86.9	65.1	47.2	36.1	HP	1.19	4.53	7.2	22.7
United States	2012	0.497	1.99	2	100.0	97.2	53.8	48.1	MM	1.16	∞	4.3	5.7
Uruguay	2009	0.623	2.65	4	80.8	79.4	50.5	49.6	MM	1.67	1.76	8.1	1.4
Vanuatu	2012	0.924	13.13	11	26.9	19.3	15.4	11.3	HP	1.33	1.20		
Zambia	2011	0.670	3.03	4	76.7	71.8	40.0	38.3	HP	1.09	1.96		6.5

* calculated by electoral alliances

elections. Botswana, until recently, was the best national example of this type; some state legislatures in the United States still fit this pattern.

3. A *moderately multi-party system* has anywhere from three to six relevant parties, but it usually has four or five, still a moderate number. This party system is fairly deconcentrated in that the top two parties have less than 80 per cent of the seats (2PSC is below 80.0). Because no one party can win an outright majority, coalition government is the norm in a moderately multi-party parliamentary system. Examples include the party systems of Austria and Germany in Europe and Costa Rica in Latin America.

4. A *two-and-a-half-party system* is a distinctive subtype of a moderately multi-party system. This system also involves from three to six relevant parties, although usually only three to five. Of these, two parties are much larger than the rest, making a clear distinction between the two main parties and the "half" party or parties. In contrast to a moderately multi-party system, a two-and-a-half-party system involves the top two parties together winning 80 per cent or more of the seats. Also, only a small gap in size between the top two parties exists, a feature measured by the ratio of seats between the top party and the second-largest party (SR 1:2 in Table 7.4). It is thus possible, but never certain, in this type of party system for one of the main parties to win an outright majority of seats. If such a single-party majority does not occur, the likely government is a coalition between one of the main parties and a smaller party. Consequently, a party that is not one of the big two (that is, the "half" party in this system) could wind up with disproportionate influence, especially if it is an acceptable coalition partner to both main parties and can play these off against each other. Long-standing examples of such a party system have existed in Australia and West Germany (pre-reunification); more recent ones are in South Korea and France.[19] Note, too, that Canada had this type of party system through the early 1980s, with the Liberals and Progressive Conservatives as the two main parties and the NDP and, for a time, Social Credit each as a smaller "half" party. One difference in the Canadian version of this party system was that hung parliaments led to minority governments and early elections rather than to coalition governments. The 2011 Canadian election may have re-established, at least briefly, a two-and-a-half-party system: the Conservatives

won a single-party majority, and the NDP became the other main party, with the Liberal Party reduced to the "half."

5. A *highly multi-party system* is very fragmented and has more than six relevant parties. There are rarely any large parties, usually only medium and small ones. Not only are coalition governments the norm in non-presidential examples of this system, as they are in countries with a moderately multi-party system, but also the coalition governments in highly multi-party systems usually involve three or more parties, so they can be quite difficult to hold together. We have already noted Brazil and Israel as current illustrations of such a party system. Belgium, Denmark, Finland, Lithuania, and the Netherlands are European examples; India and Indonesia are other non-European examples. As its name suggests, a highly multi-party system is so fragmented that, unless there is cooperation amongst the parties, governance can be difficult and the quality of government will suffer. The party system of Weimar Germany is an historical example: it featured many parties and little cooperation—indeed, parties were often clearly antagonistic and polarized—and, as noted earlier, the democratic regime ultimately broke down.

6. A *one-party predominant system* should not be confused with a pure one-party system, as in China or Cuba, which by definition is non-democratic. Rather, one-party predominant systems are multi-party systems in that they have at least three relevant parties. However, one of these parties is much larger than the rest, as evidenced by a large gap between the first and second party in both votes and seats (on seats, see SR 1:2 in Table 7.4). This one large party is so big that it both predominates in parliament and controls the government for decades or, at a minimum, for a long period of time. Such long-term control may involve outright single-party majorities, but, even when it fails to win an outright majority, the predominant party can either form a minority government or lead a coalition—and it usually has its pick of willing coalition partners. The ability of the major party in a one-party predominate system to dominate the legislature even in the absence of a majority is the key difference between this system and the imbalanced two-party system. If the traditionally dominant party fails to win a majority in the imbalanced two-party system, presumably, the traditional opposition party has done so and will take over power. In a one-party predomi-

nant system, displacing the dominant party from power involves not only that party failing to win a majority but also having most if not all of the traditional opposition parties band together—a coalition that is usually not very durable. There are two classic, long-standing national examples of this party system: the predominance in Japan of the Liberal Democratic Party (LDP) from 1955 to 1993, if not, indeed, to 2009, and the predominance in Sweden of the Social Democrats from 1932 until 1976. Other, albeit weaker, historical examples are the Christian Democrats (DC) in Italy who had one-party predominance from 1946 until 1992 (or at least until 1983) and the Mapai/Labour Party in Israel, which predominated from 1948 until 1977.[20] In terms of ongoing examples, one-party predominance definitely has existed in Namibia since 1991 with its predominant South West Africa People's Organization (SWAPO) and in South Africa since 1994 with its predominant African National Congress (ANC).

Party System Institutionalization

All of the party systems listed previously describe patterns that are both clear and durable, with, for example, the number of relevant parties in a country remaining more or less constant over several elections. In most cases, the patterns have also involved the same specific parties over several elections. However, such stability in parties is not a given in democracies. Acknowledging this fact leads us to another contemporary aspect of party systems: party system institutionalization, that is, the extent to which the party system is coherent and stable in terms of the main parties, how these parties differ in terms of ideology and core voters, and how they are tied to society. This concept was developed by Mainwaring and Scully in their 1995 edited book on Latin America.[21] An updated measure of this concept was then done for Latin America by the Inter-American Development Bank.[22] With some modifications, the Mainwaring and Scully approach has also been applied to Africa by Kuenzi and Lambright.[23] However, no cross-continent global study of party system institutionalization has ever been done. The studies that do exist have used largely the same variables in assessing institutionalization in a given country, these being:

▶ the inter-election volatility in parties' support, summed for all parties (the lower the better);

▸ the difference between presidential and legislative election support (the more people vote for the same party at both levels the better);

▸ the age of all parties with at least 10 per cent of the vote or, alternatively, of the top two parties (the older the better);

▸ the dominance of long-established parties;

▸ the general legitimacy of parties and elections, including both citizens and political leaders seeing elections as the only legitimate way to gain and hold power; and

▸ the acceptance of electoral defeat by losing parties.

To repeat, institutionalized party systems have low volatility over time, durable parties with clear roots in society (presumably based on relevant social cleavages such as ethnicity, language, religion, religiosity, class, or region), and broad support for parties and elections as legitimate political institutions. These studies rank the countries concerned on a continuum or at least suggest multiple broad categories of institutionalization, with the lowest category being called by Mainwaring and Scully "inchoate" party systems.[24]

Unfortunately, what works for one region becomes problematic when applied globally. Some countries lack credible—or any!—party vote statistics, which are needed to calculate volatility (and also disproportionality; see Table 7.4). Measuring variations in presidential and legislative voting does not require a full presidential system, as this system was defined in the previous chapter, but it does assume an elected president. Mainwaring and Scully define a long-established party as one founded by 1950. Kuenzi and Lambright note, however, that, because most African countries did not become independent until around 1960, 1970 is the relevant cut-off date for that continent. They also add, "Should one want to conduct a study that includes countries from multiple world regions, this indicator may need to be adjusted accordingly."[25] However, adjusting this indicator back and forth may cause it to lose its comparative utility.

Consequently, rather than developing a full continuum of party system institutionalization, we settle for a basic dichotomy of more institutionalized party systems versus less institutionalized ones, as listed in Table 7.5. Hard numbers have been used where they exist, but so too has been a general sense of the party system's "rootedness" in

TABLE 7.5 Party System Institutionalization (2012)

MORE INSTITUTIONALIZED PARTY SYSTEMS

Andorra	Dominica	Liechtenstein	Saint Kitts and Nevis
Antigua and Barbuda	Dominican Republic	Luxembourg	Saint Lucia
Argentina	El Salvador	Macedonia	Saint Vincent and the Grenadines
Australia	Estonia	Malta	Samoa
Austria	Finland	Mauritius	San Marino
Bahamas	France	Mexico	Senegal
Bangladesh	Germany	Moldova	Serbia
Barbados	Ghana	Montenegro	Sierra Leone
Belgium	Greece	Namibia	South Africa
Belize	Honduras	Netherlands	Spain
Botswana	Hungary	New Zealand	Sweden
Canada	Iceland	Nigeria	Switzerland
Cape Verde	India	Norway	Taiwan
Chile	Ireland	Pakistan	Thailand
Costa Rica	Israel	Panama	Trinidad and Tobago
Croatia	Italy	Paraguay	Turkey
Cyprus	Jamaica	Poland	United Kingdom
Czech Republic	Japan	Portugal	United States
Denmark	Korea, South	Romania	Uruguay

LESS INSTITUTIONALIZED PARTY SYSTEMS

Benin	Guatemala	Lithuania	Slovakia
Bolivia	Guyana	Mongolia	Slovenia
Brazil	Indonesia	Niger	Suriname
Bulgaria	Ivory Coast	Papua New Guinea	Timor-Leste (East Timor)
Colombia	Kyrgyzstan	Peru	Tunisia
Comoros	Latvia	Philippines	Vanuatu
Ecuador	Lesotho	São Tomé and Príncipe	Zambia
Grenada	Liberia	Senegal	

SYSTEMS WITHOUT POLITICAL PARTIES

Kiribati	Micronesia	Palau
Marshall Islands	Nauru	Tuvalu

society in various countries. Of particular utility for assessing this "rootedness" in developing and post-communist countries are the Bertelsmann Transformation Index's country scores for the party system, which emphasize the extent to which the party system is stable and socially rooted. Beyond less institutionalized party systems are those Pacific states with no parties at all. For the more institutionalized party systems, the various numerical features of fragmentation and specific types outlined earlier are quite likely to remain with only modest variations for a given country. However, for the less institutionalized party systems "all bets are off"; these may well look very different come their next election.

Beyond being relevant in and of itself, party system institutionalization has clear broader ramifications for comparative democratic performance and stability. The advantages of an institutionalized party system are multiple.[26] First, institutionalized parties are better able not only to articulate but also to aggregate, channel, and reach compromises among citizens' demands. Second and conversely, an institutionalized party system is obviously more accountable than one in which parties come and go or change themselves constantly. Third and consequently, in an institutionalized system, the parties have value in and of themselves, so politicians are more likely to consider the long-term effects of their decisions. Fourth, an institutionalized party system will have greater party discipline, making it easier for the legislature to function (all other things being equal in terms of fragmentation). A fifth point related to the fourth is that an institutionalized party system is more likely to be able to deliver support to the political executive, producing less gridlock and immobility than in an inchoate system. Although this point might seem applicable only to presidential systems, it in fact holds for parliamentary ones as well; for example, in the inchoate party system of Papua New Guinea, until recently, no prime minister had ever served a full parliamentary term.[27] Sixth and finally, party system institutionalization reduces the corruption that occurs under traditional patterns of personal relationships and amongst politicians who are patrons to local clients. Indeed, a comparison between the more and less institutionalized party systems in terms of the 2011 scores of Transparency International's Corruption Perceptions Index,[28] where the data exist, yields an average score of 5.554 for the more institutionalized party systems and an average score of 3.113 for the less institutionalized party systems (with a higher score indicating less corruption). A t-test here, with equal variances not assumed, gives a very high value of 8.010, which is significant at the .000 level. Overall, then, party system institutionalization can certainly be seen to lead to more effective government.

Government Formation

Parliamentary governments can be divided into four main types in terms of the number of parties in the cabinet and their seats in the legislature, as shown in Figure 7.1. Which type is formed in a given situation? With regard to post-election government

FIGURE 7.1 Types of Parliamentary Government by Number of Parties in the Cabinet and Legislative Support

PARTIES IN CABINET

	One	More Than One
More Than 50 Per Cent	single-party majority	majority coalition
50 Per Cent Or Less	single-party minority	minority coalition

LEGISLATIVE SUPPORT

formation in parliamentary systems, the formation rules provide the starting point. For example, is a formal **vote of investiture** required? (See the previous chapter.) Granted, if one party has won a majority of seats, this vote is a formality. However, in the common occurrence of a **hung parliament**, this procedure will predispose the formation of a majority coalition to win such a vote. In contrast, if no such vote is required (*negative parliamentarianism*), the largest party may simply form a minority government, or a couple of parties may form a coalition but one still lacking a majority. Scandinavia has often seen small minority governments with less than 40 per cent of the seats.[29] A single-party minority is also common in countries with a strong political convention that the largest party should form the government by itself, as is the case in Canada.[30]

Absent these features, however, a parliamentary system is likely to have a majority coalition government, and coalition formation involves a choice among various combinations, not all of which include the largest party. The different possibilities are obviously more numerous the more parties there are, in particular, in a highly multi-party system. As noted in the previous chapter, Israel from 1996 through 2001 held three separate direct elections for the prime minister, but that took it out of the realm of parliamentary systems. In a parliamentary system with a hung parliament and the need for a coalition, then, someone normally is given the first "try" (opportunity) to form a government, and that person is thus designated the **formateur**. If this would-be head of government is successful in forming a coalition and—if required—getting this coalition approved by parliament in a vote of investiture, then and only then does she or he actually become the head of government. If the first would-be formateur is unsuccessful, another is appointed, and so on. At some point, however, if no one can form a government, fresh elections may have to be called. Still, one wants to be the first formateur because there are advantages to going first, and, if the first formateur is successful, there is no opportunity for anyone else. How is the formateur determined? In Greece since 1986, the constitution specifies that the leader of the largest party becomes the first formateur, and, if that individual is unsuccessful, the leader of the second-largest party becomes the next formateur. In Ireland, the deputies propose candidates and the lower house (Dáil) votes on one, leaving the president merely to make the appointment. But, in most countries, no presupposition exists in favour of the largest party or its leader (even if that person is often asked to form the government), and, normally, the head of state decides who has the best chance of forming a government (occasionally the speaker decides, as in Sweden since 1975).[31] This role does allow a certain discretion for the head of state, if not, indeed, an outright bias, as there are often multiple feasible options in terms of both a coalition of parties and a prime minister. Presidents in parliamentary systems do use this power to favour their own parties and equally to exclude from government parties they do not like (that is, parties distant from them ideologically), when possible.[32] In countries where the head of state is a president, and especially an elected one, this bias is an accepted reality. However, the head of state who is a monarch may well want to remain scrupulously neutral (at least in appearance). In this case, the head of state might rely on an **informateur** to consult the political parties as to their coalition and policy preferences and then give advice on the selection of a formateur. The first use of an informateur was in Belgium, but informateurs have also been commonly used in other Northern European multi-party parliamentary democracies such as Denmark and the Netherlands.[33] The informateur is normally an elder statesperson or at least a politician without further ambition, someone who can provide an objective assessment of the political situation.

If a single party wins a majority, a government is normally formed quite quickly. Indeed, in the United Kingdom, a new prime minister of a single-party majority government is sometimes sworn in the day after the election, with the rest of the cabinet following shortly. However, a **hung parliament** offers no guarantee that the first formateur will be successful or that the whole process will be quick. The formation period could last a month, or two, or much longer. The record here is clearly that of Belgium, where, after the election of June 2010, a government was not finally formed and invested into office until December 2011—that is, 18 months later. (The previous government continued serving in a caretaker capacity.) Belgium's previous government formation, in 2007, took six months. Both very long formations reflect Belgium's extreme legislative fragmentation and paralysis.[34] And in Iraq, the formation period in 2010 was 290 days, the second-longest time after Belgium's. Institutionally, the only alternative here is putting a time limit on the total formation period and holding new elections if no government is formed by the end of this time. This process occurs in both Greece and Israel.

What of governmental formation in presidential systems? First, note that coalition governments can and do occur in these systems, especially in Latin America.[35] In the United States, the two-party system works against coalitions, as it does in two-party parliamentary systems. Overall, though, the government formation process in presidential systems is much simpler than in parliamentary systems. The head of government (the president) has already been directly elected by the voters and is separate from the legislature. So no **vote of investiture** is ever needed. The president can also be seen as a quasi-formateur, in that he or she is the one trying to bring other parties into government. But no government can exclude the president's party, so a lot fewer combinations are possible in a presidential system than in a parliamentary one, keeping the party system (i.e., the number and size of parties) constant. Finally, without votes of investiture or motions of non-confidence, having 50 per cent plus one legislative support does not affect government formation and survival (although it does affect the administration's ability to pass legislation), so in a multi-party system a near majority may suffice.[36]

Alternatives to Executive Coalitions

Up to this point, a coalition has meant an entity that includes more than one party in the cabinet. Strictly speaking, this is an *executive coalition*. However, parties may support the government but not get or ask for cabinet seats, and, thus, their members could avoid being bound by cabinet solidarity across all issues. These parties could still form a *legislative coalition*, in that they would vote together on matters

TABLE 7.6 Levels of Legislative Support and Coalitions

Arrangement	Duration	Policy Scope	Nature of Agreement	Ministerial and other Positions for Smaller Party
Full executive coalition	indefinite (full legislative term)	all policy areas but possible agreement to disagree in certain areas	detailed written public document	smaller party has regular ministers in cabinet with full cabinet solidarity
Contract parliamentarianism	indefinite (full legislative term)	many or most policy areas; otherwise, agreement to disagree	detailed written public document	smaller party may have ministers but these are outside cabinet
Supply and confidence agreement	can be indefinite or for a short, specific period	limited but including support on budgets and other confidence matters plus some policies desired by the smaller party; otherwise, agreement to disagree	varies; not detailed and sometimes not written	normally some committee or other positions
Cooperation agreement	can be indefinite or for a short, specific period	limited but including not opposing budgets and other confidence matters plus some policies desired by the smaller party; otherwise, agreement to disagree	varies; not detailed and sometimes not written	possibly some committee or other positions
Ad hoc support	none; issue by issue	only on the specific issue	nothing formal and public	none

of confidence, on most legislation, or on certain agreed-upon issues. A good example here is the government formed after the June 2012 elections in Greece under conservative Prime Minister Samaras. Although his government was often referred to as a three-party coalition, it is important to note that the two centre-left parties backing him and voting for his government barred their MPs from taking seats in cabinet. Instead, each party nominated two independents. In this way, the two parties presumably hoped to limit their association with the economic austerity measures of the government.

Indeed, governments can receive support from other parties or from independents in a range of ways.[37] Table 7.6 lists the main arrangements here, and this list can be nuanced even further.[38]

The first type, a full executive coalition, is fairly common, and is the standard government of much of continental Europe. It also exists since 2010 in the United Kingdom with its Conservative–Liberal Democrat coalition government. The second type is less common and has arisen recently in countries such as New Zealand and Sweden where it is called "contract parliamentarianism." This arrangement shares the permanent nature (for a given parliamentary term) and policy detail of a full coalition, but it allows the smaller party to have a minister in perhaps its main area of concern (say, the environment for a green party) while not requiring this smaller party to defend publicly everything the government does. Contract parliamentarianism can also arise if the smaller party pledged during the election campaign not to enter into coalition with the major party or with any party and wishes to keep this pledge formally. Even though legislative support from this smaller party may yield what is effectively a legislative majority (via a legislative coalition) with the same stability as a majority government, technically minority *governance* still exists in terms of the formal cabinet.[39] The next two types of support involve a smaller party or independents keeping a government in office by voting with it on non-confidence matters (under a supply and confidence agreement) or at least not voting against it on non-confidence matters (under a cooperation agreement). In return, the supporting parties or independents receive certain policy concessions. The smaller party may also get more legislative positions or "perks" in these arrangements than it would otherwise. Failing any of these arrangements, a minority government has to seek ad hoc support from other parties issue by issue. Last, it is important to note that, in a given country, more than one of these situations may occur at the same time. Thus, for example, after the 2005 elections in New Zealand, the Labour Party (with 50 out of 121 seats, just two more than its main opponent, the opposition National Party) did the following: (a) continued its minority coalition government with the Progressives (now down to one seat); (b) established contract parliamentarianism with both the New Zealand First party (with seven seats) and the United Future party (with three seats), each of which had a minister outside of cabinet (in the case of New Zealand First this was the Minister of Foreign Affairs, no small post); and (c) as additional security, reached a cooperation agreement with the Greens (with six seats).[40] The Labour-Progressive government, which was formally a minority, thus lasted the full parliamentary term.

Notes

1 David M. Farrell, *Electoral Systems: A Comparative Introduction* (Basingstoke, UK: Palgrave, 2001), 4 (italics in original).

2 See Farrell, *Electoral Systems*, 6 on these three central aspects.

3 The total number of districts is not, in itself, a relevant factor.

4 For almost all its states, the US electoral college illustrates well this winner-take-all qualification.

5 See, in particular, Arend Lijphart, *Electoral Systems and Party Systems: A Study of Twenty-Seven Democracies, 1945–1990* (Oxford, UK: Oxford University Press, 1994), 12.

6   On this phenomenon, see Alan Siaroff, "Spurious Majorities, Electoral Systems and Electoral System Change," *Commonwealth & Comparative Politics* 41, no. 2 (July 2003): 143–60.

7   John Loosemore and Victor J. Hanby, "The Theoretical Limits of Maximum Distortion: Some Analytical Expressions for Electoral Systems," *British Journal of Political Science* 1, no. 4 (October 1971): 467–77. In fact, Loosemore and Hanby's original index (see page 469) ranged from 0 to 1; however, it is standard now to measure this variable from 0 to 100. For a comparison of the Loosemore-Hanby and other measures of disproportionality, see Lijphart, *Electoral Systems and Party Systems*, 58–67.

8   Indeed, to be precise, all votes beyond one more than the second-placed candidate are "surplus" and thus wasted.

9   Farrell, *Electoral Systems*, 130.

10   The threshold is also only 2 per cent in Mexico for the proportional representation component of its electoral system.

11   The Peruvian Congress contains 120 seats, which are spread across 25 electoral districts. The district of Lima (the main city and capital) contains 35 seats, so results there are quite proportional. The other 24 districts, though, have an average district magnitude of only 3.5, which is clearly inadequate for smaller parties.

12   See Dag Anckar and Carsten Anckar, "Democracies without Parties," *Comparative Political Studies* 33, no. 2 (March 2000): 225–47.

13   See Giovanni Sartori, *Parties and Party Systems: A Framework for Analysis* (New York, NY: Cambridge University Press, 1976).

14   On this decline in Latin America, see J. Mark Payne et al., *Democracies in Development: Politics and Reform in Latin America* (Washington, DC: Inter-American Development Bank, 2002), 148.

15   Scott Mainwaring and Timothy R. Scully, "Introduction: Party Systems in Latin America," in *Building Democratic Institutions: Party Systems in Latin America*, ed. Scott Mainwaring and Timothy R. Scully (Stanford, CA: Stanford University Press, 1995), 1–34, see page 5; Payne et al., *Democracies in Development*, 127.

16   On party institutionalization see, for example, Samuel P. Huntington, *Political Order in Changing Societies* (New Haven, CT: Yale University Press, 1968).

17   For its part, Papua New Guinea had a P2%S value of 12 after its 2007 elections.

18   The United States has actually seen the most competition between its two parties at the level of the presidency.

19   On this type of party system in longstanding democracies and on the varied role of the "half" party or parties therein, see Alan Siaroff, "Two-and-a-Half-Party Systems and the Comparative Role of the 'Half,'" *Party Politics* 9, no. 3 (May 2003): 267–90.

20   On these "classic cases," see T.J. Pempel, ed., *Uncommon Democracies? The One-Party Predominant Systems* (Ithaca, NY: Cornell University Press, 1990).

21   Scott Mainwaring and Timothy R. Scully, eds., *Building Democratic Institutions: Party Systems in Latin America* (Stanford, CA: Stanford University Press, 1995).

22   Payne et al., *Democracies in Development*, Chapter 6.

23   Michelle Kuenzi and Gina Lambright, "Party System Institutionalization in 30 African Countries," *Party Politics* 7, no. 4 (July 2001): 437–68.

24   Mainwaring and Scully, *Building Democratic Institutions*, 19.

25   Kuenzi and Lambright, "Party System Institutionalization," 446.

26   Mainwaring and Scully, *Building Democratic Institutions*, 25–26; Payne et al., *Democracies in Development*, 127–28.

27   For a long time, Papua New Guinea was an extreme case of an inchoate party system, with a huge number of independents elected, frequent floor crossing (that is, MPs switching parties), and prime ministers that never lasted a full term. Political changes made in 2001 sought to produce greater stability, and these have been successful: few independents are now elected, and a prime minister did serve a full term from 2002 to 2007. That said, the overall party system in Papua New Guinea is still inchoate—but clearly not as much as before. See Benjamin Reilly, "Political Reform in Papua New Guinea: Testing the Evidence," *Pacific Economic Bulletin* 21, no. 1 (2006): 187–94.

28   See the "Corruption Perceptions Index," Transparency International: The Global Coalition against Corruption, accessed October 2012, http://www.transparency.org/research/cpi/.

29   Torbjörn Bergman, "Formation Rules and Minority Governments," *European Journal of Political Research* 23, no. 1 (January 1993): 55–66.

30   Ian Stewart, "Of Customs and Coalitions: The Formation of Canadian Federal Parliamentary Alliances," *Canadian Journal of Political Science* 13, no. 3 (September 1980): 451–79.

31   This person might not be the leader of the largest party if this party is not that large or is ideologically extreme. Both size and median position matter for becoming the party with the prime minister or other head of government. Also important is wanting to be in government, and the largest party might not want this if it has suffered an electoral loss or for other reasons. On these points, see Guy-Erik Isaksson, "From Election to Government: Principal Rules and Deviant Cases," *Government and Opposition* 40, no. 3 (Summer 2005): 329–57.

32   Shin-Goo Kang, "The Influence of Presidential Heads of State on Government Formation in European Democracies: Empirical Evidence," *European Journal of Political Research* 48, no. 4 (June 2009): 543–72.

33   Vernon Bogdanor, "The Government Formation Process in the Constitutional Monarchies of North-West Europe," in *Comparative Government and Politics: Essays in Honour of S.E. Finer*, ed. Dennis Kavanagh and Gillian Peele (London, UK: Heinemann, 1984), 49–72, see pages 57–66.

34   Marc Hooghe, "The Political Crisis in Belgium (2007–2011): A Federal System Without Federal Loyalty," *Representation: Journal of Representative Democracy* 48, no. 1 (April 2012): 131–38.

35   Daniel Chasquetti, *Democracia, presidencialismo y partidos políticos en América Latina: Evaluando la "difícil combinación"* (Montevideo: Ediciones CAUCE, 2008), especially chapters 3–5. On Brazil, see Argelina Cheibub Figueiredo, "Government Coalitions in Brazilian Democracy," *Brazilian Political Science Review* 1, no. 2 (July 2007): 182–216.

36   Jones puts this threshold at 45 per cent of the seats. Mark P. Jones, *Electoral Laws and the Survival of Presidential Democracies* (Notre Dame, IN: University of Notre Dame Press, 1995), 37–38.

37   Independents were central to determining the government after the Australian elections of 2010. However, not surprisingly, the ongoing role of independents in government formation is most clearly found in Ireland with its regular election of many independents. Liam Weeks, "Independents in Government: A Sui Generis Model?" in *New Parties in Government: In Power For the First Time*, ed. Kris Deschouwer (London, UK and New York, NY: Routledge, 2008), 137–56.

38 In fact, Boston and Bullock list eight different forms of formal governance arrangements that have occurred in New Zealand since the mid-1990s between one of the two main parties and smaller ones. Jonathan Boston and David Bullock, "Multi-Party Governance: Managing the Unity-Distinctiveness Dilemma in Executive Coalitions," *Party Politics* 18, no. 3 (May 2012): 349–68, see pages 354–56.

39 Tim Bale and Torbjörn Bergman, "Captives No Longer, but Servants Still? Contract Parliamentarism and the New Minority Governance in Sweden and New Zealand," *Government and Opposition* 41, no. 3 (Summer 2006): 422–49.

40 Boston and Bullock, "Multi-Party Governance," 358–59.

CHAPTER EIGHT

Overall Centralization versus Decentralization in Democracies

IN THIS CHAPTER YOU WILL LEARN

- what is meant by the "Westminster model";
- what the scholarly debates on classifying democracies have been;
- how to distinguish between supermajority and simple-majority rule, and how these opposite forms of majority rule vary across democracies;
- how to distinguish between localism-majoritarianism and centralism-proportionality in elections, how democracies vary in their application of these principles, and with what consequences; and
- what is meant by a decentralized democracy versus a centripetal democracy.

Chapter 6 outlined various institutional variations of democracies. An additional institutional variation, the electoral system, was explained in Chapter 7. However, in their comparative analyses, political scientists usually combine these and other factors in various ways to produce overall models of democratic regimes in terms of their allocation of power. Often non-institutional but central aspects of a democratic polity, such as its party system or the number of parties in government, are included in such types as well. The problem, though, is that these aspects of democratic regimes are more fluid. Consequently, we have decided, ultimately, to identify contrasting models of democracies that are largely based on institutional factors and that combine two measures of centralization/decentralization.

The Westminster Model

By its very name, the **Westminster model** refers to the reality of British politics in the modern era. Yet the term, in fact, applies to any political system that has this model's central features, namely, the concentration of power in a democratic parliamentary regime so that the political executive, composed of the prime minister and cabinet, governs with broad freedom and no or minimal checks and balances. That said, not only is the government and politics of the United Kingdom the basis of this model, but Britain is the former colonial power that passed this model, or at least its individual features, down to many of its colonies. As Arend Lijphart, who has done much to define this model, notes: "The British version of the Westminster model is both the original and the best-known example of this model."[1]

The actual aspects of this model vary depending on the source. For Lijphart, the model has two dimensions—an executive-parties dimension and a federal-unitary dimension—each with five aspects. For their part, Rhodes and Weller, after an exhaustive literature review, have come up with no less than 18 factors that one or more scholars attribute to the Westminster model.[2] For our purposes, though, the three core features of a Westminster democracy are as follows:

▶ a parliamentary system, with the head of state having only a ceremonial role;

▶ the concentration of political power in the executive of the central government, which experiences minimal or no checks and balances, with the executive or cabinet dominating the legislature and the prime minister, thus, a powerful political figure; and

▶ a two-party system based on a single-member plurality (SMP) electoral system— or at least a single-member electoral system—with this electoral system's bias in favour of larger parties.

To further delineate each of these points, we can describe an ideal political feature, one that exactly matches a particular aspect of the model, but note other features that certainly fit the spirit of the Westminster model. Ideally, following the British pattern, the head of state with the ceremonial role is a monarch or the governor general, the monarch's representative in various Commonwealth countries; however, a ceremonial president, such as exists in Malta, also fits the spirit of the model. The purest version of the concentration of power in the executive involves unicameralism, as in New Zealand since 1951. Of course, the United Kingdom itself is bicameral, ironically. Nevertheless, the upper house is weak in the United Kingdom; thus, as long as bicameralism is not strong, as defined in Chapter 6, the spirit of the Westminster model is preserved. Equally, the ideal type of this model has a unitary state as in New Zealand and not federalism. However, as long as any regional governments are weak and lack constitutional protection (as is true for the regional governments now within the United Kingdom), then the spirit of the model is preserved. The ideal situation typifying the third and last core feature of the Westminster model is a single-party majority government exercising the unconstrained power described as the model's second core feature and facing an opposition that is the alternative government should the voters so choose. The key here is that there are two main parties even if not only two parties. A single-party government provides clear *accountability*; that is, the voters know whom to blame if they are unhappy. Such accountability is less clear in a coalition, unless the parties are always in permanent alliance (as are, for example, the two conservative parties in Australia). Presumably, a single-party minority government would fit the spirit of Westminster accountability, but it would not have the same *decisiveness* that is also argued to be a virtue of this model.

So where do we find this model in the real world? Obviously, it has existed in the United Kingdom, although, as noted, the UK government does not have as perfect a concentration of power as it could—and since 2010 the country has had a coalition government. As implied, New Zealand was, for many decades, an even better example, but its 1996 change to the MMP version of proportional representation has shifted it away from the model in some key ways. Australia and Canada have often had single-party majorities, but the federalism in these countries is the antithesis of parts of the model. That said, the governments and politics of the Australian states and the Canadian provinces, within the areas of their jurisdiction, are usually quite good examples of the Westminster model. In terms of sovereign countries, though, those that are closest to the pure Westminster model today are the former British colonies of the Caribbean.

Majority Rule or More Than This?

Besides the work of Lijphart, several other studies exist that seek to measure majoritarianism and political centralization and their opposites.[3] Similarly, some scholars focus on the number of veto players or veto points in a political system, based on the argument that the more actors who can veto a decision or policy change or the more points at which such pressure can be applied, the less likely the change will actually occur.[4]

In this chapter, we produce a summary assessment of democracies in terms of the centralization of power versus institutional power sharing. Before we proceed, it is important to note a conceptual and definitional issue. As mentioned, Lijphart's one ideal type is majoritarian or Westminster democracy, wherein the majority (or, more accurately in terms of votes, usually the *plurality*) rules. The opposite situation he describes as consensus democracy, that is, "a democratic regime that emphasizes consensus instead of opposition, that includes rather than excludes, and that tries to maximize the size of the ruling majority instead of being satisfied with a bare majority."[5] Yet consensus is essentially a behavioural trait that can, of course, be facilitated or at least encouraged by certain institutions but that can also exist separately from such institutions. In other words, in a majoritarian system, there may well be consensus between the government and the opposition on various policies.[6] However, no consensus might exist on other issues, and, certainly, there is no ongoing consensus in the polity. Thus, it is better to emphasize the broadly inclusive nature of the majority in a structural rather than a behavioural sense. Scholars have proposed a couple of conceptual alternatives to political institutions being based on majority rule. One option here is thus to use the phrase of Schmidt: counter-majoritarianism.[7] Certainly, if a minority can and does veto the will of the majority, this is counter-majoritarian. Yet, if we focus more positively on decisions that are actually taken rather than proposals that are vetoed, then, obviously, the majority will be behind these approved decisions. So how do we determine whether decisions are supported by just the bare majority (plurality) of those in power or whether there is a broader level of agreement? It seems useful to use McGann's notion of *supermajority* versus *simple-majority* rule, in which the simple majority governs without any or with only a few constitutional or institutional checks.[8]

According to Dieter Fuchs, it is best to limit this assessment to more-or-less permanent institutional features, rather than, say, something frequently changing, such as election results or the number of parties in government.[9] Several such institutional features are measured in Table 8.1. That said, an electoral system is *not* one of these measures of supermajoritarianism. Why not? An electoral system is certainly a key political institution and will shape other, more changeable variables that are often part of this debate: e.g., electoral decisiveness, the possibility of manufactured majorities, and party systems. However, which way electoral systems "cut" is debatable. Which types of systems go with majoritarianism or supermajoritarianism and power sharing and which go with simple-majority rule? Some scholars consider proportional representation to "fit" with institutional supermajoritarianism, because proportional representation leads to multi-partism and thus more veto actors. Likewise, plurality voting and bare majority rule are both part of a simple-majority Westminster system.[10] However, other scholars argue that single-member plurality (single-member districts) are part of a decentralized and supermajoritarian structure because single-member systems make elections local whereas proportional representation (especially closed-list PR) centralizes power in national parties that take a national perspective on matters.[11] As Huber Ragin and Stephens note concerning the access of actors to political power,

> [W]e attempt to identify points of entry in the political system for influential minority groups to block legislation favored by narrow electoral (or public opinion) majorities. Proportional representation is generally accompanied by high party control over nominations and thus by stronger coherence of disciplined parties. In PR systems with party control over closed lists, revolts of backbenchers, such as those in the British system where there are single-member districts, are extremely rare. Thus, special interest organizations, such as associations of medical professionals, insurance companies, or beneficiaries of special welfare state programs have to lobby entire parties rather than individual politicians, which is a much more difficult task.[12]

Yet what remains an issue is how often party discipline breaks down in single-member systems. Certainly, the United States is a classic, if not extreme, case of a political system in which there is limited party discipline and individual politicians elected in single-member districts are subjected to endless lobbying. In summary, given this academic debate rather than scholarly consensus, we do not include the electoral system within the scale of supermajoritarianism but instead place it as part of a separate dimension in a second measure.

The Additive Index of Supermajoritarianism

A useful way of viewing the issue of supermajoritarianism is, assuming a prime minister exists, asking how much power this prime minister has in a given country, bearing in mind that the prime minister assumes this position based on his or her party's control of the lower or single house. Consequently, the prime minister's power in any given democracy depends on how much the constitution and political institutions concentrate or disperse power. In democracies with a broad dispersion of political power, a prime minister and government cannot act alone but will need to get broad agreement to do or change anything. These democracies tend towards supermajoritarianism. Conversely, in democracies having few checks on the executive, a government—certainly a majority government—can do pretty much what it likes. These democracies practise simple-majority rule.

To determine how supermajoritarian a democracy is, we measure seven factors; specific scores are given in Table 8.1. Normally, each of these measurements is on a 0 to 2 scale, and, in all cases, a higher score means more supermajoritarianism. The first factor involves the issue of whether there are relevant regional governments in a country's provinces, states, or other subnational districts, assuming these exist. Countries are scored 2 if their regional governments are constitutionally entrenched and directly elected and have collectively at least one-third of the tax revenue of the national government. (These countries, then, are listed as "more so" in Figure 6.2 to indicate that they have considerable interstate federalism.) Democracies score 1 if their regional governments are constitutionally entrenched and directly elected but lack such strong revenue or if they are not constitutionally entrenched but directly elected and have such revenue (this would be Sweden). They score 0 otherwise—if their regional governments lack constitutional entrenchment and strong revenue or if they have no regional governments. Brazil, Canada, and the United States are examples of countries that score 2 on this factor; Austria, Mexico, and South Africa are examples of countries that score 1; and France, New Zealand, and the United Kingdom are examples of countries that score 0.

Next is the issue of bicameralism in the national legislature. Countries are scored 2 if they have strong bicameralism (as that concept is defined Chapter 6); 1 if their legislatures are bicameral, but bicameralism is weak not strong; and 0 if their legislatures are unicameral. Australia, Germany, and the United States are examples of countries that score 2 on this factor; Canada, France, and the United Kingdom are examples of countries that score 1; and the Nordic countries are examples of countries that score 0.

The third factor measured is the extent to which the judicial review of legislation is practised by national supreme courts. Judicial review is certainly a much more

TABLE 8.1 Index of Supermajoritarianism (2012)

Country	Relevant Regional Governments (range of 0 to 2)	Bicameralism (range of 0 to 2)	Judicial Review (range of 0 to 2)	Powers of Separate Head of State (range of 0 to 2)	Autonomy and Legitimacy (directly elected)*	Term Non-concurrent with that of Legislature*	Referenda (range of 0 to 2)	Concordance Democracy (range of 0 to 2)	Constitutional Rigidity (range of 0 to 2)	Total (out of 16)
United States	2	2	2	2	1	1	0	0	2	12
Switzerland	2	2	0	0			2	2	2	10
Argentina	1	2	0	2	1	1	0	0	2	9
Brazil	2	2	1	2	1	0	0	0	1	9
Colombia	0	2	2	2	1	1	0	0	1	9
Mexico	1	2	1	2	1	1	0	0	1	9
Nigeria	1	1	2	2	1	0	0	0	2	9
Australia	2	2	1	0			1	0	2	8
Germany	2	2	2	0			0	1	1	8
Indonesia	1	1	1	2	1	1	0	0	1	8
Micronesia	2	0	1	2	0	1	0	0	2	8
Palau	0	1	1	2	1	0	1	0	2	8
Philippines	0	2	1	2	1	1	0	0	1	8
Canada	2	1	2	0			0	0	2	7
India	2	1	2	0			0	1	1	7
South Africa	1	1	1	2	0	0	0	0	2	7
Belgium	1	1	1	0			0	2	1	6
Comoros	0	0	0	2	1	1	0	1	1	6
Cyprus	0	0	1	2	1	1	0	0	1	6
Ireland	0	1	0	1	1	1	1	0	1	6
Italy	0	2	1	0			1	1	1	6
Korea, South	0	0	1	2	1	1	0	0	1	6
Poland	0	1	1	1	1	1	0	0	1	6
Senegal	0	1	0	2	1	1	0	0	1	6
Taiwan	0	0	1	1	1	1	0	0	2	6
Uruguay	0	1	0	2	1	0	1	0	1	6
Austria	1	1	1	0			0	1	1	5
Benin	0	0	0	2	1	1	0	0	1	5
Bolivia	0	1	0	2	1	0	0	0	1	5
Bulgaria	0	0	1	1	1	1	0	0	1	5
Cape Verde	0	0	0	2	1	1	0	0	1	5
Chile	0	1	0	2	1	0	0	0	1	5
Costa Rica	0	0	1	2	1	0	0	0	1	5
Croatia	0	0	1	1	1	1	0	0	1	5
Dominican Republic	0	0	0	2	1	1	0	0	1	5

Country	Relevant Regional Governments (range of 0 to 2)	Bicameralism (range of 0 to 2)	Judicial Review (range of 0 to 2)	Powers of Separate Head of State (range of 0 to 2)	Autonomy and Legitimacy (directly elected)*	Term Non-concurrent with that of Legislature*	Referenda (range of 0 to 2)	Concordance Democracy (range of 0 to 2)	Constitutional Rigidity (range of 0 to 2)	Total (out of 16)
Ecuador	0	0	0	2	1	0	1	0	1	5
El Salvador	0	0	0	2	1	1	0	0	1	5
France *	0	1	1	2	1	-1	0	0	1	5
Guyana	0	0	0	2	1	1	0	0	1	5
Liberia	0	1	0	2	1	0	0	0	1	5
Lithuania	0	0	1	1	1	1	0	0	1	5
Macedonia	0	0	1	1	1	1	0	0	1	5
Marshall Islands	0	0	1	2	0	0	0	0	2	5
Namibia	0	1	0	2	1	0	0	0	1	5
Paraguay	0	1	0	2	1	0	0	0	1	5
Sierra Leone	0	0	0	2	1	0	0	0	2	5
São Tomé and Príncipe	0	0	0	2	1	1	0	0	1	5
Spain	2	1	1	0			0	0	1	5
Turkey	0	0	2	1	0	1	0	0	1	5
Ghana	0	0	0	2	1	0	0	0	1	4
Guatemala	0	0	0	2	1	0	0	0	1	4
Honduras	0	0	0	2	1	0	0	0	1	4
Iraq	1	0	1	0			0	0	2	4
Kiribati	0	0	0	2	0	1	0	0	1	4
Kyrgyzstan	0	0	0	1	1	1	0	0	1	4
Liechtenstein	0	0	0	1	0	1	1	0	1	4
Mongolia	0	0	0	1	1	1	0	0	1	4
Niger	0	0	0	2	1	0	0	0	1	4
Pakistan	1	1	1	0			0	0	1	4
Panama	0	0	0	2	1	0	0	0	1	4
Peru	0	0	0	2	1	0	0	0	1	4
Portugal	0	0	0	1	1	1	0	0	1	4
Romania	0	1	0	1	1	0	0	0	1	4
Timor-Leste (East Timor)	0	0	0	1	1	1	0	0	1	4
Zambia	0	0	0	2	1	0	0	0	1	4
Antigua and Barbuda	0	1	0	0			0	0	2	3
Botswana	0	0	0	2	0	0	0	0	1	3
Czech Republic	0	1	1	0			0	0	1	3
Japan	0	1	0	0			0	0	2	3
Nauru	0	0	0	2	0	0	0	0	1	3
Netherlands	0	1	0	0			0	1	1	3
San Marino	0	0	1	0			1	0	1	3
Slovenia	0	1	1	0			0	0	1	3
Suriname	0	0	0	2	0	0	0	0	1	3
Thailand	0	1	1	0			0	0	1	3

Country	Relevant Regional Governments (range of 0 to 2)	Bicameralism (range of 0 to 2)	Judicial Review (range of 0 to 2)	Powers of Separate Head of State (range of 0 to 2)	Autonomy and Legitimacy (directly elected)*	Term Non-concurrent with that of Legislature*	Referenda (range of 0 to 2)	Concordance Democracy (range of 0 to 2)	Constitutional Rigidity (range of 0 to 2)	Total (out of 16)
Bahamas	0	1	0	0			0	0	1	2
Barbados	0	1	0	0			0	0	1	2
Belize	0	1	0	0			0	0	1	2
Estonia	0	0	1	0			0	0	1	2
Finland	0	0	0	0			0	1	1	2
Grenada	0	1	0	0			0	0	1	2
Hungary	0	0	1	0			0	0	1	2
Jamaica	0	1	0	0			0	0	1	2
Latvia	0	0	1	0			0	0	1	2
Lesotho	0	1	0	0			0	0	1	2
Luxembourg	0	0	0	0			0	1	1	2
Mauritius	0	0	1	0			0	0	1	2
Papua New Guinea	0	0	1	0			0	0	1	2
Saint Kitts and Nevis	0	0	0	0			0	0	2	2
Saint Lucia	0	1	0	0			0	0	1	2
Saint Vincent and the Grenadines	0	0	0	0			0	0	2	2
Slovakia	0	0	1	0			0	0	1	2
Sweden	1	0	0	0			0	0	1	2
Trinidad and Tobago	0	1	0	0			0	0	1	2
Andorra	0	0	0	0			0	0	1	1
Bangladesh	0	0	0	0			0	0	1	1
Denmark	0	0	0	0			0	0	1	1
Dominica	0	0	0	0			0	0	1	1
Greece	0	0	0	0			0	0	1	1
Ivory Coast	0	0	0	0			0	0	1	1
Malta	0	0	0	0			0	0	1	1
Moldova	0	0	0	0			0	0	1	1
Montenegro	0	0	0	0			0	0	1	1
New Zealand	0	0	0	0			1	0	0	1
Norway	0	0	0	0			0	0	1	1
Samoa	0	0	0	0			0	0	1	1
Serbia	0	0	0	0			0	0	1	1
Tunisia	0	0	0	0			0	0	1	1
Tuvalu	0	0	0	0			0	0	1	1
United Kingdom	0	1	0	0			0	0	0	1
Vanuatu	0	0	0	0			0	0	1	1
Iceland	0	0	0	0			0	0	0	0
Israel	0	0	0	0			0	0	0	0

* See text on pages 212–13.

common occurrence globally today than a generation ago.[13] Combining somewhat the categories of Lijphart on this issue, we score countries 2 if they have a strong practice of judicial review; 1 if they have a medium-strength practice; and 0 if they have either a weak practice or no possibility of judicial review.[14] Canada, India, and the United States are examples of countries that score 2 on this factor; France, South Africa, and Spain are examples of countries that score 1; and Japan, New Zealand, and the United Kingdom are examples of countries that score 0.

Because we are assessing constraints on a prime minister and cabinet, the role and power of any separate head of state are obviously significant. (The head of state is almost always a president in countries where the position provides a check on the executive). Specifically, then, the fourth factor is the non-symbolic political power and policy role of this head of state. A country scores 2 if the head of state is a president who is the key political actor, 1 if the head of state is not a key political actor but still has political relevance, and 0 in all other circumstances. As discussed in Chapter 6, strong heads of state can be found in straightforward presidential systems, mixed systems in which the president clearly is a key political actor, or what we call parliamentary systems with presidential dominance; relevant but not strong heads of state can be found in parliamentary systems with a presidential corrective or with a monarch that still has policy relevance, as is the situation in Liechtenstein; irrelevant heads of state are always figureheads scoring 0, even if elected presidents. France, South Korea, and the United States are examples of countries that score 2 on this factor; Ireland, Poland, and Turkey are examples of countries that score 1; and Canada, Japan, and the United Kingdom are examples of countries that score 0.

Where the head of state is at least a relevant political actor (that is, in countries scoring 2 or 1 for the powers of a separate head of state), the supermajoritarianism score is potentially modified further in a couple of ways. First, a point is given if the head of state is directly elected (including by an electoral college). In this situation, the head of state (invariably a president) has the autonomy and legitimacy to use his or her powers fully in ways that may differ from the wishes of the legislature. A separate point is given if the term of the head of state is not concurrent with that of the legislature. Compared to concurrent terms, non-concurrent terms are more likely to produce a head of state (president) with differing views than the legislature and a clearer separation of powers. A point for non-concurrent terms is also given to those presidential systems holding midterm elections (Argentina, Mexico, the Philippines, and the United States)[15] because these are more likely to go against the president, as happened, for example, in the US midterms of 2006 and 2010. This feature, then, often leads to greater divisions between the president and the assembly. Then there is France, which presents a contrary scenario in terms of the effect of non-concurrent elections. In France since 2002, the presidential and National Assembly terms are both five years, but the parliamentary election comes a month or so after the presidential one, resulting in the momentum of the president's victory carrying over into a victory of her or his supporters in the National Assembly (as has now happened three times in a row with presidents of differing parties). In this situation—what Shugart and Carey call a "honeymoon" scenario[16]—a score of *negative* 1 is given to indicate the consequent political cohesion and lack of separation of powers.

The fifth factor measured is the use of national referenda to decide policy matters, potentially, of course, against the wishes of the government of the day. Countries are scored 2 if national referenda are exceptionally frequent (held all the time); 1 if national referenda are common; and 0 if national referenda are rarely or never held. Switzerland is the one country that scores 2 on this factor (national as well as lower-level referenda are held every three months there); Australia, Ireland, and Uruguay are examples of countries that score 1; and Canada, the United Kingdom, and the United States are examples of countries that score 0. Of course, one may question why referenda are included in a scale of supermajoritarianism, as referenda often require just a simple majority to pass. The reasons are as follows. First, the majority that approves a referendum is likely to be different from the majority that put a given government in office, so referenda broaden the size of the population that "produces" policy. Second, having to pass something by referendum separate from or even in addition to gaining legislative approval certainly involves institutional power sharing or a check and balance on the legislature, which is no longer the sole deciding actor.

The sixth factor measured is the presence of consociational democracy versus competitive democracy in a country. As explained in Chapter 5, consociational democracy (also called concordance democracy) is based not on simple-majority rule as in a competitive democracy but rather—in a divided polity—on the ongoing achievement of wide consensus agreement (reflecting the consensus of the various important national segments). To repeat, this outcome arises via such methods as broad coalition governments of the main parties, minority input or even veto rights on vital issues, proportionality in the public sector (e.g., in the bureaucracy or state firms), and segmental autonomy (which may or may not involve federalism).[17] Countries are thus scored 2 if they clearly practise concordance democracy; 1 if some elements of it are still present (often these are countries that used to clearly practise it); and 0 if there is no consociationalism but rather competitive democracy. Belgium and Switzerland are the two countries that score 2 on this factor (as noted in Chapter 5); Austria, India, and Luxembourg are examples of countries that score 1; and Australia, France, and the United Kingdom are examples of countries that score 0.

The seventh and last factor of supermajoritarianism measured is the difficulty of amending the constitution. Countries are scored 2 if this difficulty is high, meaning their constitutions are quite inflexible; 1 if it is moderate; and 0 if this difficulty is low and constitutional amendment is relatively easy. Specifically, countries score 2 (high difficulty) if, in addition to receiving legislative approval, constitutional amendments must pass in a referendum with a double majority (overall and regionally) or that also requires approval from a supermajority of regions. Countries score 0 (low difficulty) if constitutional change requires only legislative approval—indeed, if approval is granted by only a basic majority and not a supermajority. This score holds even if an intervening election is required to confirm the constitutional change in a new legislature. Finally, countries are scored 1 (moderate difficulty) for all other cases. These normally involve either a threshold of greater than 50 per cent plus one in the legislature to amend the constitution or a national referendum (but with no double majority or regional supermajority requirement). Australia, Canada, and the United States are examples of countries that score 2 on this factor. Conversely, only four countries score 0: Iceland, Ireland, New Zealand, and the United Kingdom. Most other countries score 1.

The summary score of supermajoritarianism thus ranges from a potential high of 16 to a potential low of 0. Table 8.1 ranks all electoral democracies by this summary score. No country is perfectly supermajoritarian, but the most supermajoritarian democracy is the United States, followed by Switzerland—both countries' political systems contain numerous checks and balances. At the opposite end of the scale, Iceland and Israel each has a perfect minimum total score of 0, indicating that they are strictly simple majoritarian—that is, neither has any constitutional or institutional checks on the government of the day. More generally, based on the distributions of the total values produced, these summary scores can be divided into high, medium, and low categories as follows: scores of 6 or more are classified as high (supermajoritarian), 3 to 5 are classified as medium (intermediate), and 0 to 2 are classified as low (simple majoritarian). Thus, for example, the United Kingdom is classified as clearly simple majoritarian.

The consequences of this distinction between simple majoritarianism and supermajoritarianism relate to the trade-off between decisive government and consensus government. A simple-majority system allows governments to be decisive but at the risk of ignoring objections and minority opinions. Indeed, the British version of simple majoritarianism was once derided as an "elective dictatorship"; likewise, the traditional New Zealand version of the pre-1990s was critiqued for giving the government "unbridled power."[18] In contrast, a supermajoritarian system requires a broad consensus for change, so minorities may well be able to protect their interests; conversely, though, it is much harder to "get things done," that is, to govern decisively across the entire policy spectrum, under supermajoritarianism.

Centralism-Proportionality versus Localism-Majoritarianism in Elections

The second overall dimension we wish to measure relates to aspects of elections and electoral systems. Specifically, the related questions here ask whether, at one extreme, elections involve centralized competition between national parties (with proportionate party results) or whether, at the opposite extreme, elections are fought between local candidates in local constituencies (with little national proportionality). The five factors measured are shown in Table 8.2, which ranks the world's electoral democracies by their summary scores on this additive index. The first factor in this index is the ballot structure, namely, whether the voter is voting for a party, ranking a list of candidates, or voting for just one individual candidate. Countries score 2 if the ballot is a pure party ballot (closed-list PR); 1 if the ballot is a preference ballot (open-list PR, STV, dual-member plurality) or a dual ballot (mixed or parallel systems); and 0 if the ballot is a pure candidate ballot (single-member systems, SNTV, or what was called in Chapter 7 "open and completely decisive" list systems in which the vote is, in fact, for a candidate, not a party). Israel, South Africa, and Spain are examples of countries that score 2 on this factor; Ireland, New Zealand, and Switzerland are examples of countries that score 1; and Brazil, France, and the United Kingdom are examples of countries that score 0.

The second factor is the importance of the individual local candidate versus the national party in election campaigns. Measurement of this factor is based on such features as "inherited seats" (within a family), local spending or even local election organizations (such as *koenkai* in Japan), pork-barrelling of spending by politicians, individual candidate endorsements by third parties such as interest groups, and the ability of independents to get elected. Countries are scored 2 if the local candidates are of little importance (e.g., closed party list PR systems); 1 if they are of some importance; and 0 if they are of considerable importance. Argentina, Germany, and South Africa are examples of countries that score 2 on this factor; Canada, France, and the United Kingdom are examples of countries that score 1; and Brazil, India, and the United States are examples of countries that score 0.

The third factor is the average district magnitude (the number of MPs elected in a district), rounded to the nearest integer value. This reflects whether politicians compete in large regional or national constituencies or in smaller local ones. For this calculation, if a country has a separate national tier (as Sweden does), this tier is treated as one district and averaged accordingly. Countries are scored 2 if the average district magnitude is high, defined as 12 or higher; 1 if the average district magnitude is medium, defined as from 4 to 11; and 0 if this measure is low, defined as from 1 (the minimum possible) to 3.[19] Assessed separately are MMP and in-between systems that use both single-member and large regional or national districts; those that have a majority of list seats (for example, Hungary) are scored 1, whereas those that have a majority of SMP seats (for example, Japan) are scored 0. Israel, the Netherlands, and South Africa are examples of countries that score 2 on this factor; Ireland, Germany, and Spain are examples of countries that score 1; and Canada, the United Kingdom, and the United States are examples of countries that score 0.

The fourth factor is the overall nature of the electoral system in terms of proportionality versus majoritarianism, which, of course, is somewhat conditional on the average district magnitude. This measurement simply duplicates the broad overall categories assigned in Table 7.1: proportional, majoritarian, and in-between. Countries are scored 2 if the electoral system is proportional; 0 if the electoral system is majoritarian; and 1 if the electoral system is between these two extremes. Germany, the Netherlands, and South Africa are examples of countries that score 2 on this factor; Hungary, Japan, and Mexico are examples of countries that score 1; and Australia, Canada, and the United States are examples of countries that score 0.

The fifth and final factor is average turnout, which is generally argued to be higher under proportional electoral systems because votes are not "wasted" and competition occurs everywhere.[20] This factor is based on the average turnout (as a share of registered voters) in recent elections and not just on the turnout in the most recent one (unless there has been just one election since democratization). Countries are

TABLE 8.2 Index of Electoral Systems and Elections, Localism versus Centralism (2012)

	Ballot Structure: Voter Perspective (range of 0 to 2)	Importance of Local Candidate in Campaign (range of 0 to 2)	Average District Magnitude (range of 0 to 2)	Type of Electoral System (Maj. = 0, Prop. = 2; range of 0 to 2)	Turnout Level in Recent Elections of Reg. Voters (range of 0 to 2)	Total (out of 10)
South Africa	2	2	2	2	2	10
Argentina	2	2	1	2	2	9
Croatia	2	2	2	2	1	9
Guyana	2	2	1	2	2	9
Israel	2	2	2	2	1	9
Moldova	2	2	2	2	1	9
Montenegro	2	2	2	2	1	9
Namibia	2	2	1	2	2	9
Serbia	2	2	2	2	1	9
Turkey	2	2	1	2	2	9
Benin	2	2	1	2	1	8
Cape Verde	2	2	1	2	1	8
Costa Rica	2	2	1	2	1	8
Germany	1	2	1	2	2	8
Honduras	2	2	1	2	1	8
Indonesia	1	1	2	2	2	8
Italy	1	1	2	2	2	8
Kyrgyzstan	2	2	2	2	0	8
Liechtenstein	1	1	2	2	2	8
Luxembourg	1	1	2	2	2	8
Netherlands	1	1	2	2	2	8
Niger	2	2	2	2	0	8
Paraguay	2	2	1	2	1	8
Portugal	2	2	1	2	1	8
Romania	2	2	1	2	1	8
São Tomé and Príncipe	2	2	1	2	1	8
Spain	2	2	1	2	1	8
Sweden	1	1	2	2	2	8
Austria	1	1	1	2	2	7
Belgium	1	1	1	2	2	7
Cyprus	1	1	1	2	2	7
Czech Republic	1	1	2	2	1	7
Denmark	1	1	1	2	2	7
Dominican Republic	2	2	1	2	0	7
El Salvador	2	2	1	2	0	7
Greece	1	1	1	2	2	7
Iceland	1	1	1	2	2	7

	Ballot Structure: Voter Perspective (range of 0 to 2)	Importance of Local Candidate in Campaign (range of 0 to 2)	Average District Magnitude (range of 0 to 2)	Type of Electoral System (Maj. = 0, Prop. = 2; range of 0 to 2)	Turnout Level in Recent Elections of Reg. Voters (range of 0 to 2)	Total (out of 10)
Iraq	1	1	2	2	1	7
Latvia	1	1	2	2	1	7
Malta	1	1	1	2	2	7
Norway	1	1	1	2	2	7
Peru	1	1	1	2	2	7
Slovakia	1	1	2	2	1	7
Tunisia	2	2	1	2	0	7
Uruguay	1	1	1	2	2	7
Andorra	1	1	1	1	2	6
Bolivia	1	1	0	2	2	6
Brazil	0	0	2	2	2	6
Ecuador	1	1	1	2	1	6
Estonia	1	1	1	2	1	6
Finland	0	1	2	2	1	6
Hungary	1	2	1	1	1	6
Macedonia	1	1	2	1	1	6
New Zealand	1	1	0	2	2	6
Poland	1	1	2	2	0	6
Slovenia	1	1	1	2	1	6
Suriname	1	1	1	2	1	6
Bulgaria	1	1	1	1	1	5
Chile	0	1	0	2	2	5
Ireland	1	0	1	2	1	5
Mongolia	1	1	0	1	2	5
Panama	1	1	1	1	1	5
San Marino	1	1	0	2	1	5
Timor-Leste (East Timor)	1	1	0	1	2	5
Korea, South	1	1	0	1	1	4
Lesotho	0	1	0	2	1	4
Mauritius	1	1	0	0	2	4
Samoa	1	1	0	0	2	4
Switzerland	1	0	1	2	0	4
Taiwan	1	1	0	1	1	4
Thailand	·1	1	0	1	1	4
Australia	0	1	0	0	2	3
Bangladesh	0	1	0	0	2	3
Colombia	0	0	1	2	0	3
Guatemala	1	1	0	1	0	3

	Ballot Structure: Voter Perspective (range of 0 to 2)	Importance of Local Candidate in Campaign (range of 0 to 2)	Average District Magnitude (range of 0 to 2)	Type of Electoral System (Maj. = 0, Prop. = 2; range of 0 to 2)	Turnout Level in Recent Elections of Reg. Voters (range of 0 to 2)	Total (out of 10)
Japan	1	0	0	1	1	3
Liberia	0	1	0	0	2	3
Lithuania	1	1	0	1	0	3
Mexico	1	1	0	1	0	3
Philippines	1	0	0	1	1	3
Senegal	1	1	0	1	0	3
Sierra Leone	0	1	0	0	2	3
Vanuatu	0	1	1	0	1	3
Antigua and Barbuda	0	1	0	0	1	2
Bahamas *	0	1	0	0	1	2
Barbados	0	1	0	0	1	2
Belize *	0	1	0	0	1	2
Botswana *	0	1	0	0	1	2
Canada	0	1	0	0	1	2
Comoros	0	1	0	0	1	2
Dominica	0	1	0	0	1	2
France	0	1	0	0	1	2
Ghana	0	1	0	0	1	2
Grenada	0	1	0	0	1	2
Ivory Coast	1	1	0	0	0	2
Jamaica	0	1	0	0	1	2
Marshall Islands	1	0	0	0	1	2
Nauru *	1	0	0	0	1	2˘
Palau	0	0	0	0	2	2
Papua New Guinea	0	1	0	0	1	2
Saint Kitts and Nevis	0	1	0	0	1	2
Saint Lucia	0	1	0	0	1	2
Saint Vincent and the Grenadines	0	1	0	0	1	2
Trinidad and Tobago	0	1	0	0	1	2
Tuvalu	1	0	0	0	1	2
United Kingdom	0	1	0	0	1	2
Zambia	0	1	0	0	1	2
Kiribati	0	0	0	0	1	1
Micronesia	0	0	0	0	1	1
Nigeria	0	1	0	0	0	1
India	0	0	0	0	0	0
Pakistan	0	0	0	0	0	0
United States	0	0	0	0	0	0

˘ Turnout score is adjusted for very low rate of registration.

scored 2 (high turnout) if turnout averages 76 per cent or higher; 1 (medium turn-out) if turnout averages from 60 to 75 per cent; and 0 (low turnout) if turnout averages 59 per cent or less.[21] Denmark, the Netherlands, and South Africa are examples of countries that score 2 on this factor; Canada, Japan, and the United Kingdom are examples of countries that score 1; and India, Switzerland, and the United States are examples of countries that score 0.

These five measures combined produce an aggregate score of centralism-proportionality versus localism-majoritarianism in elections, and this score ranges from a maximum of 10 to a minimum of 0. At one extreme, South Africa scores a 10, indicating complete centralism and proportionality. At the other extreme, India, Pakistan, and the United States each score a 0, indicating complete localism and majoritarianism. More generally, based on the distributions of the total values produced, countries' aggregate scores can be divided into high, medium, and low categories as follows: scores of 7 to 10 are classified as high (centralized and proportional), 4 to 6 are classified as medium (intermediate), and 0 to 3 are classified as low (local and majoritarian).

The Inherent Localism-Majoritarianism Tension

Returning specifically to electoral systems, one sees that those categorized as local and majoritarian, in fact, display a systemic tension because a single-member system produces two rather different effects. It makes political competition localized, at least formally, and—assuming cohesive parties are competing—it leads to overall disproportionality in the election results, which favours single-party governments. In contrast, an electoral system using closed party list proportional representation makes political competition more centralized, but it also, as its name implies, leads to proportional overall results and coalition governments. A single transferable vote (STV) electoral system falls between these systems in terms of localization but will also produce reasonably proportionate results. Consequently, for single-member systems, the issue is whether a political party (or at least the single governing party) is normally able to direct how its members vote, occasional backbench revolts notwithstanding. In the classic Westminster model, this party control is indeed the usual reality (even if that control is less in the United Kingdom than, say, in Canada). Thus, the overall majoritarian nature of elections trumps the localized aspect. Conversely, the reverse is true if no political parties exist, obviously; if the party system is highly fragmented and inchoate, as in Papua New Guinea; and if the political system is presidential, so no incentive of government survival exists to aid party discipline. This last pattern certainly occurs in the United States and, indeed, relates to other aspects of weak party control in that country, such as over candidate nominations and election spending. In all of these non-Westminster examples of single-member electoral systems with limited party control, then, the localized aspect of politics trumps the national one. It is not a coincidence that a politician in the United States popularized the phrase "all politics is local."[22] In summary, the inherent tension between the localized aspect and the majoritarian aspect of these systems is normally resolved in favour of one or the other.

Further Consequences of Localism-Majoritarianism versus Centralism-Proportionality

For their part, localized-majoritarian systems have a strong emphasis on accountability—in terms of both the localized and majoritarian aspects of these systems—and this feature is seen as a central virtue. A local member of parliament is directly elected, or perhaps a modest number of local members are elected in a small multi-member district, as in SNTV or STV. An unpopular local member can thus be voted out. Likewise, majoritarian outcomes tend to lead to single-party governments, at least in parliamentary systems, so it is clear who is in charge. Consequently, an unpopular governing party can be specifically punished. This kind of punishment was doubtless seen most spectacularly in the 1993 Canadian election, when the incumbent Progressive Conservatives went from a single-party majority to winning only two seats out of 295. Changes of government in such localized-majoritarian systems thus normally involve a full alternation between parties: that is, a completely different one takes over (the Liberals in the 1993 Canadian example). In contrast, centralized-proportional systems use party list voting, and, often, the list is closed or hard to change even if it is open. Thus, voting out an individual deputy supported by his or her party is difficult. Also, governments under proportional systems tend to be multi-party coalitions (taking weeks if not months to form), so it may be hard to know which specific governing party to blame for something. Elections are rarely decisive in determining winners (South Africa being one key exception here); inter-party bargaining may matter as much or more. Consequently, a governing party could be unpopular and lose support but still remain in government if it bargains well with other parties or is needed numerically for a majority or a stronger minority government. A recent example of this occurrence comes from Germany. Going into its 2005 election, the Social Democrats (SPD) was the major party in a coalition with the Greens, and the SPD leader, Gerhard Schröder, was the chancellor. In the election, the SPD was seen as the main loser electorally, dropping by over 4 per cent of the vote. In contrast, the Green vote declined only slightly. Yet, although Schröder ceased to be chancellor after the elections, the SPD remained in government, now as junior partners in a coalition with the Christian Democrats. One could argue that those who wanted the SPD out of office were thus left frustrated.

In contrast, centralized-proportional systems are seen to do better in terms of *inclusiveness*. They yield a more diverse parliament, one that includes many parties representing many points of view and more women deputies. Indeed, the correlation between this scale and the number of parties with at least 2 per cent of the seats (P2%S) for the most recent election is a reasonably strong 0.374 (see Table 7.4 for P2%S values). The correlation between this scale and the percentage of women in either the lower or single house of parliament for the most recent election is an even more robust 0.467. Centralized-proportional elections also lead, at least in parliamentary systems, to a broad-based government involving multiple parties that have the support of a majority or at least a strong plurality of the population. In contrast, localized-majoritarian systems, with their biased (disproportionate) election outcomes, have not only single-party governments usually (as noted) but often single-party governments with a limited national base. For example, the British Labour Party won only 35 per cent of the vote in 2005 but formed a single-party majority based on the 55 percent of the seats that it won. Yet when this 35 per cent of the vote is combined with a turnout of only 61 per cent in that election, one sees that this particular single-party majority was directly endorsed by only a little over *one-fifth* of the electorate.

An Overall Model of Clusters of Democracies in Terms of Decentralization versus Centralization

Finally, an overall model displaying levels of decentralization versus centralization can be formed by combining the two indices outlined in Table 8.1 and Table 8.2. This model, which ranks countries in terms of high, medium, or low scores on each of these two indices, is given in Figure 8.1. Although there are nine combinations, our focus is on the democracies showing clear patterns of decentralization or centralization, not on those with medium scores on one or both indices. Four ideal types exist at the four corners of the model. First, in the lower left section or cell of Figure 8.1 are countries that are clearly categorized as simple-majority rather than supermajoritarian systems and that are localized and majoritarian (with the emphasis on majoritarian) rather than centralized and proportional in their elections. These include the Westminster model countries of the United Kingdom and the Caribbean. The three countries shown in brackets (Papua New Guinea, Tuvalu, and Vanuatu) have fragmented or non-existent party systems, so, in fact, have localized rather than majoritarian elections—making them differ from the Westminster systems that dominate this group.

In the upper left section of Figure 8.1 are what can be best described as *decentralized* systems, which combine supermajoritarianism with localized-majoritarian elections. In terms of actual scores, the United States is the most perfect real-world example of this pattern. Its North American neighbours, Canada and Mexico, also fit here. Geographic size is obviously relevant as a causal factor for this system, in that this group contains four of the world's five largest democracies by area (in descending order—Canada, the United States, Australia, and India) as well as the seventh largest by area (Mexico). Of course, there are some tiny countries in this category as well, but two of these (Micronesia and Palau) are former protectorates of the United States and thus have been influenced accordingly.

In the lower right section of Figure 8.1 are what can be called *centripetal* systems, following the term of Gerring, Thacker, and Moreno, who identify these as the alternative to decentralized systems.[23] That said, Gerring, Thacker, and Moreno lay out only two opposing types of democratic polities rather than the four presented here. A centripetal system centralizes power in the sense that government is by simple-majority rule, but it also has many parties, national rather than local competition, coalition governments, and thus an orientation to broad-based, countrywide policies. As Gerring, Thacker, and Moreno note, the three Scandinavian countries of Sweden, Norway, and Denmark are perhaps the best long-standing examples of centripetalism.[24] The fact that these countries are simple-majority systems rather than supermajoritarian ones is also a point stressed by other scholars.[25] Besides the Scandinavian countries, several other smaller democracies also have centripetal systems—the size contrast with decentralized systems is clear here. Note, too, that Greece and

FIGURE 8.1 An Overall Model of Centralism-Decentralism in Electoral Democracies (2012)

ELECTORAL SYSTEM AND ELECTION LOCALISM VERSUS CENTRALISM

		LOW	MEDIUM	HIGH
SUPERMAJORITARIANISM	**HIGH**	Australia Canada Colombia Comoros India Mexico Micronesia Nigeria Palau Philippines Senegal United States	Brazil Ireland Italy Korea, South Poland Switzerland Taiwan	Argentina Belgium Cyprus Germany Indonesia South Africa Uruguay
	MEDIUM	Antigua and Barbuda Botswana France Ghana Guatemala Japan Kiribati Liberia Lithuania Marshall Islands Nauru Pakistan Sierra Leone Zambia	Bolivia Bulgaria Chile Ecuador Macedonia Mongolia Panama San Marino Slovenia Suriname Thailand Timor-Leste (East Timor)	Austria Benin Cape Verde Costa Rica Croatia Czech Republic Dominican Republic El Salvador Guyana Honduras Iraq Kyrgyzstan Liechtenstein Namibia Netherlands Niger Paraguay Peru Portugal Romania São Tomé and Príncipe Spain Turkey
	LOW	Bahamas Bangladesh Barbados Belize Dominica Grenada Ivory Coast Jamaica (Papua New Guinea) Saint Kitts and Nevis Saint Lucia Saint Vincent and the Grenadines Trinidad and Tobago (Tuvalu) United Kingdom (Vanuatu)	Andorra Estonia Finland Hungary Lesotho Mauritius New Zealand Samoa	Denmark (Greece) Iceland Israel Latvia Luxembourg (Malta) Moldova Montenegro Norway Serbia Slovakia Sweden Tunisia

especially Malta (which are in brackets in Figure 8.1) fit less well in this category due to their two main parties and single-party governments (until recently in Greece, anyway)—although each uses a form of proportional representation.

Finally, in the upper right section of Figure 8.1 are *systems based on a broad national consensus*. That is to say, they combine supermajoritarianism with centralized-proportional rather than localized-majoritarian elections. Broad agreement is needed to make changes, but the politicians involved take a national view of things and are thus divided normally on ideological rather than geographic grounds. One interesting point to further contrast the parliamentary version of these systems with the decentralized parliamentary ones of the upper left section is that, in Germany and now Belgium, politicians go from being a regional premier to prime minister (chancellor in Germany), something that does not happen in the decentralized federal systems of contemporary Australia and Canada.

Notes

1 Arend Lijphart, *Patterns of Democracy: Government Forms and Performance in Thirty-Six Countries* (New Haven, CT: Yale University Press, 1999), 9.

2 R.A.W. Rhodes and Patrick Weller, "Westminster Transplanted and Westminster Implanted: Exploring Political Change," in *Westminster Legacies: Democracy and Responsible Government in Asia and the Pacific*, ed. Haig Patapan, John Wanna, and Patrick Weller, 1–12 (Sydney: University of New South Wales Press, 2005), 4–6.

3 These other scales are those of Evelyne Huber, Charles Ragin, and John D. Stephens, "Social Democracy, Christian Democracy, Constitutional Structure, and the Welfare State," *American Journal of Sociology* 99, no. 3 (November 1993): 711–49; Manfred G. Schmidt, *Demokratietheorien: Eine Einführung* (Opladen: Leske + Budrich, 1995), as reproduced in Manfred G. Schmidt, "When Parties Matter: A Review of the Possibilities and Limits of Partisan Influence on Public Policy," *European Journal of Political Research* 30 (September 1996): 155–83; Manfred G. Schmidt, *Demokratietheorien: Eine Einführung*, 3rd ed. (Opladen: Leske + Budrich, 2000); and Anthony J. McGann, *The Logic of Democracy: Reconciling Equality, Deliberation, and Minority Protection* (Ann Arbor, MI: The University of Michigan Press, 2006), Chapter 6.

4 On veto players, see George Tsebelis, "Decision Making in Political Systems: Veto Players in Presidentialism, Parliamentarism, Multicameralism, and Multipartyism," *British Journal of Political Science* 25 (1995): 289–325; and George Tsebelis, *Veto Players: How Political Institutions Work* (Princeton, NJ: Princeton University Press, 2002). On veto points, see Vicki Birchfield and Markus M. L. Crepaz, "The Impact of Constitutional Structures and Collective and Competitive Veto Points on Income Inequality in Industrialized Democracies," *European Journal of Political Research* 34 (1998): 175–200.

5 Lijphart, *Patterns of Democracy*, 33.

6 An analogous pattern is "bipartisanship" in the presidential system of the United States.

7 Schmidt, *Demokratietheorien: Eine Einführung*, 3rd ed.

8 Anthony J. McGann, *The Logic of Democracy: Reconciling Equality, Deliberation, and Minority Protection* (Ann Arbor, MI: The University of Michigan Press, 2006), 182.

9 Dieter Fuchs, *Types and Indices of Democratic Regimes*, WZB Discussion Paper FS III 01–203 (Berlin: Wissenschaftszentrum Berlin für Sozialforschung, 2001).

10 For such arguments, see Arend Lijphart, *Democracies: Patterns of Majoritarian and Consensus Government in Twenty-One Countries* (New Haven, CT and London, UK: Yale University Press, 1984); Lijphart, *Patterns of Democracy*; Birchfield and Crepaz, "The Impact of Constitutional Structures"; and McGann, *The Logic of Democracy*, Chapter 6.

11 For these opposing arguments, see Evelyne Huber, Charles Ragin, and John D. Stephens, "Social Democracy, Christian Democracy, Constitutional Structure, and the Welfare State," *American Journal of Sociology* 99, no. 3 (November 1993): 711–49; and John Gerring, Strom C. Thacker, and Carola Moreno, "Centripetal Democratic Governance: A Theory and Global Inquiry," *American Political Science Review* 99, no. 4 (November 2005): 567–81.

12 Huber et al., "Social Democracy, Christian Democracy, Constitutional Structure, and the Welfare State," 722, fn. 10.

13 See, generally, C. Neal Tate and Torbjörn Vallinder, eds., *The Global Expansion of Judicial Power* (New York, NY: New York University Press, 1995); on Latin America, see Rachel Sieder, Line Schjolden, and Alan Angell, eds., *The Judicialization of Politics in Latin America* (New York, NY: Palgrave Macmillan, 2005).

14 See Lijphart, *Patterns of Democracy*, 226 for his (four) scoring categories.

15 This point is awarded for Argentina even though only half of the seats in the Argentine lower house are elected at midterm.

16 Matthew Soberg Shugart and John M. Carey, *Presidents and Assemblies: Constitutional Design and Electoral Dynamics* (New York, NY: Cambridge University Press, 1992), 243. In fact, Shugart and Carey define a honeymoon legislative election as any occurring within one year after the president's inauguration. However, in our analysis, only France is scored this way because the timing of its legislative election with respect to its presidential one is structural (and thus repeated over time) rather than just an occasional coincidence.

17 See Schmidt, *Demokratietheorien: Eine Einführung*, 3rd. ed., 327–28 for the use of concordance democracy (*Konkordanz*).

18 Lord Hailsham, *The Dilemma of Democracy: Diagnosis and Prescription* (London, UK: Collins, 1978), 127; Geoffrey Palmer, *Unbridled Power: An Interpretation of New Zealand's Constitution and Government* (Auckland: Oxford University Press, 1979). Interestingly, before 1978, Lord Hailsham had served as a cabinet minister in the United Kingdom (and would later do so again), so his criticisms were based on an insider perspective. After his book's publication, Palmer served as a cabinet minister in New Zealand and also, for a year, as prime minister. While in office, he sought to "bridle" the power of New Zealand's government—and he changed the title of later editions of his book to "Bridled Power" to indicate the apparent success of this agenda.

19   The notion of larger constituencies being those with 12 seats or more is taken from Michael Gallagher, Michael Laver, and Peter Mair, *Representative Government in Modern Europe*, 4th ed. (New York, NY: McGraw-Hill, 2006), 355.

20   One can note that the fourth and fifth measures here (electoral system and average turnout) are indeed related, with a correlation being statistically significant at the .01 level.

21   However, in four countries—Bahamas, Belize, Botswana, and Nauru—the classification has been adjusted down to compensate for very low rates of registration as a share of the population.

22   This statement was made by the former House of Representatives Speaker Thomas P. (Tip) O'Neill, Jr. See his *Man of the House: The Life and Political Memoirs of Speaker Tip O'Neill*, with William Novak (New York, NY: Random House, 1987).

23   Gerring, Thacker, and Moreno, "Centripetal Democratic Governance."

24   Gerring, Thacker, and Moreno, "Centripetal Democratic Governance."

25   McGann, *The Logic of Democracy*, Chapter 6; David Arter, *Democracy in Scandinavia: Consensual, Majoritarian or Mixed?* (Manchester, UK: Manchester University Press, 2006).

CHAPTER NINE

Varieties of Autocracies: Totalitarianism, Sultanism, and Authoritarianism

IN THIS CHAPTER YOU WILL LEARN

▶ what a totalitarian regime is;

▶ how full totalitarianism differs from incomplete or pre-totalitarianism and from post-totalitarianism;

▶ what a sultanistic regime is;

▶ how authoritarianism is a residual category of autocracy and the consequent importance of noting the specific subtypes of authoritarianism;

▶ how monarchs range from being all-powerful to being mere figureheads; and

▶ how semi-liberal autocracies may have a certain level of political pluralism but not the free and fair elections of democracies.

Hitherto, we have either treated all autocracies as a group (as opposed to democracies) or simply distinguished between semi-liberal and closed autocracies. Of course, autocracies, like democracies, vary in their institutional features. Beyond these institutional variations, autocracies also differ according to the importance of ideology, the extent of their legitimacy, and the durability of their specific autocratic leaders. In this chapter, we examine three varieties of autocracy: totalitarianism, sultanism, and authoritarianism. The first and last of these varieties can be further subdivided, making a total of eight subtypes. These subtypes are outlined in Table 9.1, which follows the layout of Table 3.2. In the analysis, we do not cover every aspect given for each subtype but rather focus on the key features.

Totalitarianism

Although some authors treat totalitarianism as a subtype of authoritarianism, it is, in fact, a distinctive variant of autocracy. Existing for more or less time in all communist

TABLE 9.1 Subtypes of Autocratic Regimes

	Traditional Authoritarianism	Military Authoritarianism	Theocratic Authoritarianism	Electoral Authoritarianism
POLITICAL PARTIES AND ELECTIONS AND OVERALL POLITICAL OPPOSITION	Can range from all parties being forbidden and no elections held to a multi-party system with competitive elections and limited political opposition (but without elections actually determining the government).	Usually all parties are forbidden, but there could be one official party; limited political opposition may be tolerated.	Either one official party or all parties are forbidden, although anti-regime independents may be elected.	More than one political party; limited political pluralism and consequent political opposition; however, national elections are not free and fair enough to actually change the government.
SOCIO-ECONOMIC PLURALISM	Can range from no significant to quite extensive social pluralism; usually economic pluralism.	Some social and economic pluralism, perhaps predating the military regime.	No significant social pluralism; usually some economic pluralism.	Many autonomous actors in economy and broader society.
CIVIL LIBERTIES	Civil liberties can range from none at all to merely incomplete.	Civil liberties are non-existent or at best limited.	Civil liberties are non-existent or at best limited.	Civil liberties are usually incomplete if not indeed limited.
IDEOLOGY	Stress on deference to traditional authority.	Often very nationalistic; stress on economic and, occasionally, social development.	Ideology derived from specific religious text or school.	Stress on economic growth and social peace.
MOBILIZATION	Participation largely generated autonomously by civil society (where permitted).	Emphasis on demobilization, especially of pre-existing autonomous civil society.	Emphasis on religious mobilization.	Participation largely generated autonomously by civil society and by competing parties.
LEGITIMACY OF AUTHORITY	Traditional legitimacy.	Legitimacy comes from claims of acting in the national interest.	Legitimacy comes from religious position and the authority to interpret relevant scripture.	Legitimacy comes from the illusion of legal-rational authority.
CONSTRAINTS ON AUTHORITY	Constrained at most only somewhat by the bureaucracy, private economic actors, and general public opinion.	Constrained at most only somewhat by the bureaucracy and private economic actors and maybe by any private media.	Constrained at most only somewhat by any private economic actors or private media.	Constrained only somewhat by the constitution, the courts and the rule of law, the bureaucracy, and socio-political pluralism.
POLITICAL ACCOUNTABILITY TO POPULATION	No political accountability of the monarch, but there may be some accountability of officials.	No political accountability.	No political accountability.	No true political accountability, although regime does prefer to be popular in actuality.
LEADERSHIP DURATION	Leadership is for life and then carries on within the royal family.	Leadership is indefinite unless the military rotates power.	Leadership at the top is for life; a religious assembly chooses successors.	Leadership is indefinite unless the ruling party has internal limits (which have been as little as one term).
TRANSITION TO (LIBERAL) DEMOCRACY	The monarch and the royal family must be willing to settle for a largely figurehead role.	Transition does not usually occur until either the military loses legitimacy (for example, by losing a war) or thinks that it has sufficiently restructured the socio-political order.	Transition has never occurred willingly.	The key step is having a truly free and fair election; then it becomes improving civil liberties and government fairness.

SOURCE: Based in part on Juan J. Linz and Alfred Stepan, *Problems of Democratic Transition and Consolidation: Southern Europe, South America, and Post-Communist Europe* (Baltimore, MD: The Johns Hopkins University Press, 1996), Table 3.1 and Table 4.2, with modifications.

Pre-Totalitarianism; Incomplete Totalitarianism	Full Totalitarianism	Post-Totalitarianism	Sultanism
One official party with a monopoly of power and no political pluralism.	One official party with a monopoly of power and no political pluralism; political terror is often used initially to eliminate any possibility of organized opposition.	Still one official party with monopoly of power but beginnings of political pluralism.	There may be an official party, but it is not well institutionalized; political terror is often used to eliminate any possibility of organized opposition.
Some social and economic pluralism, perhaps predating the regime.	No significant social or economic pluralism; basically total regime control; strong hostility to pre-existing organized religion.	Limited social and economic pluralism, involving dissidents and some market actors and forces.	Some economic and social pluralism, but these are subject to arbitrary despotic intervention.
Civil liberties are non-existent or, at best, limited.	No civil liberties.	Tentative but limited civil liberties.	No civil liberties.
Elaborate and guiding ideology that includes a desired utopian vision.	Elaborate and guiding ideology that includes a desired utopian vision.	Still a state-sanctioned, elaborate, and guiding ideology but weakened faith in this.	No ideology worth its name; instead, personal glorification of leader and family.
Beginning of or partial mobilization into a wide range of regime-created obligatory organizations.	Extensive mobilization into a wide range of regime-created obligatory organizations; active participation and enthusiasm both encouraged and expected.	Still extensive mobilization into regime-sponsored organizations, but enthusiasm replaced by boredom or careerism; dissidents organize clandestinely.	Only occasional mobilization, such as of violent para-state groups.
Legitimacy comes initially more from the method of coming to power (e.g., elections or independence struggle) than from the official ideology.	Legitimacy comes from some combination of official ideology (especially its utopian goals) and the charisma of the dictator.	Legitimacy weakened by de-ideologization; shift to attempts at performance legitimacy.	Regime lacks broad legitimacy; compliance is based largely on fear, rewards, and personal ties to leader.
Constrained somewhat by any remaining separate political actors and broadly supported private actors.	Key totalitarian leader rules with undefined limits and great unpredictability; successors tend to be more predictable and bureaucratic.	Top leaders constrained by party bureaucracy and state technocrats, but not by broader civil society.	Highly personalistic and arbitrary rule that is highly unpredictable; no bureaucratic professionalism possible.
No political accountability.	No political accountability.	No political accountability, except to other party elites.	No political accountability.
For arrested totalitarianism, leadership is indefinite but effectively conditional on avoiding major policy failure.	Leadership effectively for life unless regime is defeated; usually a power struggle for new leader.	Leadership effectively for life; subject to performance; successor picked peacefully by and from party oligarchy.	Leadership effectively for life unless overthrown.
For arrested totalitarianism, the ruling party must first accept giving up or be forced to give up its monopoly of power.	Needs to go first through a post-totalitarian phase with some pluralism unless defeat in war and occupation by foreign power willing to democratize.	Depending on the maturity of the post-totalitarianism regime, scenarios can range from regime collapse followed by an interim government to a negotiated transition.	Sultan highly unlikely to abdicate so must be overthrown; however, actors close to sultan may fill the resulting power vacuum and frustrate true democratization.

regimes as well as in Nazi Germany, totalitarianism can be characterized by three key characteristics, as detailed by Linz:

▶ There is a monistic [unitary] but not monolithic center of power, and whatever pluralism of institutions or groups exists derives its legitimacy from that center, is largely mediated by it, and is mostly a political creation rather than an outgrowth of the dynamics of the preexisting society.

▶ There is an exclusive, autonomous, and more or less intellectually elaborate ideology [involving an ultimate utopian goal] with which the ruling group or leader, and the party serving the leaders, identify and which they use as a basis for policies.... [1]

▶ Citizen participation in and active mobilization for political and collective social tasks are encouraged, demanded, rewarded, and channeled through a single party and many monopolistic secondary groups. Passive obedience and apathy, ... characteristic of many authoritarian regimes, are considered undesirable by the rulers.[2]

In terms of the first point, power is monopolized by the totalitarian party and its leaders. All other parties are banned, forced to merge with the totalitarian party, or, "at best," allowed to continue as puppet parties under the control of the totalitarian party. This point does not mean that the official party always has and speaks only with one voice; differences, especially within the leadership, may exist, though these are subject to the constraints of the regime's ideology (the second feature described as characteristic of totalitarianism). However, these differences can never crystallize into political factions, and, certainly and crucially, no political pluralism exists in a totalitarian system.

Equally, no or at least no significant social and economic pluralism exist under totalitarianism either. Autonomous organizations, and thus an independent civil society, are forbidden. Any pre-existing organized religion is suppressed or heavily controlled, although many modern organizations do exist: trade unions, youth groups, sporting clubs, and so on. However, all of these are official groups with monopolies in their field: for example, there is just one trade union rather than a plurality of these. Usually, their names include that of the totalitarian party or its leader.

Moreover, people are expected to join such groups to signal *active* support for the regime (remember that demanding these demonstrations of support is the third characteristic of totalitarian regimes). Likewise, elections are not only normal under totalitarianism (albeit without partisan choice), but an intense effort is made to mobilize every possible voter so that a claim can be made of up to 99 per cent (or even 99.9 per cent) support for the regime. **Totalitarian regimes** are unique among autocracies in the extent of their mobilization efforts because, at least according to their ideologies, such regimes seek to *transform* fundamentally the existing society towards some ultimate utopia. From this perspective, totalitarianism is a modernizing type of autocracy.

In addition to the key features of monistic party power, a transformative ideology, and the extensive mobilization of citizen support, many scholarly analyses added political terror, especially in the 1950s and 1960s when Stalinism was a vivid memory. Political terror can be defined as "the arbitrary use, by organs of political authority, of severe coercion against individuals or groups, the credible threat of such use, or the arbitrary extermination of individuals or groups" as a means to achieve political control.[3] Linz argues that the extent of terror has varied under totalitarianism and that it can be found also in non-totalitarian systems, such as "sultanistic" ones or certain military regimes in Latin America.[4] Of course, as Dallin and Breslauer note, the extent of terror tends to be temporal: it is high in what they call the "mobilization phase" of totalitarianism, when society's resources are directed to achieving quickly a specific end or related ends, such as industrialization and the creation of a "new man." In contrast, in the "post-[intensive] mobilization phase," when the central goal is progressing "on track" without much resistance and, more generally, when an established process of socialization has led to the general legitimacy of the regime, terror is no longer needed, and social compliance comes basically from "peer-group pressure."[5] That said, what is unique about totalitarian terror is its ideological justification and the totalitarian regime's organizational capacity to carry it out using party cadres.[6] Consequently, political terror, per se, does not seem so much a separate feature of totalitarianism as it is a reinforcement of the second and first characteristics described previously.

Beyond these characteristics, we can note that totalitarianism has been around only since the interwar period. Some see totalitarianism—especially fascism—as a reaction to modernity, at least in part. More convincingly, it has been noted that interwar fascism had little appeal in the older, long-established countries of northern and north-western Europe; its appeal was to be found in the newer countries of Central and Eastern Europe established in the 1860s and 1870s—Austria-Hungary, Italy, Germany, and Romania (see Table 1.1). These states often experienced frustrations vis-à-vis the established powers, which seemed to block the emerging countries' desire for rapidly increasing might and respect.[7] Most crucial, perhaps, is the point that totalitarianism is, in fact, *conditional* on a certain level of modernity (and definitely on a functioning state) without which its penetrative and transformative capacities could not exist. As leading political scientist Gabriel A. Almond noted in the 1950s,

> This type of political system has become possible only in modern times, since it depends on the modern technology of communication, on modern types of organization, and on the modern technology of violence. Historic tyrannies have no doubt sought this kind of domination but were limited in the effectiveness of their means. Totalitarianism is tyranny with a rational bureaucracy, a monopoly of the modern technology of communication, and a monopoly of the modern technology of violence.[8]

Pre- and Post-Totalitarianism

What we have analysed so far can perhaps be more rigorously defined as *full* totalitarianism (see Table 9.1). However, a totalitarian regime does not come into existence the day or even the year totalitarian forces take power; instead, at least in each of Nazi Germany and the Soviet Union, totalitarianism took some time to establish, especially in terms of establishing control over or at least neutralizing previously powerful independent actors. For example, the Soviet Union under Lenin had much weaker communist control than under Stalin, especially if we consider Stalin's rule from 1929 onwards. Indeed, Lenin had to switch back toward free market capitalism in his New Economic Policy of 1921. Linz has aptly called *pre-totalitarian* those situations in which

> there is a political group of sufficient importance pursuing a totalitarian utopia but that has not yet fully consolidated its power ... a situation in which institutions like the armed forces, the churches, business organizations, interest groups, notables or tribal rulers, the courts, or even a monarch, not clearly committed to a system excluding all pluralisms even though largely favoring a limitation of pluralism, still retain considerable autonomy, legitimacy, and effectiveness.... [9]

That said, if pre-totalitarianism inevitably led to totalitarianism, it would not be worth examining here. However, in many real-world cases, this initial pre-totalitarian stage did *not* lead to full totalitarianism. Instead, the pre-totalitarian situation continued indefinitely. In other words, "the development toward totalitarianism is arrested and stabilized" although the totalitarian ideology continues to affect "considerable spheres of social life" and participation in the totalitarian party and its other organizations remains significant. Linz calls this situation "defective totalitarianism"; one could also call it incomplete totalitarianism.[10]

The most important of these "incomplete totalitarian" cases was Fascist Italy, where Mussolini remained constrained by the army, the state bureaucracy, business interests, the Catholic Church, and the monarchy—and conversely where each of these actors retained some autonomy from him and the PNF (the National Fascist Party). The autonomy of the state bureaucracy reflected the PNF's failure to establish full totalitarianism because "[o]nly when the party organization is superior or equal to the government can we speak of a totalitarian system."[11] As for the monarchy, King Victor Emmanuel III not only appointed Mussolini prime minister in 1922 but also formally removed him in 1943. (In contrast, in Nazi Germany after President von Hindenburg's death in 1934, no one was authorized to "fire" Hitler.) The central communist example of "incomplete totalitarianism" was Poland, where the Catholic Church was always able to maintain "a sphere of relative autonomy which gave it organizational and ideological capacities to resist its and the Polish nation's full incorporation into totalitarian structures."[12] Furthermore, agriculture was never collectivized in Poland because the Polish communist leaders did not see this policy as part of the "Polish road to socialism." The consequent social pluralism found in an autonomous and powerful Catholic Church and autonomous farmers not only was the central aspect of the "incompleteness" of Polish totalitarianism but also spilled over into weaker communist ideology, less communist mobilization, and an unstable party leadership.[13] In the 1960s and 1970s, many one-party regimes were established in Africa that were either basically communist in ideology or that largely copied communist rule but had a more indigenous ideology; they should be considered examples of "incomplete totalitarianism" too.

If full totalitarianism is established, one may ask whether it remains for generations. Here we are limited empirically to studying the communist systems, as Nazi Germany lasted only 12 years, rather short of Hitler's "thousand-year Reich." A critical juncture for all totalitarian communist systems has been the death of the key (and usually charismatic) initial leader—Stalin, Mao, Ho Chi Min. Their successors have tended to be less "revolutionary," in the sense of not really having transformative goals, being much less willing to use terror to achieve them, and being more concerned with preserving the status quo. Thus, they are more "conservative" and predictable. So the totalitarian system shifts from a mobilization phase to a post-mobilization, bureaucratic phase. However, such a system—for example, the Soviet Union under Khrushchev and then Brezhnev—must still be considered fully totalitarian because the regime still tolerates no real pluralism. (Of course, Khrushchev's removal from power by the rest of the communist party leadership was incongruent with full totalitarianism.)

An actual *regime* change comes with a shift from totalitarianism to *post-totalitarianism*. Post-totalitarianism certainly does *not* mean political pluralism in the sense of, say, multiple and competing political parties. However, political dissidents begin to organize or increase their organization and become somewhat more open, and there is growing social and economic pluralism as well—this movement to a more pluralistic economy is sometimes driven by necessity. Crucially, under post-totalitarianism, the official ideology becomes more and more of a facade with fewer and fewer true believers (including in the leadership). Likewise, social mobilization into state organizations becomes less passionate and more a matter of "going through the motions"; the people who join the official party are largely "careerists" or, more bluntly, opportunists. Because ideology and terror no longer motivate the ossified bureaucracy, there is a parallel increase in corruption.[14] This sort of post-totalitarianism, for better or worse, occurred in the Soviet Union under Gorbachev in the late 1980s. However, similar regimes arose earlier in parts of Eastern Europe—in Yugoslavia in the mid-1950s and in Hungary starting in 1962. On the other hand, Czechoslovakia and East Germany remained "hard line" and fully totalitarian until the collapse of communism, so each had only a brief post-totalitarian phase (and Albania had none at all). Only Bulgaria copied Gorbachev's reforms when they still seemed viable. China certainly has been post-totalitarian in economic matters since the late 1970s, but the regime remains highly repressive otherwise. Vietnam is now following a similar pattern.

Finally, it should be noted that the death of Stalin in Europe and of Mao in China would be considered the end of full totalitarianism under an alternative definition that requires a charismatic leader, political terror, and purges within the ruling party. What followed is what we have called the "bureaucratic" phase of totalitarianism but what this alternative definition considers "post-totalitarianism," which goes through "early" and "frozen" phases.[15]

Sultanistic Regimes

One communist regime not mentioned previously is Romania; another is North Korea. In fact, although these regimes have or had certain totalitarian features—above all, a communist party and related organizations—they can be better seen as examples of *sultanism*. A **sultanistic regime** is one built around an individual leader and his or her family, which, to a greater or lesser extent, plunder the country. The leader is glorified; exercises control by fear, terror, and spreading paranoia; and lacks any effective legitimacy. Chehabi and Linz offer a more thorough definition:

> a contemporary sultanistic regime ... is based on personal rulership, but loyalty to the ruler is motivated not by his embodying or articulating an ideology, nor by a unique personal mission, nor by any charismatic qualities, but by a mixture of fear and rewards to his collaborators. The ruler exercises power without restraint, at his own discretion and above all unencumbered by rules or by any commitment to an ideology or value system. The binding norms and relations of bureaucratic administration are constantly subverted by arbitrary personal decisions of the ruler, which he does not feel constrained to justify in ideological terms. As a result corruption reigns supreme at all levels of society. The staff [or cabinet] of such a ruler is constituted not by an establishment with distinctive career lines, like a bureaucratic army or a civil service, recruited based on more or less universal criteria, but largely by people chosen directly by the ruler. Among them we very often find members of his family, friends, business associates, or individuals directly involved in using violence to sustain the regime. Their position derives from their purely personal submission to the ruler, and their position of authority in society derives merely from this relation.... Although such regimes can in many ways be modern, what characterizes them is the weakness of traditional and legal-rational legitimation and the lack of ideological justification.[16]

In many ways, sultanistic regimes are the least "defendable" type of regime because they cannot claim any ultimate utopian goal, as totalitarian regimes do. Today, the main examples of sultanism are the regimes of Teodoro Obiang Nguema Mbasogo in Equatorial Guinea and Kim Jong-un in North Korea. However, there have been several important historical examples of sultanism in recent decades: the regimes of Fulgencio Batista in Cuba, Rafael Trujillo in the Dominican Republic, Jean-Claude Duvalier in Haiti, the Somoza family in Nicaragua, Muammar al-Gaddafi in Libya,

Jean-Bédel Bokassa in the Central African Republic, Gnassingbé Eyadéma in Togo, Idi Amin in Uganda, Mobutu Sese Seko in Zaire (now the Congo, DR), the Pahlavi dynasty in Iran (especially the later stages of each Shah), Saddam Hussein in Iraq, Hafez al-Assad in Syria, Ferdinand Marcos in the Philippines, Kim Il-sung and Kim Jong-il in North Korea (the grandfather and father, respectively, of Kim Jong-un), and Nicolae Ceaușescu in Romania. Note that both postwar North Korea and Romania began as communist totalitarian regimes and then shifted to sultanism in the 1960s and early 1970s respectively. Two recent examples of sultanistic rulers deposed wholly or partly by Western intervention are Saddam Hussein in Iraq and Muammar al-Gaddafi in Libya.

Sultanistic regimes generally begin as some form of authoritarianism. For example, the regimes in Iraq and Syria were initially military in that the military-backed *Ba'ath* party controlled each country. Likewise, the sultanistic rulers of the Central African Republic, Libya, Togo, and Uganda led military coups. For their part, Marcos and Nguema initially came to power via democratic elections.[17] In any case, the checks and balances of democracy or the collective rule of authoritarianism or totalitarianism gives way to personal rule by an individual under sultanism, which destroys any functioning autonomous state (assuming there was one).

Among the various bizarre features of a sultanistic regime, personalism stands out. The first element of personalism involves the ruler's personality cult, which probably compensates for this leader's general or total lack of charisma. The existence of these cults is probably most evident to the outside observer because of the many statues erected and portraits hung of these leaders. Yet, beyond such omnipresence, sultanistic rulers love to give themselves titles, not only politically formal ones, such as emperor, field marshal, or *generalísimo* (supreme commander), but more general ones such as "hero," "saviour," "Great Leader" (Kim Il-sung), or "Dear Leader" (Kim Jong-il). Sometimes they change their names to this end. For example, from 1991 until his death at the end of 2006, President Niyazov of Turkmenistan was known as "Turkmenbashi" ("Head of the Turkmen"). If not renaming themselves, sultanistic rulers (while still alive, of course) rename cities, islands, and lakes after themselves. Finally, sultanistic rulers often proclaim their own ideology because they conceive of themselves as great thinkers, and they may publish volumes of their thoughts and speeches.

The second element of personalism in a sultanistic regime is the central role played by the ruler's immediate family members, who are given formal positions. For example, Imelda Marcos (Ferdinand's wife) was a cabinet minister and mayor of Manila.

Elena Ceauşescu became the second in command of the Romanian Communist Party. Saddam Hussein's sons became as infamous as their father: Uday, for a time, oversaw the state media and national sports; his relatively more stable younger brother, Qusay, the presumed heir, controlled the security and intelligence services and the armed forces. Indeed, one of the ultimate elements of "success" for a sultanistic ruler appears to be achieving enough personal and family control so that a child will be able to take over after the ruler's death; very few sultanistic rulers have been so "successful."[18]

The "cult of personality" around certain totalitarian leaders, such as Stalin and Mao, can be considered a sultanistic feature. However, the cult of personality did not carry on to the successors of these leaders. More generally, Chehabi and Linz summarize other various differences between sultanism and totalitarianism. First, sultanistic regimes (Romania, North Korea, and the Dominican Republic excepted) have lacked any ideology worthy of the term as well as any pro-regime intellectuals who support the regime. Second, sultanistic rulers are "in it" for personal enrichment and power for its own sake whereas totalitarian rulers are exponents of a cause and often live modestly—or at least cultivate an ascetic image. Third, sultanistic regimes lack the dominant and well-organized single party and the related organizations that are central to totalitarianism. A fourth and related point is that sultanism—like authoritarianism—lacks the political mobilization that is central to totalitarianism. Fifth and finally, whereas totalitarianism penetrates all aspects of society and all areas of the country, sultanism varies in the extent of its penetration; groups or areas that are neither a source of enrichment nor a threat to the ruler are likely to be left more or less alone.[19] To these differences we can add the empirical fact that no sultanistic regime has ever lasted as long as the six decades of full totalitarianism in the Soviet Union.

Authoritarian Regimes

The last, and probably vaguest, subtype of autocracy is *authoritarianism*. Linz provides the classic definition of **authoritarian regimes**:

> political systems with limited, not responsible, political pluralism, without elaborate and guiding ideology, but with distinctive mentalities, without extensive nor intensive political mobilization, except at some points in their development, and in which a leader

or occasionally a small group exercises power within formally ill-defined limits but actually quite predictable ones.[20]

Thus, authoritarian regimes are defined largely in a negative way: they lack the ideology and mobilization characteristic of totalitarianism, and they also lack the broad arbitrariness of sultanism. Authoritarian regimes are, to some extent, a *residual category* of autocracies, which makes their definition somewhat more vague than that of totalitarian or sultanistic regimes. Furthermore, the four subtypes of authoritarianism vary in certain key ways, above all with respect to their political legitimacy.

The first subtype is **traditional authoritarianism** based on a hereditary monarchy. Today, we find such regimes not only in many Middle Eastern and North African countries—Bahrain, Jordan, Kuwait, Morocco, Oman, Qatar, Saudi Arabia, and the United Arab Emirates—but also in Swaziland in Africa, Brunei in Asia, and Tonga in the Pacific. As autocracies go, traditional monarchies have the advantage of having a clear pattern of succession, normally, which confirms the legitimacy of the new monarch. Moreover, traditional authoritarianism as a form of government still enjoys a broad legitimacy in many areas, although this form of government has certainly lost its legitimacy in Europe over time.

Although the hereditary monarch in a traditional authoritarian system can be said to be a ruling monarch by definition, in reality, these heads of state have varying degrees of power. And, as we have discussed, non-ruling hereditary monarchs play a limited political role in some democracies. Consequently, rather than just distinguishing between two categories—ruling and non-ruling monarchs—we can outline a continuum of monarchical power, moving from the most powerful monarch ruling in the most authoritarian political system to the non-ruling monarch playing a figurehead role in the most democratic one:

▶ At one extreme, the monarch holds all executive powers and rules by decree. There is no elected legislature. This is the pattern in Brunei and Saudi Arabia. This was also the pattern in Imperial Russia until 1906.

▶ The monarch still holds all executive powers and rules by decree but also "permits" the existence of an elected legislature that can comment on legislation—but whose powers are limited. This is the pattern in Oman.

▶ The monarch appoints a cabinet and a separate prime minister, but the prime minister is normally of the royal family. The monarch rules through the cabinet rather than by decree; however, the cabinet is chaired by the monarch or takes instructions from the monarch. The elected legislature has limited or, at most, some legislative powers and no power over the government. This is the pattern in Bahrain, Qatar, Swaziland, and, effectively, Kuwait. This is also essentially the pattern in the United Arab Emirates, although its legislature is only partly elected.

▶ The monarch appoints a cabinet and a separate prime minister, who is not of the royal family but is likely still a noble. The monarch rules through the cabinet rather than by decree, but the cabinet is chaired by the monarch or takes instructions from the monarch. The elected legislature has actual legislative powers but still no power over the government. This is the pattern in Monaco, where the prime ministers are civil servants from France.[21] This was also the pattern in Imperial Germany and, briefly, in Imperial Russia from 1906 to the Russian Revolution.

▶ There is a prime minister and cabinet separate from the monarch and a legislature that must approve legislation and can remove the prime minister and cabinet through a motion of non-confidence, which may be unlikely if the legislature lacks discipline and organized parties. However, the monarch picks the prime minister and cabinet, dismisses them freely, and, indeed, either directly or indirectly, still rules the country through them. The monarch also has many direct "supporters" (in a partisan sense) in the parliament, perhaps elected with the monarch's help. This is the pattern in Jordan and Morocco. This was also the historic pattern in seventeenth- and eighteenth-century Britain (in fact, up to the 1830s).

▶ There is a prime minister and cabinet separate from the monarch and accountable to the legislature, which can remove the prime minister and cabinet through a motion of non-confidence. Consequently, a prime minister and cabinet need support in the legislature to get and keep power; indeed, this support is the only means to these ends. In other words, the monarch does not determine the cabinet (at least not the civilian ministers), nor does the monarch run the cabinet. However, the monarch still has a say—if not indeed *the* say—in foreign policy or other policy areas and may even veto some legislation. This is the pattern in Liechtenstein and Thailand today, and it was the pattern in Japan in the 1920s. Bhutan appears to be aiming for this situation, once its elections have adequate competition.

▶ At the other extreme, the monarch plays absolutely no role in determining the composition of cabinet. Nor does the monarch attend cabinet meetings, have any powers over policy, or any legislative vetoes. In other words, we are describing a parliamentary system with a figurehead monarch (see Chapter 6). This is the pattern today in the United Kingdom, the Benelux countries, Scandinavia, and Spain.

Of these seven categories, the first five would be considered autocratic and the last two democratic (granted, the second-last one is borderline). Focusing on the first four categories, we can see a clear range within traditional authoritarian regimes regarding the extent of a monarch's power. Suffice it to say that countries do not suddenly switch from, say, the first category to the last one. Thus, if a traditional monarchy is going to become a democratic or constitutional monarchy with a figurehead ruler, it invariably will go through some if not most of the intermediate categories. Of course, in many places, democratization or at least political change has involved removing the monarchy altogether, especially if the monarch of the day has not wanted to "evolve."

The second subtype of authoritarianism is **military authoritarianism**. In Chapter 2, we outlined a continuum of civil-military relations in which the military's control over government ranges from being non-existent to being paramount. Within this range of categories of military influence, the last two—military rule and military control—entail military authoritarianism. Certainly, because both of these categories involve an autonomous military either running the country outright or at least exercising dominant control and oversight, regimes with either mode of government cannot be called democratic.

As of late 2012, military authoritarianism might seem to be a "dying" regime type compared with the situation in the 1960s and 1970s, but military authoritarianism in its various forms still exists in half a dozen countries (see Chapter 2), most crucially in Burma/Myanmar, which is under military control. Latin America, on the other hand, has experienced a clear swing away from military authoritarianism: as recently as the late 1970s, no fewer than 12 countries (over half of the region) were run by military regimes,[22] but now none are, and only Venezuela has a tutelary military. Of course, one of the realities of military authoritarianism is that it does not last forever inasmuch as whatever initial legitimacy it has—arising, perhaps, from the corruption and incompetence of the previous government and the military's pledge to act in the national interest—will dissipate over time. Thus, it is rare for a single military regime to last more than a couple of decades (Burma/Myanmar, under either military rule or military control since 1962, is the main exception here).

The third subtype of authoritarianism is **theocratic authoritarianism**, which involves religious-based rule. So far, all the modern examples have been cases of Islamic rule—Afghanistan under the Taliban, Iran since the 1979 Islamic Revolution, North Yemen for centuries until 1962 under the Zaydi sect, and Sudan (where Islamists are a central component and support base of the regime). Of these cases, Iran has developed the most elaborate institutionalized form of a theocratic regime. Figure 9.1 outlines the formal structure of power in Iran since 1989, when the separate post of prime minister was abolished. As can be seen, Iranians elect both a president and a parliament, which are the potentially democratic aspects of the regime. However, the Iranian president is a relatively weak head of state and government. As Buchta stresses,

> Because of constitutional shackles, the power of the presidential office is not as great as is often assumed in the West. Moreover, the high public profile of the president ... in the media and at international conferences encourages the false belief that the executive plays a dominant role in setting the domestic and foreign policy of Iran.[23]

In fact, the Iranian president is clearly second in terms of the overall power structure. The most powerful political position—and the first of three key religious-based political institutions—is the *vali-ye faqih* or "ruling jurisprudent," also referred to as the Supreme Leader. The first such "supreme jurisprudent" was Grand Ayatollah Khomeini, the leader of Iran's Islamic Revolution; after Khomeini's death, he was replaced by Ayatollah Khamenei. The *faqih* not only formally confirms the president but also is the effective head of government in terms of major policy decisions and changes, and he makes many other key appointments (see Figure 9.1). This ruling jurisprudent was initially required to be a "source of emulation" and one of the highest-ranking Shi'i clerics. However, in 1989, Grand Ayatollah Khomeini—after a conflict with Grand Ayatollah Montazeri, Khomeini's likely successor—amended the

FIGURE 9.1 The Formal Structure of Power in Iran since 1989

	Council of Guardians (six-year terms)	serves	as the de facto upper house
		functions	as a religious supreme court
	approves all candidates for		
	elects President (four-year term)	appoints	cabinet ministers (subject to parliamentary confirmation)
		controls	Planning and Budget Organization
		chairs	National Security Council
	and		
ELECTORATE	elects Parliament (four-year term)	recommends	half of the Council of Guardians (six lay members; to be appointed by the Head of the Judiciary)
	and		
	elects Assembly of Experts (eight-year term) elects Supreme Leader (life term)	serves as	Commander-in-Chief
		appoints	half of the Council of Guardians (six clerical members)
		appoints	Head of the Judiciary (who in turn appoints the lay jurists of the Council of Guardians, the Head of the Supreme Court, and the Chief Public Prosecutor)
		appoints	Expediency Council (which arbitrates between Parliament and the Council of Guardians)
		appoints	Chief of the General Staff of the Armed Forces
		appoints	commander of the the Revolutionary Guards
		appoints	president of state radio and television

SOURCE: Adapted from information provided in Wilfried Buchta, *Who Rules Iran?: The Structure of Power in the Islamic Republic* (Washington, DC: The Washington Institute for Near East Policy, 2000), 8.

constitution to lower the requirement to being a religious leader but not necessarily a leading authority.[24] This change opened up the position of *faqih* from the 20 or so Grand Ayatollahs (worldwide) to the 5,000 or so Ayatollahs in Iran.[25]

The *faqih* is chosen for life, making this position unaccountable—and meaning that Iran does not have responsible government. The choice of the supreme jurisprudent is made by the Assembly of Experts, the second religious-based political institution in Iran. The assembly is composed of 86 clerics deemed knowledgeable in Islamic jurisprudence and is elected for an eight-year term. With the supreme jurisprudent serving for life, a given Assembly of Experts may never be called on to make a selection. The Assembly of Experts itself is elected by universal suffrage, with the various regions of Iran each electing a set number based on population. In theory, the Assembly of Experts can also *remove* a supreme jurisprudent who is deemed unfit to serve, but this has never happened and seems highly unlikely.

The third religious-based political institution in Iran is the Council of Guardians, which, in various ways, ensures that Iran is ruled according to *shari'a* law. The council has 12 members: six religious clerics appointed by the supreme jurisprudent and six lay scholars recommended by parliament and formally appointed by the Head of the Judiciary (see Figure 9.1). The Council of Guardians functions as a religious supreme court. Yet it is much more than this. Because all legislation passed in parliament must be approved by the Council of Guardians, it effectively serves as Iran's upper house. (As Figure 9.1 shows, a separate Expediency Council appointed by the supreme jurisprudent is used to mediate between the two "chambers.") Finally, the Council of Guardians also oversees all national elections and referenda, not merely in the sense of organizing them but most crucially by approving on religious grounds *all* candidates for elections to the presidency, the parliament, and the Assembly of Experts. Because the Council of Guardians is free to and, indeed, does reject candidates if they are too liberal or radical, it greatly limits the range of choices given to the voters. (This system still provides a broader range of candidates than under totalitarianism, though.) For the candidates who clear this central hurdle, competition has traditionally been basically fair—and, indeed, the 1997 and 2001 presidential elections, as well as the 2000 parliamentary elections, were all won by reformist candidates in opposition to Ayatollah Khamenei, the supreme jurisprudent. Overall, then, we can characterize elections in Iran as being "unfree but fair."

The last subtype of authoritarianism is one that has been around for decades but has only recently been conceptualized by scholars: **electoral authoritarianism.**[26] In this situation, multiple political parties compete, with the winning party claiming a right to govern. Political legitimacy is based on election outcomes, which certainly sounds democratic. However, the elections are rarely free and are never fair, so the same party stays in power indefinitely. From the 1930s through the 1990s, Mexico under its Institutional Revolutionary Party (PRI) was the classic example of electoral authoritarianism. The main long-standing contemporary examples are the parliamentary systems of Malaysia and Singapore and various presidential or president-dominated systems, such as Azerbaijan, Belarus, Russia, and Seychelles. The ruling party in an electoral authoritarian regime uses a range of tactics to achieve the election numbers it wishes and so retain power: the abuse of state resources and employees, bias in state or state-controlled media, intimidation of the political opposition, and even outright fraud. (In post-Soviet countries, these tactics are known as "administrative resources.") In some cases, the announced election results are so bogus that the regime has little credibility. In other cases, however, the ruling party and leader do have a genuine base of support in the population. Both might well achieve a plurality in a free and fair election, and, indeed, this democratic reality has occurred in the past—for example, with Putin in the 2000 Russian presidential election and Lukashenko in the 1994 Belarus presidential election. However, coercion, abuse of state resources, and fraud are used to inflate their support to "impressively" high levels and keep them in power.[27] In the former Soviet Union, electoral authoritarian regimes may even create "fake" opposition parties and candidates (in the latter case, usually with the same name as the real ones) to split the opposition vote.

Singapore is a good contemporary example of electoral authoritarianism; data on its post-independence elections are given in Table 9.2. The People's Action Party (PAP) has governed Singapore continuously since independence, not only winning each election but also, until recently, winning every or almost every *seat* in each election. The PAP itself attributes its success to its highly competent and basically corruption-free governments, which have presided over Singapore's economic transformation into one of the world's most wealthy and developed countries. Nor is there any election-day fraud (such as ballot stuffing) in Singapore. Certainly, these facts and the PAP's consequent genuine popularity with many voters cannot be denied. However, it is not as if the electorate is given a free choice of alternatives. The PAP has controlled the domestic media for some time and censors the foreign media. Singapore had a diverse print media before independence and for some years thereafter, but, over time, through both direct attacks on the press and the broader Internal Security Act, the media have been made to toe the party line.[28]

Opposition parties do exist in Singapore—without them there could be no claim of competitive elections—but the government constantly harasses them. Moreover, opposition candidates are required to put up a substantial deposit (about $13,000) just to compete—limiting the freedom of elections. Perhaps the most nefarious means of

TABLE 9.2 Elections in Singapore since Independence

		PEOPLE'S ACTION PARTY			OPPOSITION	
Year	Total Seats	Seats Won	Seat Percentage	Vote Percentage	Seats Contested	Seats Won
1968	58	58	100.0	86.7	7	0
1972	65	65	100.0	70.4	57	0
1976	69	69	100.0	74.1	53	0
1980	75	75	100.0	77.7	38	0
1984	79	77	97.5	64.8	47	2
1988	81	80	98.8	63.2	69	1
1991	81	77	95.1	61.0	36	4
1997	83	81	97.6	65.0	34	2
2001	84	82	97.6	73.7	29	2
2006	84	82	97.6	66.6	47	2
2011	87	81	93.1	60.1	82	6

attacking the political opposition has been the launching of civil defamation lawsuits against individual opposition politicians when they criticize government leaders. These are invariably successful, not surprisingly given the PAP-biased judiciary, and they have, at times, resulted in sued opposition politicians being penalized by large sums and going bankrupt. In part as a consequence of these monetary factors but also as a general admission that the PAP will continue to govern, the opposition parties intentionally contested only a minority of the seats from 1991 to 2001 (see Table 9.2). Finally, for the past couple of decades, most of the seats in Singapore have been allocated through multi-member plurality, which involves "Group Representation Constituencies" (now of four to six MPs) that are winner-take-all for the plurality party list (voters can choose only between competing lists). Multi-member plurality is, of course, a rare and an extremely majoritarian electoral system, highly beneficial to the largest party. Only in the 2011 election did an opposition party in Singapore finally win a GRC.

Interestingly, as an admission that its victories have been somewhat excessive, the PAP began in 1984 to offer opposition parties up to three non-constituency members of parliament (NCMPs), to be awarded to the defeated opposition candidates who, nevertheless, got the highest share of the votes. The point here was to ensure that the opposition had a minimum of three seats in parliament, which, presumably, made the parliament look more "balanced." Of course, in the 1991 election, when the opposition parties won more than this target, no NCMPs were offered. Although the NCMPs were initially disparaged and refused by the opposition when they were introduced, today they are generally accepted as a sign of support to the voters who want an opposition. In 2010, the constitution of Singapore was amended to increase the potential number of NCMPs to nine, so that there would be an opposition of at least nine members. Yet, because the opposition won a record six seats in the 2011 election (see Table 9.2), only three NCMPs had to be offered. In addition, starting in 1990, an increasing number of nominated members of parliament (NMPs) have also been appointed; since 2010, the number of these is nine as well. These NMPs are supposed to be outstanding citizens and independent voices. In any case, they are nominated by the public and chosen by a parliamentary committee. Both the NCMPs and the NMPs can speak in parliament, take part in debates, and raise questions, but they can vote only on limited measures—nothing involving the constitution, budgets, or other matters of confidence or non-confidence in the government.[29] Thus, neither of these innovations is ever going to threaten the PAP's control of parliament.[30]

Notes

1   This ideology is central to the overall legitimacy of the totalitarian regime. Consequently, clear violations of it—that is, advocating distinctly alternative ideologies—are grounds for punishment.

2   Juan J. Linz, *Totalitarian and Authoritarian Regimes* (Boulder, CO: Lynne Rienner, 2000), 70.

3   Alexander Dallin and George W. Breslauer, *Political Terror in Communist Systems* (Stanford, CA: Stanford University Press, 1970), 1.

4   Linz, *Totalitarian and Authoritarian Regimes*, 24–26 and 100ff.

5   Dallin and Breslauer, *Political Terror*, 84–85.

6   Linz, *Totalitarian and Authoritarian Regimes*, 105, 108.

7   Stanley G. Payne, *A History of Fascism, 1914–1945* (Madison, WI: The University of Wisconsin Press, 1995), 486, 490. More generally, see his Chapter 14, "Fascism and Modernization."

8   Gabriel A. Almond, "Comparative Political Systems," *The Journal of Politics* 18, no. 3 (August 1956): 391–409, see pages 403–4 for the quotation.

9   Linz, *Totalitarian and Authoritarian Regimes*, 241.

10 Linz, *Totalitarian and Authoritarian Regimes*, 244. Finally, Linz notes, "Situations in which the strength of protototalitarian forces is reversed might be labelled 'arrested totalitarianism.'" Romania in 1941 is an example.

11 Linz, *Totalitarian and Authoritarian Regimes*, 94.

12 Juan J. Linz and Alfred Stepan, *Problems of Democratic Transition and Consolidation: Southern Europe, South America, and Post-Communist Europe* (Baltimore, MD: The Johns Hopkins University Press, 1996), 256.

13 Linz and Stepan, *Problems of Democratic Transition and Consolidation*, 256–58.

14   Keith Crawford, *East Central European Politics Today* (Manchester, UK: Manchester University Press, 1996), 51.

15   See, for example, Mark R. Thompson, "Totalitarian and Post-Totalitarian Regimes in Transitions and Non-Transitions from Communism," *Totalitarian Movements and Political Religions* 3, no. 1 (Summer 2002): 79–106, see pages 86–90.

16   H.E. Chehabi and Juan J. Linz, "A Theory of Sultanism 1: A Type of Nondemocratic Rule," in *Sultanistic Regimes,* ed. H.E. Chehabi and Juan J. Linz, 3–25 (Baltimore, MD and London, UK: The Johns Hopkins University Press, 1998), 7.

17   Chehabi and Linz, "A Theory of Sultanism," 9.

18   Chehabi and Linz, "A Theory of Sultanism," 13–16.

19   Chehabi and Linz, "A Theory of Sultanism," 3–24.

20   Juan J. Linz, "An Authoritarian Regime: The Case of Spain," in *Mass Politics: Studies in Political Sociology,* ed. Erik Allard and Stein Rokkan, 251–83 (New York, NY: Free Press, 1970), as cited in Linz, *Totalitarian and Authoritarian Regimes,* 159.

21   Given this lack of responsible government, it is unclear why Freedom House considers Monaco to be an electoral democracy. It is not treated as such in this analysis (see Table 4.3).

22   These 11 were Argentina, Bolivia, Brazil, Chile, Ecuador, El Salvador, Guatemala, Honduras, Panama, Paraguay, Peru, and Uruguay.

23   Wilfried Buchta, *Who Rules Iran? The Structure of Power in the Islamic Republic* (Washington, DC: The Washington Institute for Near East Policy and the Konrad Adenauer Stiftung, 2000), 23.

24   Buchta, *Who Rules Iran?,* 52–53.

25   Interestingly, none of the other Grand Ayatollahs actually support the principle of *velayat-e faqih* or "rule by the jurisprudent." See Buchta, *Who Rules Iran?,* 54 (his Diagram 10).

26   See, in particular, Andreas Schedler, ed., *Electoral Authoritarianism: The Dynamics of Unfree Competition* (Boulder, CO: Lynne Rienner, 2006).

27   On the phenomenon in Belarus, see Andrew Wilson, *Belarus: The Last Dictatorship in Europe* (New Haven, CT and London, UK: Yale University Press, 2011), 255–58.

28   On this history, see Francis T. Seow, *The Media Enthralled: Singapore Revisited* (Boulder, CO: Lynne Rienner, 1998).

29   Diane K. Mauzy, "Electoral Innovation and One-Party Dominance in Singapore," in *How Asia Votes,* ed. John Fuh-Sheng Hsieh and David Newman, 234–54 (New York, NY: Chatham House Publishers of Seven Bridges Press, 2002), 243.

30   Singapore is thus different from the democracy of Mauritius, where several "best losers" can also be appointed, in this case to improve ethnic balance; however, in Mauritius, these appointed "best losers" become regular MPs.

CHAPTER TEN

Democratic Transitions, Consolidations, and Breakdowns

IN THIS CHAPTER YOU WILL LEARN

- ► how democratic transition and democratic breakdown are opposite phenomena;
- ► what a wave of democratization is;
- ► where and why such waves have occurred;
- ► how and why there is some scholarly debate as to when the waves of democratization have actually occurred;
- ► what the four different processes of democratization are;
- ► which ones of these are superior and why;
- ► what the three components of democratic consolidation are;
- ► what three main challenges must be met for democratic consolidation;
- ► how, why, and when democracies break down; and
- ► how, in very exceptional circumstances, a brief democratic breakdown may be followed by democratic re-equilibration.

Democratization and Related Concepts

Simplifying somewhat the four categories outlined in Table 4.3, we can label all regimes either autocratic or democratic. When regime types are viewed in this dichotomous sense, **democratization** is the process of changing from an autocracy to a democracy or, more precisely with regard to our four categories, changing from an autocracy to at least an electoral democracy. The key step is holding free and fair elections to select the government of an individual country, as long as this government actually governs and is not just a front for a tutelary military or monarch wielding the actual power behind the scenes. If the political changes in an autocracy do not culminate in having free and fair elections for the key positions of elected power, then one should not speak of democratization. (Specifically, members of the national legislature or at least its lower house, if the system is bicameral, should be elected democratically and, in certain systems, the president should be elected as well.) Instead, if a country makes varying reforms that result in electing some lesser offices, increasing press freedoms, releasing political prisoners, or generally enlarging the scope of public debate, then one can refer to the political *liberalization* of an autocracy.[1] Such liberalization and increased openness could well involve the change from a closed autocracy to a semi-liberal one. (Remember that we use the term *semi-liberal autocracy* to distinguish its civil liberties from the full range of freedoms and their guarantees in a liberal democracy.) However, further steps—which may or may not happen—are needed to produce democratization. Finally, the change from an electoral to a liberal democracy can be called the *deepening* of democracy.[2]

In this chapter, we are concerned mainly with democratization as opposed to mere liberalization. An alternative term for the process of democratization—and the one we use most—is **democratic transition**. The opposite of a democratic transition, that is, the change from a democracy to an autocracy, is known as a **democratic breakdown**. A democratic breakdown occurs in the context of a lack of **democratic consolidation**, a deficiency of broad support for the democratic regime. (This last concept is multi-faceted and will be outlined later.) As we shall see, democratic transitions and democratic breakdowns occur in individual countries at identifiable times. Interestingly, though, countries—especially neighbouring countries—often have transitions or breakdowns fairly close in time to each other. This observation has led to the notion that there are "waves" of democratization, which we shall analyse before getting to the specifics of democratic transition, consolidation, breakdown, and related matters.

Waves of Democratization

As originally conceived by Huntington,

> A **wave of democratization** is a group of transitions from nondemocratic [autocratic] to democratic regimes that occur within a specified period of time and that significantly outnumber transitions in the opposite direction during that period of time. A wave also usually involves liberalization or partial democratization in political systems that do not become fully democratic. Three waves of democratization have occurred in the modern

world.... and during each wave some regime transitions occurred in a nondemocratic direction. In addition, not all transitions to democracy occurred during democratic waves.[3]

Thus, a wave of democratization is a clear pattern leading to an overall increase in the number of democracies, but it is also a pattern with some exceptions.

The first long wave of democratization that Huntington identifies begins in 1828 (with the US presidential election of that year) and lasts until 1926. Its roots were in the democratic ideals of the American and French revolutions of the late 1700s, and it occurred initially in Western and northern Europe and the British settler countries of the United States, Canada, Australia, and New Zealand. All these societies were experiencing social and economic development involving industrialization, urbanization, the formation of middle and working classes, growing national income, and also, eventually, somewhat of a decrease in economic inequality. Their intellectuals and many political leaders also had a strong belief in classical liberal thought. Moreover, most of these countries were either overwhelmingly or largely Protestant in religion. After World War I, this wave spread into central and Eastern Europe due to the breakup of the empires there.

According to Huntington, the second wave of democratization lasted from 1943 to 1962 and was broadly based geographically. Two factors were central in this second wave. The first was the Allied powers victory in World War II, their direct imposition of democracy on the defeated Axis powers, and their support, or, more specifically, US support (especially in the late 1940s) for democracy elsewhere, particularly in Latin America and the Mediterranean. The second factor was the decolonization occurring in Africa and Asia, which produced a huge number of new states (see Chapter 1), many of which were at least initially democratic.

The third—and ongoing—wave of democratization described by Huntington begins in 1974 with the collapse of autocracy in Portugal (although Portugal did not instantly become democratic) and spreads out from southern Europe to Latin America, Asia, and then ex-communist Europe. In the 1990s (subsequent to Huntington's book), this wave spread into Africa. Huntington argues that the third wave was multi-causal, involving global economic growth in the 1960s, the economic failures of various autocracies, a new pro-democratic attitude within the Catholic Church, renewed support for democracy by the United States and the European Community, and Gorbachev's abandonment of Soviet control over central and Eastern Europe—all reinforced in a "snowballing" way by modern communications that let people quickly know what was happening elsewhere in the world.[4] This notion of "the third wave of democratization" has become a frequent point of context in the social science literature, so students need to be familiar with it.

Huntington also argues that there have been two reverse waves of democratization, a **reverse wave** being a significant group of transitions in a nondemocratic (autocratic) direction. He states that the first reverse wave lasted from 1922 to 1942, beginning with Mussolini's March on Rome, although three more years would pass before Italian democracy was definitely over. The reverse wave then spread throughout southern and Eastern Europe, Latin America, and on to Japan. The turmoil of the post–World War I environment, the rise of both totalitarian and militaristic ideologies, and, finally, the Great Depression were central factors behind this nondemocratic wave. Of course, not all countries experienced breakdowns of democracy during this period; the breakdowns occurred mainly in places where democracy was newer and, essentially, weaker. Yet, even in the countries where democracy survived, a rise in antidemocratic movements generally occurred during this period. For Huntington, a second reverse wave of democratization took place from 1958 to 1975, most dramatically in Latin America but also in the Mediterranean, Asia, and Africa. This reverse wave in Africa involved the failure of many new democracies to get off the ground in the first place. During this period, the most common pattern of overthrowing democracy was a military coup and subsequent military rule (the patterns were more varied during the first reverse wave). Fear of communism, especially after Castro's successful revolution in Cuba and his subsequent shift to a socialist economy, was often a central factor for autocrats and their supporters in the second reverse wave, regardless of how "serious" the communist threat really was. Certainly as a consequence the United States was relatively tolerant toward the new autocracies during this period, especially if and when they pledged to be pro-Western.[5]

Methodological Critiques and Revisions of Huntington's Measurement of Waves

Huntington's analysis and classifications are commonly used, and his concept of democratic "waves" was certainly groundbreaking. That said, various criticisms can be made of his methodology. Accepting some but not all of these criticisms, we develop our own time periods of global regime change.

The first of these criticisms concerns Huntington's criteria for democracy: (1) the suffrage being held by at least 50 per cent of adult males (at least for the nineteenth century) and (2) responsible government.[6] Both Doorenspleet and Paxton criticize Huntington for establishing the first criterion, which allows a country to be called democratic even though it excludes women from voting; for her part, Doorenspleet argues for a suffrage criterion of at least 80 per cent of the adult population.[7] On the other hand Rueschemeyer, Stephens, and Stephens use a suffrage criterion of at least 60 per cent of adult males—quite close to Huntington's—or of all literate adult males because either of these is sufficient to establish multi-class suffrage rights, which is their focus.[8]

This issue could be solved by using a continuous measure of democracy: obviously, a system with both genders voting is more democratic than one with only partial male suffrage; likewise, a system with universal suffrage is more democratic than one with only 80 per cent or so of adults having the right to vote—for the latter, think of the United States prior to the Voting Rights Act of 1965. Furthermore, as noted in Chapter 4 (but not mentioned by any of the authors cited previously), is that a system with a voting age of 18 is more democratic than one with a voting age of 23 or 25. What we are talking about here is the establishment of a basic level of electoral democracy, and the notion and dating of democratic transitions are much more manageable when democracy versus autocracy is treated as a dichotomy. The relevant question is this: at what level of suffrage does the political system function in response to the needs and potential votes of more than just the elites? We use a suffrage criterion of more than 20 per cent of the 18-and-above population, even if the legal voting age is well above this; any state with more restricted suffrage, even if it has competitive elections and responsible government, is a **competitive oligarchy**. (Before 1994, South Africa was such an oligarchy because suffrage was racially restricted.)

Our cut-off is not the universal suffrage of an unqualified electoral democracy, but, certainly, it does indicate that suffrage has become broad enough so as to make politics more than an elite game. A government that meets this cut-off consequently will be called a **moderately inclusive electoral democracy** or **MIED**. Table 10.1 presents a reference list of the years in which countries have become MIEDs or in which democracy has broken down.[9] Note that every breakdown of democracy listed involved the ending of responsible government and never the reducing of suffrage rights while responsible government was maintained.

A second problem with Huntington's calculations is that he includes as countries experiencing a transition away from democracy all those European countries conquered by Nazi Germany, thus amplifying the significance and extent of his first reverse wave. As Doorenspleet points out, these conquered countries experienced the interruption rather than the breakdown of democracy.[10] Consequently, we treat such cases as incidences of occupation rather than regime change. A third problem, also noted by Doorenspleet, is that the vast increase in the number of countries in the world means a very different denominator if one is measuring the *percentage* of democracies or of autocracies.[11] Consequently, we avoid percentages and focus on the total number of changes, but we also weight these by the number of countries. A fourth and presumably obvious problem with Huntington's categories is some temporal overlap, especially between the first wave of democratization and the first reverse wave. Obviously, both a wave of democratization and its reverse cannot occur at the same time, so we determine whether transitions or breakdowns are more numerous in any given year and for all years. Fifth and related, it may not actually be the case that a wave is occurring at all in a given period. Doorenspleet uses the term "trendless fluctuation" to describe a pattern showing tiny waves of both democratizations and democratic breakdowns that cancel each other out.[12] Finally, although a wave reflects an overall pattern that may be in evidence for, say, many decades, this pattern may be more intense for a shorter period of time; consequently, when appropriate, we distinguish between phases of the "normal" and concentrated intensity of a wave.

If we use the data from Table 10.1 and apply the aforementioned qualifications, what historical patterns do we find? As shown in Table 10.2, there is indeed a long wave of democratization—in the sense of countries becoming MIEDs—from 1829 to 1922. At the end of this long wave is a particularly intense phase during and after World War I, reflecting both the democratization "trade-off" necessary to achieve legitimate mass mobilization during the war and the creation of new states as a consequence of the war. Then there is a reverse wave from 1923 through 1936. From 1937 to 1942, "nothing happens"—even though World War II saw the occupation of various democracies by Nazi Germany. Regardless of the war, no country made a transition to democracy or suffered an internal breakdown of democracy during these years. A second wave of democratization occurred from 1943 through 1957, followed not by a global reverse wave but by a period of trendless fluctuation from 1958 through 1973. This finding confirms that of Doorenspleet, although she times the start and especially the end date of this trendless period differently.[13] Note, however, that a *regional* reverse wave occurred in Latin America during the trendless period, with about half of the countries in that region undergoing a democratic

TABLE 10.1 Transitions to and Breakdowns of Democratic Regimes (MIEDs)

Country	Transition	Breakdown	Notes
Albania	1992	1995	
	1997	2009	
Andorra	1993		
Antigua and Barbuda	2004		
Argentina	1916	1930	
	1946	1948–49	
	1958	1966	
	1973	1976	
	1983		
Australia	1901		
Austria	1919	1934	
	1945		
Bahamas	1967		
Bangladesh	1980	1982	
	1991	2007	
	2009		
Barbados	1961		
Belgium	1919		occupation 1940–45
Belize	1981		
Benin	1991		
Bolivia	1952	1964	
	1982		
Botswana	1966		
Brazil	1946	1964	re-equilibration 1954–55
	1985		
Bulgaria	1919	1923	
	1990		
Burma	1956	1962	
Burundi	2005	2010	
Canada	1867		
Cape Verde	1991		
Chile	1952	1973	
	1990		
Colombia	1922	1949	
	1974		
Comoros	2006		
Congo, R	1992	1996	
Costa Rica	1928		re-equilibration 1948
Croatia	1992	1995	
	2000		
Cuba	1944	1952	
Cyprus (Greek)	1960	1974	
	1974		
Czechoslovakia	1919	1948	occupation 1939–45
Czechoslovakia/ Czech Republic	1990		
	1992		
Denmark	1915		occupation 1940–45
Dominica	1978		

Country	Transition	Breakdown	Notes
Dominican Republic	1962 1978 1996	1963 1990	
Ecuador	1948 1978	1963	
El Salvador	1984		
Estonia	1920 1992	1934	
Fiji	1970 1999	1987 2000	
Finland	1919		re-equilibration 1930–32
France	1848 1875	1850	occupation 1940–44
Gambia	1965	1994	
Georgia	1992 2004	2000 2008	
Germany/ West Germany	1919 1949	1933	
Ghana	1957 1969 1979 2000	1960 1972 1981	
Greece	1875 1910 1927 1950 1974	1909 1915 1935 1967	
Grenada	1984		
Guatemala	1945 1966 1985	1954 1970	failed autogolpe attempt in 1993
Guinea-Bissau	1994 2005	2003 2012	
Guyana	1966 1992	1970	
Haiti	1991 2006	1991 2010	
Honduras	1982 2010	2009	
Hungary	1990		
Iceland	1918		
India	1952 1977	1975	
Indonesia	1950 1999	1957	
Iraq	2010		
Ireland	1922		
Israel	1948		
Italy	1918 1948	1925	

Country	Transition	Breakdown	Notes
Ivory Coast	2011		
Jamaica	1962		
Japan	1928	1932	
	1947		
Kenya	2002	2007	
Kiribati	1979		
Korea, South	1960	1961	
	1987		
Kosovo	2008	2010	
Kyrgyzstan	2010		
Latvia	1922	1934	
	1993		
Lebanon	1943	1972	
Lesotho	2002		
Liberia	2006		
Liechtenstein	1921		
Lithuania	1922	1926	
	1992		
Luxembourg	1919		occupation 1940-44
Macedonia	1991		
Madagascar	1993	2009	failed autogolpe attempt in 2001-2
Malawi	1994	2004	
Malaysia	1957	1969	
Maldives	2008	2012	
Mali	1992	2012	
Malta	1964		
Marshall Islands	1986		
Mauritania	2007	2008	
Mauritius	1968		
Mexico	2000		
Micronesia	1986		
Moldova	1994	2005	
	2009		
Mongolia	1990		
Montenegro	2006		
Mozambique	1994	2004	
Namibia	1990		
Nauru	1968		
Nepal	1959	1960	
	1991	2002	
Netherlands	1917		occupation 1940-45
New Zealand	1890		
Nicaragua	1990	2011	
Niger	1993	1996	
	1999	2009	
	2011		

Country	Transition	Breakdown	Notes
Nigeria	1960	1966	
	1979	1983	
	1999	2003	
	2011		
Norway	1905		occupation 1940–45
Pakistan	1970	1977	
	1988/1990	1999	
	2008		
Palau	1994		
Panama	1956	1968	
	1989		
Papua New Guinea	1975		
Paraguay	1993		failed coup attempt in 1996
Peru	1956	1962	
	1963	1968	
	1979	1992	
	2001		
Philippines	1946	1972	
	1986	2004	
	2010		
Poland	1922	1926	
	1990		
Portugal	1910	1926	
	1975		
Romania	1992		
Russia	1993	2003	
Saint Kitts and Nevis	1983		
Saint Lucia	1979		
Saint Vincent and the Grenadines	1979		
Samoa	1991		
San Marino	1906	1923	
	1945		
São Tomé and Príncipe	1991		failed coup attempts in 1995 and 2003
Serbia	1880	1883	
Serbia / Yugoslavia	1903	1929	
Serbia	2000		
Senegal	2000	2007	
	2012		
Sierra Leone	1998		
Slovakia	1992		
Slovenia	1991		
Solomon Islands	1978	2000	
Somalia	1960	1969	
South Africa	1994		
Spain	1931	1936	
	1977		
Sri Lanka	1947	2010	
Suriname	1975	1980	
	1987	1990	
	1991		

Country	Transition	Breakdown	Notes
Sweden	1921		
Switzerland	1848		
Syria	1944	1949	
	1954	1956	
Taiwan	1987		
Thailand	1945	1947	
	1949	1951	
	1974	1976	
	1992	2006	
	2011		
Timor-Leste (East Timor)	2003		
Trinidad and Tobago	1962		
Tunisia	2011		
Turkey	1950	1960	
	1961	1970	
	1973	1980	
	1983		
Tuvalu	1978		
Ukraine	1991	1999	
	2005	2012	
United Kingdom	1885		
United States	1829		
Uruguay	1918	1973	re-equilibration 1933–42
	1984		
Vanuatu	1980		
Venezuela	1959	2006	failed coup attempts in 1992 (twice) and 2002
Zambia	1991	1996	
	2006		

breakdown during this time. Finally, a third wave of democratization began in 1974 (as Huntington argues) and is still ongoing. This third wave was particularly intense from 1990 through 1994, when it reached central and Eastern Europe and Africa. It has been much weaker overall since then, although the "Arab Awakening" that started at the end of 2010 has produced, as of late 2012, one new democracy in Tunisia (where the uprisings began) with the possibility of a couple more to come.

The Processes of Democratic Transition in Sovereign States

A transition to democracy in an already sovereign state can occur in one of four ways,[14] as is shown in Table 10.3, which gives various illustrative postwar examples as opposed to a complete list. First, the process of democratization can be *dictated*

TABLE 10.2 Waves of Democratization, 1800 to Present

	Number of Transitions	Number of Breakdowns	Difference	TOTAL N	Difference Weighted by Total States at the End of the Period (absolute values, in percentages)
FIRST WAVE, 1829–1922	36	4	+ 32	64	50%
moderate phase, 1829–1914	*15*	*3*	*+ 12*	*56*	21%
intense phase, 1915–22	*21*	*1*	*+ 20*	*64*	31%
REVERSE WAVE, 1923–36	4	15	– 11	66	17%
STABILITY, 1937–42	0	0	0		
SECOND WAVE, 1943–57	29	10	+ 19	88	22%
FLUCTUATION, 1958–73	26	25	+ 1	144	1%
THIRD WAVE, 1974–present (2012)	128	54	+ 74	195	38%
moderate phase, 1974–89	*40*	*11*	*+ 29*	*167*	17%
intense phase, 1990–94	*45*	*5*	*+ 40*	*191*	21%
moderate phase, 1995–present	*43*	*38*	*+ 5*	*195*	3%

by those in power, as it was, for example, by the Brazilian military or the Hungarian communists. This transition is a top-down process. Second, formal *negotiations* between the regime and the leaders of the pro-democratic opposition can take place, as happened between the Polish communists and the Solidarity movement as well as between the whites-only government of South Africa and the African National Congress.[15] Third, the autocratic regime can collapse, in which case the leaders *abdicate* power and simply walk away. Such a regime collapse can occur because of the military defeat of a military regime, which happened to Greece in Cyprus and to Argentina in the Falkland Islands. Alternatively, autocracies have collapsed due to the combination of the withdrawal of external support and massive public demonstrations (think of the communist regimes of Czechoslovakia and East Germany) or because of massive public demonstrations that cause a regional "spillover" (think of the Arab Awakening). All of these are essentially if not totally internal processes. Fourth and finally, after military defeat and foreign occupation, the occupying powers may choose to *impose* democracy on the occupied country, as was done in Germany and Japan after World War II.[16] Overall, in terms of the internal processes, the *dictated* process occurs when the ruling autocrats are stronger than any opposition, the *negotiated* process occurs when the ruling autocrats and those in opposition are roughly equal in power (at least to the extent that neither can impose their wishes), and the *abdicated* process occurs when the ruling autocrats (often quite quickly) become weaker than the political opposition.

Of these four processes, the negotiated and dictated ones (in that order) are seen to be "superior" in the sense of being more likely to produce a durable democracy. This durability results from elements of the old regime helping to produce the new democratic regime, thus lending it "forward legitimacy," especially among the supporters of the old regime who, presumably, were not in favour of such a change. The negotiated scenario adds to this "forward legitimacy" a separate legitimacy amongst the supporters of the political opposition, whose leaders have agreed to the specifics of the regime change. In contrast, when an autocratic regime abdicates or is conquered, key figures of the old regime work against democratization, and its supporters remain to not only oppose the new democratic regime but to actively try to undermine it—and they may well be strong enough to be effective. For example, politics in Weimar Germany followed this pattern after the country's military defeat in World War I.[17] In the imposed democracy scenario, a major and long-term military occupation is likely necessary to root out and marginalize the key figures and activists of the old regime, as happened, for example, during the "denazification" of Germany after 1945.

Yet, for either a dictated or negotiated process to occur, the ruling autocrats have to be less than fully autocratic; that is, they have to be willing to open up the political process. As noted, initially, this loosening of autocratic control may involve a desire for liberalization but not full democratization, with the former change then snowballing into the latter. In any case, the leadership of the ruling autocracy has to be in the hands of a reformer rather than a hard-line "standpatter"—a King Juan Carlos and not a *Generalísimo* Franco, a Gorbachev and not a Brezhnev. Indeed, a country may go through more than one reform leader during the process of democratization or even liberalization, and the reformist course can be interrupted by a "standpatter."[18] Moreover, in either a dictated or a negotiated process, the leader willing to reform has to have the foresight to want to change things before change is forced on the leadership; although it may seem obvious that it is better to be in control of the process of change, if only to be able to negotiate from a position of relative strength, if the ruling autocracy is fairly powerful still, then there is usually a great temptation to do nothing in the way of reforms. Equally, for a negotiated transition to occur, an *organized* political opposition with recognized leaders must exist: massive spontaneous protests are not enough. Additionally, the reality is that, under full totalitarianism

TABLE 10.3 Processes of Transition to Democracy

| | NON-DEMOCRATIC REGIME TYPE | | | | | | |
PROCESS	Racial Oligarchy	Electoral Authoritarian	Military Authoritarian	Theocratic Authoritarian	Incomplete Totalitarian or Post-Totalitarian	Full Totalitarian	Sultanistic
DICTATED		Mexico Taiwan	Brazil Chile (Spain) Turkey		Bulgaria Hungary		
NEGOTIATED	South Africa		South Korea Uruguay		Mongolia Poland		
ABDICATED		Tunisia	Argentina Greece Portugal			Czechoslovakia East Germany	Philippines (under Marcos) Romania (under Ceauşescu)
IMPOSED BY OUTSIDE POWERS		Grenada	Japan Panama			Nazi Germany	Iraq

NOTE: European traditional authoritarian regimes tended to become competitive oligarchies.

SOURCE: Adapted from information in Table 3.1 of Samuel P. Huntington, *The Third Wave: Democratization in the Late Twentieth Century* (Norman, OK: University of Oklahoma Press, 1991), 113.

or sultanism, an organized political opposition, by definition, does not and cannot exist. Thus, as Table 10.3 indicates, when these regime types do make a transition to democracy, they follow less favourable processes (see Chapter 9, especially Table 9.1, for an outline of the characteristics of full totalitarianism and sultanism).

Democratic Transitions and Consolidation

The transition to democracy needs to be kept separate from what follows it, which is ideally the consolidation of democracy. Gunther, Puhle, and Diamandouros are clear and useful in this regard:

Transition and consolidation are conceptually distinct aspects of ... [democratic development], although in practice they may temporally overlap or sometimes even coincide. Transition begins with the breakdown of the former ... [autocratic] regime and ends with the establishment of a relatively stable configuration of political institutions within a democratic regime. Consolidation ... refers to the achievement of substantial

attitudinal support for and behavioral compliance with the new democratic institutions and the rules of the game which they establish. In most cases, the consolidation
of democracy requires more time than the transition process ... consolidation is much
more complex and it involves a much larger number of actors in a wider array of political arenas. The outcomes of these processes are also distinct: transition results in the
creation of a new regime; consolidation results in the stability and persistence of that
regime, even in the face of severe challenges.[19]

Consequently, no democratic consolidation is possible without a democratic transition; however, a democratic transition will not necessarily be followed by democratic
consolidation.

We can see a "successful" pattern of democratic transition and consolidation in
Figure 10.1. The sequence goes as follows. At some instant, there is an autocracy or
perhaps an oligarchy (as in South Africa); this is period A. This regime could hold
elections (certainly the case in a competitive oligarchy), but these elections do not
produce responsible government or they might not involve an even moderately inclusive franchise. Pressures build up for regime change, perhaps from within, perhaps
because of international opinion. A reformist leader or leadership decides to open
up the system; this decision, which might involve agreeing to negotiate with pro-
democracy leaders, is point *b*. Alternatively, the autocracy collapses or is conquered,
and the new authorities seek to make the system more open and democratic; this is
another version of point *b*. A transition begins. However, for this to be a transition
to democracy, indicated as period C, various events must occur. First, as we have
noted, there has to be agreement, especially by the ruling autocrats if they have not
abdicated or been conquered, that democracy is the actual goal rather than just
some limited liberalization. The mechanics of the new democratic regime—that is,
its main institutional features (e.g., whether it is a parliamentary or presidential
democracy)—have to be agreed to. This agreement can involve deciding on a new
constitution. Any direct control or tutelary power by a monarch or national military
or regional warlords must be given up. Such a requirement may not be "obvious" if
this power was exercised behind the scenes in the outgoing autocracy, but the step is
necessary nevertheless. The central element in a transition for oligarchies and, possibly, a required step for some autocracies is the extension of the franchise to make
it sufficiently broad; in the contemporary context, the presumption is universal adult
suffrage. Finally, a date is set for the founding elections of the new democracy; these

FIGURE 10.1 Stages of Democratic Transition and Consolidation

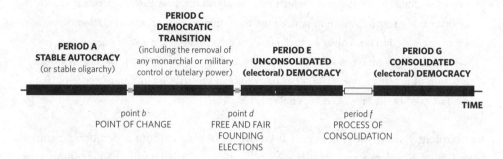

elections are point *d*. (If, prior to these elections, the country held separate elections for a constitutional assembly to produce a new constitution, those elections remain part of the transition stage.)

Still, things can go "wrong" at the transition stage. In particular, transitions or liberalizations that might become transitions to democracy could fail before getting to the founding elections if the ruling autocrats or other key players within the regime "change their minds" and restore autocracy, for example, by replacing the reformist leader with a hardliner. Examples of such reactions include hardliner Dimitrios Ioannidis's coup in Greece in 1973 (although Greece had a successful democratic transition the following year) and the military assumption of direct rule that ended the pro-democracy uprising in Burma in 1988. The crackdown in China in 1989, including the crushing of the student demonstrations in Tiananmen Square, should also be seen in this light.[20] Yet, even if elections are not only agreed to but also held, responsible government is not produced if the military or the monarch remains in effective control. The latter is the current situation in Bhutan, whose 2008 elections *cannot* be seen as the founding elections of a new democracy. On the other hand, if we look on the bright side, a country can be considered at least an electoral democracy after all the necessary events of the transition (period C) occur and once the founding elections (point *d*) are free and fair with everyone accepting the results and the new government taking office. Getting to and then past point *d* is certainly reason to cheer, but it is not reason to be complacent. What guarantee do we have that the country concerned will still be a democracy in five or ten years, or even the next year?

Such a question returns us to the concept of democratic consolidation. Democratic consolidation involves three components.[21] The first is *law-abidingness*; a democratic regime is consolidated when political leaders and other elites, as well as most of the population, obey the laws and the constitution, compete peacefully for power through the specified procedures and institutions, and avoid political violence. The second is *partisan behaviour*; a democratic regime is consolidated when political elites respect each other's right to compete, are tolerant of opposing views, hand over power unconditionally when defeated in elections, recognize as legitimate duly elected governments of other parties, do not sympathize with or apologize for any extremists on their side of the political spectrum, and do not attempt to use the military or foreign agents for partisan advantage. In this sense, we can speak of political parties in opposition being a *loyal opposition* once democracy is consolidated, as opposed to a disloyal or semi-loyal one.[22] Third and finally, in terms of *political attitudes* or *beliefs*, a democratic regime is consolidated when the leaders of all significant political parties, most other elites and opinion makers, and an overwhelming majority of the people consistently believe that democracy is the best form of government both theoretically and specifically for their country. Diamond argues that the threshold of "overwhelming public support" for democracy is having at least 70 to 75 per cent of the people holding such pro-democratic beliefs and conversely no more than 15 per cent of the people definitively preferring some form of non-democratic government. (The remainder of the population would not have any clear or strong opinion one way or another, presumably.) Consequently, no anti-democratic movement or party, existing or hypothetical, would have a significant mass following.[23]

These three components of democratic consolidation reinforce each other; however, they do not necessarily develop in perfectly parallel patterns. For example, the elites of a country might be strongly committed to democracy, but the masses could be rather indifferent; one suspects that this was the case in early post-independence India. On the other hand, certain political leaders may trail their population in terms of commitment to democracy, which happened, for example, in Argentina in the 1990s. There, President Carlos Menem used undemocratic means (especially stacking the judiciary) to expand and maintain his power and interests as well as those of his cronies when mass support for democracy was at the 70 per cent and above level.[24] Thus, in Figure 10.1, we refer to a multifaceted *process* of consolidation (*f*), at the end of which one has a consolidated democracy (period G). In contrast to point *b* and point *d*, "period *f*" has no specific point in time, as it is more of a conceptual outcome than a precise one. In other words, we can certainly identify consolidated democracies, but we cannot easily refer to a specific date at which they become fully consolidated.[25] According to scholarly analysis and, if available, survey data, most democracies that have been around continuously since before the "third wave" (that is, before 1974; see Table 10.2), as well as the newer democracies of southern Europe and several in central and Eastern Europe, are generally considered to be consolidated. In contrast, most of the other "third wave" democracies, especially those in Africa, are considered to be unconsolidated, especially at the mass level.[26]

Following Diamond, we can note that the main challenges of democratic consolidation are threefold.[27] The first of these tasks is the need to "deepen" and thus improve democracy so that it becomes more comprehensive, accountable, and fair. In the typology of our analysis, this deepening involves going from an electoral democracy to a liberal one. Indeed, very few electoral but not liberal democracies are considered consolidated; India remains the main consolidated electoral democracy, but we can also add Jamaica and the idiosyncratic case of Liechtenstein. Democratic "deepening" and improvement are central for democratic consolidation inasmuch as the latter involves both the elites acting democratically and the mass public strongly supporting democracy. Consequently, as Diamond notes,

> The less respectful of political rights, civil liberties, and constitutional constraints on state power are the behaviors of key political actors, the weaker is the procedural consensus underpinning democracy. Consolidation is, by definition, obstructed. Furthermore, the more shallow, exclusive, unaccountable, and abusive of individual and groups rights is the electoral regime, the more difficult it is for that regime to become legitimated at the mass level (or to retain such legitimacy) [because its citizens, with reason, tend to have a low opinion of democracy as they experience and see it], and thus the lower are the perceived costs for the elected president or the military to overthrow the system. [28]

Illustrations of this logic have occurred, for example, in both Pakistan and Bangladesh, where, after their respective 1999 and 2007 military coups, the army disparaged its country's previous electoral democracy as something so flawed that it was not "real democracy" and thus not worth returning to (although both countries have since done so). For example, at a news conference in April 2007, the Bangladesh army chief, Lieutenant General Moeen U Ahmed, said, "We do not want to go back to an elective democracy where corruption becomes all pervasive, governance suffers in terms of insecurity and violation of rights, and where political criminalisation threatens the very survival and integrity of the state."[29]

A second task of democratic consolidation is to achieve successful regime performance in terms of public policy outcomes, thus producing a "virtuous circle." Policy effectiveness not only produces legitimacy but is easier to achieve when there is legitimacy and consolidation: regimes with higher levels of legitimacy can solve problems more easily than those with lower levels because, in the former case, politicians are more likely to cooperate and the public is more likely to be patient while necessary reforms are undertaken. The final task of democratic consolidation is political institutionalization, so political institutions (including, as was discussed in Chapter 7, political parties) can function with greater coherence, effectiveness, adaptability, and autonomy. This task is, in a sense, antecedent to the other two. Political institutionalization, especially of the judiciary and the legislature, means better "checks and balances" on the executive, so power is not abused. Political institutionalization also facilitates the ability of the regime to aggregate the desires of the citizenry and to produce effective responses to these, as well as solving crises and adapting to global or local change.

Of course, all of these facets of consolidation can be reversed. That is, a democratic regime that is consolidated (and perhaps has been for decades) could experience an outburst of political violence, as Uruguay did in the 1960s. Its political incumbents could make elections less competitive although still democratic. Such a regime could weaken its commitment to civil liberties or to civilian control over the military, perhaps because of regional insurgencies, as happened in Colombia, India, and Sri Lanka. It could slide into economic stagnation for decades, as in postwar Uruguay, or become less adept at solving problems. It could simply become more corrupt, as happened in Venezuela in the 1980s. Finally, such a regime could see political de-institutionalization if, for example, judicial independence is eroded, as it was in Argentina under Menem, or the established political parties become less responsive to voters, which happened in Venezuela and also in Italy in the 1980s. These negative developments, especially if there are more than one of them, will produce **democratic deconsolidation**, as is illustrated in Figure 10.2. Democratic deconsolidation happens when a consolidated democracy (period G) experiences a process (not a point) of deconsolidation (*h*), and thus reverts to an unconsolidated stage (period E). Of course, differences could exist between the unconsolidated period after democratic deconsolidation and the earlier unconsolidated period, especially concerning which crucial categories remain to be consolidated, but let us still use the term "period E" for both.

FIGURE 10.2 Stages of Democratic Transition, Consolidation, and Deconsolidation

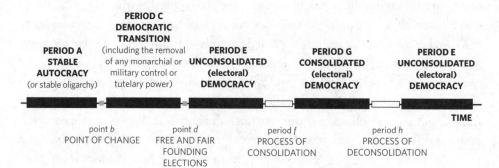

The Hows and Whys of Democratic Breakdown

Is it important that a given democracy is consolidated rather than unconsolidated (or deconsolidated)? The answer is a definite yes, and, as for why, one only has to think of Weimar Germany historically or Pakistan and Sri Lanka in the contemporary era. Democracies that are unconsolidated and that are faced with serious crises will tend to break down and be replaced by autocracies, perhaps for a couple of years, perhaps for a couple of decades or more. Figure 10.3 outlines the sequence under which, instead of consolidating, a democracy suffers a breakdown (at point *i*), and the country reverts to an autocracy lasting for period J. Note that, in any given country, the autocracy of period J may be different than the one that existed in period A (for example, the first could be a traditional authoritarian and the second a military regime), hence the different label.

How have democratic breakdowns occurred? The answer is in various ways, specifically, four:

▸ A military coup d'état overthrows a democratically elected government. Many of these have already been noted.

▸ A "self-coup" (*autogolpe* in Spanish) occurs. In other words, the democratically elected leader suspends or violates the constitution (or replaces it undemocratically) and proceeds to rule indefinitely as an autocrat. Self-coups happened, for example, in parts of Eastern Europe in the 1920s and 1930s, with Perón in Argentina in the late 1940s, and with Fujimori in Peru in 1992. An alternate

FIGURE 10.3 Stages of Democratic Transition, Crisis, and Breakdown

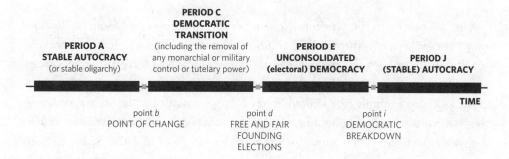

version of this scenario has a democratically elected leader ceasing to behave democratically and rigging his re-election or that of his party to usher in electoral authoritarianism. For example, such "electoral self-coups" were carried out by President Kuchma of Ukraine in his presidential re-election of 1999 and President Putin of Russia in both the Duma elections of 2003 and his presidential re-election of 2004. As the examples suggest and as has been shown, these endogenous breakdowns are more likely in presidential systems than in parliamentary ones.[30]

▶ A "royal coup" occurs. A monarch who had not been directly running the country, in that the state was run by a prime minister and a cabinet responsible to the legislature, decides to assume all power (see Chapter 9 for the varying power of monarchs in authoritarian regimes). A "royal coup" occurred in Yugoslavia in 1929.

▶ An antidemocratic mass party "wins" an election (in the sense of coming first) and is then handed power. The Nazi Party came to power in this way in Germany in 1933, as did the communists in Czechoslovakia in 1948. If we accept that electoral fraud often is a feature of democratic breakdown, we can place here the actions of the Popular Front in Spain, which, in 1936, "improved" its winning election results to consolidate power. One could argue that the largest party or alliance in parliament should have the right to govern or at least to be part of the government, but what if its intent is to end democracy? In Algeria in

1992, the military intervened to prevent such an outcome. Of course, Algeria is still under military tutelage today.

One *absence* from the previous list is important to note—revolution. No democracy has ever been overthrown by revolution. And the corollary is this: all successful revolutions have been against some form of autocracy. Nor have any democracies ended because of civil war. In reality, either a civil war has been won by the democratic side (for example, the United States North continued to be an MIED during the US Civil War, including holding regular elections) or, more usually, neither side in a civil war has been democratic (for example, Russia 1917 to 1922, Spain 1936 to 1939, or Angola 1975 to 2002). Note also that we are not considering as democratic breakdowns the conquest of democracies by hostile foreign powers, such as the conquest of Western European democracies by Nazi Germany.

A specific event can be seen as being the "trigger" that leads to a breakdown. However, *why* breakdowns occur is more important—the larger context in which they happen. Five broad factors can be noted: (1) external "shocks" like the Great Depression; (2) more generally, a high "load" on the system—in other words, many difficult problems to solve; (3) political polarization and wide social and political divisions, including the strength of radical leftists, which frightens conservatives into supporting or even calling for a military coup, and "excessive nationalism" on the part of the political right; (4) negative external pressures, or at least the lack of positive external support for democracy; and, in the more contemporary period, (5) economic mismanagement and corruption. Each of these factors feeds into the key contextual point here, which is the *loss of legitimacy* (or its absence in the first place) of the democratic system. By definition, as Linz notes,

At the very least, legitimacy is the belief that in spite of shortcomings and failures, the existing political institutions are better than any others that might be established, and that they therefore can demand obedience. Ultimately it means that when the rulers who hold power constitutionally demand obedience, and another group questions that demand in the name of alternative [non-democratic] political arrangements, citizens will voluntarily opt for compliance with the demands of those in authority.... Ultimately, democratic legitimacy is based on the belief that for that particular country at that particular historical juncture, no other type of regime could assure a more successful pursuit of collective goals.[31]

Democratic legitimacy is thus a relative concept—democracy must be considered more legitimate than other regime types—and one based very much on outputs or "ends."

Consequently, democratic legitimacy itself is produced, maintained, and ideally increased but potentially decreased (even to the point of "deconsolidation") by the *system performance* of the democratic regime. We can define system performance more precisely as not only a regime's general ability to achieve broadly desired goals, such as economic and social development, but also its ability to find and implement acceptable solutions for any problems that might arise. Following Linz, we distinguish between the efficacy and the effectiveness of a regime; the first refers to the regime's ability to produce solutions and the second to how well it can implement them.[32] Ultimately, if the democratic system is seen as dysfunctional *and* if key elites (presumably with a certain level of public support or at least indifference) consider some type of autocracy more likely to deliver the desired "ends," then a successful breakdown may well occur. Of course, an actor or a group could try to seize power for its own sake without any intention of improving the public interest, but such an actor or group invariably claims to be acting in the national interest even if this claim is a lie. The issue, again, is whether the level of dissatisfaction with the democratic regime is sufficient for the lie to be widely believed. If not and if a reasonably high level of democratic political culture exists in the country, then this seizure of power will ultimately fail.

Not all governments are equally competent, of course, but successful democracies generally have competent (or at least not totally incompetent) governments most of the time. All other things being equal, democratic legitimacy will increase over time in a generally successful democracy as more and more people see the positive outputs of the democratic regime. This progression usually continues until legitimacy reaches a high level (which is, as noted, 70 to 75 per cent or more of the population viewing democracy as the best form of government for the country). Such an increase will not necessarily be linear; there could be a "two steps forward, one step back" pattern. However, new democracies face two particular challenges with regard to democratic legitimacy. The first is that they may well lack a "reserve" of legitimacy. In older democracies, democratic legitimacy is broadly based and more or less taken for granted, so a badly performing regime can "coast" for a while if need be. In contrast, a new democratic regime tends to be under greater pressure to prove itself continually because the democratic regime in itself may not have any broad support in the population. Of course, this "pressure" will vary depending on the performance of the previous autocratic regime; if that regime was incompetent or corrupt, the bar will not be very high for the new democratic regime, inasmuch as legitimacy is a relative concept. Second and related is the issue of distinguishing the regime as a political system from the government of the day. In older democracies, an incompetent or corrupt government is likely to lead to that particular government being unpopular but not to any delegitimation or deconsolidation of democracy per se. Why? People can remember previous competent governments and assume (or hope) that future ones will be better than the current one. In other words, people may wait impatiently for the next election, so they can throw out an incompetent and unpopular government, but they do not wish to throw out democracy—at least, not after just one bad government. In contrast, however, people may find it hard to distinguish the government of the day in a new democracy, especially if it is the first such democratic one, from the democratic political system in which it operates because there is no previous competent democratic government (perhaps of another party) to serve as a reference point. Dissatisfaction with the government of the day, then, can easily become dissatisfaction with democracy as a political regime.

The Duration of Democracies That Breakdown

A democracy may last indefinitely. Many Western democracies—qualifying these as MIEDs in terms of suffrage—have lasted over a century to date. On the other hand, some democracies have lasted only a matter of months. Haiti made a transition to democracy in February of 1991 with the coming to power of newly elected President Jean-Bertrand Aristide. His party also won a plurality of seats in the Chamber of Deputies. A few months later, in September of 1991, Aristide was overthrown in a military coup. Obviously, then, in a new democracy, a democratic breakdown can occur rapidly, sometime later on, or never at all. However, scholars note that breakdowns come quite quickly on average, that "democratic regimes are particularly vulnerable in their early years."[33] Conversely, the longer a democracy exists, the more likely it is to last indefinitely. So, at a certain point, breakdown is less likely and, perhaps, very unlikely if the democracy has consolidated. Looking at the 108 cases of democratization that at some point broke down (see Table 10.1), we can calculate that the median duration of these democracies is eight years—so democratic breakdown is often quick. Conversely, the extreme cases of a long time until a democratic breakdown are Sri Lanka, after 63 years of democracy; Uruguay, after 55 years of democracy (including a decade-long period of re-equilibration); and Venezuela, after 47 years of democracy. As noted, in each case it can be argued that the country underwent deconsolidation in the years preceding the breakdown. If we rank these 108 cases from longest to shortest duration before breakdown, the 10th percentile (separating out the countries for which breakdown took the longest) comes in just above the 11th country, or at 26 years. Consequently, to use a rounder number, if a democracy can last 25 or so years, it is probably consolidated,[34] and it is unlikely to break down without worsening circumstances that both damage democracy and lead to deconsolidation. In other words, odds are that, after 25 or 26 years of democracy, a country's political system will continue to be democratic indefinitely.

Democratic Re-equilibration

Finally, in exceptional circumstances, a political crisis in an unconsolidated democracy may not lead to a political breakdown but rather to what Linz has called a re-equilibration of democracy. He defines **democratic re-equilibration** as follows:

> Reequilibration of a democracy is a political process that, after a crisis that has seriously threatened the continuity and stability of the basic democratic political mechanisms, results in their continued existence at the same or higher levels of democratic legitimacy, efficacy, and effectiveness. It assumes a severe jolting of these institutions, a loss of either effectiveness or efficacy, and probably legitimacy, that produces a temporary breakdown of the authority of the regime.... Breakdown followed by reequilibration of democracy can be effected by anti- or aconstitutional means, by the interference in the normal democratic processes of a political actor (like a charismatic leader) whose initial legitimation is ademocratic, or by the use of force, as in a military putsch.... The new regime might be established illegally, but it must be legitimated by the democratic process afterward, and above all, it must operate thereafter according to the democratic rules.[35]

Assuming that the new or modified regime does have higher levels of legitimacy, we can suggest that re-equilibration will produce consolidation, as suggested in Figure 10.4. The issue here is whether re-equilibration occurs at a specific point or is an ongoing process. It does seem to be the latter, although key events are part of the

FIGURE 10.4 Stages of Democratic Transition, Crisis, and Re-equilibration

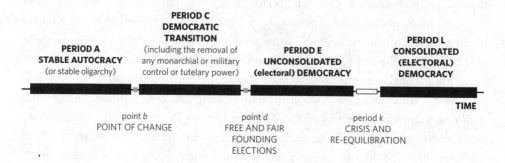

process. This process (*k*) leads to a consolidated democracy, period L, where there was not one before, but it does so in a very different way than under process *f* of Figure 10.1.

The classic example of democratic re-equilibration is France in 1958, when its regime changed from the Fourth to the Fifth Republic. The Fourth Republic was an unconsolidated democracy with little love for its political institutions, extreme political polarization, highly unstable governments, and, by the mid-to-late 1950s, an unsolvable crisis created by the Algerian War. With divisions over Algeria threatening to produce a military coup and possibly a civil war, Charles de Gaulle, the war hero who had resigned his position as leader of the French Provisional Government in 1946, offered to come back to "save France"—on his own terms, of course. The traditional political leaders acquiesced and made de Gaulle what amounted to a temporary dictator for several months. During this time, he produced a new constitution with a powerful president, although this constitution did not, technically, create a presidential system (see Chapter 6). He then proceeded to submit this constitution successfully to a national referendum and get himself elected as the first president of the new Fifth Republic. We thus see an after-the-fact confirmation and legitimation of de Gaulle's "seizure of power." His charisma, prestige, and legitimacy, which extended beyond that recognized by his direct supporters, were crucial in this process, just as they and his World War II military leadership were key in bringing the French Army back under control. It took a few years for de Gaulle to "solve" the Algerian crisis (ultimately by granting that country its independence), but, overall, the Fifth Republic, with de Gaulle at its head for the first decade, proved to be more efficacious at solving problems than the Fourth Republic ever was (except in economic matters).

Besides France in 1958, Finland in 1930–32 (with Pehr Evind Svinhufvud playing the "de Gaulle" role), Costa Rica in 1948–49, and, to some extent, Uruguay in 1933–42 can be seen as cases of re-equilibration. Overall, though, there have been few such cases, as re-equilibration requires (1) political leadership that has been hitherto untainted by the major crisis and the resulting loss of legitimacy of the regime, (2) the ability of this leadership to be acceptable to both supporters and opponents of the old regime; and (3) a willingness on the part of the leadership of the old regime; to transfer power to what is formally an anti-regime actor who has no constitutional claim to this power but who can be assumed to be the only saviour of democracy.[36] Needless to say, very few unconsolidated democracies have both a de Gaulle of their own waiting around in the wings and traditional parties that are willing to grant this "saviour" power, when push comes to shove. Consequently, re-equilibration should not be seen as a likely option. The reality is that the vast majority of unconsolidated democracies must slowly consolidate, by the various means noted above, if they are to be truly durable.

Notes

1   Samuel P. Huntington, *The Third Wave: Democratization in the Late Twentieth Century* (Norman, OK: University of Oklahoma Press, 1991), 9.

2. For example, see Larry Diamond, *Developing Democracy: Toward Consolidation* (Baltimore, MD: The Johns Hopkins University Press, 1999), 74.

3   Huntington, *The Third Wave*, 15. Bold added to stress key concept.

4   Huntington, *The Third Wave*, 16–46 *passim*.

5   Huntington, *The Third Wave*, 16–21.

6   Huntington, *The Third Wave*, 16.

7   Renske Doorenspleet, "Reassessing the Three Waves of Democratization," *World Politics* 52 (April 2000): 384–406, suffrage criterion on 391; Pamela Paxton, "Women's Suffrage in the Measurement of Democracy: Problems of Operationalization," *Studies in Comparative International Development* 35, no. 3 (Fall 2000): 92–111.

8   Dietrich Rueschemeyer, Evelyne Huber Stephens, and John D. Stephens, *Capitalist Development and Democracy* (Chicago, IL: University of Chicago Press, 1992), suffrage and other minimum criteria of democracy on 303.

9   The dates given are either (1) the date of independence of a colony on which a government elected in a free and fair election with at least moderately inclusive suffrage became a responsible government;

or (2), for already sovereign states, the year a government that was elected based on the first free and fair elections with moderately inclusive suffrage came into office, not the election year per se (thus 1829 not 1828 for the United States and 1990 not 1989 for Chile's re-democratization) and not the year when the suffrage law was changed (thus 1928 not 1925 for Japan). On this last point, see Doorenspleet, "Reassessing the Three Waves," 391, fn 26.

10   Doorenspleet, "Reassessing the Three Waves," 394–95.

11   Doorenspleet, "Reassessing the Three Waves," 395.

12   Doorenspleet, "Reassessing the Three Waves," 386, 398–99.

13   Doorenspleet, "Reassessing the Three Waves," 399, Table 1.

14   Note that we use the phrase "an already sovereign state" to make a distinction between these states and former colonies that become democracies upon independence; former colonies do not always fit into the four methods of transitioning to democracy described here.

15   This second process could also involve a political pact or settlement among various party leaders who are equally democratic but sharply divided on partisan, ideological, and sociological grounds, such as with the Dutch "Pacification Settlement" of 1913–17 or the Punto Fijo Pact in Venezuela and the related "Declaration of Principles" and "Minimal Program for Government" of 1958. Because of these pacts, this second process is sometimes called a "pacted transition."

16   Huntington, *The Third Wave*, 113. Note that we are using what are hopefully clearer terms for the different processes and that some changes have been made to Huntington's classifications.

17   In terms of the schema in Table 9.3, Germany in 1918 should be placed with Argentina, Greece, and Portugal as a case of *military abdication*. Although pre-1914 Imperial Germany was certainly an example of traditional authoritarianism, this regime was changed by the world war. As Smith remarks, "As the 1914–18 war progressed, the country slithered towards military dictatorship. Nominally responsible to the Emperor, the German High Command became increasingly contemptuous of any restrictions on its power." Once they realized that the war was lost, the High Command found it expedient to hand power over to a civilian government, which would reach an armistice and thus take the blame. See Gordon Smith, *Democracy in Western Germany: Parties and Politics in the Federal Republic*, 3rd ed. (New York, NY: Holmes and Meier, 1986), 16.

18   Huntington, *The Third Wave*, 130–33.

19   Richard Gunther, Hans-Jürgen Puhle, and P. Nikiforos Diamandouros, "Introduction," in *The Politics of Democratic Consolidation: Southern Europe in Comparative Perspective*, ed. Richard Gunther, Hans-Jürgen Puhle, and P. Nikiforos Diamandouros, 1–33 (Baltimore, MD and London, UK: The Johns Hopkins University Press, 1995), 3.

20   Huntington, *The Third Wave*, 135.

21   Juan J. Linz and Alfred Stepan, *Problems of Democratic Transition and Consolidation: Southern Europe, South America, and Post-Communist Europe* (Baltimore, MD: The Johns Hopkins University Press, 1996), 6; Diamond, *Developing Democracy*, 69. Their various categories have been modified somewhat here.

22   On this component, see also Juan J. Linz, *The Breakdown of Democratic Regimes: Crisis, Breakdown, and Reequilibration* (Baltimore, MD and London, UK: The Johns Hopkins University Press, 1978), 16, 27–37.

23   Diamond, *Developing Democracy*, 68–69.

24   Diamond, *Developing Democracy*, 70.

25   One may be tempted here to use a specific crisis point that was successfully overcome, such as the failed coup in Spain in 1981; however, such a democratic success is more a demonstration of being on the road to democratic consolidation. Indeed, Spanish democracy was probably not fully consolidated until the change in government from the centre to the socialists after the elections of 1982.

26   For an alternative definition of consolidation with respect to post-communist Europe that focuses solely on elites (including the bureaucracy) but has no "requirements" in terms of mass attitudes, see Stephen E. Hanson, "Defining Democratic Consolidation," in *Postcommunism and the Theory of Democracy,* ed. Richard D. Anderson, Jr., M. Steven Fish, Stephen E. Hanson, and Philip G. Roeder, 126–51 (Princeton, NJ: Princeton University Press, 2001), 141–42.

27   Diamond, *Developing Democracy*, 73ff.

28   Diamond, *Developing Democracy*, 74–75.

29   "B'desh Democracy Fails, Army Says," *BBC News*, 4 April, 2007, http://news.bbc.co.uk/2/hi/south_asia/6517887.stm.

30   Ko Maeda, "Two Modes of Democratic Breakdown: A Competing Risks Analysis of Democratic Durability," *The Journal of Politics* 72, no. 4 (October 2010): 1129–43.

31   Linz, *The Breakdown of Democratic Regimes*, 16–17, 18.

32   Linz, *The Breakdown of Democratic Regimes*, 18–23.

33   Ethan B. Kapstein and Nathan Converse, *The Fate of Young Democracies* (New York, NY: Cambridge University Press, 2008), 41.

34   Writing in the 1990s, Kitschelt put the break-point at 20 years: "As a rule of thumb, after 20 years of democracy anti-system parties have tacitly accepted the democratic rules and will not stage a revolt." Herbert Kitschelt, "Formation of Party Cleavages in Post-Communist Democracies: Theoretical Propositions," *Party Politics* 1, no. 4 (October 1995): 447–72, see page 460.

35   Linz, *The Breakdown of Democratic Regimes*, 87.

36   Linz, *The Breakdown of Democratic Regimes*, 87–88.

CHAPTER ELEVEN

Postscript: Democracies and Autocracies in the Future

IN THIS CHAPTER YOU WILL LEARN

▶ which autocracies might experience viable democratic transitions in the not-too-distant future and why;

▶ which democracies might experience democratic breakdowns and why, or, more specifically, what factors threaten the world's democracies, and how many of these factors different democracies currently have; and

▶ which countries have generally oscillated back and forth between electoral democracy and autocracy.

It was some 30 years ago that Samuel Huntington wrote an article entitled "Will More Countries Become Democratic?"[1] Overall, he concluded that, outside of South America, the prospects for the further spread of democracy were "not great." Wisely, however, he qualified this conclusion by noting that it assumed no major changes in world developments.[2] The collapse of the Soviet Union and the ending of its empire a few short years later led to the democratization of most of central and Eastern Europe. The 1990s also saw a peaceful transition to democracy in what had been the racial oligarchy of South Africa. More surprising has been the spread of democracy to many other countries in Africa, countries that have quite low levels of development.

All this goes to show that political science cannot predict precisely the future of democracy any more than it can other political events. In part, predicting democratization is tricky because democracy can, in fact, be imposed from outside on a country or, more commonly, established by national political elites as a clear political decision regardless of the level of development of the country.[3] So any of the world's autocracies of today could be a democracy (at least an electoral one) 10 or 20 years from now. That is possible, yes, but how probable? Or, to phrase the question differently, if democracy were introduced into a current autocracy, would it survive and ultimately consolidate? This question is obviously central for new democracies such as Iraq and Tunisia, but it applies to all autocracies today and, indeed, to various new democracies. Echoing Huntington's scepticism of two decades ago, the probability of *both* democratization and democratic survival does not seem "great" for the world's remaining autocracies as a group. As has been noted, most of these suffer from low levels of development, very unequal distributions of what wealth they have, a lack of democratic political culture or any democratic history, and a high degree of militarization.

The best prospects for democratic survival should democracy be established would be in the more developed autocracies, specifically Bahrain, Jordan, the United Arab Emirates, and especially Singapore. None of these have a large population. All have capitalist market economies, a strong factor favouring democracy. The only other autocracies with a capitalist market economy appear to be Georgia and Qatar. We have also noted the strong relationship between years of schooling and democracy, and, indeed, mean years of schooling is high (8.0 or more) in each of Bahrain, Jordan, the United Arab Emirates, and Singapore—although not very high (10.0 years or more).[4] That said, Bahrain, Jordan, and the United Arab Emirates have traditional authoritarian regimes, and their non-figurehead monarchies are clearly the central factor keeping them autocratic. Singapore has no monarchy, of course, and thus stands out as a uniquely developed autocracy, as noted earlier. (Indeed, going back to Chapter 5, we see that the Model Two prediction for Singapore is clearly that it should be a democracy.)

Of course, inasmuch as the world today contains fewer autocracies than democracies, it is not a stretch to argue that most of the autocracies left are the least viable ones for democracy. Flipping this point, we note that never have there been so many democracies as there are in the contemporary world. How confident should we be that all of these will remain democracies? An answer to this question is a two-step process. The first consideration is to note the global trends in democratization. As pointed out in Chapter 10, we appear to be in a third wave of democratization, albeit in a rather modest phase of this wave. Since 1995, the world has seen a net gain of five democracies. However, nothing is "stopping" world or at least regional circumstances from leading to a reverse wave at some point. Obviously, one cannot predict if or when this reversal might occur, but the lesson of history is that it is likely: both previous waves of democratization were followed by setbacks.

FIGURE 11.1 Newer Democracies and Threatening Factors

(YEAR OF TRANSITION IN BRACKETS)

		CONSTRAINTS ON EXECUTIVE		
		NOT	WEAK	
CIVILIAN CONTROL OVER THE MILITARY	**ADEQUATE**	Andorra (1993) Bulgaria (1990) Cape Verde (1991) Chile (1990) Croatia (2000) Czech Republic (1992) Estonia (1992) Latvia (1993) Lesotho (2002) Lithuania (1992) Macedonia (1991) Moldova (2009) Mongolia (1990) Montenegro (2006) Palau (1994) Peru (2001) Philippines (2010) Poland (1990) Romania (1992) Samoa (1991) Serbia (2000) Slovakia (1992) Slovenia (1991) South Africa (1994) Timor-Leste (East Timor) (2003) Zambia (2006)	Antigua and Barbuda (2004) Dominican Republic (1996) Guyana (1992) Hungary (1990) Iraq (2010) Ivory Coast (2011) Kyrgyzstan (2010) Namibia (1990) Panama (1989) Senegal (2012) Tunisia (2011)	
	NOT	Benin (1991) Ghana (2000) Indonesia (1999) Paraguay (1993) São Tomé and Príncipe (1991) Thailand (2011)	Bangladesh (2009) Comoros (2006) Honduras (2010) Liberia (2006) Mexico (2000)	Niger (2011) Nigeria (2011) Pakistan (2008) Sierra Leone (1998) Suriname (1991)

NOTE: Newer democracies are defined as those of less than 25 years as of 2012.

The second consideration or question is the following: if democracy does, in fact, break down in a reasonable number of countries at some point in the next generation, in which countries might this occur? Chapter 10 suggests that breakdowns are rare—but still possible—once a country has 25 or so years of democracy. Note, then, that of all the democracies extant today (late 2012), 53 have been democratic for less than 25 years—a substantial minority. These are the most likely places for democratic breakdown. Given that democratic breakdowns have resulted most frequently from either military coups (including recently in Guinea-Bissau and Mali) or self-coups (including recently in Nicaragua, Sri Lanka, and Ukraine), minimizing the threat of either a military coup or a self-coup is key.[5] Figure 11.1 assesses these issues for the 53 newer democracies. The vertical divide separates countries based on whether they have adequate civilian control over military, defined here as having civilian control or civilian supremacy (see Chapter 2 and Table 2.1). The horizontal divide separates countries based on whether they have weak constraints on their executives, something that makes a self-coup more likely.[6] By weak constraints on the executive we mean some combination of a dominant president (including a president with decree powers), a weak legislature,[7] a legislature controlled by the executive or by the party of the executive (versus one controlled by the opposition control or a hung parliament), a high judiciary without political independence, and a general lack of checks and balances. Having these last two characteristics would tend to make a democracy electoral, not liberal. Also, having weak constraints might be ongoing or could reflect a recent consolidation of power by the executive. Countries in the upper right of the figure are thus at risk of a self-coup, those in the lower left risk a military coup, and those in the lower right risk both. On the other hand, the newish democracies in the upper left are likely to remain democratic. Indeed, 42 per cent of the countries in this group are liberal democracies, whereas there are *no* liberal democracies in any of the other three groups. This point is important: because liberal democracies are more democratic than electoral democracies (that is, they are democratic in more areas), they have "further to fall" to be reversed to an autocracy. Electoral democracies, conversely, have "less far to fall."

Oscillating States

For some of the countries in Figure 11.1, the prognosis is even bleaker. Not only might they have a democratic breakdown in the near future, they have had one— or more—in recent decades. Indeed, several countries have gone back and forth between democracy and autocracy. Huntington identifies this cyclical pattern as one in which neither democracy nor autocracy can institutionalize effectively.[8] Let us call countries with this pattern "oscillating states." Now, such a pattern is not necessarily permanent. In the period after World War II, Argentina and Turkey were clear examples of such oscillation due to military coups. However, both have remained democratic since 1983—though each has faced challenges to its democracy. Yet,

TABLE 11.1 Oscillating States in the Third Wave

			FREQUENCY SINCE 1974		
	Regime in 1973	Regime as of (late) 2012	Democratic Transitions	Democratic Breakdowns	Total Regime Changes
Bangladesh	autocracy	democracy	3	2	5
Niger	autocracy	democracy	3	2	5
Nigeria	autocracy	democracy	3	2	5
Suriname	autocracy	democracy	3	2	5
Thailand	autocracy	democracy	3	2	5
Albania	autocracy	autocracy	2	2	4
Georgia	autocracy	autocracy	2	2	4
Guinea-Bissau	autocracy	autocracy	2	2	4
Haiti	autocracy	autocracy	2	2	4
Pakistan	democracy	democracy	2	2	4
Ukraine	autocracy	autocracy	2	2	4
Croatia	autocracy	democracy	2	1	3
Fiji	democracy	autocracy	1	2	3
Ghana	autocracy	democracy	2	1	3
Honduras	autocracy	democracy	2	1	3
Moldova	autocracy	democracy	2	1	3
Peru	autocracy	democracy	2	1	3
Philippines	autocracy	democracy	2	1	3
Zambia	autocracy	democracy	2	1	3

currently, various countries are certainly in a back-and-forth cycle between autocracy and democracy.

Looking at the period since 1974 (the start of the third wave of democratization in which the overall trend, by definition, is to more democracy globally), we find 19 countries that have oscillated, as shown in Table 11.1. Each has had more than one transition or more than one breakdown. Many have even had more than one of both. (If Georgia makes a democratic transition after its presidential election in 2013, following its democratic parliamentary election in 2012, then it would move into the top group of this list.) As shown in Table 11.1, these countries are concentrated in post-communist Europe, sub-Saharan Africa, and Asia—but not so much in Latin America as would have been the case a generation ago. Quite likely, some of the oscillating states that are now autocratic will return to democracy—at least for a time. As for those that are democratic, they will need to break out of their cycle to remain so.

Notes

1   Samuel P. Huntington, "Will More Countries Become Democratic?" *Political Science Quarterly* 99, no. 2 (Summer 1984): 193–218.

2   Huntington, "Will More Countries Become Democratic?" 218.

3   Adam Przeworski and Fernando Limongi, "Modernization: Theories and Facts," *World Politics* 49, no. 2 (1997): 155–83, see page 177.

4   Average years of schooling are higher in various other autocracies, usually communist or post-communist ones.

5   Ko Maeda, "Two Modes of Democratic Breakdown: A Competing Risks Analysis of Democratic Durability," *The Journal of Politics* 72, no. 4 (October 2010): 1129–43.

6   Ethan B. Kapstein and Nathan Converse, "Why Democracies Fail," *Journal of Democracy* 19, no. 4 (October 2008): 57–68, see page 64.

7   On parliamentary power and regime type, see M. Steven Fish, "Stronger Legislatures, Stronger Democracies," *Journal of Democracy* 17, no. 1 (January 2006): 5–20; on parliamentary power across the world, see M. Steven Fish and Matthew Kroenig, *The Handbook of National Legislatures: A Global Survey* (New York, NY: Cambridge University Press, 2009).

8   Huntington, "Will More Countries Become Democratic?" 210.

Glossary of Selected Key Terms

Authoritarian Regime: In effect, this is a residual category of **autocracy** defined largely in a negative way: an authoritarian regime is an autocratic regime that lacks the ideology and mass mobilization found in a **totalitarian regime** and that also lacks the broad arbitrariness of a **sultanistic regime.**

Autocracy: Literally, absolute rule by one individual, the autocrat, but, more, generally, rule by an individual or group that is effectively unaccountable to the population. Autocracy is thus the opposite of **democracy.**

Bureaucracy: In the Weberian sense, a system of government administration based on a rational hierarchy of authority and employing full-time civil servants who are hired and promoted based on training and experience and by formal contracts. These bureaucrats have defined rights and duties and fixed salaries, and they are expected to serve the public neutrally and without using their positions for direct personal gain.

Civilian Supremacy: The ability of a civilian government to conduct general policy without interference from the military; to define the goals, size, resources, and general organization of the military; to formulate and conduct defence policy knowledgeably; and to monitor effectively the implementation of said defence policy. This category of civil–military relations is the most democratic because, in it, civilians have the most control over the military.

Clientelism: An informal power relationship between unequals in which a higher status "patron" provides benefits to a client or clients. These clients in turn reciprocate by providing the patron with support, including voting for the patron or for a third party of the patron's wish.

Collapsed State: One in which the state authority has totally disintegrated to be replaced by anarchy, multi-actor civil war, or fragmentation into various autonomous regional areas.

Competitive Oligarchy: A **political regime** with responsible government and competitive elections but with 20 per cent or less of the 18-and-above population eligible to vote.

Confederation: A group of sovereign entities forming a common government for specific and limited purposes. **Sovereignty** remains with the constituent governments, which take all key decisions. The common government requires unanimity amongst the constituent governments, does not directly act upon the population, and leaves matters of implementation to the constituent governments.

Consociational Democracy: A political system found in certain heterogeneous democracies, which is based on power-sharing—especially in terms of broad coalition cabinets that include most if not all of the key groups—as opposed to pure majoritarianism.

Critical Mass: A sufficiently large minority group. Critical mass theory suggests that there will be a qualitative change in the nature of collective group behaviour and within-group interactions only when the minority group reaches such a critical mass, perceived to be around 30 per cent of the whole.

De Facto State: A **state** with effective internal control, control over its borders, and domestic legitimacy but lacking international recognition.

De Jure State: A **state** that is recognized as a state by the international community but that is so weak or illegitimate that it cannot actually control most of its own people or its borders.

Democracy: A **political regime** that involves, at a minimum, the competition of political elites for public support and the accountability of elected politicians to the voters. Within these broad parameters, there are key differences between **liberal democracy** and **electoral democracy**.

Democratic Breakdown: The collapse of a **democracy**. More formally, this means the change from a democracy to an **autocracy**; thus, it is the opposite of a **democratic transition**.

Democratic Consolidation: Broad support for a democratic regime, involving law-abidingness, partisan behaviour consistent with **democracy**, and broadly held democratic values and beliefs.

Democratic Deconsolidation: The loss of support for both a democratic regime and the general legitimacy of **democracy**, involving increased lawlessness, undemocratic partisan behaviour, and an increase in antidemocratic values and beliefs.

Democratic Re-equilibration: A political process that, after a crisis involving the paralysis and delegitimation of national democratic institutions and a temporary breakdown of the authority of the regime, results in their continued existence or speedy re-creation at the same or higher levels of democratic legitimacy, efficacy, and effectiveness. A central role here is normally played by a charismatic national leader, who may come to power through undemocratic means but thereafter governs democratically.

Democratic Transition / Democratization: The process of changing from an **autocracy** to a **democracy** or, more precisely, changing from an autocracy to at least an **electoral democracy**. The key step here is the holding of free and fair elections to select the government, under the qualification that **responsible government** also exists in the state—in other words, that elected national politicians are the ones in control of a sovereign state.

Dissolution: The breakup of a sovereign state into its component parts, each of which becomes a new sovereign state, with the previously existing **state** ceasing to exist.

District Magnitude: The number of seats to be filled in (or members to be elected from) an electoral district or constituency. For example, for the Canadian House of Commons, the district magnitude has been one everywhere for some decades now.

Earned Majority: An election outcome in which a party wins a majority of seats based on its winning a majority of the popular vote (even if its vote percentage is still less than its seat percentage). This outcome is contrasted with a **manufactured majority**.

Effective State: A **state** that controls its national territory and borders and that has sufficient tax-raising capacity, bureaucratic autonomy and competence, domestic penetration, and broad legitimacy to ensure that national laws and policies are actually in effect throughout the country.

Electoral Authoritarianism: Authoritarianism based on a ruling party or president that does not allow free and fair elections but that derives authority from election victories (indeed claiming that these are free and fair). Elections are held regularly, and some opposition parties or candidates are allowed on the ballot so as to maintain a pretense of competition. If this regime is based on a president, sometimes referenda (again, not free and fair) are used to extend the president's term or at least the term limits.

Electoral College: A group of people chosen by elections or by virtue of their office whose task is to select a president. This group performs no other subsequent function, so it is unlike the legislature that, in various parliamentary systems, selects the president, in other words, the country's head of state.

Electoral Democracy: A **political regime** that contains the following three elements (sufficiently although perhaps not perfectly)—**responsible government**, free and fair political competition, and full and equal rights of political participation—but that is deficient in terms of civil liberties or a legally based, limited, but well-functioning state.

Electoral System: The process used for voting (e.g., the ballot structure) and then for translating votes into seats in the context of an election, thereby determining the partisan composition of the legislature but not specifically the government.

Federalism: A political system with a central government and constitutionally entrenched regional governments with similarly entrenched powers, as well as some role in national politics. Domestic

sovereignty is thus shared between the two levels, but only the central government exercises international sovereignty.

Flawed State: A state lacking some combination of tax-raising capacity, bureaucratic autonomy and competence, domestic penetration, and broad legitimacy, thus rendering it less effective and usually unable to produce successful national policies.

Formateur: A politician designated to try to form a government and thus, if operating within a parliamentary system, given the opportunity to become prime minister if successful.

Human Development Index (HDI): A measure of the United Nations that combines three factors: (1) life expectancy, (2) years of schooling, and (3) per capita income, which is corrected for variations in purchasing power and is adjusted by being logged. These combined factors lead to a standardized score in which a higher value indicates a higher level of development.

Hung Parliament: A parliament in which no one party has a majority of the seats. A hung parliament is parallel to a "hung jury" because of both its lack of decisiveness and the inconclusiveness that results. Often this situation is called a minority government, but a minority government is only one possible outcome of a hung parliament—even if it is the "normal" one in Canada. Alternatively, for example, two or more parties can get together in a hung parliament to form a majority coalition government.

Index of Disproportionality: As used in this analysis, a mathematical index that sums the absolute value of each party's vote share (percentage) to seat share difference and then divides this total by two to get a value between zero and 100. The higher the number, the greater the disproportionality.

Informateur: In a multi-party democratic monarchy, a person who, after consulting with the various political parties, advises the head of state on who has the best chance of forming a government and thus being designated **formateur**. The informateur is normally a senior politician, perhaps retired, who can provide an objective assessment of the political situation.

Liberal Democracy: A **political regime** that combines the following five elements: **responsible government**, free and fair political competition, full and equal rights of political participation, civil liberties, and a legally based, limited, but well-functioning state.

Manufactured Majority: An election outcome in which a party wins a majority of seats despite winning a minority of the popular vote, the majority of seats thus being "manufactured" by the **electoral system**. This outcome is contrasted with an **earned majority**. The manufactured majority may even be won by the party second in popular votes; this reversal of vote and seat finish is called a "spurious majority."

Military Authoritarianism: Authoritarianism based on an autonomous military running the country either outright or indirectly.

Moderately Inclusive Electoral Democracy (MIED): A **political regime** with **responsible government**, competitive elections, and more than 20 per cent of the 18-and-above population eligible to vote—but without the universal suffrage of an unqualified **electoral democracy**.

Parliamentary System: A political system with a dual executive and with the head of government (and the government generally) accountable to the legislature, not least because of the possibility of a motion of non-confidence.

Party System: The relationship among the various political parties (there must be at least two) in a territory, that is, their total number, relative size, competitiveness, and so on.

Political Culture: The attitudes, values, and beliefs that individuals have with respect to their **political regime** or system and the ways it allocates power and resolves political conflicts.

Political Development: The achievement, where this does not exist, of national autonomy, political order, **political institutionalization**, and possibly also **democracy.**

Political Institutionalization: The process by which political organizations (for example, executives, legislatures, and judiciaries, but also political parties) and political procedures become complex (with formal internal structures and hierarchies), adaptable, coherent, stable, and autonomous from other institutions.

Political Regime: The method or system of government, including both formal and informal structures of the state, governmental roles and processes, and the method of selection of these. A political regime is broader than the government of the day.

Power Resources: A term developed by Tatu Vanhanen referring to the economic, intellectual, and organizational resources that an individual or group can bring to bear in the struggle for political power. The deconcentration (wide diffusion) of these resources facilitates **democracy;** the concentration of these resources works against democracy.

Presidential System: A political system with a single executive, chosen by the voters (perhaps indirectly via an **electoral college**) and not accountable to the legislature.

Rechtsstaat: A "state subject to law." The law thus protects the citizens against the power of the **state,** specifically the abuse (i.e., arbitrary use) of this power by the police or other state actors.

Republic: In the modern sense, the opposite of monarchy; that is, a regime in which the head of state is not a hereditary monarch.

Responsible Government: Not only a government that is responsible to the people in the sense of accountability "downwards" (at least by way of elections) but also a government that is *only* responsible to the people and not to a monarch or military that may be "pulling the strings" either openly or secretly.

Reverse Wave (of Democratization): Within a specified period of time, a significant number of transitions in an autocratic (non-democratic) direction that outnumber **democratic transitions** during that period of time. One could call this a "wave of autocratization" if that were a word.

Secession: The creation of a new **state** on territory that had been part of an existing **state**, which continues to exist within its remaining territory.

Sovereignty: The sense of a **state** being the highest authority in a territory and exercising this authority with respect to its domestic population, its borders, and its interactions with other states. Sovereignty also has the connotation of its possessors enjoying a monopoly on the legitimate use of force within a territory.

State: A political entity defined in two different ways: (1) a sovereign power effectively ruling over the population within a fixed territory; and (2) the organizationally differentiated political, bureaucratic, legal, and usually military system of a country. The first usage is "a state"; the second is "the state."

Strong Bicameralism: Having two legislative chambers in which the upper house truly matters because (1) both houses are equal or relatively equal in terms of legislative powers, (2) the upper house has the legitimacy to use its powers, and (3) the upper house is composed or elected in a different way from the lower house.

Sultanistic Regime: An autocratic regime that is built around an individual and her or his family, which, to a greater or lesser extent, plunder the country; that glorifies this leader; that exercises control by fear, terror, and spreading paranoia; and that lacks any effective legitimacy. An alternative term here is "personalistic regime."

Theocratic Authoritarianism: Authoritarianism in which the ruling power is a religious leader or elite.

Totalitarian Regime: An autocratic regime having (1) a ruling party, (2) an official and genuine ideology, and (3) an active mobilization of the population into supporting the regime, including membership in various regime-sponsored organizations.

Traditional Authoritarianism: Authoritarianism in which the ruling power is a monarch.

Vote of Investiture: A formal vote by the parliament on a would-be prime minister and, sometimes, a proposed cabinet—a vote that must be won for those proposed to take office or remain in office after an election. Such a procedure makes the system one of positive parliamentarianism because actual parliamentary endorsement of the government is required; negative parliamentarianism requires no such formal vote.

Wave of Democratization: Within a specified period of time, a significant number of transitions from autocratic to democratic regimes that outnumber transitions in the opposite direction (**democratic breakdowns**) during that period of time. A wave of democratization also usually involves political liberalization in some autocratic political systems that nevertheless remain autocratic.

Weak State: A state lacking control over some or even much of the national territory or borders, having parts of the country clearly outside of effective state control, and experiencing frequent predatory behaviour by state elites, thus rendering the state unable to impose national policies throughout the country and produce effective national development.

Westminster Model: Based on the British political system, the concentration of power in a democratic parliamentary regime so that a single-party executive (prime minister and cabinet), as opposed to a coalition, governs with broad freedom and no or minimal checks and balances between elections.

Recommended Sources for Further Research

Web References

The United Nations' annual *Human Development Report* is available online: http://www.undp.org/content/undp/en/home/librarypage/hdr/.

New York-based Freedom House's annual *Freedom in the World* is the most cited international survey of political rights and civil liberties: http://www.freedomhouse. org/reports. It also publishes a separate, more detailed yearly analysis of post-communist countries called *Nations in Transit* and an annual survey of media independence, *Freedom of the Press*.

The Organization for Security and Co-operation in Europe has an Office for Democratic Institutions and Human Rights (OSCE/ODIHR) that provides documents on international standards of elections as well as field reports on elections observed by the ODIHR in Europe, Central Asia, and the United States: http://www.osce.org/odihr.

The Berlin-based Transparency International annually publishes its *Corruption Perceptions Index*, as well as a *Global Corruption Report*: http://www. transparency.org/research/.

The Bertelsmann Transformation Index (BTI) assesses political and economic transformations (toward liberal democracy and capitalism) in developing and post-communist countries: http://www.bti-project.org/home/index.nc (website and index available in German and English).

The World Bank measures six dimensions of good governance for the countries of the world: see the website *Worldwide Governance Indicators*, http://info. worldbank.org/governance/wgi/index.asp.

Chronological lists of national and subnational leaders can be found at the *Rulers* website edited by B. Schemmel: http://www.rulers.org.

For election results, the traditional reference site *Elections around the World*, edited by Wilfried Derksen of the Netherlands, has been assumed by *Wikipedia*; see their "Elections by Country" page: http://en.wikipedia.org/wiki/Elections_by_country.

A comprehensive site of international electoral information and election statistics is from Australia, namely, *Psephos: Adam Carr's Election Archive*: http://psephos. adam-carr.net.

The Geneva-based Inter-Parliamentary Union also provides the most recent national election results for almost every country and with (usually) a couple of paragraphs of commentary: see the PARLINE database on national parliaments at http://www.ipu.org/parline-e/parlinesearch.asp.

For elections in Europe, including those in major subnational territories, the *Parties and Elections in Europe* website is quite thorough and gives the ideology, transnational affiliation, and founding dates for all parties winning seats, as well as an archive of historical election results for each country: http://www.parties-and-elections.eu.

Finally, the International Foundation for Election Systems in Washington, DC, in conjunction with the Consortium for Elections and Political Process Strengthening (CEPPS) has a very thorough global *Election Guide* for background information: http://www.electionguide.org.

Academic Journals

The *Journal of Democracy* publishes short, highly informative articles that are very up-to-date as these things go (http://www.journalofdemocracy.org/).

Electoral Studies includes detailed analyses of elections in most major and many other countries but certainly not in all countries (http://www.journals.elsevier.com/electoral-studies/).

Chronological References

By far, the most thorough chronology is the ongoing monthly *Keesing's Record of World Events,* which has been published since 1931 (http://www.keesings.com/).

Also useful is the six-volume, regionally based *Political Chronologies of the World,* published in 2001 by Europa Publications. Europa also publishes the very comprehensive *Europa World Year Book* (previously the *Europa Year Book*), which goes back to 1959.

Bibliography

Agüero, Felipe. *Soldiers, Civilians, and Democracy: Post-Franco Spain in Comparative Perspective*. Baltimore, MD: The Johns Hopkins University Press, 1995.

Alagappa, Muthiah. "Asian Civil–Military Relations: Key Developments, Explanations, and Trajectories." In *Coercion and Governance: The Declining Political Role of the Military in Asia*, ed. Muthiah Alagappa, 433–98. Stanford, CA: Stanford University Press, 2001.

Alagappa, Muthiah. "Investigating and Explaining Change: An Analytical Framework." In *Coercion and Governance: The Declining Political Role of the Military in Asia*, ed. Muthiah Alagappa, 29–66. Stanford, CA: Stanford University Press, 2001.

Almond, Gabriel A. "Comparative Political Systems." *Journal of Politics* 18, no. 3 (August 1956): 391–409. http://dx.doi.org/10.2307/2127255.

Ambrosio, Thomas. *Authoritarian Backlash: Russian Resistance to Democratization in the Former Soviet Union*. Farnham, Surrey, UK: Ashgate, 2009.

Ambrosio, Thomas. "Constructing a Framework of Authoritarian Diffusion: Concepts, Dynamics, and Future Research." *International Studies Perspectives* 11, no. 4 (November 2010): 375–92. http://dx.doi.org/10.1111/j.1528-3585.2010.00411.x.

Anckar, Dag. "Democracy as a Westminster Heritage." *Taiwan Journal of Democracy* 7, no. 1 (July 2011): 47–71.

Anckar, Dag. "Democratic Standard and Performance in Twelve Pacific Microstates." *Pacific Affairs* 75, no. 2 (Summer 2002): 207–25. http://dx.doi.org/10.2307/4127183.

Anckar, Dag, and Carsten Anckar. "Democracies without Parties." *Comparative Political Studies* 33, no. 2 (March 2000): 225–47. http://dx.doi.org/10.1177/0010414000033002003.

Asian Development Bank. "The Rise of Asia's Middle Class." Special chapter in
    Key Indicators for Asia and the Pacific 2010, 41st ed., 3–60. Manila: Asian
    Development Bank, August 2010.

Bale, Tim, and Torbjörn Bergman. "Captives No Longer, but Servants Still?
    Contract Parliamentarism and the New Minority Governance in Sweden and
    New Zealand." *Government and Opposition* 41, no. 3 (Summer 2006): 422–49.
    http://dx.doi.org/10.1111/j.1477-7053.2006.00186.x.

Baumgartner, Jody C., and Rhonda Evans Case. "Constitutional Design
    of the Executive: Vice Presidencies in Comparative Perspective."
    Congress and the Presidency 36, no. 2 (2009): 148–63. http://dx.doi.
    org/10.1080/07343460902948105.

Bergman, Marcelo. *Tax Evasion and the Rule of Law in Latin America: The
    Political Culture of Cheating and Compliance in Argentina and Chile*. University
    Park, PA: The Pennsylvania State University Press, 2009.

Bergman, Torbjörn. "Constitutional Design and Government Formation: The
    Expected Consequences of Negative Parliamentarianism." *Scandinavian
    Political Studies* 16, no. 4 (December 1993): 285–304. http://dx.doi.
    org/10.1111/j.1467-9477.1993.tb00042.x.

Bergman, Torbjörn. "Formation Rules and Minority Governments." *European
    Journal of Political Research* 23, no. 1 (January 1993): 55–66. http://dx.doi.
    org/10.1111/j.1475-6765.1993.tb00348.x.

Bertelsmann Stiftung. *Bertelsmann Transformation Index* (accessed various years
    November 2012): http://www.bti-project.org/index/.

Binder, Leonard, James S. Coleman, Joseph LaPalombara, Lucian W. Pye, Sidney
    Verba, and Myron Weiner. *Crises and Sequences in Political Development*.
    Princeton, NJ: Princeton University Press, 1971.

Birch, Sarah. *Electoral Malpractice*. New York: Oxford University Press, 2011.
    http://dx.doi.org/10.1093/acprof:oso/9780199606160.001.0001.

Birchfield, Vicki, and Markus M.L. Crepaz. "The Impact of Constitutional
    Structures and Collective and Competitive Veto Points on Income Inequality in
    Industrialized Democracies." *European Journal of Political Research* 34, no. 2
    (1998): 175–200. http://dx.doi.org/10.1111/1475-6765.00404.

Blais, André, Louis Massicotte, and Antoine Yoshinaka. "Deciding Who Has the Right to Vote: A Comparative Analysis of Election Laws." *Electoral Studies* 20, no. 1 (2001): 41–62. http://dx.doi.org/10.1016/S0261-3794(99)00062-1.

Bogdanor, Vernon. "The Government Formation Process in the Constitutional Monarchies of North-West Europe." In *Comparative Government and Politics: Essays in Honour of S.E. Finer*, ed. Dennis Kavanagh and Gillian Peele, 49–72. London, UK: Heinemann, 1984.

Boston, Jonathan, and David Bullock. "Multi-Party Governance: Managing the Unity-Distinctiveness Dilemma in Executive Coalitions." *Party Politics* 18, no. 3 (May 2012): 349–68. http://dx.doi.org/10.1177/1354068810382937.

Buchta, Wilfred. *Who Rules Iran? The Structure of Power in the Islamic Republic.* Washington, DC: The Washington Institute for Near East Policy and the Konrad Adenauer Stiftung, 2000.

Butler, David, and Austin Ranney. *Referendums around the World: The Growing Use of Direct Democracy.* Washington, DC: American Enterprise Institute, 1994.

Centeno, Miguel Angel. "Blood and Debt: War and Taxation in Nineteenth-Century Latin America." *American Journal of Sociology* 102, no. 6 (May 1997): 1565–605. http://dx.doi.org/10.1086/231127.

Central Intelligence Agency. *The World Factbook*. Washington, DC: CIA, 2012. https://www.cia.gov/library/publications/the-world-factbook.

Chasquetti, Daniel. *Democracia, presidencialismo y partidos políticos en América Latina: Evaluando la "difícil combinación."* Montevideo: Ediciones CAUCE, 2008.

Chehabi, H.E. "Small Island States." In *The Encyclopedia of Democracy*, ed. Seymour Martin Lipset, 1134–37. Washington, DC: Congressional Quarterly, 1995.

Chehabi, H.E., and Juan J. Linz. "A Theory of Sultanism 1: A Type of Nondemocratic Rule." In *Sultanistic Regimes,* ed. H.E. Chehabi and Juan J. Linz, 3–25. Baltimore, MD and London, UK: The Johns Hopkins University Press, 1998.

Coggins, Bridget. "Friends in High Places: International Politics and the Emergence of States from Secessionism." *International Organization* 65, no. 3 (Summer 2011): 433–67. http://dx.doi.org/10.1017/S0020818311000105.

Collier, David, and Steven Levitsky. "Democracy with Adjectives: Conceptual Innovation in Comparative Research." *World Politics* 49, no. 3 (April 1997): 430–51. http://dx.doi.org/10.1353/wp.1997.0009.

Collier, Paul. *The Bottom Billion: Why the Poorest Countries are Failing and What Can Be Done about It.* New York, NY: Oxford University Press, 2007.

Collier, Ruth, and David Collier. *Shaping the Political Arena: Critical Junctures, the Labor Movement, and Regime Dynamics in Latin America.* Princeton, NJ: Princeton University Press, 1991.

Colomer, Josep M. "Introduction." In *Political Institutions in Europe*, ed. J.M. Colomer, 1–16. London, UK and New York, NY: Routledge, 1996.

Crawford, Keith. *East Central European Politics Today.* Manchester, UK: Manchester University Press, 1996.

Crisis States Research Centre. "Crisis, Fragile and Failed States: Definitions used by the CSRC." Last modified March 2006. http://www2.lse.ac.uk/internationalDevelopment/research/crisisStates/download/drc/FailedState.pdf.

Dahl, Robert A. *Democracy and its Critics.* New Haven, CT: Yale University Press, 1989.

Dahl, Robert A. *Polyarchy: Participation and Opposition.* New Haven, CT: Yale University Press, 1971.

Dallin, Alexander, and George W. Breslauer. *Political Terror in Communist Systems.* Stanford, CA: Stanford University Press, 1970.

Diamond, Larry. *Developing Democracy: Toward Consolidation.* Baltimore, MD: The Johns Hopkins University Press, 1999.

Diamond, Larry. "Economic Development and Democracy Reconsidered." *American Behavioral Scientist* 35, no. 4–5 (March/June 1992): 457–60.

Diamond, Larry, Jonathan Hartlyn, and Juan J. Linz. "Introduction: Politics, Society, and Democracy in Latin America." In *Democracy in Developing Countries: Volume 4, Latin America*, 2nd ed., ed. Larry Diamond, Jonathan Hartlyn, Juan J. Linz, and Seymour Martin Lipset, 1–70. Boulder, CO: Lynne Rienner, 1999.

Diamond, Larry, Juan J. Linz, and Seymour Martin Lipset. "Introduction: What Makes for Democracy?" *Politics in Developing Countries: Comparing Experiences with Democracy,* 2nd ed., ed. Larry Diamond, Juan J. Linz, and Seymour Martin Lipset, 1–66. Boulder, CO: Lynne Rienner, 1995.

Dix, Robert H. "History and Democracy Revisited." *Comparative Politics* 27, no. 1 (October 1994): 91–105. http://dx.doi.org/10.2307/422219.

Doorenspleet, Renske. "Reassessing the Three Waves of Democratization." *World Politics* 52, no. 03 (April 2000): 384–406. http://dx.doi.org/10.1017/S0043887100016580.

Eckstein, Harry. *Division and Cohesion in Democracy: A Study of Norway.* Princeton, NJ: Princeton University Press, 1966.

Elklit, Jørgen, and Palle Svensson. "What Makes Elections Free and Fair?" *Journal of Democracy* 8, no. 3 (July 1997): 32–46. http://dx.doi.org/10.1353/jod.1997.0041.

Evans, Peter. *Embedded Autonomy: States and Industrial Transformation.* Princeton, NJ: Princeton University Press, 1995.

Farrell, David M. *Electoral Systems: A Comparative Introduction.* Basingstoke, UK: Palgrave, 2001.

Fearon, James D. "Ethnic and Cultural Diversity by Country." *Journal of Economic Growth* 8, no. 2 (2003): 195–222. http://dx.doi.org/10.1023/A:1024419522867.

Felipe, Jesus. *Tracking the Middle-Income Trap: What Is It, Who I7s in It, and Why? (Part 1).* ADB Economics Working Paper No. 306. Manila: Asian Development Bank, March 2012.

Felipe, Jesus. *Tracking the Middle-Income Trap: What Is It, Who Is in It, and Why? (Part 2).* ADB Economics Working Paper No. 307. Manila: Asian Development Bank, March 2012.

Figueiredo, Argelina Cheibub. "Government Coalitions in Brazilian Democracy." *Brazilian Political Science Review* 1, no. 2 (July 2007): 182–216.

Finer, Samuel E. *The Man on Horseback: The Role of the Military in Politics.* 2nd rev. ed. Boulder, CO: Westview Press, 1962.

Fish, M. Steven. "Stronger Legislatures, Stronger Democracies." *Journal of Democracy* 17, no. 1 (January 2006): 5–20. http://dx.doi.org/10.1353/jod.2006.0008.

Fish, M. Steven, and Matthew Kroenig. *The Handbook of National Legislatures: A Global Survey*. New York, NY: Cambridge University Press, 2009. http://dx.doi.org/10.1017/CBO9780511575655.

Fitch, J. Samuel. *The Armed Forces and Democracy in Latin America*. Baltimore, MD: The Johns Hopkins University Press, 1998.

Forrest, Joshua B. *Lineages of State Fragility: Rural Civil Society in Guinea-Bissau*. Athens, OH: Ohio University Press, 2003.

Forum of Federations. *Handbook of Federal Countries 2005*. Edited by Ann L. Griffiths. Montreal, QC and Kingston, ON: McGill-Queen's University Press, 2005.

Fuchs, Dieter. *Types and Indices of Democratic Regimes*. WZB Discussion Paper FS III 01–203. Berlin: Wissenschaftszentrum Berlin für Sozialforschung (WZB), 2001.

Fukuyama, Francis. *The Origins of Political Order: From Prehuman Times to the French Revolution*. New York, NY: Farrar, Straus and Giroux, 2011.

Gallagher, Michael, Michael Laver, and Peter Mair. *Representative Government in Modern Europe*. 4th ed. New York, NY: McGraw-Hill, 2006.

Ganguly, Sumit. "Six Decades of Independence." *Journal of Democracy* 18, no. 2 (April 2007): 30–40. http://dx.doi.org/10.1353/jod.2007.0024.

Geddes, Barbara. *Politician's Dilemma: Building State Capacity in Latin America*. Berkeley and Los Angeles, CA: University of California Press, 1994.

Gerring, John, Strom C. Thacker, and Carola Moreno. "Centripetal Democratic Governance: A Theory and Global Inquiry." *American Political Science Review* 99, no. 4 (November 2005): 567–81. http://dx.doi.org/10.1017/S0003055405051889.

Glaeser, Edward L., Giacomo A. M. Ponzetto, and Andrei Shleifer. "Why Does Democracy Need Education?" *Journal of Economic Growth* 12, no. 2 (June 2007): 77–99. http://dx.doi.org/10.1007/s10887-007-9015-1.

Gunther, Richard, Hans-Jürgen Puhle, and P. Nikiforos Diamandouros. "Introduction." In *The Politics of Democratic Consolidation: Southern Europe in Comparative Perspective*, ed. Richard Gunther, Hans-Jürgen Puhle, and P. Nikiforos Diamandouros, 1–32. Baltimore, MD and London, UK: The Johns Hopkins University Press, 1995.

Hadenius, Axel. *Democracy and Development*. Cambridge, UK: Cambridge University Press, 1992. http://dx.doi.org/10.1017/CBO9780511549731.

Hailsham, Lord. *The Dilemma of Democracy: Diagnosis and Prescription*. London, UK: Collins, 1978.

Halperin, Morton H., and Kristen Lomasney. "Guaranteeing Democracy: A Review of the Record." *Journal of Democracy* 9, no. 2 (April 1998): 134–47. http://dx.doi.org/10.1353/jod.1998.0026.

Handelman, Howard. *The Challenge of Third World Development*. 3rd ed. Upper Saddle River, NJ: Prentice Hall, 2003.

Hanson, Stephen E. "Defining Democratic Consolidation." In *Postcommunism and the Theory of Democracy*, ed. Richard D. Anderson Jr., M. Steven Fish, Stephen E. Hanson, and Philip G. Roeder, 126–51. Princeton, NJ: Princeton University Press, 2001.

Harris, Dan, Mick Moore, and Hubert Schmitz. *Country Classifications for a Changing World*. IDS Working Paper 326. Brighton, UK: Institute of Development Studies, University of Sussex, May 2009.

Herbst, Jeffrey. *States and Power in Africa: Comparative Lessons in Authority and Control*. Princeton, NJ: Princeton University Press, 2000.

Holsti, K.J. *Taming the Sovereigns: Institutional Change in International Politics*. Cambridge, UK: Cambridge University Press, 2004. http://dx.doi.org/10.1017/CBO9780511491382.

Hooghe, Marc. "The Political Crisis in Belgium (2007–2011): A Federal System Without Federal Loyalty." *Representation: Journal of Representative Democracy* 48, no. 1 (April 2012): 131–38.

Howard, Michael. *War and the Nation State*. Oxford, UK: Clarendon Press, 1978.

Huber, Evelyne, Charles Ragin, and John D. Stephens. "Social Democracy, Christian Democracy, Constitutional Structure, and the Welfare State." *American*

Journal of Sociology 99, no. 3 (November 1993): 711–49. http://dx.doi. org/10.1086/230321.

Huber, Evelyne, Dietrich Rueschemeyer, and John D. Stephens. "The Paradoxes of Contemporary Democracy: Formal, Participatory, and Social Dimensions." *Comparative Politics* 29, no. 3 (April 1997): 323–42. http://dx.doi. org/10.2307/422124.

Huntington, Samuel P. "The Goals of Development." In *Understanding Political Development*, ed. Myron Weiner and Samuel P. Huntington, 3–32. Glenview, IL: Scott, Foresman / Little, Brown, 1987.

Huntington, Samuel P. *Political Order in Changing Societies.* New Haven, CT: Yale University Press, 1968.

Huntington, Samuel P. *The Third Wave: Democratization in the Late Twentieth Century.* Norman, OK: University of Oklahoma Press, 1991.

Huntington, Samuel P. "Will More Countries Become Democratic?" *Political Science Quarterly* 99, no. 2 (Summer 1984): 193–218. http://dx.doi. org/10.2307/2150402.

International Institute for Strategic Studies. *The Military Balance 2011.* Washington, DC: International Institute for Strategic Studies, 2011.

International Telecommunication Union. *ICT Data and Statistics.* http://www.itu. int/ITU-D/ict/statistics/.

International Telecommunication Union. *ICT Indicators Database.* http://www.itu. int/ITU-D/ict/publications/world/world.html.

Isaksson, Guy-Erik. "From Election to Government: Principal Rules and Deviant Cases." *Government and Opposition* 40, no. 3 (Summer 2005): 329–57. http:// dx.doi.org/10.1111/j.1477-7053.2005.00154.x.

Jackson, Robert H. *Quasi-States: Sovereignty, International Relations and the Third World.* Cambridge, UK: Cambridge University Press, 1990.

Jenne, Erin K., and Cas Mudde. "Hungary's Illiberal Turn: Can Outsiders Help?" *Journal of Democracy* 23, no. 3 (July 2012): 147–55. http://dx.doi.org/10.1353/ jod.2012.0057.

Johnson, Chalmers. *MITI and the Japanese Miracle: The Growth of Industrial Policy, 1925–1975*. Stanford, CA: Stanford University Press, 1982.

Jones, Mark P. *Electoral Laws and the Survival of Presidential Democracies*. Notre Dame, IN: University of Notre Dame Press, 1995.

Kang, Shin-Goo. "The Influence of Presidential Heads of State on Government Formation in European Democracies: Empirical Evidence." *European Journal of Political Research* 48, no. 4 (June 2009): 543–72. http://dx.doi.org/10.1111/j.1475-6765.2009.00840.x.

Kapstein, Ethan B., and Nathan Converse. *The Fate of Young Democracies*. New York, NY: Cambridge University Press, 2008. http://dx.doi.org/10.1017/CBO9780511817809.

Kapstein, Ethan B., and Nathan Converse. "Why Democracies Fail." *Journal of Democracy* 19, no. 4 (October 2008): 57–68. http://dx.doi.org/10.1353/jod.0.0031.

Karatnycky, Adrian. "Muslim Countries and the Democracy Gap: The 2001 Freedom House Survey." *Journal of Democracy* 13, no. 1 (January 2002): 99–112. http://dx.doi.org/10.1353/jod.2002.0009.

Karl, Terry Lynn. "Electoralism." In *International Encyclopedia of Elections*, ed. Richard Rose. Washington, DC: CQ Press, 2000.

Karl, Terry Lynn. "The Hybrid Regimes of Central America." *Journal of Democracy* 6, no. 3 (July 1995): 72–86. http://dx.doi.org/10.1353/jod.1995.0049.

Katz, Richard S. *Democracy and Elections*. New York, NY: Oxford University Press, 1997. http://dx.doi.org/10.1093/acprof:oso/9780195044294.001.0001.

Kingston, Paul, and Ian S. Spears, eds. *States within States: Incipient Political Entities in the Post–Cold War Era*. New York, NY: Palgrave Macmillan, 2004.

Kitschelt, Herbert. "Formation of Party Cleavages in Post-Communist Democracies: Theoretical Propositions." *Party Politics* 1, no. 4 (October 1995): 447–72. http://dx.doi.org/10.1177/1354068895001004002.

Kohn, Richard H. "How Democracies Control the Military." *Journal of Democracy* 8, no. 4 (October 1997): 140–53. http://dx.doi.org/10.1353/jod.1997.0060.

Krasner, Stephen D. "Abiding Sovereignty." *International Political Science Review* 22, no. 3 (July 2001): 229–51. http://dx.doi.org/10.1177/0192512101223002.

Kuenzi, Michelle, and Gina Lambright. "Party System Institutionalization in 30 African Countries." *Party Politics* 7, no. 4 (July 2001): 437–68. http://dx.doi.org/ 10.1177/1354068801007004003.

Kuhonta, Erik Martinez. "Walking a Tightrope: Democracy Versus Sovereignty in ASEAN's Illiberal Peace." *Pacific Review* 19, no. 3 (September 2006): 337–58. http://dx.doi.org/10.1080/09512740600875119.

Lane, Philip R., and Gian Maria Milesi-Ferretti. "The External Wealth of Nations Mark II: Revised and Extended Estimates of Foreign Assets and Liabilities, 1970–2004." *Journal of International Economics* 73, no. 2 (November 2007): 223–50. http://dx.doi.org/10.1016/j.jinteco.2007.02.003.

Levitsky, Steven, and Lucan A. Way. *Competitive Authoritarianism: Hybrid Regimes after the Cold War.* New York, NY: Cambridge University Press, 2010. http://dx.doi.org/10.1017/CBO9780511781353.

Lewis, M. Paul, ed. *Ethnologue: Languages of the World.* 16th ed. Dallas, TX: SIL International, 2009. http://www.ethnologue.com.

Liebenow, J. Gus. *African Politics: Crises and Challenges.* Bloomington and Indianapolis, IN: Indiana University Press, 1986.

Lijphart, Arend. "Changement et continuité dans la théorie consociative." *Revue Internationale de Politique Comparée* 4, no. 3 (1997): 679–97.

Lijphart, Arend. *Democracy in Plural Societies: A Comparative Exploration.* New Haven, CT: Yale University Press, 1977.

Lijphart, Arend. *Electoral Systems and Party Systems: A Study of Twenty-Seven Democracies, 1945–1990.* Oxford, UK: Oxford University Press, 1994.

Lijphart, Arend. *Patterns of Democracy: Government Forms and Performance in Thirty-Six Countries.* New Haven, CT: Yale University Press, 1999.

Lijphart, Arend. "The Puzzle of Indian Democracy: A Consociational Reinterpretation." *American Political Science Review* 90, no. 2 (1996): 258–68. http://dx.doi.org/10.2307/2082883.

Lindblom, Charles E. *Politics and Markets: The World's Political-Economic Systems*. New York, NY: Basic Books, 1977.

Linder, Wolf. *Swiss Democracy: Possible Solutions to Conflict in Multicultural Societies*. 2nd ed. Basingstoke, UK: Macmillan, 1998.

Linz, Juan J. "An Authoritarian Regime: The Case of Spain." In *Mass Politics: Studies in Political Sociology*, ed. Erik Allard and Stein Rokkan, 251–83. New York, NY: Free Press, 1970.

Linz, Juan J. *The Breakdown of Democratic Regimes: Crisis, Breakdown, and Reequilibration*. Baltimore, MD and London, UK: The Johns Hopkins University Press, 1978.

Linz, Juan J. *Totalitarian and Authoritarian Regimes*. Boulder, CO: Lynne Rienner, 2000.

Linz, Juan J., and Alfred Stepan. *Problems of Democratic Transition and Consolidation: Southern Europe, South America, and Post-Communist Europe*. Baltimore, MD: The Johns Hopkins University Press, 1996.

Linz, Juan J., and Alfred Stepan. "Toward Consolidated Democracies." *Journal of Democracy* 7, no. 2 (April 1996): 14–33. http://dx.doi.org/10.1353/jod.1996.0031.

Lipset, Seymour Martin. *Political Man: The Social Bases of Politics*. Expanded ed. Baltimore, MD: Johns Hopkins University Press, 1981.

Lipset, Seymour Martin. "The Social Requisites of Democracy Revisited: 1993 Presidential Address." *American Sociological Review* 59, no. 1 (February 1994): 1–22. http://dx.doi.org/10.2307/2096130.

Lipset, Seymour Martin. "Some Social Requisites of Democracy: Economic Development and Political Legitimacy." *American Political Science Review* 53, no. 1 (March 1959): 69–105. http://dx.doi.org/10.2307/1951731.

Loosemore, John, and Victor J. Hanby. "The Theoretical Limits of Maximum Distortion: Some Analytical Expressions for Electoral Systems." *British Journal of Political Science* 1, no. 4 (October 1971): 467–77. http://dx.doi.org/10.1017/S000712340000925X.

López-Pintor, Rafael. *Electoral Management Bodies as Institutions of Governance*. New York, NY: Bureau for Development Policy, United Nations Development Program, 2000.

Lynch, Allen C. *How Russia Is Not Ruled: Reflections on Russian Political Development*. Cambridge, UK: Cambridge University Press, 2005. http://dx.doi. org/10.1017/CBO9780511614361.

Maddison, Angus. Maddison Project. http://www.ggdc.net/maddison/maddison-project/home.htm.

Maddison, Angus. *The World Economy: A Millennial Perspective*. Paris, France: OECD, 2001.

Maeda, Ko. "Two Modes of Democratic Breakdown: A Competing Risks Analysis of Democratic Durability." *Journal of Politics* 72, no. 4 (October 2010): 1129–43. http://dx.doi.org/10.1017/S0022381610000575.

Mainwaring, Scott, and Timothy R. Scully. "Introduction: Party Systems in Latin America." In *Building Democratic Institutions: Party Systems in Latin America*, ed. Scott Mainwaring and Timothy R. Scully, 1–34. Stanford, CA: Stanford University Press, 1995.

Mann, Michael. "The Autonomous Power of the State: Its Origins, Mechanisms and Results." In *States in History*, ed. John A. Hall, 109–36. Oxford, UK: Basil Blackwell, 1986.

Mauzy, Diane K. "Electoral Innovation and One-Party Dominance in Singapore." In *How Asia Votes*, ed. John Fuh-Sheng Hsieh and David Newman, 234–54. New York, NY: Chatham House Publishers of Seven Bridges Press, 2002.

McAlister, Lyle N. "The Military." In *Continuity and Change in Latin America*, ed. John J. Johnson, 136–60. Stanford, CA: Stanford University Press, 1964.

McGann, Anthony J. *The Logic of Democracy: Reconciling Equality, Deliberation, and Minority Protection*. Ann Arbor, MI: The University of Michigan Press, 2006.

Merquior, J.G. "Patterns of State-Building in Argentina and Brazil." In *States in History*, ed. John A. Hall, 264–88. Oxford, UK: Basil Blackwell, 1986.

Migdal, Joel S. *Strong Societies and Weak States: State-Society Relations and State Capabilities in the Third World*. Princeton, NJ: Princeton University Press, 1988.

Moniruzzaman, M. "Party Politics and Political Violence in Bangladesh: Issues, Manifestation and Consequences." *South Asian Survey* 16, no. 1 (March 2009): 81–99. http://dx.doi.org/10.1177/097152310801600106.

Moore, Barrington. *Social Origins of Dictatorship and Democracy: Lord and Peasant in the Making of the Modern World*. Boston, MA: Beacon Press, 1966.

Munck, Gerardo L. *Authoritarianism and Democratization: Soldiers and Workers in Argentina, 1976–1983*. University Park, PA: Pennsylvania State University Press, 1998.

Nordlinger, Eric A. "Political Development: Time Sequences and Rates of Change." *World Politics* 20, no. 3 (April 1968): 494–520. http://dx.doi.org/10.2307/2009779.

Nordlinger, Eric A. *Soldiers in Politics: Military Coups and Governments*. Englewood Cliffs, NJ: Prentice-Hall, 1977.

OECD. List of Member Countries. http://www.oecd.org/general/listofoecdmembercountries-ratificationoftheconventionontheoecd.htm.

Oldenburg, Philip. *India, Pakistan, and Democracy: Solving the Puzzle of Divergent Paths*. New York, NY: Routledge, 2010.

Ott, Dana. *Small is Democratic: An Examination of State Size and Democratic Development*. New York, NY and London, UK: Garland Publishing, 2000.

Ottaway, Marina. *Democracy Challenged: The Rise of Semi-Authoritarianism*. Washington, DC: Carnegie Endowment for International Peace, 2003.

Palasik, Mária. *Chess Game for Democracy: Hungary between East and West, 1944–1947*. Translated by Mario Fenyo. Montreal, QC and Kingston, ON: McGill-Queens University Press, 2011.

Palmer, Geoffrey. *Unbridled Power: An Interpretation of New Zealand's Constitution and Government*. Auckland: Oxford University Press, 1979.

Patapan, Haig, John Wanna, and Patrick Weller, eds. *Westminster Legacies: Democracy and Responsible Government in Asia and the Pacific*. Sydney: University of New South Wales Press, 2005.

Paxton, Pamela. "Women's Suffrage in the Measurement of Democracy: Problems of Operationalization." *Studies in Comparative International Development* 35, no. 3 (Fall 2000): 92–111. http://dx.doi.org/10.1007/BF02699767.

Payne, J. Mark, Daniel Zovatto G., Fernando Carrillo Flórez, and Andrés Allamand Zavala. *Democracies in Development: Politics and Reform in Latin America.* Washington, DC: Inter-American Development Bank, 2002.

Payne, Stanley G. *The Collapse of the Spanish Republic, 1933–1936: Origins of the Civil War.* New Haven, CT and London, UK: Yale University Press, 2006.

Payne, Stanley G. *A History of Fascism, 1914–1945.* Madison, WI: The University of Wisconsin Press, 1995.

Pempel, T.J., ed. *Uncommon Democracies? The One-Party Predominant Systems.* Ithaca, NY: Cornell University Press, 1990.

Pion-Berlin, David. "Defense Organization and Civil-Military Relations in Latin America." *Armed Forces and Society* 35, no. 3 (April 2009): 562–86. http://dx.doi.org/10.1177/0095327X08322565.

Pritchett, Lant, and Michael Woolcock. "Solutions When *the* Solution is the Problem: Arraying the Disarray in Development." *World Development* 32, no. 2 (February 2004): 191–212.

Przeworski, Adam. *Democracy and the Market: Political and Economic Reforms in Eastern Europe and Latin America.* New York, NY: Cambridge University Press, 1991. http://dx.doi.org/10.1017/CBO9781139172493.

Przeworski, Adam, and Fernando Limongi. "Modernization: Theories and Facts." *World Politics* 49, no. 02 (1997): 155–83. http://dx.doi.org/10.1353/wp.1997.0004.

Ravallion, Martin. "The Developing World's Bulging (but Vulnerable) Middle Class." *World Development* 38, no. 4 (April 2010): 445–54. http://dx.doi.org/10.1016/j.worlddev.2009.11.007.

Reilly, Benjamin. "Political Reform in Papua New Guinea: Testing the Evidence." *Pacific Economic Bulletin* 21, no. 1 (2006): 187–94.

Rezvani, David A. "The Basis of Puerto Rico's Constitutional Status: Colony, Compact, or 'Federacy'?" *Political Science Quarterly* 122, no. 1 (Spring 2007): 115–40.

Rhodes, R.A.W., and Patrick Weller. "Westminster Transplanted and Westminster Implanted: Exploring Political Change." In *Westminster Legacies: Democracy and Responsible Government in Asia and the Pacific*, ed. Haig Patapan, John Wanna, and Patrick Weller, 1–12. Sydney: University of New South Wales Press, 2005.

Rokkan, Stein. *Citizens, Elections, Parties: Approaches to the Comparative Study of the Processes of Development*. New York, NY: David McKay, 1970.

Rose, Richard, and Doh Chull Shin. "Democratization Backwards: The Problem of Third-Wave Democracies." *British Journal of Political Science* 31, no. 2 (April 2001): 331–54. http://dx.doi.org/10.1017/S0007123401000138.

Rotberg, Robert I. "The New Nature of Nation-State Failure." *Washington Quarterly* 25, no. 3 (Summer 2002): 85–96. http://dx.doi.org/10.1162/01636600260046253.

Rowen, Henry S. "The Tide Underneath the 'Third Wave.'" *Journal of Democracy* 6, no. 1 (January 1995): 52–64. http://dx.doi.org/10.1353/jod.1995.0018.

Rueschemeyer, Dietrich, Evelyne Huber Stephens, and John D. Stephens. *Capitalist Development and Democracy*. Chicago, IL: University of Chicago Press, 1992.

Rustow, Dankwart A. "Transitions to Democracy: Toward a Dynamic Model." *Comparative Politics* 2, no. 3 (April 1970): 337–63. http://dx.doi.org/10.2307/421307.

Rustow, Dankwart A., and Robert E. Ward. *Political Modernization in Japan and Turkey*. Princeton, NJ: Princeton University Press, 1964.

Sartori, Giovanni. *Parties and Party Systems: A Framework for Analysis*. New York, NY: Cambridge University Press, 1976.

Schedler, Andreas. "Elections without Democracy: The Menu of Manipulation." *Journal of Democracy* 13, no. 2 (April 2002): 36–50. http://dx.doi.org/10.1353/jod.2002.0031.

Schedler, Andreas, ed. *Electoral Authoritarianism: The Dynamics of Unfree Competition*. Boulder, CO: Lynne Rienner, 2006.

Schmidt, Manfred G. *Demokratietheorien: Eine Einführung.* Opladen: Leske + Budrich, 1995.

Schmidt, Manfred G. *Demokratietheorien: Eine Einführung.* 3rd ed. Opladen: Leske + Budrich, 2000.

Schmidt, Manfred G. "When Parties Matter: A Review of the Possibilities and Limits of Partisan Influence on Public Policy." *European Journal of Political Research* 30, no. 2 (September 1996): 155–83. http://dx.doi.org/10.1111/j.1475-6765.1996.tb00673.x.

Schmitt, Carl. *Verfassungslehre.* Berlin: Duncker and Humblot, 1970. First published in 1928. Excerpts translated by Rune Slagstad, "Liberal Constitutionalism and its Critics: Carl Schmitt and Max Weber." In *Constitutionalism and Democracy,* ed. Jon Elster and Rune Slagstad, 103–29. Cambridge, UK: Cambridge University Press and Oslo: Norwegian University Press, 1988.

Schmitter, Philippe C., and Terry Lynn Karl. "What Democracy Is ... and Is Not." *Journal of Democracy* 2, no. 3 (Summer 1991): 75–88. http://dx.doi.org/10.1353/jod.1991.0033.

Schneider, Friedrich. "Shadow Economies around the World: What Do We Really Know?" *European Journal of Political Economy* 21, no. 3 (September 2005): 598–642. http://dx.doi.org/10.1016/j.ejpoleco.2004.10.002.

Schumpeter, Joseph A. *Capitalism, Socialism, and Democracy.* 3rd ed. New York, NY: Harper and Brothers, 1950.

Seow, Francis T. *The Media Enthralled: Singapore Revisited.* Boulder, CO: Lynne Rienner, 1998.

Siaroff, Alan. "Comparative Presidencies: The Inadequacy of the Presidential, Semi-Presidential, and Parliamentary Distinction." *European Journal of Political Research* 42, no. 3 (May 2003): 287–312. http://dx.doi.org/10.1111/1475-6765.00084.

Siaroff, Alan. "Spurious Majorities, Electoral Systems and Electoral System Change." *Commonwealth and Comparative Politics* 41, no. 2 (July 2003): 143–60. http://dx.doi.org/10.1080/14662040412331310131.

Siaroff, Alan. "Two-and-a-Half-Party Systems and the Comparative Role of the 'Half.'" *Party Politics* 9, no. 3 (May 2003): 267–90. http://dx.doi.org/10.1177/13 54068803009003001.

Sieder, Rachel, Line Schjolden, and Alan Angell, eds. *The Judicialization of Politics in Latin America*. New York, NY: Palgrave Macmillan, 2005.

Shugart, Matthew Soberg, and John M. Carey. *Presidents and Assemblies: Constitutional Design and Electoral Dynamics*. New York: Cambridge University Press, 1992. http://dx.doi.org/10.1017/CBO9781139173988.

Slagstad, Rune. "Liberal Constitutionalism and its Critics: Carl Schmitt and Max Weber." In *Constitutionalism and Democracy*, ed. Jon Elster and Rune Slagstad, 103–29. Cambridge, UK: Cambridge University Press and Oslo: Norwegian University Press, 1988.

Smith, Anthony D. "State-Making and Nation-Building." In *States in History*, ed. John A. Hall, 228–63. Oxford, UK: Basil Blackwell, 1986.

Smith, Gordon. *Democracy in Western Germany: Parties and Politics in the Federal Republic*. 3rd ed. New York, NY: Holmes and Meier, 1986.

Spence, Michael. *The Next Convergence: The Future of Economic Growth in a Multispeed World*. New York, NY: Farrar, Straus and Giroux, 2011.

Spero, Joan Edelman. *The Politics of International Economic Relations*. 4th ed. New York, NY: St. Martin's Press, 1990.

Spruyt, Hendrik. *The Sovereign State and Its Competitors: An Analysis of Systems Change*. Princeton, NJ: Princeton University Press, 1994.

Stepan, Alfred. *Arguing Comparative Politics*. New York, NY: Oxford University Press, 2001.

Stepan, Alfred, Juan J. Linz, and Yogendra Yadav. *Crafting State-Nations: India and Other Multinational Democracies*. Baltimore, MD: Johns Hopkins University Press, 2011.

Stewart, Ian. "Of Customs and Coalitions: The Formation of Canadian Federal Parliamentary Alliances." *Canadian Journal of Political Science* 13, no. 3 (September 1980): 451–79.

Stokke, Kristian. "Building the Tamil Eelam State: Emerging State Institutions and Forms of Governance in LTTE-Controlled Areas in Sri Lanka." *Third World Quarterly* 27, no. 6 (September 2006): 1021–40. http://dx.doi.org/10.1080/01436590600850434.

Sutton, Paul. "Democracy in the Commonwealth Caribbean." *Democratization* 6, no. 1 (Spring 1999): 67–86. http://dx.doi.org/10.1080/13510349908403597.

Tate, C. Neal, and Torbjörn Vallinder, eds. *The Global Expansion of Judicial Power.* New York, NY: New York University Press, 1995.

Thompson, Mark R. "Totalitarian and Post-Totalitarian Regimes in Transitions and Non-Transitions from Communism." *Totalitarian Movements and Political Religions* 3, no. 1 (Summer 2002): 79–106. http://dx.doi.org/10.1080/714005469.

Tilly, Charles. "Reflections on the History of European State-Making." In *The Formation of Nation-States in Western Europe*, ed. Charles Tilly and Gabriel Ardant, 3–83. Princeton, NJ: Princeton University Press, 1975.

Trinkunas, Harold A. "Crafting Civilian Control in Argentina and Venezuela." In *Civil–Military Relations in Latin America: New Analytical Perspectives*, ed. David Pion-Berlin, 161–93. Chapel Hill, NC: The University of North Carolina Press, 2001.

Trudeau, Pierre Elliott. "Some Obstacles to Democracy in Quebec." *Canadian Journal of Economics and Political Science* 24, no. 3 (August 1958): 297–311. http://dx.doi.org/10.2307/138618.

Tsebelis, George. "Decision Making in Political Systems: Veto Players in Presidentialism, Parliamentarism, Multicameralism, and Multipartyism." *British Journal of Political Science* 25, no. 3 (July 1995): 289–325. http://dx.doi.org/10.1017/S0007123400007225.

Tsebelis, George. *Veto Players: How Political Institutions Work.* Princeton, NJ: Princeton University Press, 2002.

United Nations. *Human Development Index (HDI)–2011 Rankings.* http://hdr.undp.org/en/statistics/.

United Nations. *Human Development Report 2011.* New York, NY: Oxford University Press for the United Nations Development Programme (UNDP), 2012.

United Nations, Department of Economic and Social Affairs, Population Division. *World Population Prospects: The 2010 Revision.* New York, NY: United Nations, May 2011. http://esa.un.org/unpd/wpp/index.htm.

United Nations Conference on Trade and Development. *Statistics.* http://unctad. org/en/Pages/Statistics.aspx.

Urdal, Henrik. "A Clash of Generations? Youth Bulges and Political Violence." *International Studies Quarterly* 50, no. 3 (September 2006): 607–29. http:// dx.doi.org/10.1111/j.1468-2478.2006.00416.x.

Valenzuela, Arturo. "Chile: Origins and Consolidation of a Latin American Democracy." *Democracy in Developing Countries: Latin America,* 2nd ed. Ed. Larry Diamond et al., 191–247. Boulder, CO: Lynne Reinner, 1999.

Valenzuela, J. Samuel. "Democratic Consolidation in Post-Transitional Settings: Notion, Process, and Facilitating Conditions." In *Issues in Democratic Consolidation: The New South American Democracies in Comparative Perspective,* ed. Scott Mainwaring, Guillermo O'Donnell, and J. Samuel Valenzuela, 57–104. Notre Dame, IN: University of Notre Dame Press, 1992.

Vanhanen, Tatu. *The Process of Democratization: A Comparative Study of 147 States, 1980–88.* New York, NY: Crane Russak, 1990.

Wade, Robert. *Governing the Market: Economic Theory and the Role of Government in East Asian Industrialization.* Princeton, NJ: Princeton University Press, 1990.

Walker, Edward W. *Dissolution: Sovereignty and the Breakup of the Soviet Union.* Lanham, MD: Rowman & Littlefield, 2003.

Watts, Ronald L. *Comparing Federal Systems.* 2nd ed. Montreal, QC and Kingston, ON: McGill-Queen's University Press, 1999.

Weber, Max. *Economy and Society.* Vol. 2. Edited by Günther Roth and Claus Wittich. New York, NY: Bedminster Press, 1968.

Weber, Max. *The Theory of Social and Economic Organization.* Edited by Talcott Parsons. Translated by A.M. Henderson and Talcott Parsons. New York, NY: The Free Press, 1964. Reprint of translation first published in 1947 by Oxford University Press.

Weber, Max. "The Theory of Social and Economic Organization." In *From Max Weber: Essays in Sociology*, ed. H.G. Gerth and C.W. Mills, 342–45. New York, NY: Oxford University Press, 1946.

Webster, Andrew. *Introduction to the Sociology of Development*. 2nd ed. Basingstoke, UK: Macmillan, 1990.

Weeks, Liam. "Independents in Government: A Sui Generis Model?" In *New Parties in Government: In Power For the First Time*, ed. Kris Deschouwer, 137–56. New York, NY: Routledge, 2008.

Whittlesey, Derwent. *The Earth and the State: A Study of Political Geography*. New York, NY: Henry Holt and Company, 1944.

Wilson, Andrew. *Belarus: The Last Dictatorship in Europe*. New Haven, CT and London, UK: Yale University Press, 2011.

Woo-Cumings, Meredith, ed. *The Developmental State*. Ithaca, NY: Cornell University Press, 1999.

World Bank. *Atlas of Global Development*. 3rd ed. Washington, DC: The World Bank, 2011.

World Bank. *China 2030: Building a Modern, Harmonious, and Creative High-Income Society*. Washington, DC: The World Bank, 2012.

World Bank. *World Development Indicators 2012*. Washington, DC: The World Bank, 2012.

World Bank. *World Development Report 2003*. Washington, DC: The World Bank and New York, NY: Oxford University Press.

World Economic Forum. *Global Competitiveness Report 2011–2012*. Geneva: World Economic Forum, 2012.

Yom, Sean L., and F. Gregory Gause III. "Resilient Royals: How Arab Monarchies Hang On." *Journal of Democracy* 23, no. 4 (October 2012): 74–88. http://dx.doi.org/10.1353/jod.2012.0062.

Zartman, I. William, ed. *Collapsed States: The Disintegration and Restoration of Legitimate Authority*. Boulder, CO: Lynne Rienner, 1995.

Index